9 x 6/18
9x 6/18 - 8/20
D0060015

For Sale—American Paradise

For Sale—American Paradise

How Our Nation Was Sold an Impossible Dream in Florida

Willie Drye

Guilford, Connecticut

An imprint of Rowman & Littlefield

Distributed by NATIONAL BOOK NETWORK

British Library Cataloguing in Publication Information Available

Library of Congress Cataloging-in-Publication Data Available

ISBN 978-0-7627-9468-3 (hardcover)
ISBN 978-1-4930-1899-4 (e-book)

∞™ The paper used in this publication meets the minimum requirements of American National Standard for Information Sciences—Permanence of Paper for Printed Library Materials, ANSI/NISO Z39.48-1992.

To the memory of two dear friends

"We find that whole communities suddenly fix their minds upon one object, and go mad in its pursuit; that millions of people become simultaneously impressed with one delusion, and run after it, till their attention is caught by some new folly more captivating than the first."

—*Charles Mackay,* Memoirs of Extraordinary Popular Delusions

Contents

CHAPTER ONE

An Old Man's Memories

On Tuesday, March 18, 1986, Edwin A. Menninger was the reluctant guest of honor at his ninetieth birthday party, thrown by the chamber of commerce in Stuart, Florida.

"I tried to talk them out of it," Menninger told a *Miami Herald* reporter a few days earlier. "But they decided I needed a party, so I guess we'll have one."

More than one hundred guests showed up. Menninger, frail and going blind, wore a pink camellia pinned to his lapel and a garland of purple azaleas draped around his neck. He seated himself in a rattan chair and took in the festivities like an aged, decorated chieftain being honored by his tropical tribe.

"My, there's quite a gang of people here, isn't there?" Menninger murmured softly. When some of the guests wished him "Happy birthday," a mischievous grin flashed across his face.

"Merry Christmas!" he responded impishly.

Despite the old man's gentle irascibility, the guests made it clear that they adored him. The mayor said a new park would be named in his honor. One of the guests rose to speak about Menninger's long and productive life.

As Menninger listened to the tribute, the Florida that he had played a small part in creating hummed with activity that held the attention of people around the world. Wealthy snowbirds who'd fled the frigid Northeast several months earlier were enjoying their oceanfront homes at Palm Beach or Jupiter Island or Ocean Reef, or they were cruising aboard their yachts in the Keys or off Sanibel Island. Others were basking in the sunshine at small stadiums throughout the state as they watched Major League baseball players get ready for the upcoming season.

In Port St. Lucie, Port Charlotte, and other rapidly growing retirement towns, retirees of more modest means were relaxing in their 2,000-square-foot homes on 10,000-square-foot lots, chatting on the phone with their grandkids back home in freezing places like Pittsburgh and Perth Amboy.

In Orlando, thousands of excited families from all over the world were enjoying the squeaky-clean fantasies at Walt Disney World. And in Miami Beach, beautiful people and their entourages from Milan and Barcelona and other centers of European style were displaying themselves at trendy cafes and nightclubs on Ocean Drive.

A few days before Menninger's birthday party, millions of Americans had watched the latest irony-laden episode of *Miami Vice*, a trend-setting TV show in which stylish cops fought a ceaseless battle against fiendish and even more stylish criminals. Men across the country were cultivating the three-day stubble constantly sported by the show's hero, vice cop Sonny Crockett. And they were copying Crockett's fashionable South Florida wardrobe—linen slacks, loafers with no socks, and pale pastel-color T-shirts worn under expensive, unstructured Italian sports jackets. The look was becoming so popular that Macy's department stores would soon open a *Miami Vice* section in its men's clothing departments.

The show's set designers were making stars of Miami and Miami Beach. Every week, Miami's flashy skyline, South Beach's Art Deco architecture, and the cities' gritty tropical streetscapes were captivating the show's huge audience.

But Edwin Menninger, who had once been a driving force in South Florida's evolution from a swampy frontier to America's winter playground, could no longer participate in what he'd helped set in motion. Now, all he could do was listen to the accolades of an admiring speaker.

"Ed, we love you," the speaker said in conclusion. The other guests stood and applauded.

As the crowd sang "Happy Birthday," Menninger struggled gamely to his feet and raised his right arm in acknowledgment. He seldom allowed his left arm—mangled in a long-ago accident in a college chemistry lab—to be displayed.

Moments such as this stir the emotions and sometimes prompt old memories to come swirling into our thoughts. As Menninger looked around the room at the applauding crowd, he might have remembered a moment more than sixty years earlier when he'd been part of another festive crowd that was applauding a great man of that era.

It was a breezy day in late June 1925, and Menninger, twenty-nine years old, was among a gathering of about four thousand people who had assembled in Pocahontas Park in Vero Beach. The wind off the ocean made the early summer heat bearable and fanned the tantalizing aroma of barbecue over the gathering, which had assembled to celebrate the creation of Indian River County.

William Jennings Bryan probably caught a whiff of the sizzling beef and pork as he rose from his seat and walked ponderously across a wooden platform that overlooked the throng. His substantial bulk underscored his well-known fondness for such simple food. As the acerbic journalist H. L. Mencken had noted, Bryan "liked the heavy, greasy victuals of the farmhouse kitchen."

Bryan—a three-time candidate for president of the United States and one of the great orators in American history—approached the railing at the edge of the platform. This was the day's main event, a moment to tell one's grandchildren about, and the people sharpened their focus and prepared to absorb Bryan's every word.

They had been listening politely all morning to local politicians congratulate themselves for the vision and brilliance they'd displayed in persuading the state legislature in distant Tallahassee to approve the creation of the new county, which would officially come into existence at midnight, with Vero Beach as the seat. They'd heard local business boosters predict well-deserved prosperity for the good residents, and they'd heard the politicians vow to enact new programs to guarantee that prosperity.

In the summer of 1925, however, it didn't take a politician's promise to guarantee Florida's prosperity. The state was immersed in a mad, frenzied boom in real estate speculation, and money was everywhere, almost as though the ubiquitous palm trees were sprouting dollar bills instead of coconuts. The frantic land sales in Florida amounted to a boom within a boom. Americans had more discretionary income than ever before, and they were looking for places to spend it. Millions of dollars were pouring into Florida banks in a ceaseless flow from all across the United States.

So much cash had been stuffed into South Florida banks that a pack of backwoods bandits known as the Ashley Gang had, until recently, been hauling away sacks of greenbacks and vanishing into the eerie, trackless Everglades. Their spree had ended only six months earlier a few miles up the road from Vero Beach. Sheriff's deputies had killed leader John Ashley and three gang members after stopping them at the Sebastian River bridge. The deputies claimed the gang members tried to grab their concealed weapons, but tales were circulating that the cops put handcuffs on the robbers and then shot them in cold blood.

Rumor had it that John Ashley had hidden more than $110,000—about $1.5 million in twenty-first-century dollars—somewhere around the gang's hideout, and a few adventurous souls were braving the damp, deadly wilds of the Glades, looking for the loot.

It seemed likely that a dredge operator would find the treasure. Developers were boldly talking of draining the alligator-infested Everglades and building elegant, perfect cities where life would be lived as it had never been lived on this Earth. At times their plans seemed to be the fevered dreams of lunatics, but the developers really did have reason to believe that they could, in effect, sell land by the gallon. Every day, trains were bringing as many as seventy-five Pullman cars full of would-be millionaires into Miami, where the population had exploded from about 29,000 in 1920 to 175,000 in the summer of 1925.

Thousands more were pouring into Florida on the recently opened Dixie Highway, which brought winter-weary Midwesterners to the land of perpetual sunshine. Everybody came with wads of cash and letters of credit, and they were eager to buy land—any land anywhere, even if it was soaking wet. With all the dredging, draining, filling, and landscaping going on, land that was under a foot of black swamp water today would be high and dry in a few weeks and selling for eight or ten times the original price.

This swarm of eager buyers was driving up land prices so fast that accountants were working as hard as the dredge operators. "It was easy to lie to a prospect in those days," said Walter Fuller, who was making so much money selling real estate in St. Petersburg that he claimed he didn't have time to count it. "The typical prospect already had his cupidity whetted to a point his tongue was hanging out. Any old story would be accepted."

The speculation mania had spread like a tropical fever to smaller towns such as Vero Beach, Sarasota, Fort Myers, Stuart, and throughout the state. Men of great wealth and vision—the kind of men that Americans loved to idolize in the 1920s—were buying great chunks of land in Florida and promising spectacular things—an end to poverty, plenty of work for everybody, a long and healthful life in the sun, and permanent wealth for anyone willing to invest a few bucks for a plot of land.

Famed Hearst Newspapers columnist Arthur Brisbane—whose nationally syndicated "Today" column was read by millions daily—had visited Stuart three times in less than a year, and local business boosters were fervently hoping he would buy land there.

Jesse Livermore, the legendary stock market manipulator and peerless profiteer, was interested in Stuart, and everyone knew a man like Livermore wouldn't buy anything unless he was dead certain it would soon be worth many, many times more than he paid for it.

In neighboring Palm Beach County, architect Addison Mizner and his madcap brother Wilson were selling $2 million worth of property every week in Boca Raton. Publicly, Addison touted his development as a city with "every atom of beauty that human ingenuity can add to a land endowed by nature," and his inspired vision for the city had buyers waiting in line to purchase his beautiful Spanish Mediterranean homes.

But the rowdy roaring vortex of the speculation madness was in Miami, where even William Jennings Bryan, the Bible-thumping, teetotaling advocate for the rights of the common man, was caught up in the mania. He'd moved from Nebraska to Miami in 1912, and he loved pontificating about the wonders of his adopted state. Miami developer George Merrick was paying Bryan $100,000 a year in cash and property—more than President Calvin Coolidge or even baseball superstar Babe Ruth was earning—to tell people what a wonderful place Coral Gables was.

At Coral Gables, Bryan looked out at hundreds of eager fortune seekers gathered around the beautiful Venetian Pool to hear him speak. They came from all over the United States, lured by countless stories in newspapers about ordinary people who'd come to Florida, made modest investments in real estate, and quickly resold their property for staggering profits.

CELEBRATE WORLD OCEANS DAY

FREE INSULATED TOTE BAG WITH ANY PURCHASE

JUNE 8 ONLY

Present this coupon for a free insulated tote bag.

Offer valid in restaurant only on 6/8/18, while supplies last. One bag, one coupon, per person. Purchase required. No cash value/no cash back. Code: TOTE BAG

Get a free taco when you join our Beach Club at rubios.com

Highly respected mass-circulation magazines such as the *Saturday Evening Post*, the *New Yorker*, *Harper's*, and *Literary Digest* also were publishing stories about Florida in nearly every issue.

The lure of quick, easy riches was bringing thousands of newcomers into Florida every day, and Menninger and Bryan, among others, were doing their part to fuel the expectations of instant wealth.

As incredible as Bryan's claims seemed, there was a grain of truth to them. In the summer of 1925, sales of property in Coral Gables were averaging $4 million a month—more than $53 million in today's dollars—and when Merrick started selling lots in the new Sylvania Heights section of Coral Gables, he raked in an astonishing $21 million in a single business day.

Bryan believed that Florida had a limitless future, and he professed this faith with the same zealous certainty he attached to his belief in the literal truth of the Bible's scriptures. His appearance in Vero Beach was another opportunity for him to preach the gospel of Florida prosperity. Crowds were as important to him as home cooking—perhaps more so, because William Jennings Bryan had a compulsive need to be the center of attention. "I never see a crowd of people that I do not wish to address them," he'd once said.

But Bryan gave something back to his listeners in return for their attention. Somehow, he could connect at a primal level with his audience, sensing their fears and confusions, their frustrations, dreams, hopes, and joys. He absorbed and synthesized this inarticulate mass of human emotions and returned it to his listeners in the form of beautiful, flowing oration that ennobled their dreary lives of struggle and toil. His great, mystical gift was the ability to make ordinary people who lived ordinary lives in insignificant places—wheat farmers in Kansas, silver miners in Nevada, tobacco farmers in Virginia, mill hands in North Carolina—feel important, dignified, and hopeful.

He'd been doing it since 1896, when he had stepped up to the podium at the Democratic National Convention in Chicago and delivered a speech that turned a debate on the merits of a silver-backed monetary system versus one backed by gold into a stunning, stirring, impassioned hymn to the common man. When he finished, the twenty thousand delegates didn't simply applaud—they nearly started a riot. The cheering "came like a burst of artillery," one reporter wrote. They were "demented," another journalist observed, tearing off their coats and vests and flinging them into the air.

The speech propelled Bryan, at the age of just thirty-six, to the Democrats' nomination for president of the United States. He became the standard-bearer not only for his party's political hopes, but also for a way of life and a system of beliefs. He became the champion for millions of Americans who fervently believed in a simple, moral universe ruled by an omnipotent Christian God that unfailingly rewarded good and punished evil. He also fought loudly and diligently for the rights of the underprivileged, and in the process he became known as "The Great Commoner."

But Bryan failed three times in his quest for the White House. After a brief stint as secretary of state under President Woodrow Wilson, Bryan returned to his beautiful Mediterranean-style home in Miami and busied himself with speaking engagements and real estate investments. The urge to make the world a better place and the lust for political power still burned fiercely within him, however. A few years earlier Bryan had toured Florida, campaigning to become a state delegate to the 1924 Democratic National Convention. But the canny old political warhorse also had seriously contemplated a run for one of Florida's seats in the US Senate, and he was sizing up the way the state's voters responded to him. When Arthur Brisbane and his boss, William Randolph Hearst, visited Bryan in Miami in February 1924, Brisbane reported in "Today" that Bryan's political ambitions were stirring again. "It will please all to know that Mr. Bryan has the old fire in his eye," Brisbane wrote. "He can smell the battle afar off."

By the summer of 1925, Bryan had maneuvered himself into the unusual position of exerting great influence within two groups in Florida, with dramatically different values and agendas. Although Bryan lived among relentless sinners in Miami, he was a leader among staunch social conservatives who were determined to impose dramatic restrictions on Americans' thoughts and behaviors. Bryan had worked for passage of the Eighteenth Amendment to the US Constitution, which forbade the manufacture and sale of alcoholic beverages, and he had been a driving force behind an effort to forbid the teaching of Charles Darwin's theory of evolution in public schools.

But while Bryan was a puritan, he had no qualms about helping Florida businessmen grab as much cash as they could from the ever-growing hordes flocking to the state to escape annoying restrictions—Prohibition, income taxes, speed limits—and frolic in a land of tropical excesses. He was happy to stand before these throngs of scofflaw hedonists and tell them they'd truly found Paradise.

So as Bryan stepped up to the railing at Vero Beach and prepared to address the audience, he wasn't talking to a group of celebrants. He was talking to thousands of potential voters. And for the first time in Bryan's career, about half of those voters were women. The Nineteenth Amendment had given women the right to vote in 1920, and they had cast their first ballots in a presidential election in 1924.

But the younger women in the Vero Beach crowd were a different creature from the women of Bryan's Victorian youth. Many had their hair clipped very short and peered at Bryan from beneath the tiny brims of tightly fitting cloche hats pulled down almost to their eyebrows. The dresses they wore—thin, revealing, with hemlines at the knee—had horrified Albert A. Murphree, president of the University of Florida and a friend of Bryan's. Murphree was convinced that such dresses were "born of the Devil and his angels, and are carrying the present and future generations to chaos and destruction."

To make matters worse—at least from Murphree's standpoint—the modern woman wore makeup, and lots of it. When Murphree had been a young man in the nineteenth and early-twentieth centuries, makeup had been used only by prostitutes and actresses.

In the mid-1920s, however, the fashion dictated a stark contrast between dark eye makeup, dark lipstick, and very pale skin. Two factors influenced this look—the discovery of the tomb of the ancient Egyptian king Tutankhamun in 1922, and the growing influence of the Hollywood film industry.

Young women fascinated with the look of ancient Egypt laid on dark eye shadow and eyeliner. And they carefully applied lipstick to create the "Cupid's lips" outline brought to the silver screen by actress Clara Bow.

Some of the women even dared to light up cigarettes and apply their makeup in public. And they talked of getting drunk—referred to as "blotto"—and kissing lots of men.

They were the epitome of the "flapper" look that had swept the country. The word may have originated as a slang term for English prostitutes, and it greatly annoyed T. Drew Branch, a member of the Florida state legislature who hailed from, of all places, Liberty County. Branch said that calling a woman by this name "offended the dignity" of the people of Florida. He had recently introduced a bill in Tallahassee that would make it illegal for newspapers or magazines to refer to any woman in the great state of Florida as a flapper. The proposal was defeated.

Many younger men in the crowd were sporting the "Palm Beach" look, which consisted of a sports jacket worn with knickerbockers, known as "plus fours"—because they ended four inches below the knee—and knee socks. The ensemble was topped with a round, flat-brimmed straw hat called a "boater." It was a look that was especially popular among real estate salesmen.

As the men listened to earlier speakers and awaited Bryan's speech, they did as men have done for as long as they've worn slacks—they dug their hands into their pants pockets and jingled their loose change. But the coins they fingered on that day in 1925 were quite different from those of today. There were fewer coins with presidents, for starters—no Jefferson nickel or Roosevelt dime or Washington quarter. Lincoln was on the penny, but he'd only been there since 1910, so there were still lots of pennies with the profile of an Indian chief on them.

Instead, the men jingled nickels with an Indian head and a buffalo on them, and everything else—quarters, half-dollars, and dollars, all made of silver—showed Lady Liberty in some form.

The silver dollars—heavy, and nearly the same diameter as a golf ball—were magnificent coins, and in 1925 one of them had the purchasing power of more than $12 in twenty-first-century dollars.

The crowd greeted Bryan with generous, prolonged applause, and as he waited for it to subside he looked out over the faces gazing expectantly up at him. In his somber dark suit, floppy bow tie, and gleaming black shoes, Bryan was the embodiment of the stern nineteenth-century morals that still tugged at the sleeve of American society in the 1920s.

Edwin Menninger, who was editor of the *South Florida Developer* in nearby Stuart, had been breathlessly chronicling Florida's roaring boom in the pages of his newspaper, and he'd been a leader in Stuart's successful effort to create a new county on the St. Lucie Inlet. The turnout and festivities in Vero Beach impressed Menninger, but he felt certain that Stuart would outdo this gathering in January when the town hosted the celebration for the creation of Martin County, named after Florida governor John Martin. As bright and promising as Indian River County's future seemed, Martin County's was even brighter, as far as Menninger was concerned. People and money were pouring into Stuart, and plans were being laid that would propel the little town to greatness.

The applause faded, and Bryan began to speak. He started with a self-deprecating quip about his futile campaigns for the White House. He noted that the previous speaker, T. J. Campbell, had been introduced as the next state senator from Indian River County. "I hope the prediction of the man who introduced Mr. Campbell is more reliable than were those of the men who introduced me as 'the next president,'" he said.

When the chuckling subsided, Bryan told his listeners that he'd learned a lot about Florida during his campaign to become a delegate to the 1924 Democratic National Convention. He expected to learn more about the state in the coming months, and promised to tell as many people as he could what a wonderful place it was. "This year I am going to every tourist city in which they will let me speak and tell the tourists who are there that Florida is the greatest opportunity of this generation," he said.

Bryan then began preaching his now-familiar gospel of the glittering future that lay ahead for Florida. It was a classic Bryan oration, full of noble, uplifting ideals and flowery phrases.

"We are sometimes asked, 'When will Florida's prosperity fail?'" Bryan said. "My answer is, 'Not until the sunshine fails and the ocean breezes cease to carry healing in their wings.'"

But Bryan also wanted residents of his adopted state to use its gifts for more than just enriching themselves. "I want us to make Florida the nation's leading state in material wealth and prosperity and also first politically, intellectually, and morally," he said. "God has blessed the state of Florida as he has blessed no other state in the union, and for this reason, if for no other, we should remember Him in all that we do."

As Bryan mingled with the crowd after his speech and waited for his helping of barbecue, Edwin Menninger walked up and introduced himself. The eager young editor quickly outlined some of the wonderful things happening a few miles down the road in Stuart, and invited Bryan to speak at Martin County's upcoming official birthday party.

Bryan gratefully accepted the invitation. "I would feel lost if I were not there on that occasion," Bryan said. "Helping start new counties is one of my specialties."

Sixty years after Menninger chatted with the loquacious American icon, his friends gathered in Stuart to honor him for the role he'd played in helping to realize the grandiose prophecies of the 1920s. The beautiful county where they lived had become one of the wealthiest counties in the nation, and Florida had become synonymous with the fulfillment of dreams and fantasies. Miami was now a glitzy international city that spoke three or four languages and moved much faster than the posted speed limits.

But as the smiling old man took in the outpouring of love and respect at his ninetieth birthday party, he could have told you that Florida's path to prosperity had taken some bizarre and brutal turns in the months after he shook hands with William Jennings Bryan.

CHAPTER TWO

Railroad to Dreamland

THOUSANDS OF YEARS AGO, FRIGHTENED PEOPLE SPENT MANY WINTER NIGHTS shivering and staring fearfully into the cold darkness beyond the fires at the entrances of dank, smoky caves that were their homes. Surely, they thought, there must be a place somewhere beyond the firelight where life is easier—a warm, idyllic place of lush year-round vegetation, where food is abundant and clothing is optional, where they wouldn't have to spend all of their waking hours just trying to keep their bellies filled and worrying about when they would die.

And so in some way approximating this, the human dream of finding a paradise was formed. That dream became as essential to human existence as air and water: Life shouldn't be this hard; there must be a better place somewhere, and one day I'll find it.

The vision of paradise in this life or beyond eventually became enshrined in the world's major religions. Its usual depiction was a lush garden where there was no toil, no struggle, no death, and no worry, only perpetual peace and contentment.

As civilizations developed, the longing for a paradise spanned eras and cultures. The immortal Greek warrior Alexander the Great is said to have sought the gates of Paradise in the fourth century BC. Medieval European Christians longed to find the legendary kingdom of Prester John, said to contain a fountain whose waters made people young again.

Tales of a fountain in a land somewhere to the north whose waters restored youth circulated among pre-Columbian residents of Cuba, Mexico, and Central America. Adventurers determined to find this wondrous fountain set out in small canoes. When they didn't return, the friends they'd left behind assumed they'd found the fountain and did not want to leave the land of eternal youth.

In the fifteenth and sixteenth centuries, Renaissance explorers crossed unknown seas and traveled thousands of miles from the comfort and familiarity of their homes because they thought they would find a place where living was easier.

Juan Ponce de León went in search of such a place in 1513. He'd lost a political power struggle to a well-connected rival and had been unseated as the Spanish governor of Puerto Rico, so he set out with three ships and a band of conquistadores to find a better place.

In early April 1513, Ponce de León landed in a lush, subtropical world. It's doubtful that he was the first explorer to set foot in this land, but he claimed naming rights for Spain. It was the Easter season, called Pascua Florida, or "Festival of Flowers" by the Spanish. So to honor the season, Ponce de León named his landing place La Florida—Place of Flowers. The explorer is thought to have landed near present-day Cape Canaveral, where, more than four centuries later, a new breed of explorers would ride fireballs into the heavens.

Ponce de León went ashore for a few days; then, thinking that La Florida was an island, he sailed southward, intending to circumnavigate it.

For about two months, Ponce de León's ships hugged the coast of the peninsula. Legend has it that along the way he sailed into the mouth of the present-day St. Lucie River, about one hundred miles south of Cape Canaveral in present-day Martin County. He is said to have dropped a stone cross into the St. Lucie to claim the area for Spain.

Ponce de León's name is inextricably linked with his alleged search for a mystical fountain whose waters would restore youth to anyone who drank from it. But historians generally think that, like most Europeans who came to the New World four hundred or five hundred years ago, he was more interested in finding gold, slaves, and converts to Christianity.

Ponce de León and his three ships continued their explorations in the waters around Florida into the summer of 1513. Then, leaving one ship to continue exploring, Ponce de León returned to Puerto Rico.

He led another expedition to Florida in 1521, this time intent on establishing a Spanish colony. Ponce de León and about two hundred would-be colonists landed on the southwest coast of Florida, probably near present-day Charlotte Harbor. The Calusa Indians, however, wanted nothing to do with European settlers. They attacked the Spaniards and drove them off. Ponce de León received a nasty wound to the thigh from an arrow that may have been dipped in poison.

The conquistador and his ships left Florida and sailed for Havana. But Ponce de León's wound would not heal. Eventually infection set in. There was nothing Spanish doctors could do, and he died soon after arriving in Havana.

Juan Ponce de León would not be the last person to come to Florida seeking a better life and be bitterly disappointed.

In the summer of 1559, Spain sent another expedition to Florida, this time under the conquistador Tristán de Luna y Arellano, who led a company of men intent on planting a colony at what is now Pensacola, at the western tip of the Florida Panhandle. But it was a rough summer on the Gulf of Mexico. On September 19, 1559, a powerful hurricane swept in from the Gulf and devastated the settlement.

The colonists hung on for a while after the hurricane, but when a Spanish ship arrived a year later and offered passage to Cuba to anyone who wanted to leave, most of the colonists left. The Spanish government soon abandoned the colony.

A hurricane would deposit more visitors on a Florida beach in 1696. Jonathan Dickinson had been a planter in Jamaica until he converted to the Religious Society of Friends, better known as Quakers.

Dickinson and his family left Jamaica in August 1696. Accompanying him were Robert Barrow, an elderly leader of the Friends, and Dickinson's slaves. They sailed on the *Reformation* for Philadelphia to join William Penn's experiment in religious freedom in the colony of Pennsylvania.

On the night of September 23, 1696, a hurricane tossed the *Reformation* aground on what is now Jupiter Island, in present-day Martin County.

About two dozen castaways, including Dickinson's party and the crew of the *Reformation*, were shipwrecked in a strange and savage land. Their impression of Florida was quite different from that of Juan Ponce de León's Place of Flowers.

Dickinson later wrote that "the wilderness country looked very dismal, having no trees, but only sand hills covered with shrubbery palmetto, the stalks of which were prickly, there was no walking among them."

The nearest outpost of European civilization was the Spanish settlement at St. Augustine, about 250 miles up the coast. Today the trip from Jupiter Island to St. Augustine can be driven in about four hours. In 1696, it was weeks away on foot.

Nevertheless, Dickinson and his party trudged northward up the beach. Along the way they were alternately helped and harassed by Indians. They were terrified when they saw the tracks of large animals in the sand. Aggressive, stinging insects constantly buzzed around them.

"We had little comfort," Dickinson wryly noted later.

Despite the fears and discomforts and the deaths of two members of their party along the way, Dickinson and his group maintained a resolute faith that God would see them safely through their perilous journey. Six weeks later they tramped wearily into St. Augustine. In April 1697, they finally reached Philadelphia.

In the early nineteenth century, Dr. Jacob Motte, a US Army surgeon, was another reluctant visitor to Florida. The United States had acquired La Florida from Spain in 1821, and it became the US Territory of Florida.

The Seminole Indians caused problems with American efforts to settle Florida, and the US government wanted to kick them out of their home. In 1832, Seminole chiefs signed an agreement to leave Florida and move west, but a few Seminole leaders refused to comply with the treaty and disappeared into the trackless Everglades.

Motte, who was Harvard-educated and accustomed to the comforts and refinements of civilization, accompanied US Army troops sent to Florida in 1837 to drive out the stubborn Seminoles. He later wrote about his experience in *Journey into Wilderness*, in which he articulately explained his fascination and disgust with the strange land of Florida.

Florida, Motte wrote, "is certainly the poorest country that ever two people quarreled for." The climate was impossibly uncomfortable, too warm even in winter and impossibly hot in the summer.

It was "a most hideous region," and the only creatures who could live in such a setting were Indians, alligators, snakes, and "every other kind of loathsome reptile."

Common sense seemed to dictate that the Seminoles should keep Florida, Motte said.

But at times, Motte, the weary, miserable soldier far removed from his customary comforts, was dazzled by Florida's wild tropical beauty.

In late January 1838, Motte's unit moved from Fort Pierce a few miles down the coast to the headwaters of the St. Lucie River in present-day Martin County. The landscape enchanted him, and he wrote about it in gushing prose. Instead of a nasty swamp fit only for Seminoles and snakes, Motte saw "picturesque clumps of cypress trees and willows, ornamentally clothed with long hanging moss, gracefully and fantastically disposed in festoons, forming fairy-looking islets reposing in verdant loveliness on the bosom of the water."

Instead of a lair for loathsome reptiles, it was the habitat "for the genii of those unearthly regions, which come nearest the description of that fabulous place, that we read of, which was neither land, water, nor air," Motte wrote.

The deeper the soldiers went into the wilderness, the more rhapsodic Motte's descriptions became. "Nothing, however, can be imagined more lovely and picturesque than the thousand little isolated spots, scattered in all directions over the surface of this immense sheet of water, which seemed like a placid inland sea shining under a bright sun," he wrote. "Every possible variety of shape, colour, contour, and size were exhibited in the arrangement of the trees and moss upon these islets, which, reflected from the limpid and sunny depths of the transparent water overshadowed by them, brought home to the imagination all the enchanting visions of Oriental description."

Motte "felt the most intense admiration, and gazed with a mingled emotion of delight and awe" at the ethereal landscape.

Florida became the twenty-seventh state in March 1845. It is a quirky state geographically, simultaneously the southernmost continental state and yet, in some ways, it was only marginally a part of the antebellum Old South that bordered it to the north. It is the only state that both touches the Atlantic Ocean and sprawls across two time zones. Its easternmost city, Palm Beach, overlooks the Atlantic, but if you head due north from Florida's westernmost city, Pensacola, you will eventually arrive in Chicago. It's a 540-mile trip down the state's eastern coastline from Fernandina Beach near the Georgia border to Key West, only ninety miles from Havana, Cuba.

Only a few white settlers lived between Tampa and Key West before the Civil War. But Fort Dallas, an outpost of the US military from the Seminole Wars, which were fought sporadically between 1816 and 1858, remained as a settlement near the shores of the Biscayne Bay after the struggle ended. The Everglades covered most of southern Florida, and the Glades were inhabited by the handful of Seminoles who had eluded US troops sent to subdue them or drive them out.

The Civil War could easily have started in Florida several months before Confederate troops fired on Fort Sumter in Charleston, South Carolina, in April 1861.

By 1860, the long-simmering dispute about the extension of slavery into US territories had become unresolvable. South Carolina furiously severed its political connection with the United States government on December 20, 1860.

Mississippi left the Union on January 9, 1861, and Florida seceded on January 10. That same day, Lieutenant Adam Slemmer, in charge of US forces in Pensacola, moved his federal troops into Fort Pickens on Santa Rosa Island, a barrier island just offshore from the city.

Colonel William Chase, a West Point–educated army engineer who had decided to cast his lot with the Confederacy, led troops to Fort Pickens and demanded that Slemmer surrender. Slemmer refused, and Chase contemplated storming the fort, an act that surely would have sparked war. But he decided against it, and Fort Pickens became one of the few US forts in the Confederacy to remain in Union hands for the entire war.

After the Civil War ended in 1865, the reunited nation—or at least the victors—got down to the serious business of becoming wealthy. Ulysses S. Grant, the former Union general who finally figured out a way to beat Confederate general Robert E. Lee, was elected president in 1868—although Texas, Mississippi, and Virginia had not been readmitted to the Union and did not vote in that presidential election.

Author Oliver Carlson noted that President Grant "ushered in that hustling period of the 1870s, when the dominant dream of America was to get rich."

The Reconstruction era gave rise to "new Americans" who were "primitive" and "ruthless" souls who didn't trouble themselves with scruples. They were "a race of buccaneers," Carlson said.

While the Old South languished in poverty, mythologized its bloodily defeated "Lost Cause," and endured military occupation by US troops, men such as Cornelius Vanderbilt, Andrew Carnegie, Jay Gould, Jim Fisk, John D. Rockefeller, Henry Flagler, and "a tribe of other swindlers and railroad wreckers, rascals one and all," amassed huge fortunes in the final decades of the nineteenth century.

"But to the man in the street, these were heroes to be cheered for their audacity," Carlson wrote. "Those who grumbled at their ways were told, 'You'd do the same thing if you only had the chance.'"

In 1867, Congress passed the Reconstruction Act over the veto of President Andrew Johnson, and the former Confederate States were occupied by Union troops and placed under military rule. That same year, author Harriet Beecher Stowe—whose book, *Uncle Tom's Cabin*, supposedly was cited by President Abraham Lincoln as the cause of the Civil War—bought property on the St. Johns River near Jacksonville and built a winter home there. Her twofold purpose was to build a school for African Americans and allow her son to take advantage of the Florida climate to recover from severe wounds he'd suffered as a Union soldier during the war.

Stowe also wrote a book about Florida called *Palmetto-Leaves*. She echoed Jacob Motte's rhapsodic description of Florida. "No dreamland on earth can be more unearthly in its beauty and glory than the St. Johns in April," she wrote.

But she also was aware of Florida's faults, comparing its climate to "an easy, demoralized, indulgent old grandmother, who has no particular time for anything, and does everything when she happens to feel like it."

Stowe cautioned newcomers to Florida. "Don't hope for too much," she warned, and don't expect "an eternal summer."

"For ourselves," she wrote, "we are getting reconciled to a sort of tumbledown, wild, picknicky kind of life—this general happy-go-luckiness which Florida inculcates."

If Florida was a woman, Stowe wrote, she would be what today would be called a "hot mess"—a brunette, dark and attractive, with beautiful skin and "a general disarray and dazzle, and with a sort of jolly untidiness, free, easy, and joyous."

Florida tourism got another boost in 1869 when Dr. Daniel G. Brinton, who had served as a surgeon in the Union Army of the Potomac during the Civil War, wrote *A Guide-Book of Florida and the South for Tourists, Invalids and Emigrants*. Brinton praised Florida's winter climate, saying it was "in some respects unsurpassed by any portion of the United States."

He was effusive in his praise of Fort Dallas and Biscayne Bay.

"Undoubtedly the finest winter climate in the United States," Brinton wrote, "both in point of temperature and health, is to be found on the south-eastern coast of Florida. It is earnestly to be hoped, for the sake of invalids, that accommodations along the shore of Key Biscayne and the mouth of the Miami [River], will, before long, be provided, and that a weekly or semi-weekly steamer be run from Key West thither."

He backed up his praise of the healthful winters with a quote from Dr. R. F. Simpson, an army surgeon who had served at most of the antebellum military bases in Florida. Simpson said Biscayne Bay "has a climate, in every respect, perhaps, unsurpassed by any in the world."

In 1873, another New England Yankee came to Florida and was enthralled. Massachusetts-born author and journalist Edward King took an extended tour of the old Confederacy and wrote a series of stories about each Southern state for

Scribner's Magazine. The stories later were collected into a book, *The Great South: A Record of Journeys*, published in 1875.

In his essay about Florida, King praised the climate and tropical beauty of "our new winter paradise."

"In the winter months, soft breezes come caressingly; the whole peninsula is carpeted with blossoms, and the birds sing sweetly in the untrodden thickets," he wrote. "It has the charm of wildness, of mystery; it is untamed; civilization has not stained it."

In the eight years since the Civil War had ended, King noted, Florida had become a haven for winter-weary Northerners and those suffering from tuberculosis and other debilitating diseases.

King noted that Florida's Silver Spring, south of Gainesville, was attracting fifty thousand tourists a year in the early 1870s. And he was charmed by Palatka, a "cheery, neat" town on the St. Johns River south of Gainesville and about thirty miles inland from St. Augustine.

King drew a languid, lyrical sketch of Palatka and its waterfront.

"Little parties lazily bestow themselves along the river bank, with books or sketching materials, and alternately work, doze or gossip, until the whistles of the ascending or descending steamers are heard, when everybody flocks to the wharves," he wrote. "At evening a splendid white moonlight transfigures all the leaves and trees and flowers; the banjo and guitar, accompanying [N]egro melodies, are heard in the streets; a heavy tropical repose falls over the little town, its wharves and rivers."

George Colby, a twenty-seven-year-old New Yorker, was a different kind of restless dreamer who came to Florida in 1875. He was not drawn by Florida's mild winter climate or sent there to recover from illness. Colby claimed to have been led there by a spirit guide he called Seneca, who wanted him to establish a community of like-minded spiritualists in the Florida wilderness.

Seneca was quite specific about where he wanted Colby to establish this community: It would be near a spring that discharges into the St. Johns River and seven pine-covered hills overlooking a group of lakes.

In early November 1875, Colby, supposedly following Seneca's instructions, set out in a mule-drawn wagon through the woods of interior Florida. Soon he found seven pine-covered hills overlooking some lakes near Blue Spring. He chose this spot to establish Cassadaga, a small village of spiritualists near DeLand.

Ulysses Grant left the White House in 1877 after serving two terms; however, his staunchest supporters wanted him to seek a third term in 1880, after his Republican successor, President Rutherford B. Hayes, announced he would not seek reelection. Despite the fact that serving a third term would break George Washington's sacred precedent of serving only two terms, Grant did not discourage the idea.

But Grant's supporters started worrying that voters would tire of the former and possibly future president as he made a cross-country trip in 1879. They convinced him to get out of the country for a while. Grant set off for Cuba and Mexico.

In early January 1880, Grant and his family reached Florida, en route to Havana. He was impressed, and realized that Florida had great potential.

"I am very much pleased with Florida," he wrote in a January 18, 1880, letter to a friend. "The winter climate is perfection, and, I am told by Northern men settled here, that the summers are not near so hot as in the North, though of longer continuance. This state has a great future before it."

A month later in Havana, he complained about the "sultry" weather in Cuba, "just such as we run from at home in the Dog Days." Florida was a much better winter resort than muggy Havana, he wrote.

Florida appealed to different passions in politicians and businessmen. Their dreams focused on figuring out a way to package and sell the state's most abundant asset—lots and lots of undeveloped land—for huge profits.

Florida's leaders thought they could pull the state out of the postwar wreckage and political chaos in the former Confederate States by giving twenty-two million acres—more than half the state—to railroad companies and then issuing state bonds to pay for laying track. They assumed that railroads would lure business investments that would in turn create jobs and prosperity. But industry wasn't interested, and the money to pay off the bonds didn't come.

Desperate to prevent the state from defaulting on its ill-conceived bonds, Governor William Bloxham made one of history's biggest land deals. He persuaded wealthy Philadelphia industrialist Hamilton Disston to buy four million acres—an area larger than the state of Connecticut—at 25 cents an acre. Disston's first payment of $500,000 in May 1881 kept the state solvent.

Disston boasted that he'd turn Kissimmee, a scrubby little cattle town in central Florida near Orlando, into a "magic city." He also expected to greatly increase his wealth in the process.

But Disston badly miscalculated the amount of money, work, and plain old good luck he'd need to make his venture pay off. He struggled for more than a decade, but the deep economic depression that followed the Panic of 1893 finally put him under. Despondent because of his huge losses, Disston shot himself.

He had no way of knowing, however, that his huge land purchase had laid the foundation for Florida's economic salvation, because it did eventually attract the railroads, and they were willing to lay their own tracks. A few years after the unhappy, unlucky Disston was laid to rest, there were five thousand miles of rails in the state.

Thanks to the railroads, Dr. Brinton's guidebook, and Yankee writers like Harriet Beecher Stowe and Edward King, northern physicians were prescribing winter trips to Florida for their patients who suffered from lingering, debilitating diseases. In 1878, a plutocrat who was amassing one of the great fortunes of the nineteenth century took his ailing wife to St. Augustine, hoping the gentle climate there would restore her frail health.

That visiting tycoon was Henry Flagler. He was as much of a dreamer as any of the others who found their way to Florida in the closing decades of the nineteenth century. But unlike the others, Flagler had the means to reconfigure an entire state in the shape of his dreams. After Flagler was gone and new dreamers seeking overnight fortunes were pouring into the state at the peak of its wild, untamable land boom in 1925, W. L. George would note that Florida "is still conscious of Flagler, looks back to him much as Noah may have looked back to Adam."

Flagler, the son of a poor Presbyterian minister, was an oddity among the great fortune-gatherers of America's Gilded Age. He believed that great wealth could only be acquired by hard, even obsessive work and self-sacrifice, and he rejected taking money from enterprises he considered immoral.

Flagler's father earned $400 a year as a minister. When he was fourteen, Flagler decided it was time to strike out on his own to ease his father's financial burdens.

He set out on foot, carrying only a carpetbag for luggage. Eventually, he arrived in the small town of Republic, Ohio, about thirty miles southeast of Toledo. He had five cents in silver, four copper pennies, and a French five-franc coin.

He went to work in a country store for $5 a month plus board. "I worked hard and saved my money," he said in a 1907 newspaper interview with journalist James B. Barrow of the *Norwalk* (Ohio) *Reflector*.

A few years later, Flagler took his meager savings to nearby Bellevue, Ohio, and went into the business of buying and selling grain. He met John D. Rockefeller, who sold grain on commission in Cleveland. Rockefeller became Flagler's agent for wheat sales.

Flagler also bought an interest in a distillery—a perfect place to sell his grain for a nice profit. But the son of the Presbyterian minister was uneasy about making money from whiskey, and he soon sold his interest.

Still, Flagler did quite well as a grain merchant and accumulated a small fortune of $50,000—more than $750,000 in twenty-first-century dollars. He decided to take his capital to Saginaw, Michigan, and go into the business of manufacturing salt.

It was one of the few bad decisions Flagler ever made. After three years, his $50,000 investment was gone and he owed another $50,000 in unpaid wages to his employees.

He borrowed money from in-laws—at 10 percent interest—to pay off his debts, and moved on to Cleveland to reenter the grain business.

By now, his old associate John D. Rockefeller was a partner in an oil refining business. Once again, Flagler borrowed money from an in-law and bought a partnership in the business in 1867. Three years later, they dissolved the partnership and organized the Standard Oil Company.

"We worked night and day, making good oil as cheaply as possible and selling it for all we could get," Flagler said.

Standard Oil grew like a weed. Years later, Rockefeller said Flagler had been the brains behind the company's rapid and profitable growth.

Perhaps heeding the advice of a physician who believed in Florida's healing powers, Flagler took his wife, Ida Harkness Flagler, to St. Augustine in 1878, hoping to restore her failing health. The city's graceful antiquity charmed Flagler, and it was a visit he would remember.

Flagler remarried after Ida died in 1881. Remembering the charms of St. Augustine, Flagler took his new bride to the city for their honeymoon. But while the city impressed him, he was unimpressed by St. Augustine's hotels.

So, with the same inspiration that had enabled him to turn Standard Oil into a profit-spewing giant, Flagler hit upon an idea. If he liked St. Augustine, other visitors likely would as well. If he didn't think much of the hotels, neither would other well-heeled worldly travelers. So he'd build a hotel that would satisfy the discerning and expensive tastes of these visitors.

And he had another idea. He could build and own the means of transportation that could bring hundreds of those visitors to St. Augustine every day—the railroad.

This formula was one Flagler would repeat for two decades—extending his Florida East Coast Railway down the state's Atlantic coast, and building sumptuous hotels along the way. His first hotel, the sprawling, 544-room Ponce de León Hotel, opened in St. Augustine in 1885.

That same year, young Thomas Edison was attending the World Industrial and Cotton Centennial in New Orleans when he heard that bamboo grew to towering heights near Fort Myers on the Florida Gulf Coast. Since bamboo was used as the filament in his incandescent lightbulbs, he decided to go to Fort Myers to take a look.

Edison, thirty-eight years old and recently a widower, decided to build a winter home in Fort Myers. He would spend winters there for six decades, and his presence would help to transform Fort Myers from a rustic village where cattle roamed the unpaved streets into a bustling city.

By the last decade of the nineteenth century, more dreamers and schemers were finding their way to Florida. One of them was Cyrus Teed, a doctor, who claimed that he was visited by an angel in 1870 in his laboratory in Utica, New York.

Teed said that the angel—blonde, beautiful, and dressed in a gorgeous gold-and-purple gown—had explained to him that conventional science was wrong about the nature of the universe. The sun and the orbiting solar system didn't exist, she said. The Earth actually was hollow, and the universe existed inside it. The continents were on the inner walls of the hollow sphere, and the sun and heavens were suspended in the center of the sphere.

Teed, who started calling himself "Koresh," thought such a revelation was worthy of a religious movement, but he had trouble attracting followers until 1886, when he spoke to the National Association for Mental Sciences in Chicago.

Koresh explained his theories, and his audience was amazed. They elected him president and gave him a free hand to reshape the organization as he wished. Soon it became the Koreshan Unity.

Koresh's followers eventually made him a wealthy man, but Chicago newspapers were skeptical of the self-proclaimed religious leader, "whose brown, restless eyes glow and burn like live coals." And Koresh was branded a home-wrecker and reportedly was nearly lynched by angry Chicago husbands whose wives had succumbed to his charismatic appeal and joined his group.

Teed started looking into Florida real estate, and, with winter approaching, he bought about three hundred acres near Fort Myers in November 1894. The seller was an immigrant farmer named Gustave Damkohler, who was dazzled by Teed's plans to build the utopian city of New Jerusalem, where, he predicted, ten million people of all races would live in harmony.

The winter of 1894–95 began as a typically mild Florida winter. But before it ended, bitterly cold weather would change the course of Florida's history.

On Christmas Day, the temperature climbed into the 80s in Orlando, the center of Florida's growing citrus industry. But the warm temperature would prove to be especially cruel for the state's orange and grapefruit trees.

A few days after Christmas, citrus growers gathered in Orlando's San Juan Hotel. On December 28, a cold front from the northwest pushed rain and plummeting temperatures into northern and central Florida. The following morning, the citrus growers awoke to a temperature of 24 degrees Fahrenheit in Orlando—stunning cold for Florida.

Had cooler temperatures prevailed in northern and central Florida earlier in December, the citrus trees would have started going dormant and thus been a little better prepared for the cold snap. Still, some oranges and grapefruit trees might have survived even the plunge into the mid-20s had the cold been brief. But the warm Christmas Day temperature followed by the sudden, brutal, and prolonged cold snap was the end of the citrus crop. Even the fruit that had been hanging on the trees at the time of the plunge in the temperature froze.

Panic spread through the San Juan Hotel. Around nine p.m. on the evening of December 29, a handsome, middle-aged man wearing a Stetson hat and a fashionable frock coat stepped out of the hotel to check the temperature. He looked at the thermometer and groaned aloud. Then he pulled out a pistol and put a bullet into his brain.

A few days into the New Year, temperatures warmed, and by late January the few trees that had somehow managed to survive the December freeze were recovering. But on February 7, 1895, an even colder icy blast dropped the temperature in northern and central Florida to 17 degrees. Manatees froze to death in the Sebastian River near Melbourne, and a bizarre icy appearance descended on the tropical landscape.

"It was a strange experience to walk over the frozen sand and see every little puddle covered with ice, on a trail overhung by the sub-tropical vegetation of a

Florida hammock with a north wind blowing in my face that chilled me to the bones," Outram Bangs recalled in an article for *The American Naturalist* a few months later.

It would be years before the citrus crop recovered. And the twin freezes of December and February started a domino-like effect of failing businesses and then failing banks. Before the freezes, eight banks operated in Orlando and surrounding Orange County. Only one bank survived the economic chaos after the freeze.

While orange and grapefruit trees in Florida were being killed by icy weather, a vicious winter storm was forming off the Atlantic coast, and bitterly cold temperatures plunged much of the nation into a deep freeze. Dallas, Texas, reported a temperature of 0 degrees Fahrenheit on the morning of February 7, 1895, and towns in Colorado reported temperatures of 8 below. Railroad traffic was hopelessly snarled by ice and snow. In Memphis, a railroad flagman slipped on ice and fell in front of a moving train.

The storm slammed into New England with terrific force. It had been a long time since the old-timers on Cape Cod had seen anything like the blizzard that walloped them with winds approaching hurricane strength on February 8, 1895.

But while the rest of the nation was shivering and cursing the cold, the temperature on Biscayne Bay near the tip of the Florida peninsula stayed above the freezing mark. Julia Tuttle, a shrewd local businesswoman and landowner who had been trying to persuade Henry Flagler to extend his railroad to Fort Dallas, decided to make one more try. Legend has it that she sent fresh flowers and orange blossoms to Flagler to impress upon him that while the rest of the nation was frozen, Fort Dallas and Biscayne Bay were untouched by the awful winter.

So as the nation dug itself out from the arctic blast of February 1895, two men made decisions that would have dramatic effects on Florida's future. In St. Augustine, Henry Flagler—with or without the orange blossoms from Tuttle—decided to extend his railroad to Fort Dallas. And in Massachusetts, Reverend Solomon Merrick, a Congregationalist minister who had ridden out the blizzard with his family on Cape Cod, decided he'd had enough of New England winters. He was going to move his family to a little settlement on the balmy shores of Biscayne Bay. His young son George would later figure prominently in Florida's development.

By April 1896, Flagler had extended his railroad to Fort Dallas. Along the way he'd built hotels in Jacksonville, Ormand Beach, and Palm Beach, as well as a second hotel in St. Augustine. He had also built a lavish mansion in Palm Beach for his third wife, Mary Lily Kenan Flagler.

Flagler also was working on a new hotel in the little settlement that had been named after the old Seminole Wars fort. The utilitarian military name had been changed to something more lyrical in July 1896. Taking its name from the river that flowed into Biscayne Bay, the settlement was now called Miami. And in January 1897, the sumptuous hotel that inevitably followed Flagler's railroad opened—the Royal Palm Hotel. The yellow-and-white, six-story hotel included a swimming pool and docks for guests' yachts.

Flagler bought land from Julia Tuttle and the Brickell family, and he intended to build a city around his railroad. But before Tuttle sold the land to Flagler, she made him agree to an unusual clause she'd inserted into the deed to his new property. Before Flagler could resell the land, the prospective buyer had to agree not to buy, sell, or manufacture alcoholic beverages on the property. If a landowner violated this clause, the land immediately reverted to Flagler.

As soon as Miami was established, however, determined entrepreneurs set up saloons less than twenty feet from the new city limits. It was the beginning of a battle between "wets" and "drys" in the city that would continue for decades.

In the summer of 1896, as Miami started to transform itself from a drowsy, isolated tropical village, the United States was in the process of choosing its twenty-fifth president.

In Chicago, Democrats were divided about their nominee until a young Nebraska lawyer took the podium to address the crowd. When William Jennings Bryan, only thirty-six years old, finished, he had electrified the convention and galvanized the Democrats around his candidacy.

Bryan's oration became known as the "Cross of Gold" speech. It was an impassioned demand for fairness toward the common man, whose economic struggles were made immensely more difficult by the nation's adherence to the gold standard that was staunchly supported by the Republican Party.

Bryan wanted to make the United States into his vision of the Promised Land, where everyone, no matter how humble their circumstances, could enjoy a life of opportunity, comfort, and security. And when humble men united behind a just cause, they were invincible, he said.

"The humblest citizen in all the land when clad in the armor of a righteous cause is stronger than all the whole hosts of error that they can bring," Bryan said.

His stirring speech called for everyday working Americans to stand up against "the encroachments of aggregated wealth" and demanded that the "humbler members of our society" receive the benefits they had earned for helping to create the nation's prosperity.

"We will say to the Republican Party in this campaign," Bryan intoned in the closing of his speech, " 'you shall not press down upon the brow of labor this crown of thorns; you shall not crucify mankind on a cross of gold.' "

There was a moment of silence as Bryan ended his speech and prepared to step down from the podium. Then twenty thousand delegates exploded into applause.

"Then from the remotest wall to the speaker's stand, from end to end of the gigantic hall, came like one great burst of artillery the answer of the convention," the *Newark* (Ohio) *Daily Advocate* reported. "Roar upon roar, crash upon crash of fierce, delirious applause."

The delegates stood on their chairs, threw hats into the air, and waved handkerchiefs, "tossing like whitecaps on the winter sea," the *Advocate* said.

"The orator was literally whirled off his feet and borne on by the struggling masses of his frantic friends," the *Advocate* said. "From that hour, Hon. Wm. J. Bryan was as good as nominated for President, despite the efforts of leaders and friends of other candidates to stop the tremendous tide."

Bryan would lose the election to Republican William McKinley, and he would lose two other attempts at the White House in 1900 and 1908. But three attempts at the presidency would establish Bryan as a staunch advocate and spokesman for the common man, make his name a household word, and lay the groundwork for a profitable career in Florida real estate a few decades later.

Bryan paid his first visit to Florida in 1898, when unrest in Cuba finally brought Spain and the United States to war. Cuban rebels who wanted independence from Spain had been clashing with loyalists for years. And some, including Cuban poet and patriot José Martí, had been planning and organizing their efforts against Spain in Cuban communities in Tampa and Key West.

In January 1898, rioting erupted in Havana. On January 24, the United States dispatched the powerful battleship USS *Maine* from Key West to Havana, hoping that a show of force would cool passions.

On the evening of February 15, about half an hour after a US Marine bugler had blown the mournful notes of "Taps" aboard the *Maine*, there was a muted explosion in or near the battleship. Then came a second explosion, powerful enough to lift the ship's bow out of the water and toss the massive turret of one of its ten-inch guns off the deck.

More than 260 American sailors were killed. Historians are still arguing about whether the explosion was caused by a bomb planted by Spanish loyalists hoping to provoke a war with the United States or by volatile gases that ignited in the battleship's coal bunker. But after an investigation, American officials decided the deadly blast had been caused by a bomb planted by Spanish saboteurs.

Goaded on by sensationalistic newspaper stories about the explosion of the *Maine* and Spanish atrocities in Cuba, the United States declared war on Spain in April 1898.

The US Navy immediately took the war to the Pacific Ocean. On May 1, an American fleet under Commodore George Dewey destroyed a Spanish fleet of warships in Manila Bay in the Philippines.

But the US Army was much slower to gear up for war. The United States had not had a major mobilization of troops since the end of the Civil War. When war on Spain was declared, the US Army had only about twenty-eight thousand men under arms. It would take time to field a force against Spain. And because of Florida's proximity to Cuba, it was a logical place for the army to prepare 125,000 new soldiers for battle.

It made sense to train troops in Jacksonville and Tampa, two cities with excellent harbors where troops and war matériel could easily be moved in and out. It made less sense to station troops in Miami, which, even with Flagler's railroad, was still little more than a settlement and did not have a harbor comparable to Tampa, Jacksonville, and Key West.

An army inspector filed two reports saying that Miami was not a good place to put soldiers, but Miami residents believed their frontier town would be a target for Spanish ships, and Flagler thought it would be good for his railroad to have an army base there.

So troops were sent to Miami.

The city was still a frontier village with a few hundred residents in April 1898. The town started changing, however, when the troops came. Money and people poured in. Many soldiers weren't impressed with South Florida in the summer, however; a Louisiana soldier described Miami as "a waste wilderness as can be conceived only in rare nightmares."

American military leaders thought Tampa would be a good place to assemble and train troops for an invasion of Cuba. The declaration of war on Spain and the call for 125,000 recruits had stirred patriotic passions in young American men, who flocked to recruiting stations. Soon they were pouring into Tampa, at the time a city of about twelve thousand.

Commanding General of the Army Nelson Miles was dismayed by the conditions when he arrived in Tampa in June 1898. All was chaos. Miles pronounced the confusion "inextricable." But eventually, American troops were ready to invade Cuba.

William Jennings Bryan volunteered his services to the US Army, and in July, he arrived in Jacksonville as a colonel commanding a regiment of troops from Nebraska. The war moved quickly once American troops invaded Cuba in mid-June, so the conflict ended with Bryan still in the army camp in Jacksonville.

Still, Bryan would not forget his first trip to Florida.

Julia Tuttle died the same month the war ended, and about half the land in Miami went to her heirs. The executor of her will, Harry Tuttle, wasn't as fussy about booze as his mother had been. In 1900, he sold a lot inside the city limits without the "no alcohol" clause.

The new owner promptly opened a saloon.

The railroads continued to bring wealthy visitors to Florida who liked what they saw and bought property. Louis Comfort Tiffany and William Luden, the cough drop millionaire, were among the super-rich who built huge houses in Miami.

When Flagler sat down to talk with journalist James Barrow in 1907, he was only a few days past his seventy-seventh birthday, and had recently started his most ambitious—some would say craziest—project. In those long-ago days before labor unions, the Occupational Safety and Health Administration, and the Environmental Protection Agency, he was extending his railroad from Miami,

128 miles down the remote, ecologically fragile Florida Keys to Key West, the nation's southernmost city.

It was a Herculean undertaking that would require unheard-of feats of engineering.

But Flagler didn't intend to stop at Key West. The bustling maritime city of about twenty thousand—accessible only by boat, and about as much Caribbean as American—was only ninety miles from Havana, Cuba. Flagler intended to extend rail passenger and freight service to Cuba. Tourists could board a train in New York and ride to Key West, where the passenger cars would be loaded on a special ferry for the crossing to Havana. When the ferry arrived in the Cuban capital, departing passengers would board the passenger cars for the return trip to Key West and points north.

The frugal minister's son who had set off on his own as a teenager with a handful of coins in his pocket was worth somewhere around $60 million—about $1.5 billion in twenty-first-century dollars. Flagler recalled the early days when he was broke and in debt and trying to recover and learn from his mistakes.

"I carried a lunch in my pocket until I was a rich man," he told Barrow. "I trained myself in the school of self-control and self-denial."

Flagler acknowledged that the self-imposed frugality hadn't been easy, but it was better than working for someone else.

"It was hard on [me], but I would rather be my own tyrant than have someone else tyrannize over me," he said.

His nineteenth-century upbringing as the son of a poor-but-honest preacher had had a dramatic influence on his attitude toward great wealth.

"If money is spent for personal uses, to promote idleness, luxury, and selfishness, it is a curse to the possessor and to society," Flagler told Barrow. "Wealth brings obligation, moral and governmental. It has but one legitimate function, and that is its employment for the welfare of the nation. The man who builds a factory or digs a mine serves his country."

It was a properly moral Victorian attitude of noblesse oblige. And he expressed another old-fashioned opinion about acquiring great wealth: It took an awful lot of hard work and self-sacrifice, and required a single-minded, almost fanatical devotion.

"To succeed may cost one's health, or it may mean separation from one's family and friends and banishment to the desert, the mine, or the forest," he said. "But no matter the way and no matter the price, success always demands unremitting toil, self-denial, and enthusiasm."

Henry Flagler would live just long enough to see his railroad to Key West—called the Overseas Extension—completed in 1912. He died after taking a bad fall a year later at his magnificent home in Palm Beach.

Flagler's construction crews employed hundreds of men to clear the right-of-way and lay the tracks for the railroad down Florida's east coast. Among the men who hired on was Joe Ashley, a backwoodsman who was a highly skilled trapper and marksman.

Joe Ashley brought his family from the state's Gulf Coast and joined Flagler's construction crew in 1904, the year Flagler made the decision to extend his railroad to Key West. Among Joe Ashley's sons was eleven-year-old John, who had inherited his father's remarkable skill as a marksman with a rifle and a pistol. John preferred to spend his time in the wilds, trapping otters. The skills the youngster was developing would serve him well in another, more lucrative occupation in a few years.

In 1905, Flagler's work crews began clearing the right-of-way to lay rails to the tip of the Florida peninsula, where they would start building bridges and laying tracks across the Florida Keys. Florida's mild winters and rail connections to populous northeastern cities were getting more attention across the country. The January 1906 edition of *National Geographic* magazine noted that southern Florida was "the only truly tropical land" that was connected by rail to the eastern United States. "It is indeed a wonder that when cold weather comes, this region is not completely overrun with people," writer John Gifford said.

As the first decade of the new century ended, Florida was not running over with people, but it was starting to get noticed. The 1910 US Census showed that the state's population had increased from just over 528,000 in 1900 to about 753,000 in 1910.

The population increase for Dade County—which included Miami—was especially impressive. In 1900, when Dade County extended one hundred miles up the coast from Miami, its population was about 4,600. Ten years later, Dade's boundaries had been shrunk to create Palm Beach and St. Lucie Counties to its north. But even within the diminished boundaries, Dade's 1910 population had more than doubled in a decade, to just under 12,000. And the combined population of the new counties that occupied Dade's old boundaries was approaching an additional 9,700 newcomers.

Americans were beginning to realize that an earthly version of Paradise lay at their doorstep. Florida was a long way from being tamed, but the tangled, unearthly wilderness that had terrified Jonathan Dickinson and alternately disgusted and enthralled Jacob Motte did not seem quite so wild and impenetrable anymore. As the first decade of the new century ended, more newcomers were coming to Florida, bringing their dreams, ideas, and money. As they worked to carve an idyllic paradise out of the wilderness, a homegrown gang of opportunistic thieves—daring, ruthless, clever, and intimately familiar with the wilds of southern Florida—were determined to grab as much of the new wealth as they could carry away to their hideout, deep in the Everglades.

After all, they told themselves, they were entitled to it.

CHAPTER THREE

Dreamers and Thieves

A LIFETIME OF WRESTING A LIVING FROM THE WILDS OF SOUTHERN FLORIDA had made Joe Ashley a hard man. But it also had made him resourceful, practical, and determined, and it had relieved him of any lingering concerns about laws. He was not one to let ethics or propriety stand between him and a dollar. In his book, if you saw a chance to make—or take—a dollar and you stopped to think about right and wrong, you'd probably miss your opportunity. And only a fool would hesitate to take what he could. If the other man wasn't quick enough or smart enough or strong enough to hold on to it, that was his problem.

Ashley and his family—his wife, five sons, and four daughters—moved from a small settlement near the mouth of the Caloosahatchee River on Florida's Gulf Coast to the state's Atlantic coast in 1904. Ashley went to work on one of the crews clearing right-of-way for the Florida East Coast Railway's relentless southward march to the tip of the peninsula and beyond. Some said that Ashley moved his family because he'd gotten into a gunfight and his seriously wounded opponent had sworn revenge when he recovered.

Aside from matters of style and social graces, Joe Ashley and his clan weren't too different from many of the other dreamers and fortune seekers who started coming to Florida in a steady stream in the first two decades of the twentieth century. They wanted lots and lots of money. But unlike the persevering preacher's son who'd opened the door to the state, many of the newcomers felt they were entitled to wealth, and they didn't have time to work for a lifetime to accumulate it. They wanted it now.

Joe Ashley's son John had inherited his old man's worldview, as well as his uncanny skill with firearms. It was said that John could lay a whiskey bottle on its side on a tree stump and, from thirty paces away, put a bullet through the bottleneck so cleanly that only the bottom of the bottle would be broken.

John also inherited his father's skills as a woodsman. And something—perhaps Joe's spare-no-rod parenting style—had made John just plain mean.

In late 1911, John, now in his early twenties, went on a hunting and trapping expedition in the Everglades northwest of Fort Lauderdale. During this hunting trip, his youthful greed and impulsiveness and his inherent ruthlessness would prompt him to kill a young husband and father because he wanted something that was worth a small fortune. And he wanted it immediately.

Only the man he killed saw John Ashley commit the crime, but the evidence against him was airtight. He should have swung from the gallows soon after he was arrested and charged with the murder, and the world would have been rid of him. But clever lawyers played the legal system to keep the noose from Ashley's neck. And his backwoods cunning, his cold-blooded daring, and some plain old good luck took over from there.

For a decade after John Ashley dodged the hangman's noose, he and his family, aided by a few career criminals who joined them, did pretty much as they pleased in southeastern Florida between Fort Pierce and the Florida Keys. They robbed banks and bootleggers. They made and sold moonshine and hauled whiskey from the Bahamas. They made fools of some cops and killed others, and they eluded capture by intimidating all who would offer evidence against them. And when things got too hot, they disappeared into the Everglades.

John Ashley's criminal career started with a hunting trip.

In early November 1911, John left his family's home just south of Stuart for a hunting and trapping expedition in the Everglades. He loaded camping gear, food, a tent, several guns, and dozens of traps into his canoe. He was especially interested in trapping otters. Otter fur was valuable and would fetch a handsome price in Miami and Fort Lauderdale.

But as Christmas approached, Ashley had nothing to show for more than a month in the wilds. On December 19, Ashley stopped at the encampment of Homer Tindall, a young man about his own age who was on a hunting expedition with his father. The Tindalls were camped near the dredge *Caloosahatchee*, a floating earth-mover that was working on the North New River Canal, a drainage canal being built about twenty-five miles west of Fort Lauderdale.

Ashley stayed in the Tindalls' camp a couple of days. He and Homer watched Seminole Indians coming and going on the canal, and Ashley wondered if the Indians had had better luck with their traps than he'd had with his.

On the morning of Thursday, December 21, Ashley left the Tindalls' camp and paddled up the canal to a Seminole encampment a few miles from the *Caloosahatchee*.

The Seminoles had indeed had better luck, accumulating a pile of eighty-four otter pelts, cured and ready for market. They were worth a lot of money, and John Ashley eyed them enviously.

Among the Seminoles was Desoto Tiger, twenty-five years old and oldest son of Tom Tiger, a Seminole chief who had died about a decade earlier. Like his father, Desoto Tiger was highly respected by his tribesmen. He spoke perfect English and was married with two small children—a boy, four, and an infant daughter.

After eyeing the otter hides, Ashley disappeared for a couple of days.

The crew of the *Caloosahatchee* shut down to take a Christmas holiday, but on Christmas Day, John Ashley showed up at the dredge with a couple gallons of whiskey. The Seminoles, who were camped nearby, came to the dredge and joined Ashley for an evening of Christmas cheer. Word spread, and soon a sizable crowd had assembled.

It was a relatively tame party for a gang of young men gathered deep in the Everglades with gallons of whiskey. Still, there was a mishap. One of the Seminoles who'd had too much to drink fell from the upper deck of the dredge. Although he was seriously injured, the party continued.

After an evening of boozing, Ashley showed up at the Seminoles' camp around daybreak. He showed no interest in resuming his hunting and trapping expedition. Instead, he parked himself in the Indians' camp and started guzzling whiskey. He stayed there several days, drinking. And apparently the way he eyed the Indians' stack of pelts made them uneasy. The Seminoles tried to get Ashley to leave, but he wouldn't budge. So they decided to move their valuable stash to the *Caloosahatchee*, where it would be more secure.

Desoto Tiger was chosen to move the hides to the dredge. Early Friday morning, December 29, 1911, Tiger and Ashley watched other Seminoles load the furs into Tiger's canoe, which was equipped with a sail. As Tiger got into the canoe to start the trip to the dredge, Ashley asked to join him, saying he wanted to go to the dredge to buy some food. Ashley brought his rifle—a handsome, .38-55 caliber, Model 1894, lever-action Winchester—with him, but left all of his other gear at the Seminoles' camp. Desoto Tiger placed a pistol in the canoe next to where he would stand to propel the vessel with a pole.

John Ashley and Desoto Tiger left the camp shortly before eight a.m. Around ten a.m., the crew aboard the *Caloosahatchee* saw John Ashley glide by in a canoe. He was alone.

Later that day, another Seminole took his tribesman who'd been injured Christmas night to Fort Lauderdale to see a doctor.

The following day, Desoto Tiger's uncle, Jim Gopher, was worried. His nephew hadn't returned to camp, nor had he been seen since the previous morning when he'd gotten into the canoe with John Ashley. Jim Gopher set out to find his nephew.

He went first to the *Caloosahatchee*, but the crew there hadn't seen Desoto Tiger.

Jim Gopher kept looking. He found an oar in the saw grass next to the canal. It was his nephew's. Clearly something had gone wrong during the short trip from the Seminoles' camp to the *Caloosahatchee*.

Jim Gopher went back to the dredge. There, he met his tribesman who'd taken the injured Seminole to Fort Lauderdale. He told Jim Gopher that he'd seen John Ashley in the canal near Fort Lauderdale around four p.m. the previous day. Ashley's own boat was still in the Seminoles' camp in the Everglades.

On Sunday morning, December 31, Melville Forrey, the captain of the *Caloosahatchee*, led a search party seeking Desoto Tiger. Jim Gopher took them to the spot where he'd found the oar. As the wake from their small boat rolled toward the canal bank, a human body suddenly floated to the surface. It was Desoto Tiger. He'd been shot twice.

One bullet had struck him between the eyes and exited the back of his head. The other had struck him in the chest but hadn't exited. Forrey got out his knife and dug out the bullet. It was a .38-55 caliber slug.

James Girtman couldn't believe that the sunburned young man who came to his store on Saturday morning, December 30, was John Ashley. The last time he'd seen Ashley, he was a little kid in short breeches. But here he was, and he had otter pelts to sell, eighty-four of them.

Girtman made Ashley an offer—$584 for the lot, and not a nickel more. Ashley thought that was a mighty cheap price. But, he admitted, he hadn't gone to a lot of trouble to get the hides. He'd trapped some of them and swapped for the others. So he was willing to sell them for what Girtman offered.

Girtman gave Ashley $84 in cash and told him to come back shortly for the rest of the money. When Ashley returned, he was decked out in new clothes. He went with Girtman to a bank, where Girtman cashed a check and gave $500 to Ashley.

It was a lot of walking-around money for 1911—more than $14,000 in twenty-first-century dollars. John Ashley hired a cab to drive him to West Palm Beach. The cabbie dropped him off in what was delicately referred to in those days as the "red-light district." Flush with cash, Ashley went into a whorehouse, intent on a night of single-minded pleasure.

Ashley's exuberance got the better of him, however, and soon the cops were hauling him off to jail for recklessly shooting up the house. No one was injured, but Ashley had raised quite a ruckus. The West Palm Beach police hadn't heard about the killing in the Everglades. Ashley paid his $25 bail, collected his guns—including his prized Winchester—and left town aboard the northbound Florida East Coast Railway passenger train. It was New Year's Eve, 1911. John Ashley didn't know it, but he was a wanted man. And it wasn't because he'd skipped bail for shooting up a whorehouse. He was wanted for murder.

Stories about the brutal murder of a respected Seminole Indian in the Everglades started appearing in newspapers soon after New Year's Day, and the name "J. H. Ashley" was connected to the crime. Word reached Joe Ashley's house that the cops were looking for his son. On January 3, 1912, John Ashley said good-bye to his family and headed west for New Orleans. From there, he made his way to San Francisco, and then north to the Pacific Northwest, where he hired on with a logging crew out of Seattle.

The police would learn nothing about John Ashley's whereabouts from his family. But they didn't give up the search, nor did the Seminole Tribe.

On January 12, nine days after Ashley's hasty departure from Florida, a dignified and well-spoken Sioux Indian from Muskogee, Oklahoma, sat down for a special meeting with the Palm Beach County Board of Commissioners. The Native American's name was James W. Strongheart. He was the grandson of the famous warrior Sitting Bull, and he was related to Desoto Tiger by marriage. He'd come to Florida to try to track down the man who'd killed his in-law.

Strongheart had been to the Everglades, where he'd made his own inquiries into the death of Desoto Tiger. He was convinced that John Ashley had killed Desoto Tiger for the otter pelts.

Strongheart wanted the county commissioners to offer a reward for Ashley, but county attorney H. L. Bussey said the county wasn't allowed to use public money for that purpose. The commissioners could, however, request Florida governor Park Trammell to offer a reward, and they were willing to do that.

Strongheart was convinced that a large reward would be more likely to get results. So a week after his meeting with the Palm Beach County commissioners, he met with a multimillionaire businessman who'd recently arrived in Miami. The new resident was a Midwesterner, a dynamic, energetic man who had a few ideas for a real estate venture.

Strongheart described the details of the death of Desoto Tiger and explained what he was trying to do. The man who'd killed his in-law was little more than an animal. He had to be captured and brought to justice. A big reward would be a powerful inducement for someone to come forward with information that could lead to his capture and conviction.

The businessman listened to Strongheart's request and agreed. Tell the newspapers that I'll kick in a contribution to the reward fund, he said.

Strongheart was elated. He talked to a reporter for the *Miami Daily Metropolis* at Girtman Bros. Groceries on Twelfth Street, where John Ashley had sold his ill-gotten otter hides a few weeks earlier.

The January 18, 1912, edition of the *Metropolis* published a front-page, above-the-fold story saying that Carl G. Fisher, "a wealthy resident who is from Indiana," would pay a $500 reward for information that led to the conviction of the murderer of Desoto Tiger.

The reward for Desoto Tiger's killer was one of Fisher's earliest investments in Florida. Before he was finished, he would sink millions more into the community.

Fisher was a grade-school dropout who had made a fortune by inventing the automobile headlight. He was also a founding partner of the Indianapolis 500 in 1911. In 1910 he bought a mansion on a stretch of Brickell Avenue overlooking Biscayne Bay that came to be known as "Millionaires' Row."

Fisher bought the mansion sight unseen as a winter vacation home. He would become one of several powerful, wealthy men who became fascinated with Florida around the start of the second decade of the new century. These men—Fisher, William Jennings Bryan, Barron Collier, and others—would build on Henry Flagler's investment and lay the foundation for Florida's spectacular growth—and wild real estate speculation—a decade later.

Around the same time that Fisher agreed to offer a reward for the arrest of John Ashley, he met John Collins, who, at the age of seventy-five, had bought property on a swampy, mosquito-infested barrier island about two and a half miles offshore. Collins called his island Ocean Beach, and he was trying to build a wooden bridge across Biscayne Bay to his property. But he'd run out of money.

Collins impressed Fisher, and he loaned Collins $50,000 to complete the bridge. Collins gave Fisher two hundred acres on his island.

Carl Fisher's wife Jane visited the island with her husband and saw a jungle swarming with mosquitoes. She had no idea why her husband wanted it.

But Fisher, like other dreamers who'd come to Florida before him, saw a paradise.

As Jane Fisher swatted mosquitoes, her husband stood in the middle of the swamp and told her that he was going to build a city here—"a city like magic," she recalled, "like romantic places you read and dream about but never see."

Jane Fisher said it was Carl's "greatest and craziest dream." He was going to create Miami Beach.

Like Henry Flagler, Carl Fisher realized that his vision for his magic city could only be accomplished if more people came to Florida. But unlike Flagler, whose notion of transportation was the nineteenth-century steam-powered passenger train, Fisher was plugged into the transportation of the future—the automobile. And before automobiles could bring hordes of newcomers to Florida, good roads would have to be built.

So Fisher became a driving force behind two major arteries that would open Florida to the automobile—the Dixie Highway, which ran from the Midwest to Miami, and the Lincoln Highway, which ran from San Francisco to New York City.

The bridge to John Collins's swampy island opened in June 1913—one month after Henry Flagler died after falling down a flight of stairs in his Palm Beach mansion. The bridge was billed as the longest wooden bridge in the world.

Fisher bought more land, hired a construction crew to clear away mangroves and build bulkheads, and started pumping sand from Biscayne Bay onto his property. In a few years he'd raised most of Ocean Beach to at least five feet above sea level. He planted grass and trees, built tennis courts and golf courses, and planned to turn the island into a sun-and-fun destination that catered to the wealthy. He was so determined that Ocean Beach be associated only with carefree fun that he forbade cemeteries on the island.

But in November 1913, just as Fisher was putting the finishing touches on Ocean Beach, his hopes of attracting tourists were dealt a serious blow when Dade County voters narrowly approved a referendum banning the sale of alcoholic beverages. The polls had scarcely closed, however, before bootleggers were doing a flourishing business.

If Fisher was upset by the vote, the referendum undoubtedly pleased his Brickell Avenue neighbor, William Jennings Bryan, a longtime and passionate advocate of Prohibition. At the same time the bridge to Fisher's dream-city-to-be was being completed, workmen were putting the finishing touches on Bryan's new waterfront home overlooking Biscayne Bay. Bryan had decided to build a winter home in Florida for a now-familiar reason: He hoped the climate would improve his wife's fragile health.

Bryan first visited Miami on Christmas Day, 1909, when he delivered a speech that came to be known as "The Prince of Peace" lecture, in which he affirmed his faith in religion and disputed Charles Darwin's theory of evolution.

Bryan visited Fort Myers and Miami in January 1912, and hinted that he and his wife were thinking about building a winter home in Miami. He took a quick look at the Everglades and made a boat trip across Lake Okeechobee. The farmer's son was impressed by the lake area's rich, dark soil.

"One could hardly believe that there was such an enormous wealth of soil undeveloped, and the area of it amazes me," he told *Miami Daily Metropolis*. "I regard the reclamation of the Everglades as one of the greatest enterprises of its kind on record."

He brought his wife to the village of Miami and Mary Bryan was charmed from the moment she stepped off the Florida East Coast Railway train in May 1912.

"As soon as I breathed the balmy air of Miami I knew this was the place, and began to investigate," she later recalled.

The Bryans started work on their home on Brickell Avenue soon after he became secretary of state under President Woodrow Wilson in 1913. Bryan rolled up his sleeves and helped the stonemasons build a garden wall on the property.

The *Miami Daily Metropolis* of April 11, 1913, described Bryan's new home overlooking Biscayne Bay as a "magnificent and stately structure" that had been designed by Mary to resemble "an old Spanish castle."

Miami wasn't the only part of Florida that was getting the attention of wealthy, powerful men. In 1911, Barron Gift Collier, a high school dropout who'd become a millionaire by the age of twenty-six, visited Useppa Island, near Fort Myers on Florida's Gulf Coast. He liked it so much he bought it, and then he started buying more property, eventually creating his own empire on Florida's southwest coast.

By 1911, Miami had about six thousand residents, and apparently that was big enough for the federal government to decide to put a US Weather Bureau station there.

At the time, the Weather Bureau was a branch of the Department of Agriculture. The science of meteorology was in its infancy, and a college degree in the field was not required in order to be in charge of a Weather Bureau station. Station chiefs made observations on such things as wind speed and direction, temperatures and barometric pressure readings, forwarding the information on to Washington, DC.

All weather forecasts for all parts of the country came from Washington.

In early May 1911, Richard W. Gray arrived in Miami to be the first "official in charge" of the Weather Bureau station there. His qualifications for the post were meager—a high school diploma from Charlotte, North Carolina, and "various special courses" that included two years' study of mathematics and languages, according to Department of Agriculture inspection reports written a few years after Gray took the post.

Despite his sparse training in meteorology, Gray's abilities and efficiency were considered "excellent," inspector H. C. Frankenfield wrote. But under "special qualifications" for the post, the inspector noted "None."

Gray, thirty-six years old when he took the job, was "a tall, slender young man of pleasing personality and address," Frankenfield noted. "His habits are good and his standing in the community is excellent. So far as is known he lives within his means, and he has no source of income other than his official salary.

"Mr. Gray appears to have read and studied extensively, and has passed all of the Weather Bureau examinations with high percentages," Frankenfield wrote. "He is ambitious and energetic, and can do work of a better class than is required here. He likewise has confidence in his own abilities, and would be glad to change stations, if advanced in grade."

Gray was "a good man," Frankenfield concluded, although, at times, he could be "a trifle too loquacious."

A month after Richard Gray had set up shop at Miami's new US Weather Bureau station, Solomon Merrick, the minister who had left behind New England's bitter winters for a sunny citrus farm in Florida, died after an extended illness. His son George, who'd been studying law at New York University, dropped out of school and came home to take over the family's citrus plantation.

George was an artistic young man who wrote poetry and had won a prize for one of his short stories. It occurred to him that maybe there was a better use for the farm than growing grapefruit. He started thinking about building a city—a beautiful, perfect city.

By late 1913, John Ashley had been away from Florida for two years. He'd spent some of that time working as a logger in the Pacific Northwest. He also claimed later that he'd crossed into Canada and robbed a bank.

He was getting homesick. Although there was the problem of the price on his head and the cops looking for him, he didn't care. He made his way back home to the family house at the edge of the Everglades.

Still, being a wanted man made him edgy.

On January 27, 1914, Floyd Chaffin, a civil engineer, was riding his motorcycle on a stretch of the Dixie Highway between Stuart and West Palm Beach. Near the little community of Fruita, John Ashley and his younger brother Bob suddenly stepped out of the thick vegetation that lined the highway, pointed guns at Chaffin, and ordered him to stop.

John Ashley aimed a shotgun at Chaffin, identified himself, and accused Chaffin of being a deputy sheriff sent to arrest him. He said he was going to kill all of the deputies in Palm Beach County. I'm a bad man, and I'm wanted all over the country, Ashley told Chaffin. Killing one more man won't make any difference to me.

Chaffin protested, telling the brothers that he was not a lawman. But it didn't matter to them. John Ashley hit the engineer with the butt of his shotgun several times, and then Bob pistol-whipped him. But instead of killing Chaffin, they left him lying in the road, injured but alive.

After the attack on the engineer, every cop and sheriff in the area knew John Ashley was back. On February 21, Palm Beach County Sheriff George Baker sent two deputies, S. A. Barfield and Rob Hanlon, to arrest him. The deputies were walking along the Dixie Highway, looking for a break in the jungle-like undergrowth, when John Ashley and brother Bob appeared before them, guns drawn.

The brothers disarmed the deputies and told them to go back to West Palm Beach. But Ashley couldn't resist taunting the lawmen. Tell Sheriff Baker not to send any more "chicken-hearted men" after him, he said.

It was hard for the Ashley clan to understand why the law was going to so much trouble to arrest John. The dead man was a Seminole Indian. What was all the fuss about?

Finally, the family made a cynical calculation. John would turn himself in and stand trial for the murder of Desoto Tiger. The way the Ashleys figured, there weren't twelve men—women couldn't serve on juries at the time—in Palm Beach County who would convict an Ashley for shooting a Seminole. No one who was a friend of the family would vote for a conviction. And anyone who wasn't a friend knew they'd face the furious wrath of the clan if they voted to convict John Ashley of a crime that could send him to the gallows.

Ashley made arrangements through an attorney to surrender to Palm Beach County sheriff's deputies. He promised to behave himself under two conditions: He didn't have to submit to being handcuffed when he was moved from the jail to the courtroom during the trial, and his father could bring his supper every night to the Palm Beach County Jail. Sheriff Baker agreed, and Ashley turned himself in on April 27, 1914.

Ashley's trial began in West Palm Beach a couple of months later. The Ashleys' gamble was shrewd, but not quite shrewd enough. On July 1, the jury retired to deliberate. When they returned, they told the judge they were deadlocked. Nine of their twelve members had voted, as the Ashleys figured they would, for acquittal. But three had dared to vote to convict John Ashley of murder.

It wasn't quite enough to get John Ashley off the hook. He'd have to stand trial again. Still, he continued to behave as a model prisoner. And undoubtedly he still believed, with good reason, that there weren't twelve men in Palm Beach County who'd be crazy enough to convict him.

In the closing days of John Ashley's trial in West Palm Beach, while the jury of twelve listened to attorneys sparring over how a man was killed in the wilds of the Everglades more than two years earlier, another man was killed in Europe.

On June 28, 1914, an angry young man with a gun killed a member of the ruling family of Austria-Hungary and his wife, who were visiting Sarajevo, Austria. The young gunman's name was Gavrilo Princip. Like countless assassins throughout history, Princip, a Serbian, believed that by killing Archduke Franz Ferdinand, heir to the throne of Austria-Hungary, he was striking a blow against a monstrous evil. What he'd actually done, however, was tip the first domino in a sequence of events that would ignite four years of slaughter in Europe.

The carnage that followed the deaths of two people in Sarajevo would change the world almost beyond recognition.

Before the war ended in 1918, more than sixty-five million servicemen from the United States, Britain, Germany, France, and many other countries around the world would be engaged in the conflict. More than eight million of them would die, along with nearly seven million civilians.

Although the murder of Franz Ferdinand and his wife was a brutal act, it did not have to ignite the greatest conflagration that the world had ever seen. The war happened because the assassination activated an entanglement of alliances and treaty obligations that quickly divided Europe into two opposing armed camps. In a sense, the conflict that came to be called the Great War happened because honor demanded it. And the weapons the belligerents wielded were frighteningly efficient, modern killing machines—rapid-fire machine guns, powerful artillery, airplanes, battleships, and submarines. It was the first time such deadly weapons had been deployed on so large a scale.

"All this madness, all this rage, all this flaming death of our civilization and our hopes has been brought about because a set of official gentlemen, living luxurious lives, mostly stupid, and all without imagination or heart, have chosen that it should occur rather than that any one of them should suffer some infinitesimal rebuff to his country's pride," British philosopher Bertrand Russell wrote in August 1914.

The story of the faraway assassination received prominent play on the front page of the *Miami Daily Metropolis* of June 29, 1914, although the killer was referred to as a "Servian" student. In fact, the newspaper's editors misspelled "Serb" and "Serbian" throughout the story as "Serv" and "Servian."

On the day that Franz Ferdinand and his wife Sophie were gunned down, the world still moved at a relaxed, nineteenth-century pace. Four-legged horsepower still was a primary means of transportation. Steam powered the locomotives that pulled trains and powered ships at sea, but there were plenty of sleek schooners that used the ancient propulsion of the wind.

Still, the technology that would change the world in a few years had appeared. Airplanes, primitive though they were, had been around for a decade, and would play a role in the war that was about to erupt in Europe. Automobiles powered by gasoline-fueled internal combustion engines were becoming common, although for long trips Americans still used the steam-powered passenger train.

The United States had ratified the Seventeenth Amendment to the Constitution in 1913, allowing voters in each state to choose the two senators who would represent them in the US Senate. Before the amendment, US senators had been chosen by individual state legislatures.

But the voters who went to the polls to choose those senators were males only, just like the jury in West Palm Beach that had been unable to come to a decision about whether John Ashley was guilty of murder. Women could not vote, nor could they serve on juries.

The outbreak of war in Europe in 1914 proved to be the undoing of William Jennings Bryan as secretary of state. Bryan was a firm believer that civilization was steadily moving humanity to a utopian destiny, when hunger, poverty, and wars would be eliminated. He was horrified as Europe stumbled inexorably toward a massive armed conflict. As Germany and the Central Powers squared off against the Allies—primarily Great Britain and France—Bryan insisted on a policy of strict neutrality toward the belligerent nations.

That was in line with President Woodrow Wilson's stated policy—at least, technically. But while Bryan had volunteered for military service during the Spanish-American War, he abhorred war and wanted to stop the fighting in any way possible, even if it left Britain and France at a disadvantage. And his concept of neutrality was so strict and narrow that he even refused to publicly condemn Germany when a German submarine torpedoed the British passenger liner *Lusitania* in May 1915. The sinking killed 1,198 civilians, including 128 Americans.

Germany claimed that the ship had been carrying war munitions for the Allies and therefore was a legitimate target of war. Bryan didn't dispute the German assertion.

Relations between Bryan and President Wilson became tense. Bryan submitted his resignation on June 8, 1915. He was a private citizen again, free to pursue other interests.

After the mistrial a few months earlier, John Ashley had spent the summer and much of the fall of 1914 behind bars in West Palm Beach, awaiting a new trial. No judge in his right mind was going to allow bail for a prisoner who had eluded cops for two years before turning himself in. Ashley kept his bargain about behaving, however, so he was never handcuffed, and he was allowed to receive home-cooked suppers from his mother while he was in jail.

Ashley's second trial started on November 11, 1914. The courtroom was packed with spectators and men called to serve as potential jurors. Judge Pierre Branning called the courtroom to order, then told the 150 potential jurors that any of them who were sick or deaf or had urgent business would be excused from duty.

"In an instant there was a rush to the front of the courtroom and about every ailment known to doctors was given out," reported the *Stuart Times*. "In fact, Judge Branning was surprised to hear of so much sickness."

About seventy-five jurors—half the pool—were excused. When all of those who remained had been questioned by prosecution and defense attorneys, only two had been chosen. It was abundantly clear that there were not a dozen men in Palm Beach County who were willing to sit in judgment of an Ashley.

The Ashleys didn't need an attorney to tell them that if a jury couldn't be selected in Palm Beach County, the judge would grant the prosecution's relentless requests to move the trial to another county. And a trial in another county in front of a jury they couldn't control either through friendship or intimidation could mean an unhappy outcome for John Ashley.

The Ashleys didn't like the odds. So on Saturday, November 15, Joe Ashley and his clan executed what could be called the "pork chop plan" to free John Ashley from jail.

Court was in session that day, but once again, no jurors were chosen. After the session ended but before John Ashley left the courthouse, Joe Ashley asked his son what he wanted for supper.

"John, do you want some good beefsteak for supper?" Joe Ashley asked.

"Yes," John answered.

"Wouldn't you rather have pork chops?" Joe suggested in a way that Sheriff Baker thought was a bit odd.

"Sure," John answered.

John Ashley then left with Robert Baker, a deputy sheriff who was the jailer, and also the son of Sheriff George Baker.

As usual, Ashley was not in handcuffs when he got into an automobile with Baker for the short ride from the courthouse to the jail. It was a dark and rainy night as Baker drove through the streets of West Palm Beach with his prisoner. Still, it wasn't dark enough to prevent Baker from recognizing Joe Ashley and one of his sons standing across the street from the jail.

As Ashley and Baker were walking from the car into the jail compound, Baker's wife called to him from the cottage next to the jail that she shared with her husband. She handed Baker a plate of pork chops that Joe Ashley had left for his son.

Baker and John Ashley walked to the entrance of the jail, and Baker handed his prisoner the plate so he could have both hands free to unlock the gate. He turned and put the key into the lock.

The next thing he heard was the sound of breaking glass, and when he turned around, he saw John Ashley disappearing around the corner. Still, there was a ten-foot fence surrounding the compound. No one could scale that without help.

Baker drew his gun and raced after his prisoner. In the darkness he heard Ashley blindly run into the fence. He fired a shot in the direction of the sound, and then ran to the fence.

Ashley was gone. The fence was intact. It was as though Ashley had simply melted through the wire. Baker took off in the direction that he thought Ashley would have gone, but there was no trace of him.

Sheriff George Baker told the *Daily Tropical Sun* of West Palm Beach that he thought the conversation between father and son about supper was a prearranged signal. His father's suggestion that John have pork chops for supper was a signal that it was time for him to break out of jail.

"It is supposed that a skiff or canoe with weapons and provisions had been furnished by his friends and put in some place known only to them and him so that he knew where to go and by this time is a long ways out in the Glades," the *Tropical Sun* concluded.

John Ashley stayed out of sight for a couple of months after his escape. But in February 1915, with winter tourists and money coming into Florida, the clan came out of hiding.

In 1894, the Florida East Coast Railway built a railroad drawbridge across the St. Lucie River, just north of Stuart. Eventually, seagulls learned that when a passenger train crossed the bridge, there was a good chance that food scraps would be thrown out of the dining car.

Soon Stuart residents could tell when a passenger train was approaching because gulls would alight on the bridge to await the train. They would be on the bridge long before the train's whistle was heard. Residents noted that they never assembled on the bridge in advance of freight trains.

Shortly after sundown on Sunday, February 7, 1915, the gulls settled on the bridge in anticipation of the arrival of a southbound trainload of tourists on the *Palm Beach Limited*. It was the peak of the winter season, and the luxurious Florida East Coast (FEC) Railway train, nicknamed "The Millionaires' Special," was hauling a load of well-heeled northern visitors—many of them New Yorkers—to Palm Beach. The train included an observation car with an open-air platform, where passengers could watch the tropical vista slide by.

Steam-powered locomotives were required to make regular stops to take on water for their boilers, and the *Palm Beach Limited* stopped at a water tank in Stuart. As the train started pulling away from the tank, but before it could pick up speed, four agile young men wearing masks dashed out of hiding and climbed onto the observation platform. They pulled out pistols and told the passengers to raise their hands.

Some of the women screamed at the sight of the guns, but one of the would-be robbers shouted that they did not want anything from the women. One of the men herded the women into another passenger car.

The bandits started to demand valuables from the men, but someone pulled the emergency stop cord, and the train screeched to a sudden halt. The bandits leapt off the train and ran.

For all of their gun-waving, they hadn't made much of an impression on the Yankee tourists.

"They were young fellows, and they looked like farmers," Margaret Wilson, a passenger from New York City, told the *New York Times*. "They seemed frightened."

Still, an armed holdup of a passenger train full of wealthy tourists made national headlines. "Bandits Lose Nerve and Run from Prey," read a front-page headline in the *Washington Herald* edition of Monday, February 8, 1915.

A sheriff's posse mounted a vigorous effort to capture the would-be train robbers, and soon had four suspects in custody in Stuart. But the men turned out to be drifters who'd been in the wrong place at the wrong time, and they were released.

With the release of the tramps, however, suspicion automatically turned to the Ashleys, and Sheriff Baker and his posse were determined to find them. They continued beating the bushes through the night and into the next morning. This set the stage for an ironic comedy of errors that could have had a tragic ending, but luckily led only to embarrassment.

It so happened that silent film director George Terwilliger was filming a shoot-'em-up thriller in Florida for Lubin Studios of Philadelphia. The film starred two heartthrobs of the early days of motion pictures, Ormi Hawley and Earl Metcalfe.

The script included a scene in which armed robbers boarded a train and robbed the passengers, and Terwilliger had made arrangements to shoot it on the FEC's tracks, just across the St. Lucie River from Stuart.

On Monday morning, the southbound train carrying Terwilliger and his film crew and actors stopped at the raised drawbridge that spanned the river. Terwilliger started putting his actors through a very realistic rehearsal. Men with guns climbed aboard the train and pointed them at passengers, who appeared to be horrified.

The sheriff's posse, still hunting for the previous night's robbers, saw what was happening.

"Then," reported the Philadelphia *Evening Ledger*, "things started."

"Several shots were fired, whether as a signal to other sheriffs or at the Lubin players has not been cleared up as yet," the *Ledger* said, "but from every direction armed man-hunters carrying rifles appeared."

The actors, now genuinely terrified, scattered as men brandishing weapons swarmed aboard the train.

"Some fled into the train—others stood still, frightened still, thinking they were about to be held up by a band of Florida robbers," the *Ledger* reported. "Three of the sheriffs grabbed two of the Lubin 'robbers.' Everyone talked, no one understood."

Amid the chaos and shouting, director Terwilliger noticed that one of the men waving a gun was wearing a lawman's badge. Terwilliger grabbed the man by his suspenders and shouted "Moving pictures! Moving pictures!"

"Light then began to dawn on both sides," the *Ledger* said. "The sheriff explained to Terwilliger and the latter explained to the sheriff."

Guns were lowered and holstered, pounding heartbeats subsided; there may even have been a few laughs. And the posse apparently was stagestruck.

"After the company had recovered from fright, rehearsals were resumed," the *Ledger* reported, "and the sheriff and his deputies, at their own request, acted in the pictures and then resumed their manhunt."

A guide leading a group of hunters in the Everglades may have accidentally found what lawmen had been seeking—one of the Ashleys' hideouts. Around nightfall on February 16, C. C. Myers and a boatload of tourist hunters were about to land on a canal bank to set up camp for the night. Suddenly a man with a shotgun appeared on the opposite bank of the canal.

"If you want to see blood, make your campfire there!" the man shouted. Then he raised the shotgun and fired.

Myers was hit in the back by the pellets. The hunters fled. Myers survived the painful attack.

They couldn't identify the angry gunman who'd shot Myers, but the cops assumed it was an Ashley. And lawmen also thought the Ashleys had robbed a store in Deerfield, a small village south of West Palm Beach, a few days later.

On Tuesday, February 23, the Ashleys committed the crime that would clearly demonstrate to local lawmen that they were dangerous criminals. On that morning, teller A. R. Wallace was absorbed in taking a deposit from a customer at the Bank of Stuart. A movement caught his eye and he glanced up.

He was looking up the muzzle of a rifle that was pointed at him by Bob Ashley, kid brother of John Ashley.

"Hands up!" Bob said.

Wallace thought he was joking.

"Hands up!" Bob Ashley repeated more forcefully.

Wallace glanced around and saw that John Taylor, the bank's cashier, had his hands in the air.

"Better put 'em up, Wallace," Taylor said. "He means it."

Wallace raised his hands "All right," he said. "What's next?"

John Ashley, a gun in each hand, waved one of his pistols at Wallace. He tossed a sack at the teller. "Throw it in here, that's what's next," he said.

There was about $4,300 in bills and coins within sight of the robbers, and Wallace started tossing it into the sack. But he did not open any drawers containing more cash, and Ashley apparently was unaware that there was more cash at hand.

Wallace picked up a sack containing about $30 in pennies.

"Throw it in," Ashley commanded.

Another gun-toting robber appeared. His name was "Kid" Lowe, a hardened criminal from Chicago who'd come south and somehow connected with John Ashley.

Lowe asked how much money was in the sack.

Told there was about $4,300, Lowe was angered.

"Where's the rest?" he demanded, shoving a gun in Wallace's face.

"There is no more," Wallace said. "This is a small bank and has only a small supply of cash."

Lowe grabbed Wallace and shoved him into the lobby, where several other terrified customers were waiting.

"Which one of you fellows can run a car?" Lowe demanded.

A customer named Frank Coventry said he could drive a car, and Lowe ordered him to drive the three robbers out of town.

What happened next has been debated for nearly a century.

Somehow, John Ashley was shot in the head but miraculously not killed. One account of the incident says Bob Ashley fired his gun in jubilation at the successful holdup and accidentally hit his brother. Another account says that as Coventry was driving out of town, Kid Lowe turned to fire a shot to discourage anyone who might be pursuing them, and the bullet struck one of the car's window frames, ricocheted, and struck Ashley. Still another explanation was that Ashley accidentally shot himself with his own gun. And Ashley later would claim that Lowe was trying to kill him so he wouldn't have to give Ashley a share of the loot.

However the shot was fired, the bullet struck Ashley below the chin and lodged behind his right eye. Somehow, he was not killed, but it was a severe wound—one that probably would have been fatal if left unattended.

Coventry sped south on the Dixie Highway. Ashley was losing a lot of blood from his wound and passed out briefly, Coventry said later. About ten miles south of Stuart, Coventry was ordered to stop. The three robbers got out. Coventry was told to return to Stuart, and if he so much as looked back as he was driving away, they'd kill him.

Coventry later told police that the three had horses waiting for them when they got out of his car. Despite his wound and weakness from loss of blood, John Ashley was still able to mount a horse and gallop into the swamp, Coventry said.

As they disappeared into the Everglades, carloads of heavily armed men were speeding after them. They knew the fugitives would head for their familiar hideouts. At one point that afternoon, the lawmen were certain they had their quarry surrounded. But John Ashley's intimate knowledge of the Everglades saved them, and somehow they eluded the posse.

By nightfall, about a hundred men, some of them on horseback, were thrashing through the Glades, looking for the bank robbers. John Ashley, still losing blood, was weakening and in intense pain. Still, he managed to elude the posse for two days.

Finally, he'd had enough. Ashley gave himself up on the morning of February 25.

But Bob Ashley and Kid Lowe were still on the run, and they'd taken the money with them.

The cops took John Ashley straight to a surgeon's office in West Palm Beach. By that night, he was back in the Palm Beach County Jail. Eventually, he would wear a glass eye in the socket where his right eye had been.

While the cops-and-robbers drama was playing out in the wilds of southern Florida, Edwin Menninger, a student at Washburn College in Topeka, Kansas, was busy preparing for a career in medicine. He hadn't given too much thought to his choice of professions. His father was Dr. Charles F. Menninger, a renowned psychiatrist. His brothers Karl and Will were also planning careers in medicine. It was a family tradition.

In 1915, Edwin Menninger was a senior at Washburn. He'd studied chemistry for three years, and now was applying himself to organic chemistry.

But he had other interests, including journalism. As a boy, he'd shown unusual skill in managing his newspaper-delivery routes. They were well-organized, and he had developed an effective system for collecting from his subscribers and adding new ones.

He was associate editor of the student-produced newspaper, the *Washburn Review*. And he enjoyed the art of legerdemain.

He also enjoyed experimenting with chemicals. This, however, was a pleasure that would change the course of his life.

On March 2, 1915, Menninger and a fellow student were experimenting with chemicals in a laboratory in Rich Hall on the Washburn campus. They mixed phosphorus and potassium chlorate in a test tube. Menninger knew that he'd created a volatile, highly unstable combination. They decided to take the mixture outside to test it.

Menninger carried the glass test tube in his right hand. Without thinking, he shifted the tube to his left hand, upending it in the process.

That slight movement of the chemicals was all that was needed to agitate and ignite the compound. There was a blinding flash and the test tube was shattered in a shower of sparks and broken glass. Like John Ashley, Menninger lost his right eye, and his left hand was severely mangled. His plans to become a medical doctor were destroyed as well. When he recovered, he would leave Kansas for New York City to enroll in the Columbia University School of Journalism.

While Dr. Charles Menninger tried doggedly to save what remained of his son's left hand, a grand jury in West Palm Beach heard evidence against John Ashley for robbing the Bank of Stuart the previous month. On March 10, Ashley was indicted, along with Kid Lowe and Bob Ashley, on charges of bank robbery. Lowe and the younger Ashley were still on the run, however.

John Ashley still had to answer for the death of Desoto Tiger.

On March 22, Ashley was in court in West Palm Beach for the third time to face the charge of murdering the Seminole Indian. Prosecuting attorneys had made a vigorous effort to get the trial moved to another county, arguing that a jury in Palm Beach County would be afraid to bring in a guilty verdict. But Judge Pierre Branning had sided with Ashley's defense attorneys in refusing a change of venue.

The judge soon changed his mind, however. Attorneys questioned 112 potential jurors, trying to seat a dozen to hear the evidence. Only two were chosen. All of the others told Branning that they'd already made up their minds about whether John Ashley was guilty or innocent and thus could not be impartial.

Branning gave up. The trial would be moved to Dade County.

John Ashley was in jail when the judge made his decision. It was a serious blow to his hopes for being acquitted of the murder charge. Nevertheless, he put up an optimistic front.

"All I want is a fair and impartial trial, and I believe I can get it in Miami as well as I could here," he told a reporter for the *Daily Tropical Sun*.

Whether John Ashley actually believed what he said is another question.

In 1909, L. D. Reagin, publisher of the *Sarasota Times*, set out on an automobile trip from Tampa to Jacksonville. At the time, those cities were two of Florida's leading seaports.

There's no record of what kind of car Reagin was driving, but at the time a Ford Model T was capable of forty to forty-five miles per hour on a good road. And the roads between Tampa and Jacksonville were not the best.

It was a trip of around three hundred miles. Had Reagin been traveling in a Model T on roads that would have allowed him to push the car to its top speed for the entire distance, he could have made the trip in roughly six and a half to seven and a half hours.

Reagin made the journey in nineteen hours, for an average speed of about sixteen miles per hour. Still, in 1909, it was the fastest anyone had ever made the trip between Tampa and Jacksonville in an automobile.

By 1915, it was becoming abundantly clear to Florida's business leaders that there had to be a better way to link the state's Gulf and Atlantic coasts. And businessmen on the Florida Gulf Coast especially wanted an overland route from southwest Florida to Miami, which even then was on its way to becoming an important seaport on the state's east coast.

But between Tampa and Miami lay hundreds of miles of dense jungle and saw-grass prairies. Most engineers took one look at terrain that was as mysterious as the surface of the moon and concluded that a road simply could not be built through that impenetrable swamp.

Still, a few dreamers were willing to try. In April 1915, Francis W. Perry, president of the Fort Myers Chamber of Commerce, and James F. Jaudon, the tax assessor for Dade County, sat down in Tallahassee to talk about a road connecting Tampa and Miami. They got a map of the state from Florida commissioner of agriculture William McRae and studied it closely.

Lake Okeechobee, the giant, shallow lake that serves as a holding pond for water before it flows slowly southward through the Everglades, was the northern boundary of the Glades. From the southern shore of the lake to the tip of the peninsula was almost entirely covered by jungle, saw-grass prairie, and a shallow sheet of water sliding through the Glades to Florida Bay.

You could travel by automobile on roads of varying quality from Tampa southward to Fort Myers, a distance of around 145 miles. But the only way to get from Fort Myers to Miami was to either go by boat southward around the tip of the peninsula or embark on an automobile trip of perhaps 750 miles that would have required going north to somewhere around Gainesville, then turning east to St. Augustine, and finally, a trip of more than 300 miles south down the east coast to Miami.

As Jaudon and Perry studied the map, they knew that carving a road through the Everglades would be a fiendishly difficult task. But even their unbridled imaginations couldn't conceive just how difficult it would be.

"The unknown character of the immense terra incognita through which the highway was projected could not be determined by engineers trudging through miles of aquatic prairie," an anonymous author wrote in a booklet about the construction project in 1928. "Not until actual construction was attempted did the discouraging features of the undertaking become adequately known."

Had Jaudon, Perry, and others who took up the cry to pierce the Everglades known what they actually were up against, they might not have taken on the project. No one would have blamed them for throwing up their hands and declaring that it couldn't be done.

Still, it was an age when anything seemed possible. The Panama Canal had been built to link the Atlantic and Pacific Oceans, and Henry Flagler had laid down a railroad across the Florida Keys to Key West. Why couldn't a road be built through the Everglades?

Jaudon and Perry started talking to other movers and shakers in Florida. The idea started gaining momentum.

Judge Pierre Branning issued some special instructions to guide the selection of the dozen Dade County men who would sit in judgment of John Ashley in his third trial for the murder of Desoto Tiger: They must have no prejudice against Indians, they must be willing to consider an Indian's testimony the same as they would a white man's, they must have no prejudice against hearing testimony through an interpreter translating the Seminole language, no reluctance to impose the death sentence should evidence convince them beyond a reasonable doubt that the defendant was guilty, and no predetermined opinion about John Ashley's guilt or innocence.

It took a couple of days to get through the selection process, but on April 2, 1915, a jury in Miami started hearing the evidence. Newspaper reporters covering the first day of testimony wrote that the accused was in good spirits.

But his mood changed as the trial progressed.

The jury heard the story of Desoto Tiger's death—valuable otter pelts belonging to the Seminoles, Tiger found dead from two gunshot wounds, pelts sold by Ashley in Miami.

Ashley still wore bandages around his head from the gunshot wound he'd suffered after the robbery of the Bank of Stuart two months earlier. Bandages completely covered where his right eye had been.

"For the most part he sits grim and silent," the *Miami Daily Metropolis* reported, "thin lips pressed tightly together—always watching the witness."

His mother, Lugenia, equally grim, sat beside him with his lawyers at the defendant's table. "Never a change comes across her countenance, except when she turns to speak a word to her son in answer to some question," the *Metropolis* reported. "Statement after statement comes from the witnesses, never causing her to wince or smile."

A few days into the trial, the prosecution brought in a surprise witness who sent defense attorneys into paroxysms of protest. His name was Homer Tindall, and he'd talked with John Ashley when Ashley dropped by his campsite a few days before Desoto Tiger was killed.

Tindall had not testified during Ashley's first trial that had ended in a hung jury in West Palm Beach. After hours of heated arguments that stretched over two days, Judge Branning ruled that Tindall's testimony could be heard by the Miami jury.

Homer Tindall and his father had been camped about a mile and a half from the *Caloosahatchee*, the dredge that had been working on the drainage canal. Ashley spent the night of December 19 at the Tindalls' camp.

Around noon the following day, Ashley and the younger Tindall watched two Seminoles glide past their camp in a canoe in the canal.

"The Indians were coming up to the camp and they were some little distance away, and he, Ashley, asked me if I knew them and I told him I did not," Tindall testified, "and he asked me if I reckoned they had any hides, and I told him I didn't know, and he said, 'If they have let us kill them and get the hides.' He said, 'We can do it and no one will ever know it,' and I told him 'No,' and he said, 'If I could find one with a large quantity of hides I wouldn't any more mind killing him than I would of shooting a buzzard,' and at that time the Indians were at the camp and there wasn't any more said."

Tindall said Ashley had stayed in their camp until December 21 and then left; he'd had no further contact with him.

The jury also heard James Girtman testify that he had bought eighty-four otter pelts from Ashley for $584.

When Ashley took the stand, he said he and Desoto Tiger had discussed the hides privately in Ashley's tent, and that Ashley had wanted to buy the pelts but first wanted to get an opinion about what they were worth. Ashley said he told Tiger that he'd go to Fort Lauderdale to get an estimate, and that Tiger had insisted that he bring back whiskey.

Ashley said when he returned, he paid Tiger $400 for the hides on December 28, and this transaction also was in the privacy of his tent. He denied saying to Tindall that he would as soon shoot a buzzard as an Indian, and accused Tindall of accepting a bribe in exchange for his testimony.

Ashley told the jury that he'd shot Desoto Tiger in self-defense while they were in Tiger's boat. The Seminole had pointed a pistol at him and threatened to kill him unless he gave him whiskey.

"He had his pistol pointing at me, and I, hearing the click of the pistol, grabbed my gun and started shooting as fast as I could," Ashley told the jury.

Desoto Tiger tumbled out of the canoe and into the canal, Ashley said.

But the jury didn't buy John Ashley's story. On April 8, 1915, they pronounced Ashley guilty of murder. The following day, Judge Branning sentenced Ashley to hang. When he heard the sentence, Ashley looked toward the attorney who had led the prosecution's case against him. A cool, chilling smile slowly came to his lips.

Ashley's court-appointed defense attorney, Crate D. Bowen, said he would appeal the conviction. In the meantime, Ashley would be held in the Dade County Jail in Miami awaiting trial on charges of robbing the Bank of Stuart a few months earlier.

Some people who were acquainted with Joe Ashley attributed his contempt for the rule of law to the fact that he grew up in the post–Civil War South during Reconstruction, when US troops occupied the former Confederate States for more than a decade. Whatever the reason, he certainly did not respect traditional boundaries of behavior and property ownership.

He saw no harm in robbing banks. In fact, he considered it a public service. The money they took was insured and would be replaced by "some damned Yankee insurance company." So the bank did not lose anything, the depositors didn't lose anything, and since the Ashleys would spend the money locally, it was actually a form of economic stimulus. So instead of forming posses to chase them down, "Everybody ought to help us," was the way Joe Ashley saw it.

So it stood to reason that Joe Ashley and his family were not going to allow the state of Florida to hang his son for the murder of a Seminole.

Dade County Sheriff Dan Hardie knew he had a slippery prisoner on his hands, and that John Ashley's family was likely to try to free him. He added locks and chains to increase security.

The Ashleys' jailbreak attempt came in a sudden, brutal, and deadly fashion on June 2, 1915.

Workers at a multistory parking garage across the street from the Dade County Jail talked to three men—one older, the other two younger—who were hanging around the garage that morning as though they were waiting for something to happen.

The men wanted to make sure a Ford automobile parked in the garage would start with no problems. They bought new batteries for the car and installed them.

"I tried to talk to them but none of them seemed very talkative and our conversation was not long," E. T. Wells, who worked at the garage, told the *Daily Tropical Sun* later. "The men all seemed to be nervous, and I remember now that one or the other frequently went to the doors or windows and looked out."

One of the younger men was Bob Ashley, John Ashley's kid brother. Ashley had bought a bottle of whiskey earlier that day, and he was carrying a curious package, something long and slender and wrapped in blue paper. A garage employee later said Ashley occasionally went to a window or door of the garage to communicate in sign language with someone in the jail across the street.

Around 12:30 p.m. Bob Ashley made a daring move. He crossed the street from the parking garage to the jail and knocked on the door of the adjoining house, where Deputy Sheriff Robert Hendrickson, the jailer, lived with his wife. When Hendrickson came to the door, Bob Ashley shot him dead with a rifle that had been wrapped in the blue paper. He grabbed the keys to the jail, and ran.

Hendrickson's wife grabbed a shotgun and aimed at the fleeing Bob Ashley, but the gun either misfired or wasn't loaded.

In the parking garage across the street, Joe Ashley and Kid Lowe were talking to employees on the second deck of the building when they heard a gunshot. Ashley and Lowe ran to a window. They watched for a few moments, then started down the stairwell, one of them remarking that Miami didn't seem to be a very safe town, and that they'd better leave and go home.

Across the street, the gunshot that had killed the jailer was attracting a crowd, and Bob Ashley apparently lost his nerve. He dropped the keys and fled back into the garage. Not seeing his father or Kid Lowe, he ran to the Ford with the recently installed new batteries.

But Bob Ashley couldn't operate a car. He pointed his gun at a man standing nearby and ordered him to get in the car and drive it. The man replied that he did not know how to drive a Ford.

Ashley leveled his gun at a second man and demanded that he get in the car to drive. But that man also said he did not know how to drive a Ford.

So Ashley accosted a third man and shouted to him to get in the car. But the man was hard of hearing, and when he cupped his hand around an ear and asked Ashley to repeat what he'd said, the young gunman gave up and ran from the garage and out onto the street.

Ashley waved his gun and stopped a man driving a cycle car, a small, cheap automobile with room for only the driver and a passenger or two. Ashley shoved the gun in the driver's face and ordered him to drive him out of town. The driver realized the police were after Ashley and refused, but Ashley became enraged and threatened to kill him. Reluctantly, the driver made room for Ashley in his small car and drove away.

But after going a few blocks, the car stalled and the driver got out, raised the hood, and started tinkering with the engine. By this time, Miami police officer Robert Riblett had overtaken Bob Ashley. Riblett pointed his gun at Ashley and ordered him to surrender.

Again, there are varying accounts of what happened next. Some say that Riblett and Ashley grappled hand to hand before the shooting started. Others say Ashley whirled and fired twice at Riblett, and then the police officer managed to get off a shot that hit Ashley in the abdomen.

Both men were mortally wounded. Riblett died shortly afterward at a hospital. Bob Ashley was examined by a doctor, who said there was nothing he could do. He was taken to a jail cell. Sheriff Dan Hardie sat down on his bunk, hoping to get deathbed information from Ashley. Ashley admitted he'd planned to break his brother out of jail, but he refused to tell Hardie anything more about his family, and soon he was dead.

John Ashley, of course, denied knowing anything about a plot to spring him. Jailers then discovered that he'd secretly been using a spoon to tunnel his way out of his cell, and was on the verge of succeeding. He was moved to a more secure cell, presumably to await his date with the hangman's noose. But the Florida Supreme Court had agreed to hear the appeal of his conviction for the murder of Desoto Tiger, so he had escaped the gallows—at least for the time being.

A few days later, Sheriff Hardie received a crudely written letter, addressed to "Mr. Dan Hardie, high sheriff of Dade County."

"Dear Sir," it began, "we were in your city at the time one of our gang young Bob Ashley was brutally shot to death by your officers and now your town can expect to feel the results of it any hour. And if John Ashley is not fairly delt with and given a fair trial and turned loose simply for the life of a god damned Seminole indian, we expect to shoot up the hole god damned town, regardless of the results might be. We expect to make our appearance at an early date, signed, Ashley gang."

The letter was signed "Kid lowe Arizona kid ike Mitchell and others name not mentione."

Nothing came of the threat, and Hardie dismissed it as a hoax. Apparently, the Ashleys were willing to wait for the state Supreme Court to decide on the appeal.

While lawmen in Miami and Palm Beach counties tried to contain and curtail the crude but crafty savagery of the Ashley clan, local politicians moved forward with plans to try to tame a natural force that was wilder than the Ashleys—the Everglades.

A week after the gunfight in downtown Miami, in which three men were killed, a group of businessmen met in Orlando to form the Florida Highway Association. Among the discussion items on their agenda was the proposed highway through the Everglades, linking Tampa and Miami. It needed a catchy name. The Tamiami Trail—a clever name that managed to be both alliterative and combine the names of the cities that would be linked—emerged from the discussion.

Preliminary plans called for the Trail to go through only two counties, Dade on the east coast and Lee on the Gulf Coast. Each county would be responsible for paying for the portion passing through it.

In 1915, the boundaries of Lee and Dade met in the middle of the state near the tip of the peninsula. Both were large counties, and in 1915, Lee County—which included Fort Myers—was bigger than the state of Delaware. Dade County's segment of the Trail would be around thirty-five miles. Lee County's portion would be more than twice that. Lee did not have the rapidly growing population and tax base that Dade had, and thus had fewer resources to pay for its share of the highway.

On September 8, the Dade County Board of Commissioners—who would have to approve any plan to pay their county's share of the construction costs—heard from some of the doubters about building the Trail. J. H. Tatum told the commissioners that draining the Everglades to build the road would flood Dade County, and he was unalterably opposed to spending so much money to simply flood the county. He also had doubts about whether Lee County would ever build its share of the highway, and that would mean all the money Miami spent on the road would be wasted because it would be a road to nowhere.

At times the debate over whether to build the road grew heated. Then the meeting was interrupted by a telegram. The Lee County Board of Commissioners had just decided to hold an election on October 19 to determine whether the county would issue bonds to pay for its portion of the Tamiami Trail. Dade County voters would decide the same issue on the same date.

Around the same time that Dade and Lee County leaders were discussing the Tamiami Trail, representatives from the ten states through which the Dixie Highway would pass, from Michigan to Florida, met in Chattanooga, Tennessee, to discuss the road's route. Regardless of where the highway meandered from its origin in Montreal, however, it would end in Miami, functioning like a pipeline for winter-weary Midwesterners seeking sunshine.

Lee County and Dade County voters approved issuing bonds to build the Tamiami Trail. Miami boosters were ecstatic about the bond approval. The day after the vote, the *Miami Herald* predicted that, within eighteen months, "the traveler may go over a splendid road from this city to Tampa."

Surveyors had the Dade County portion of the highway laid out by March 1916, and on August 15, giant excavators started hacking westward toward the Dade-Lee county line.

In Miami, Dade County jailers kept a close eye on their most infamous prisoner, as John Ashley's murder conviction awaited consideration by the Florida Supreme Court. On August 4, A. J. Rose, one of Ashley's court-appointed attorneys, received a telegram from Tallahassee. It was from the clerk of the state Supreme Court. Ashley's conviction had been reversed, and a new trial was ordered.

There was no explanation in the telegram for why the court had made this decision.

On September 14, Palm Beach County Sheriff George Baker, accompanied by a judge and a newspaper reporter, arrived in Miami to pick up Ashley. The old gentlemen's agreement about no handcuffs was forgotten. Ashley left the jail handcuffed between two of the Palm Beach County delegation. He was taken back to West Palm Beach for his fourth trial for the death of Desoto Tiger.

The following afternoon, an Overland touring car with four riders rolled to a stop in front of the Bank of Homestead, about forty miles southwest of Miami.

Two men got out of the car and walked into the bank. One of the men wrote a check for $10 to Thomas Dice, signed it Dan Wilson, and the two men stepped up to a teller's window and presented the check.

The teller didn't know the men and called the bank's cashier over to take a look at the check. As the cashier was examining the check, the men each pulled out revolvers.

"Hands up, gentlemen," one of them said. "We have been in the Glades long enough."

The men left with all of the cash in the bank—about $6,500. They headed west in the Overland—toward the Everglades.

For the next two weeks, the robbers fought a running gun battle with a posse that pursued them through the Everglades and into the Florida Keys. Three members of the posse were killed by "friendly fire" from other posse members in a shoot-out with the bandits on the morning of Sunday, September 17. But by October 2, two of the robbers were dead and the other two were in jail. There were reports that Kid Lowe, who was still wanted for the Bank of Stuart holdup, had planned the Homestead stickup.

John Ashley sat in the Palm Beach County Jail for two months until the date for his fourth trial arrived in November. But apparently no one saw any point in putting him on trial again for murder in a county where one previous trial had ended in a hung jury, and a jury couldn't even be seated for a second trial. Prosecutors agreed to drop the murder charge if Ashley would plead guilty to robbing the Bank of Stuart in February 1915.

He was sentenced to seventeen years in the Florida State Prison in Raiford, about forty miles north of Gainesville.

In early 1917, Tamiami Trail boosters got a jolt of reality about how difficult it was going to be to push a highway through the Everglades. On February 10,

Miami engineer John W. King, his son, John Jr., and eighteen-year-old William Catlow Jr. left Miami to survey land that had recently been purchased from the state for the Trail's right-of-way. They thought it would take them about two weeks to work their way through the Glades to the Gulf Coast.

By late February, they hadn't reached their destination, nor had they been heard from since they left Miami. On February 27, two experienced Everglades guides—a trapper and a Seminole Indian—went looking for the group.

Other search parties joined the hunt, but after more than a week, the three missing surveyors still hadn't been found. On March 9, aviator Phil Rader and surveyor Burt Tubbs took off in a Curtiss military biplane and flew over the Everglades. It was a risky flight. Pilots had learned to avoid flying over the Everglades because of treacherous air currents over the vast swamp that could cause planes to suddenly drop hundreds, or thousands, of feet.

Rader pushed his plane to an altitude of 14,000 feet—a record for that time—partly to add a margin of safety in case he encountered a sudden downdraft, partly so that he and his passenger could see a bigger expanse of land. They saw a few people moving through the Glades, but they turned out to be search parties.

King and his two young companions were indeed having a rough time. The story of their trek through the Glades became the subject of an eight-part series by writer W. Livingston Larned that was published in 1918 in *Forest and Stream* magazine, a popular mass-circulation magazine that included among its contributors former president Theodore Roosevelt.

The elder King badly miscalculated what it would take to cross the formidable Everglades. He was "fairly familiar" with the outer edge of the Glades, and had not expected any major problems, Larned wrote.

But the interior of the great swamp was far different from what King had anticipated—impassable in some places, bewildering in others, and always eerily quiet, despite the obvious presence of so much wildlife.

"It seems past belief that, almost within hearing of Miami's church bells, we should thus face absolute helplessness," King wrote in the diary that formed the basis for Larned's stories. "My faith in my own knowledge of the area is beginning to weaken."

The story of the men lost in the Everglades made national headlines, and raised such concern for their safety that a group of Miami spiritualists offered their assistance in finding the lost exploration party. And J. F. Jaudon, for whom King was doing the exploration, seriously considered taking them up on their offer.

Even when the group was almost within sight of their Gulf Coast objective, they couldn't find a path through the final stretch of the Glades. They could see distant waterspouts that occasionally formed over the Gulf of Mexico, but could not find a way out. They were weak and disoriented from hunger, and King began to wonder if they'd make it.

Finally, on March 14, a telegram arrived from Key West for J. F. Jaudon in Miami. The three missing men had made it to the mouth of the Shark River on the Gulf Coast, near the southwest tip of the peninsula. There, they'd come across a small processing operation owned by the Manetto Company, which extracted tannic acid from palmetto trees. The company's superintendent had taken them by boat to Key West—the closest town—so they could tell the world that they were safe.

Suddenly the *Miami Herald*'s prediction about pushing a road through a couple hundred miles or so of the Everglades in eighteen months seemed a little optimistic.

John Ashley was back to his old tricks at the Florida State Prison in Raiford. He was behaving like a prisoner who sincerely wanted to mend his ways and hasten his return as a productive member of society. Prison officials noticed his exemplary behavior, and soon he was rewarded. In March 1918 he was transferred from Raiford to a prison work camp in Milligan, in the western Florida Panhandle, about fifty miles east of Pensacola.

Ashley was assigned to a chain gang. Every day, he and other prisoners, wearing pants with broad, alternating black-and-white horizontal stripes, climbed into what essentially was a cage on wheels and were taken to a site where they did manual labor on roads.

For three months, Ashley did his job, swinging picks and pushing shovels. But summers in the Florida Panhandle can be stunningly hot. And he was getting homesick again. He decided he'd had enough, and on July 11, 1918, he and another prisoner slipped away from the chain gang.

The western Panhandle was a long way from Ashley's home, but somehow, he made it back to his familiar haunts down on the peninsula south of Stuart, and soon he was again spending most of his time in the Everglades. He found a new occupation: He and his father were operating three moonshine stills in the Glades.

And there was romance in John Ashley's life.

Laura Upthegrove was not a delicate, feminine beauty. Author Hix C. Stuart described her as an "Amazon" who never left home without her .38 caliber revolver.

"There was nothing striking in Laura's appearance to which might be attributed John's devotion," Stuart wrote. "Dark, unkempt hair, a tawny weather-beaten complexion, prominent cheekbones, squinting yet sharp black eyes, and generally untidy in appearance; there was nothing attractive about Laura," Stuart wrote.

Yet Laura and John had magic moments together. An undated photo of the two shows a happy couple obviously in love and posing cheek to cheek for the camera against the backdrop of the Florida wilderness. Ashley, a few inches taller, stands behind Laura, his arms wrapped around her neck and shoulders.

He's wearing a white shirt, dark slacks, and what appears to be an army garrison cap. Laura, buxom and beaming at the camera, is dressed in women's outdoor clothing of the late 1910s—a drab dark long coat and calf-length skirt, high-top shoes, and dark leggings. She's holding on to John's forearms.

Taken out of context, they appear to be merely a young couple very much in love instead of two desperadoes who would spend the rest of their brief lives on the run.

While dreamers were telling themselves that spanning the Everglades with a highway would be no big deal, and lawmen in southern Florida were spending a lot of their time seeking members of the Ashley clan in that vast swamp, world events were inexorably dragging the United States into the war raging in Europe.

Americans' ire had been roused in May 1915 when a German submarine torpedoed the British passenger liner *Lusitania*, killing 1,198 people, including Americans. Germany, however, had realized what a potent weapon its undersea boats were, and was reluctant to curtail its attacks on Allied ships, regardless of whether they were warships. Even the *Lusitania* had been carrying war supplies along with its passengers, making it a legitimate target of war as far as Germany was concerned.

In March 1916, a German sub torpedoed a French passenger liner in the English Channel. No one was killed, but among the injured were a few Americans.

President Wilson warned Germany that the United States would cut its diplomatic ties with Germany if they continued to attack civilian shipping, and Germany responded by saying its submarines would not sink merchant ships without warning and would allow passengers and crew to abandon ship before sinking it.

President Wilson continued his efforts to mediate a peace between the Allies and the Central Powers, but German leaders had little interest in the negotiations because they thought they could eventually win the war outright rather than settle for a negotiated peace. Even the threat of American intervention didn't concern them because they thought they could win the war before American troops were ready for combat.

In January 1917, Germany announced that it was lifting the restrictions it had imposed on its U-boats and would resume "unrestricted submarine warfare." The United States severed diplomatic ties with Germany, and in March 1917 German subs sank five American merchant ships.

Then came the ultimate German insult to the United States. British intelligence agents intercepted a message circulating among some German officials suggesting that if America declared war on Germany, Germany should seek an alliance with Mexico. The inducement for Mexico to form this alliance would be the opportunity to recover the territory it had lost in its war with the United States from 1846 to 1848—territory that had become the states of Texas, New Mexico, and Arizona.

President Wilson released the message to American newspapers, and the nation was infuriated.

Former secretary of state William Jennings Bryan was in Miami in the months leading up to the US entry into the war. He was horrified that the United States was being dragged into a conflict that, he would later say, was caused by the same science that "manufactured poisonous gasses to suffocate soldiers" and was preaching "that man has a brute ancestry," and eliminated "the miraculous and the supernatural from the Bible."

Bryan rushed to Washington, DC, hoping to head off the move to war. But there was nothing he could do. On April 4, 1917, the United States declared war on Germany. Bryan had lost his bid to preserve peace, but he promptly sent a note to President Wilson telling him that he would do whatever he could to help the war effort.

Congress approved a draft that eventually would require all men between the ages of eighteen and forty-five to register for military service. Before World War I ended, about 2.8 million American men had been drafted.

One forty-five-year-old man who didn't have to worry about the draft was an out-of-work architect named Addison Mizner. Suffering from a leg injury that wouldn't heal, Mizner was shivering through the winter of 1917–18 in Port Washington, New York, overlooking Manhasset Bay on Long Island's North Shore. The winter was made more miserable by a coal miners' strike, leaving heating fuel very scarce.

Through a mutual friend, Mizner happened to meet Paris Singer, heir to a portion of the Singer Sewing Machine Company fortune that had been amassed by his father, Isaac Singer.

Paris Singer and Mizner quickly became friends, and Singer's personal nurse suggested that Mizner's leg would benefit from warmth and sunshine. So in January 1918 Mizner, Singer, and the nurse boarded a southbound Florida East Coast Railway train in New York City.

Mizner's good health returned in the warm Florida winter, and he started designing a hospital that Singer wanted to build in Palm Beach for convalescing American soldiers returning from World War I. Soon, the jobless architect who had been shivering and suffering from a gimpy leg in a chilly Long Island apartment would become the toast of Palm Beach. The Roaring Twenties were just around the corner, and nowhere would they roar louder than in Florida.

CHAPTER FOUR

Leave Your Brain at Home

When the bloody Great War ended in November 1918, the world's psyche had been dramatically altered. More than fifteen million people were dead, and the comfortable Victorian fantasy that Western civilization was steadily moving the world toward a time of universal peace and prosperity had been shredded by four awful years of systematic, mechanized slaughter. Self-denial and sacrifice suddenly seemed silly and pointless; it was better to surround yourself with luxuries and enjoy life to the utmost while you could.

"There was an immense, all-pervading disillusionment," Bruce Catton later wrote in *American Heritage* magazine. "The nation's highest ideals had been appealed to during the war, so that to win the war seemed the holiest of causes; the war had been won, but it was hard to see that anything worth winning had been gained; the idealism had been used up, and people had an uneasy feeling that they had been had."

So, with traditional beliefs shattered, "lots of people became materialists," Catton wrote.

"It was easier, indeed, it was almost necessary, to center one's attention on the material things that were going on in this country," he wrote.

And yet, there was a subconscious longing—part memory, part fantasy—for a past that seemed simpler and safer. People wanted desperately to escape the harsh, frightening new realities that confronted them. In his book *Only Yesterday: An Informal History of the 1920s*, Frederick Lewis Allen noted that Americans yearned for a place where they could escape "into the easy-going life and beauty of the European past, into some never-never land which combined American sport and comfort with Latin glamour—a Venice equipped with bathtubs and electric ice boxes, a Seville provided with three eighteen-hole golf courses."

The Florida that emerged during the 1920s would, in many ways, resemble these fantasies—for a few years, at least.

Although Florida had been part of the United States since 1845, it was still very much a work in progress as a state in 1920. It had frontiers that were every bit as untamed, undeveloped, and unexplored as the American West of the nineteenth century.

The changes wrought in American society and the world by the Great War would not be noticed immediately. Still, the transition would be steady, and it would unfold over the coming decade. During this seminal ten years, many comfortable beliefs, social mores, and public attitudes would be peeled away until the fading vestiges of the nineteenth century were gone.

A denizen of the twenty-first century transported back to the United States of 1925 would, of course, be struck by many differences. Automobiles would not be sleek and aerodynamically designed computers on wheels. They would resemble the boxy horse-drawn carriages and buggies they were replacing. Telephones, on the other hand, would be stylishly designed, but they would be attached to a wire. Any reference to "wireless" would be referring to radios.

Still, there would be much that would be familiar to modern sensibilities. Automobiles, though boxy and primitive in appearance, would exist. Their numbers were steadily increasing, and their profound influence on society was becoming apparent. Henry Ford was perfecting a manufacturing technique that would lower the cost of automobiles so that even people of modest means could afford a family flivver. They would reshape American society.

Telephones and radios were primitive by modern standards, but they were bringing instant communications to the masses. Popular culture, influenced by radio and the growth of the motion picture industry, was steadily changing the way Americans thought, spoke, dressed, and behaved. And Americans were buying the postwar era's new technological marvels without paying for them with cash on the barrelhead, a practice that would have appalled their Victorian grandparents.

The visitor from the future also would see the often bitter conflict between progressive and conservative social forces so familiar to the early twenty-first century.

When Wyoming became the thirty-sixth state to ratify the Eighteenth Amendment in January 1919, the manufacture and sale of alcoholic beverages would become illegal a year later. The Ku Klux Klan would be railing against immigrants, and the Klan's membership would steadily increase through the 1920s. Conservative Christians—including William Jennings Bryan, whose politics were a sometimes bewildering mix of progressivism and conservatism—would be insisting that Darwin's theory of evolution not be taught in public schools.

But at the same time, progressive forces were moving the country away from other traditional restrictions, and among the most obvious changes were new freedoms for women. The ratification of the Nineteenth Amendment—also supported by Bryan—gave women the right to vote beginning in 1921, and they were demanding and seizing freedoms their grandmothers wouldn't have dreamed of asking for.

When the decade began, however, only 644 people lived in Miami Beach—which had changed its name from Ocean Beach when it was incorporated in 1915—and Carl Fisher was wondering whether his vision for the island as a playground would ever materialize. Miami's population was about 30,000, and George Merrick was still a year away from selling his first lot in Coral Gables. Florida's national banks held just over $88 million in deposits and had loans totaling almost $67 million.

The state's population was just over 968,000.

All of those figures would change dramatically in just a few years.

It took a while for the US economy to readjust after the Great War ended, and the nation endured a brief economic slump in 1920. Still, more people were coming to Florida, despite the downturn.

When Republican Warren Harding was elected president in November 1920, Americans figured that prosperity would follow. In his inaugural address in March 1921, Harding sounded a theme that he was sure would be well received. With the Great War behind them, Americans were ready for a return to normalcy.

"I would like to acclaim an era of good feeling amid dependable prosperity and all the blessings which attend," Harding said.

The prewar "normalcy" that Harding wanted to restore was gone, however, blasted away by the carnage on the European battlefields. "Dependable prosperity" might be at hand, but the attendant "good feeling" might be a bit more elusive, since Prohibition loomed.

On November 23, 1921, a group of real estate brokers gathered in Miami heard Gordon Nye, editor of the *Florida Real Estate Journal*, tell them that Florida was not being properly sold to the nation, and that its efforts to grow and develop were being seriously hampered by derogatory stories about the state being published in out-of-state newspapers and magazines.

"We are not doing anything to combat this propaganda except issuing Chamber of Commerce booklets once a year and letting it end there," he said.

There was no mention in the *Miami Daily Metropolis* of whether George Merrick attended this meeting, and he was known to avoid public functions. But Merrick was about to launch a pro-Florida selling campaign that would far exceed anything Nye had in mind.

In November 1921, Merrick had added several thousand acres to his father's citrus farm, and accumulated $500,000 in capital. He was ready to start building his carefully planned city. Eventually, Coral Gables would be acclaimed as a landmark accomplishment in urban planning.

But when Merrick—who had what a novelist might describe as a "broad, honest face"—sold his first lots for $600 each on November 27, 1921, there were more doubters than believers in his ambitious undertaking.

Kenneth Roberts, who wrote a series of articles about Florida for the *Saturday Evening Post* in the mid-1920s, said knowledgeable people thought Merrick's plans were doomed to failure. Coral Gables was too far from the water—too far from anything, in fact. The doubters "could understand paying almost any price for waterfront property—even as much as $5,000 for a lot, or $10,000 even. But not $600 for a lot six miles from anywhere!"

Merrick had great difficulty raising additional capital, Roberts said.

"Merrick, for a time, was avoided as though he had a touch of the plague when he attempted to raise money to carry out his building schemes for Coral Gables," Roberts wrote. "Forward-thinking financiers would stare mournfully at one another after Merrick had attempted to wrench a little money from them, and express a moderate amount of near-sympathy for the wretched individual who might eventually decide to take a chance with him."

Still, Merrick worked his carefully crafted plan. All the money that came in from sales went back into the development of Coral Gables. Streets were widened and a few houses were built. Because of the improvements, the price of lots went up the following year. Most were sold for $1,200 each, but a few brought $2,500.

Merrick continued building wide streets and added meticulous landscaping touches such as oak and royal palm trees.

But again, the money that came in was plowed back into the development. And Merrick continued to seek investors.

Finally, the Jefferson Standard Life Insurance Company of Greensboro, North Carolina, was willing to invest in Coral Gables. It was a lifeline for Merrick. As work progressed, Jefferson Standard was satisfied enough with the results to put more money into the project. Eventually Jefferson Standard's confidence prompted the Missouri State Life Insurance Company to make an investment, and then the Mortgage and Securities Company of New Orleans came on board.

"It then began to be fairly apparent to the more astute financiers that Merrick was not, as they had first supposed, in need of the gentle attention of a corps of alienists," Roberts wryly noted.

Like Merrick, Carl Fisher struggled at first to get Miami Beach under way.

In 1915, Roberts wrote, Fisher's property "consisted of a desolate-looking sand-spit."

Like Merrick, many observers questioned Fisher's judgment as he pushed ahead with his project, using a dredge to pile up sand from Biscayne Bay and actually create real estate where none had existed before. And although his cash flow had improved, all of the money Fisher brought in was going back into his development.

Fisher's wife Jane said that her husband was "practically down to his last dollar" when he opened the magnificent Flamingo Hotel in Miami Beach in 1920.

But Fisher, the tenacious opportunist, managed to get the ultimate VIP to stay at his hotel soon after it opened. President-elect Warren G. Harding decided to take a Florida vacation after winning the nation's highest office in November 1920. When Fisher learned Harding was coming to Miami, he was determined to get him into the Flamingo.

Jane Fisher said her husband "shanghaied" Harding "right out from under the nose" of a Miami reception committee. Fisher hustled Harding aboard his own yacht, the *Shadow VI*, and took him to the Flamingo's penthouse, "where a poker game and plenty of scotch were waiting," she wrote.

Fisher installed Harding in one of the luxurious villas he'd built on the grounds of the Flamingo. The four-bedroom house, specially decorated for Harding, included a fireplace and a porch overlooking Biscayne Bay. Fisher even obtained several days' worth of newspapers from Marion, Ohio, so the president-elect could catch up on news from his hometown.

The *Miami Daily Metropolis* reported that Harding was "carefully guarded against annoyances at Miami Beach" while he played golf, took a dip in the ocean, and toured the city.

Harding was delighted with the villa. "It's just an ideal little place," he said.

Meanwhile, Fisher masterfully played the herd of newsmen trailing Harding, knowing that Miami Beach and his new hotel would be mentioned in news stories being sent around the world.

The *Metropolis* reported that the hospitality shown the reporters and photographers was "of a different character than anywhere else in Florida," and had brought "the highest praise" from the newsmen.

Harding—minus the reporters and photographers—spent a night at Fisher's exclusive fishing camp, Cocolobo Key, in Biscayne Bay. He returned with a sunburned face and blistered hands from hauling in a sailfish, an amberjack, and a wahoo.

The president-elect also dropped in for a visit with William Jennings Bryan, now a full-time Miami resident. The *Metropolis* didn't report what Harding and Bryan discussed, but it's likely that Bryan told Harding of his frustrations at how casually Prohibition was being violated in Miami.

But if forbidding the manufacture, sale, and transport of alcoholic beverages was an impediment to Fisher and other movers and shakers in Florida, it was a golden opportunity for the Ashley Gang.

For years, John Ashley and his felonious family had been operating three moonshine stills from the safety of their Everglades hideouts, so they were already on the wrong side of the nation's alcoholic beverage laws when Prohibition went into effect. But when booze was outlawed everywhere, they saw a chance to increase their income by getting into the business of bootlegging.

And with typical Ashley ruthlessness, they figured they could increase their income even more by eliminating the competition and taking their profits as well.

By 1921, when the president-elect was vacationing just down the coast from their hideout, the Ashleys were making a regular seventy-mile run across the Straits of Florida between Palm Beach County and West End in the British-owned Bahamas. There, they were loading up their small skiff with booze and hauling it back across open water to their lair.

The most obvious—and probably most popular—indication of Florida's indifference to the restrictions of the rest of the world was the state's unofficial attitude toward enforcing Prohibition. Supporters of the Eighteenth Amendment—including Miami's most famous resident, Bryan—had hailed it as a noble measure that would save the nation from perdition, but millions of otherwise law-abiding Americans paid no attention to it. They bought their booze from bootleggers at outrageous prices, and the fact that they'd broken the law to get it only seemed to enhance their pleasure as they hoisted their glasses.

In Miami, Prohibition was regarded more as a challenging inconvenience than the law of the land. Every day, bootleggers in small, speedy boats—many of them powered by military airplane engines left over from the war—left Miami and other towns on the state's southeast coast and made the run to the Bahamas to buy whiskey. They could make their choices and have a free lunch while their purchases were loaded. By nightfall, the whiskey was being poured into glasses and sold for huge profits in Florida.

Selling booze to Florida bootleggers was such an economic boon to the Bahamas that in 1920 the islands' governor brought some unexpected good news to his legislature. Their worries about an expected $150,000 budget shortfall had been completely erased. So much whiskey was being hauled over to Florida that sales taxes had created a $500,000 surplus in the Bahamian treasury.

Bryan was horrified when he learned that the Bahamian government had no intention of helping the United States enforce Prohibition, and actually was almost gleeful that income from American bootleggers had erased their government's debt.

Rum-running between Florida and the Bahamas was becoming such an annoyance to Bryan that he made a dramatic proposal to end it: The United States should buy the Bahamas from Great Britain, or insist that Great Britain hand them over to pay off its debt to the United States from World War I.

The traffic of seagoing bootleggers had prompted the Ashley Gang to expand its illegal operations. They'd gone into piracy. Armed to the teeth, John Ashley, brothers Ed and Frank, and Kid Lowe would stop small boats loaded with booze from the Bahamas. The gang would force the unlucky bootleggers to hand over their liquor and any cash they might be carrying.

Sometimes, the gang would surprise unlucky bootleggers as they were coming ashore after completing their run. The rum piracy proved to be a lucrative sideline business for the Ashleys.

On June 1, 1921, DeSoto County Sheriff John Poucher got a tip that bootleggers were unloading a shipment of booze at a garage just outside the small town of Wauchula, Florida. When Poucher and a deputy arrived, they searched a car parked outside the garage and found two pistols. Then two men came out of the garage. Unarmed and seeing that they were confronting cops, the men surrendered peacefully and were taken to the county jail.

One of the bootleggers said his name was Davis. He was put into a holding cell.

But the man's face was familiar to one of the other prisoners in the DeSoto County Jail, who asked for a private word with Sheriff Poucher.

That man's name is not Davis, the prisoner said. That's John Ashley. *The* John Ashley.

Three days later, Ashley was behind bars again in the Florida State Prison in Raiford. Eventually, he was moved to a prison in Holmes County in the Florida Panhandle between Tallahassee and Pensacola. It had been a sizable stretch of freedom—nearly three years—for Ashley. But he did not intend to stay in jail to serve out the remainder of his long term.

The loss of their most slippery member didn't curtail the rest of the gang members from their profitable activities on the seas between Florida and West End. But greed or perhaps the fury of other bootleggers tired of losing their profits to the Ashleys proved fatal to two gang members.

Just after dark on Wednesday, October 19, 1921, Ed and Frank Ashley climbed into a small skiff. The presence of a Coast Guard cutter just off the St. Lucie Inlet near Stuart didn't deter them in the slightest. They ran without lights, and they muffled their small engine so that it was practically noiseless.

Their tactics worked. They slipped past the cutter undetected and began their journey to West End.

The following day, the brothers insisted that their boat be loaded with as much booze as it could possibly carry. Although the Bahamian liquor dealers had no compunctions about selling booze to American bootleggers, they warned Ed and Frank that their boat was too heavily loaded. With typical Ashley bravado, the brothers laughed off the warning and insisted that more booze be loaded.

Still, the sky was threatening and it looked like rough weather was coming. Despite their indifference to the dangers of carrying such a heavy load, the brothers decided to wait a day before leaving.

On Friday, October 21, 1921, the skies were overcast and the seas were choppy—so choppy that the scant freeboard caused by the Ashleys' load of liquor would make for a very dangerous return to Florida in their small boat.

They were advised to wait another day, but Ed and Frank were itching to get their hands on the cash that their haul would bring. With choppy seas licking at their gunwales, the brothers set out for home.

They were never seen again.

John Ashley would later say that the same night his brothers had set out on the choppy seas, he'd had a dream about their fate.

Author Hix Stuart, who claimed to have had the only interview John Ashley ever granted to a writer, later wrote about Ashley's dream.

"He seemed to hover right over the liquor-laden skiff as it plowed through the moonlit sea," Stuart wrote. "Suddenly out of the night appeared another craft, larger and faster, skimming directly toward his brothers' boat. . . . To Ed and

Frank the contour of the boat placed it as just another rum boat going to the island for a load. But John, in his eerie vantage, recognized its crew of three as Jim White, Bo Stokes, and Alton Davis—hijackers on land and liquor pirates at sea. A fusillade of shots and John awoke, weak and frightened, convinced that something had happened to his brothers."

Stuart said that Joe Ashley visited his son in prison, and John Ashley told his father about his dream. Not long after, Jim White, Bo Stokes, and Alton Davis disappeared at sea.

Bootleggers mysteriously vanishing on the high seas didn't have the slightest deterrence on the availability of booze in Florida, however. In one of his stories for the *Saturday Evening Post*, Kenneth Roberts reported that prices for bootleg liquor in Miami were low compared to the prices in larger northern cities, where tipplers "have been paying $120 a case for stuff that is only fit for cleaning the nicotine out of pipe stems."

A case of twelve bottles of scotch whisky that cost $24 in the Bahamas could be bought in Miami for $50—about $690 in twenty-first-century dollars. Taxi drivers then were selling the booze for $10 a bottle to hotel guests, pocketing $70 in profits in the process, Roberts wrote.

Some cigar stores and newsstands operated punchboards, offering as their top prizes bottles of expensive scotch and rye.

Roberts warned tourists who wanted "to bring back a wee nip of Scotch with them from Florida" to be cautious about how they concealed the booze. All trunks were searched, he said. They were more likely to get away with it if they kept the liquor in hand-carried luggage.

But Miami's bootleggers had become so sophisticated that they'd devised ways to move large shipments of liquor out of the city right under the noses of federal agents. They'd load a train car with booze, then buy grapefruit or tomatoes or other perishable fruit to cover the whiskey for shipment by rail to wherever it was wanted.

Some of the smugglers owned schooners and made night runs to the Bahamas, where, because of the larger quantity they bought, they paid $18 a case for liquor.

The easy availability of liquor in Miami was infuriating federal agents, who were determined to stop it. By early 1922 they'd been watching bootleg traffic long enough to devise a plan. On March 20, shortly after William Jennings Bryan had proposed that the United States acquire the Bahamas, federal lawmen under Colonel L. G. Nutt, the acting federal Prohibition director, executed raids. Among those hauled in by the federal dragnet was a vice president of a Miami bank, who was charged with conspiracy for allegedly agreeing to be the bagman for a bootlegging transaction. He'd apparently agreed to hold four $1,000 bills and a $50 bill until a shipment of booze was delivered.

The raid was a brief embarrassment for a few Miami officials, but soon the liquor was flowing freely again.

Handford Mobley didn't look like a tough guy. In 1922, Mobley was seventeen years old, small and slender, with delicate, almost effeminate facial features.

But Handford Mobley was John Ashley's nephew, and he greatly admired and looked up to his uncle. And while Uncle John was in jail, Mobley made his bones, so to speak, with the family.

Business was usually quiet in the mid-afternoons at the Bank of Stuart, so when two people walked into the lobby at that time on May 22, 1922, the only others in the bank were the cashiers.

E. P. Hyer was in a teller's cage filing checks when the pair walked in. He was absorbed in his task and didn't notice them until he heard someone order him to "throw up my hands."

"I was too busy to pay much attention to the first order, but when someone repeated it and shoved a .45 caliber revolver in my face through the bars of the cage, I realized it was a holdup and complied," Hyer told the *Palm Beach Post*.

The young man who shoved the gun in Hyer's face was J. Clarence Middleton. He was nattily attired in what was referred to as a Palm Beach suit—a lightweight white suit with a double-breasted jacket. With him was "a young fellow disguised as a woman wearing a heavy black veil," Hyer said.

The young man in drag was Handford Mobley. He also carried a revolver.

Mobley started shoving cash into a pillowcase, then ordered cashier Percy Fuge to open the bank vault. Fuge fiddled with the vault's locking mechanism, but instead of opening it, he activated the time lock so that the vault could not be opened.

An unfortunate customer came into the bank to make a deposit. Apparently, the gang had finally realized that it was best to bring their own driver when they pulled a stickup, and the customer was followed into the bank by Roy Matthews, who was driving the getaway car. Matthews had blackened his face with soot or burnt cork as a disguise.

In his haste to cram as much cash as possible into the pillowcase, Middleton spilled trays of silver coins onto the floor. He ordered the customer to pick up the silver.

Meanwhile, Mobley was getting impatient with Fuge for not opening the vault. Brandishing his pistol, Mobley sneered, "Open that vault or I'll blow your brains out."

"It's too late now, boys," Fuge replied. "I've already set the time lock on it."

Mobley was infuriated, but did not carry out his threat to kill Fuge. The robbers left with about $8,100. The vault had contained another $20,000.

The robbers drove around Stuart a few times to confuse anyone trying to follow them, then crossed the St. Lucie River and headed north toward Fort Pierce.

But Palm Beach County Sheriff Robert Baker—the former jailer who had succeeded his father as sheriff—wasn't thrown off by the trick, and set off after them.

Baker chased the fugitives for more than two hundred miles. The gang eluded Baker near the town of Sebring, but Baker telephoned a description of the gang to police in nearby towns.

Mobley and Middleton checked into a hotel in Plant City, but the clerk became suspicious, and when the two went to their room, he called the cops.

When the police arrived, the two men had left. But an alert motorcycle cop arrested the pair at a nearby train station. They each had a ticket to Savannah, Georgia.

A man thought to have been the third robber managed to slip aboard the northbound Seaboard Air Line train. The train's conductor told police a passenger said he'd lost his ticket and paid for his fare in cash.

Mobley and Middleton—who told the police his name was J. Clarence Jones—had about $2,300 on them when they were captured. Mobley seemed to enjoy bantering with lawmen after he'd been arrested. He said he didn't have the rest of the money. He told the cops an imaginative tale about being forced at gunpoint to rob the bank by two threatening accomplices they'd just met in a nearby park. Those two men had the rest of the money from the robbery, Mobley said.

"Mobley gave every outward evidence of being very chipper and rather pleased with himself," the *Palm Beach Post* reported. "He had not needed the money, he said, always had plenty of money, one or two thousand dollars, but he liked the excitement."

A few days later, police in Griffin, Georgia—about forty miles south of Atlanta—arrested Roy Matthews and charged him with being one of the bank robbers.

In October, the three were in the Palm Beach County Jail in West Palm Beach awaiting trial. But on October 25, 1922, a judge ordered their trial postponed because several witnesses for the defense weren't available to testify. Defense attorneys said they hadn't had enough time to summon these key witnesses, who would swear under oath that these young men hadn't been anywhere near Stuart on the day of the robbery.

The three accused robbers did not seem at all concerned about the trial. "They seemed altogether at ease and during the intervals in the court procedure chatted and laughed with relatives and friends," the *Palm Beach Post* reported.

The judge agreed to postpone the trial until February 1923, and signed an order allowing Mobley, Matthews, and Middleton to be temporarily transferred to a jail in Fort Lauderdale because repairs and renovations were being made to the Palm Beach County Jail.

Mobley and Matthews would not be around for the new trial date, however. On December 14, the young daredevils forced open a skylight in the Fort

Lauderdale jail. They went through the opening and, using sheets and blankets tied together as a rope, lowered themselves out of the jail and made straight for the Everglades.

Mobley was off for more excitement.

It was starting to seem unlikely that construction crews would ever be able to push a road through the Ashley Gang's hideout. By early 1923, it was clear that Lee County was not going to be able to pay for its stretch of the Tamiami Trail. But Barron Collier, the young advertising millionaire from Cincinnati, was buying hundreds of thousands of acres of land in Lee County, and he was determined to make his investments pay.

He couldn't get a return on his huge investment, however, if no one could get to the land. And completing the Tamiami Trail would be the best way—the only way, really—to open his land for development.

So if Lee County couldn't pay for building the Trail, Collier would. But first he wanted his own county.

In February 1923, Collier bought a dredge that had been used on the construction of the Florida East Coast Railway. The dredge's one-cubic-yard bucket could move about one-quarter of a ton of dirt with every bucketful. Collier moved the dredge to the Gulf Coast to go to work on the Tamiami Trail.

Still, by early April, work on the road was flagging. In Fort Myers, civic and business leaders decided that something had to be done to revive public interest in finishing the Trail. So at 7:30 a.m. on April 4, with much fanfare, about two dozen business boosters set out from Fort Myers to cross the Everglades in seven automobiles—even though there was no road where they would be going. They would be joined by two Seminole Indian guides.

They called themselves the Tamiami Trailblazers, and they expected their ambitious stunt to get the attention of newspapers and provide a much-needed publicity boost for the construction project. The Trailblazers said they thought it would take three days to get through the Glades and reach Miami.

They were right about the publicity they would receive, but, like John King in 1917, they were way off on how long it would take them to complete their journey. And the length of that journey and the uncertainty of their fates would be what got newspapers' attention.

Heavy rains soaked the Everglades shortly after the Trailblazers left. On April 7, the day the Trailblazers were due in Miami, there was no sign of them. A search party from Miami went into the Everglades looking for the missing men, but couldn't find a clue as to their whereabouts.

Newspapers across the country picked up the story of the Trailblazers missing in the mysterious Everglades. Some thought that the drenching rain had made it impossible for them to continue, so they'd turned around and headed back to Fort Myers.

Others, however, speculated that they'd met the type of fate that only the Everglades could have dealt them.

"The outside world had no knowledge of how the trail blazers were faring in their undertaking," recalled Russell Kay, who'd been one the Trailblazers. "Exaggerated stories were released from Miami by a few news service writers, who, drawing on their imagination, pictured the men as lost in the wilderness and fighting for their lives against wild animals, alligators, and snakes.

"Most reports concluded that the convoy was hopelessly lost, without food or help," Kay said. "This was all 'hogwash' and untrue; the men knew generally where they were all the time, and they were only delayed because of the difficult terrain."

To describe the terrain as "difficult" was an understatement. During much of the trip, the Trailblazers were able to travel only a mile or so each day, and traveling after sunset was out of the question. Sometimes the cars bogged down in mud to their axles, and had to be pushed and pulled out. Sometimes streams had to be forded, and when they were too deep, primitive log bridges had to be built.

There was saw grass that tore at the men's clothing. And there were also the native denizens of the Glades—snakes, alligators, panthers.

The Trailblazers came across dozens of water moccasins in a large pool near the Turner River. Frightened by the sight of so many poisonous snakes, one of the men killed two with a shovel.

"This so angered the Indians, they threatened to desert then and there," Kay said.

One of the Trailblazers was Stanley Hanson, an agent for the federal Office of Indian Affairs. Hanson managed to calm the infuriated Seminole guides, then explained their anger to the Trailblazers.

"He explained that the Indians never kill wantonly, and that they respected the snakes because they contended that the reptiles had more right to be there than humans," Kay said.

The Seminoles believed it was a crime to kill the snakes without cause. One of them walked barefoot among the moccasins. He didn't look down at the snakes and kept a steady pace as he walked through them.

The moccasins didn't touch the Seminole, Kay said.

On April 11, the *Miami Herald* sent a reporter aloft in an airplane to look for the Trailblazers. After three hours of zigzagging at perilously low altitude, the pilot and reporter saw no sign of the men.

The Trailblazers, however, had seen the plane. They tried quickly to get a signal fire started to attract the attention of the fliers, but couldn't get it lit in time.

The men realized that people were worried. They were days overdue, and no one had heard a word from them since they'd left Fort Myers.

So while most of the men continued wrestling the cars through the Everglades, three men pushed ahead to Miami to let the world know that the Trailblazers were unharmed and still working their way to Miami. The small advance party reached Miami early on the morning of April 12, but the main group was still several days behind them.

As the Trailblazers coaxed their cars through the Everglades, fretting about water moccasins and alligators as they drew nearer to their destination, tempers were flaring in Fort Myers and Tampa. Barron Collier was mounting an all-out effort in the Florida state legislature to persuade the lawmakers to create a new county that would be named after him.

In Fort Myers, people were furious that two of the men among their delegation to the legislature were showing signs of supporting Collier's effort. On April 18, dozens of angry Lee County residents gathered at a public meeting in the county seat of Fort Myers to protest Collier's political manipulations.

The following day, an irate telegram was dispatched to legislator Walter O. Sheppard. The opponents called the effort to create a new county a betrayal of their trust, claiming that "90 percent" of the people in Lee County opposed the move.

That same day, the *Fort Myers Press* confidently reported that Collier might be losing his effort to carve out a new county.

"Barron Collier, of New York and the Everglades, seems to have gone about as far as he can get," the *Press* said on its editorial page. "His plan for the county of Collier was so unfair on the face of it that it seems to be losing."

The *Press* said plans for chopping up Lee County would be "nothing short of a mutilation" of "this grand old county."

Lee County, named after Confederate general Robert E. Lee, had been formed in 1887, right about the time that Northerners were starting to notice Florida's balmy winters. More counties were formed as the state's population continued to grow in the early twentieth century. Between 1905 and 1921, sixteen new counties had been created, and Lee County voters had already approved creating another new county, Hendry, from a portion of Lee County.

But Collier taking another chunk of Lee for another new county had not been publicly discussed, nor had it been put before the voters, the *Press* noted.

Allowing Barron Collier to have his county, the *Press* said, would make the residents of that new county "subject to the autocratic whims and fancies of one man, benevolent though he might be."

The *Tampa Tribune* also had some reservations about creating a county for Barron Collier. The *Tribune* acknowledged that Collier had promised to bring industry and jobs to southwest Florida. But, the newspaper said, he should be required to make some of those improvements first, noting that "it would seem to be a bad idea to create a new county for the benefit and at the request of one man."

Meanwhile, on the other side of the peninsula, the Tamiami Trailblazers—bruised, ragged, insect-bitten, hungry, and sore—finally emerged from the

Everglades, nearly three weeks after they'd started their "three-day" trip. Their cars were battered, dented, and dirty. They'd realized that such luxuries as running boards and fenders on automobiles were an inconvenience when they were trying to cross a swamp, so those parts had been removed and discarded long ago.

But they'd kept the automobiles in good operating condition otherwise, and around six p.m. on April 19, the Trailblazers finally rolled into Miami. The *Miami Herald* said that the Trailblazers had made history, and proclaimed that "the last frontier of the United States was crossed by the automobile party."

The publicity stunt had paid off. The uncertainty about the fate of the Trailblazers lost in the infamous Everglades had attracted cameramen from Warner-Pathé News and Fox Movietone News, who accompanied the Trailblazers for the last fifty miles or so of their trip. Soon, movie audiences across the country would be learning about the effort to build the Tamiami Trail through Florida's wild, exotic Everglades.

Still, the conquest of the Glades was nowhere near complete.

Back on the Gulf Coast, the fracas about whether to create a county for Barron Collier was heating up. The *Tampa Times* commented that Collier's first name was indeed appropriate, for he was "one of the real old-time barons of the middle ages, who took what they wanted by virtue of the 'mailed fist,' and asked nobody."

Like several other Gulf Coast newspapers, the *Times* did not trust the wealthy Yankee advertising tycoon, and wanted him to spread around some of his wealth before he was given his own county.

"Some of the Lee County folks, who have less money and less gall than the northern baron, suggest that the development should come first," the *Times* opined. "They would like to see the color of his money before they hand over to him the best part of Lee County for a principality of his own."

"The state should be suspicious of the wealth that seeks to monopolize the land of the people," the *Times* concluded.

On April 21, a state House of Representatives subcommittee voted six to three to make an unfavorable report on the bill to create Collier's county. Collier apparently realized he was losing the battle of public opinion. On April 24, he arrived in Tallahassee and immediately went into a long meeting with state representative R. A. Henderson and others whom the irate *Fort Myers Press* referred to as "henchmen."

The following day, the committee voted to reopen its hearings on the bill so that Collier could make a statement to the panel.

Late that evening, it appeared that Collier, the public relations genius, was turning the legislature his way. Legislator S. Watt Lawler Jr. telegraphed Collier opponents in Fort Myers: "Collier forces very active. Things are getting complicated. Additional hearing this afternoon. We need reinforcements."

On Friday, April 27, the *Press* was practically foaming at the mouth at Collier's "monarchistic" plans and the new developments in Tallahassee that seemed to be going in Collier's favor.

Who will build schools for the new county, the *Press* asked, and who will support them? What might happen if, God forbid, Barron Collier were to die soon after the new county was formed? Would the promised development happen then? And how would the Tamiami Trail be completed?

Even Fort Myers ministers got involved in the fight, sending a letter to Governor Cary Hardee saying they had "grave concerns" that the creation of the county would imperil the "moral welfare" of all citizens of southwest Florida. The preachers didn't say it outright in the telegram, but there had been rumors circulating that Collier intended to open gambling casinos once he got his county, and since he would be boss of his domain, who knew what other sinful pleasures he might bring to his fiefdom?

The fight dragged on into May, when two giants of American industry came out strongly against the creation of the county. Thomas Edison, the wizard of science who'd been wintering in Fort Myers since 1885, joined his winter neighbor, Henry Ford, in hiring lobbyists to go to Tallahassee to try to convince the legislature to turn down Collier's request.

The *Press* reported that neither Edison nor Ford thought there were enough people or development prospects to justify forming a new county. But even the opposition of these two titans couldn't sway the Florida legislature. On Thursday, May 3, 1923, both houses approved the creation of Collier County by wide margins. The new county would come into existence on July 9, 1923. The small town of Everglade, renamed Everglades, would become the county seat.

Collier immediately started transforming the isolated, backwater hamlet into a modern town, building docks, laying out streets, providing electricity and phone lines. Eventually, he built a school, a movie theater, a fire department, and a courthouse, among other amenities.

After the legislature voted, Collier granted his first interview to one of his most bitter opponents, the *Press*. He told the reporter that he didn't think he'd been fairly treated by newspapers on the Gulf Coast, but he didn't hold a grudge against anyone who had opposed the creation of the new county.

He wanted the new county created because he thought he could accomplish more with a group of county administrators who were friendly to his efforts rather than administrators who were more concerned with Fort Myers's interests.

Collier went through a list of improvements he planned to make. He pledged to start a steamboat connecting Collier County with Miami and to improve railroad connections in the county as well. He also promised to add telephone lines.

And he vowed to buy new machinery and work it around the clock to complete the Tamiami Trail through Collier County to the Dade County line.

"I do not blame the people of Fort Myers and the rest of Lee County for the attitude they have taken," Collier told the *Press*, "but want to assure them that the development that will be made in Collier County will help all of the West Coast of Florida; and I believe that I have relieved the rest of Lee County of a section that they might not have been able to do as much with as I can."

After his life-changing accident in the chemistry lab at Washburn College in 1915, Edwin Menninger moved to New York, studied journalism at Columbia University, and went to work for the *New York Tribune*. But during the winter of 1921–22, he came down with a severe case of the flu. His doctor told him that the only way he'd recover was to get out of the bitter New York winter and go to Florida.

Menninger went to West Palm Beach and was hired as the night city editor at the *Palm Beach Post*.

After a few months on his new job, Menninger learned that the *Post* published a weekly newspaper called the *South Florida Developer*. The *Developer* had been launched two years earlier as a public relations tool for the Model Land Company, which had been formed by Henry Flagler in 1896 as he extended his railroad down Florida's east coast.

To launch the *Developer*, the land company paid for ten thousand subscriptions for its customers, but after a couple of years the company stopped paying, and the subscriptions had dwindled to about 1,200.

Learning about the *Developer* stirred Menninger's boyhood memories of his well-managed newspaper routes and rekindled his ambition to own his own newspaper. So he talked to Donald H. Conkling, who published the *Developer* for the *Palm Beach Post*.

After some discussion, Conkling essentially gave the *Developer* to Menninger. The deal was finalized on January 1, 1923. No cash actually changed hands in the transaction, although Menninger agreed to pay Conkling $500 for the *Developer*'s list of subscribers and another $500 for an old printing press. Conkling told Menninger he could pay off that debt by printing the *Palm Beach Post* for him.

Menninger moved to Stuart in August 1923, borrowed $400 from one of his brothers, put $200 down on a linotype machine, and was in business as the publisher of the *South Florida Developer*.

Menninger, the former newspaper delivery boy who had run his routes with such precocious efficiency, had an unusual combination of talents, being both a savvy journalist and a shrewd businessman.

Florida was about to undergo a dramatic transformation from a rowdy frontier to a stylish national fad. Edwin Menninger, an ambitious young journalist, would become a chronicler of, a participant in, and a commentator on an outlandish and colorful episode of unfettered American capitalism in all its grandeur and delusion. He would become caught up in the mania and hysteria of the wild real estate speculation that was about to engulf Florida, yet he would also display his down-to-earth Kansas common sense. Occasionally, he would step back from the dreams and chaos swirling around him and, like the classic Greek chorus, make insightful comments in the *South Florida Developer*. And like a character in a novel, he would evolve as he watched events unfold.

When it was over, he would realize the harsh lesson that he and others had learned as they'd watched what they thought was a permanent paradise plunge into bottomless ruin.

But in the late summer of 1923, he was a young man only twenty-seven years old, about to embark on the adventure of running his own newspaper.

Apparently there wasn't a jail in Florida that could hold John Ashley.

After his arrest in Wauchula for transporting whiskey, he had been sent to a state prison in Holmes County in the western Florida Panhandle between Tallahassee and Pensacola. On September 27, 1923, Ashley and another convict, a US Navy deserter who was doing time for grand larceny, found a few loose bars in a jail cell. They forced the bars out and climbed through.

Once again, John Ashley was free. He vowed never to see the inside of a jail again, and his reasons likely went beyond merely not wanting to be confined.

The prison work camps run by the state of Florida in the late-nineteenth and early-twentieth centuries were quite different from a county jail where friends and family lived nearby. The work camps were hellholes in which prisoners were treated like slave labor.

The same year Ashley escaped the prison in Holmes County, the state's prison system was engulfed in scandal when Martin Tabert, a twenty-two-year-old North Dakota farm-boy who was traveling through Florida, ran out of money in Tallahassee. He was arrested for vagrancy. His parents sent him money, but by the time it reached Tallahassee, the young man had been sent to a prison work farm for a sixty-day sentence.

He died from a whipping administered by a prison guard. In 1923, flogging prisoners was legal in Florida.

So Ashley's life may well have been as much in danger at the hands of wardens and guards in the prison as it was from sheriffs and police officers on the outside.

Ashley worked his way across the Panhandle and down the peninsula, and soon he was back in his familiar hideout in the wilds of Palm Beach County. He was reunited with his partners in crime. It was just like old times again.

"Automobiles were stolen, burglaries committed, and general terror reigned in the territory in which they operated," author Hix Stuart wrote.

They also continued making moonshine and making runs to the Bahamas to bootleg whiskey from West End. And they resumed their highly profitable piracy of other bootleggers in the waters between Florida and the Bahamas.

They were always a few steps ahead of the law, and the Everglades was always nearby when lawmen got too close. But by late 1923, as more and more winter visitors were coming to Florida, cops and sheriffs in southern Florida were becoming more determined to stop their crimes, one way or the other.

President-elect Warren Harding's visit to Miami Beach in February 1921 and a persistent shortage of coal during two subsequent winters helped start a flow of cold-weather visitors to Florida that would turn into a torrent in a few years.

Beginning in November 1922 and continuing into the winter months of 1923–24, many smaller newspapers—especially in the Midwest—ran a story with the headline "Running Away from Winter."

It read more like an advertisement than a news story: "With cold weather and the coal shortage, the greatest pilgrimage to the southland known in years has begun. Southern Atlantic seaports report a steady stream of yachts moving southward, indicative of an unusually heavy season. Southern resort managers say, however, the pilgrimage will not be confined to what is commonly known as America's smart set, but will include as many if not more persons of moderate means."

The story, which did not carry a byline, was accompanied by a spread of enticing photos—several young women in skimpy (for the time) bathing suits climbing a palm tree, and two more sitting by a pool, mounted polo players, and President Harding on a Miami Beach golf course.

The layout of the story was identical in every newspaper. Neither the copy nor the photos were removed or altered. The story obviously was aimed at enticing chilly Midwesterners to climb into their Fords and spend a few weeks in the warm Florida sunshine.

The writer, undoubtedly a crafty press agent, acknowledged "it is society that gets the greatest notoriety at winter resorts."

"Yet those whose names do not appear in the society columns are there in just as great numbers and have just as much fun, or more, than those who dress for dinner every evening and worry about beach capes and pretty polo coats," the story said.

Whoever wrote the story also emphasized that Florida was not that far away by train.

"To the man up north who has been shoveling coal into a voracious furnace that threatens to eat up the meagre supply, a sudden view next day of pretty bathing girls in one-piece suits disporting themselves on a sunny beach holds a thrill that is likely to be remembered," the story said.

President Harding's post-election visit to Miami Beach had been an invaluable publicity coup for Carl Fisher, but Fisher and other ambitious developers were still regarded with some suspicion when the 1922–23 winter season arrived. *Saturday Evening Post* writer Kenneth Roberts noted that in 1923, Florida developers who were standing in the middle of pine trees and palmettoes, picking sandspurs off their socks and talking to developers about their plans to spend millions of dollars on hotels, casinos, and golf courses, often were regarded as "addicts to the potent loco-weed."

Still, construction statistics for four Florida cities in early 1923 were impressive. In February, building permits issued for Miami Beach, Miami, and Tampa totaled more than $995,000, dwarfing even the combined totals of Savannah, Georgia, and Charleston, South Carolina. In fact, Miami Beach's total alone surpassed those of Savannah and Charleston, which were much larger cities.

The *Miami Herald* also predicted that 1923 would be a year of exceptional industrial growth for the city, noting that demand was increasing for products manufactured in Miami.

There were other indicators of rapid economic growth. In February 1923, Burdines, a leading department store, reported sales were up 34 percent from the same time in 1922, and sales for the following month increased by more than 32 percent from March 1922.

There were about 8,700 telephones in Miami in December 1923, and Southern Bell expected to add another 1,500 in the following two months. The telephone company had had to add more than $500,000 worth of new equipment to keep up with telephone-service demands in 1923, and expected to spend at least that much in 1924.

Still, as the "Running Away from Winter" story noted, Miami and Miami Beach also had become the winter home of more captains of American industry, including cough drop producer William Luden; tire tycoon Harvey Firestone; William K. Vanderbilt II, heir to the great Vanderbilt fortune; and T. Coleman du Pont, a retired general and a US senator representing Delaware. And there were others, including J. C. Penney, owner of the department stores, and automobile manufacturer William Durant.

The presence of the upper strata of society also attracted some lawbreakers with far more finesse and skill than the homegrown Ashley Gang. In late January and early February 1923, sophisticated and skilled jewel thieves made off with hundreds of thousands of dollars' worth of jewelry from the homes of wealthy winter residents in Dade County.

On January 31, about $250,000 worth of jewelry was stolen from the Brickell Avenue mansion of Chicago millionaire David Joyce. A neighbor's chauffeur who hastily departed Miami for Boston was detained for questioning, but he did not have any of the jewelry in his luggage, and police confirmed his explanation that he'd left in a hurry because his father-in-law was dying.

Five days later, second-story thieves broke into the Miami Beach mansion of automobile parts manufacturer Robert H. Hassler and made off with thousands of dollars' worth of gold and diamond jewelry.

Miami's continuing struggles with Prohibition made huge headlines in the *Miami Daily Metropolis* at the same time the jewel thieves were hauling away their loot. On February 2, three federal agents raided the Plantation Inn, a roadhouse just west of Miami.

But the raid turned into a fierce fistfight when proprietor Wilbur Phelps punched an agent in the face so hard that he went tumbling down a flight of steps. Another agent started fighting Phelps. Waiters brandishing liquor bottles started to come to Phelps's aid, but the third agent pulled a gun and backed them off.

Phelps finally was subdued and handcuffed. He was charged with possession of liquor, maintaining a nuisance, and resisting arrest.

The following day, a Dade County deputy sheriff served arrest warrants on the federal agents who had raided the Plantation Inn. They were charged with assault with intent to kill Wilbur Phelps.

That same day, Miami reporters got a few minutes to chat with Georgia governor Thomas Hardwick, who passed through the city after a fishing trip in the Florida Keys. Hardwick said he thought laws "modifying" Prohibition would eventually be passed, and pointed out that the only people who seemed to support the Volstead Act were hard-line moralists and the bootleggers who were getting rich from it.

"As long as there is so much public sentiment against the federal act, there is little hope to remedy conditions because juries will not convict violators even though evidence is produced," Hardwick said.

His comments were prophetic.

A grand jury indicted Wilbur Phelps on charges of violating the Volstead Act, and that indictment nullified the assault charges against the federal agents who had raided the Plantation Inn.

But on April 23, a jury decided that Phelps was not guilty of the possession and sale of whiskey. The *Miami Daily Metropolis* reported that Phelps was one of three defendants found not guilty that day of violating the Volstead Act.

At times, it did seem as though bootleggers were running Miami, Miami Beach, and the other rapidly growing cities on Florida's southeast coast. A man who reported bootleggers to cops was beaten up by those bootleggers in broad daylight on the street.

The *Chicago Daily News* reported that booze purchases in Nassau, the Bahamas, had increased from about 37,000 gallons a year in 1917 to more than 1.3 million gallons in 1922, and that anyone could easily buy whiskey in Miami for $5 a quart.

"Any Prohibition enforcement agent that didn't have lead in his shoes and a daub of mud in both eyes . . . could easily get the goods on twenty or thirty Miami bootleggers in a day," Kenneth Roberts wrote for the *Saturday Evening Post*.

Crime or no crime, President Harding had become a fan of Miami Beach. The chief executive came back for another visit in March 1923. As the houseboat transporting the president from Jacksonville chugged slowly into Biscayne Bay on the morning of March 14, Carl Fisher's speedy yacht, the *Shadow VI*, raced across the bay to meet Harding.

The president, eager to get on the golf course, gratefully climbed aboard, and the yacht zipped back across the bay at thirty miles an hour. In just a few minutes, Harding had stepped up to the first tee and whacked a respectable drive of about 180 yards down the fairway.

The *Miami Daily Metropolis* noted that Harding "looked a little greyer, a little heavier, a little older" than in February 1921, when he'd made his first visit to Miami Beach. But once again, he'd put Miami Beach into newspapers across the United States.

While Miami and Miami Beach were receiving an increasing flow of visitors and evolving into modern cities, Edwin Menninger—who moved from West Palm Beach to Stuart in August 1923—was taking stock of his new home. In some ways, the small town, at the time one of the northernmost communities in Palm Beach County, still retained vestiges of the nineteenth century.

The only time the town's electric plant operated during the day was on Tuesday afternoons, so housewives could iron their hand-washed laundry. Otherwise, the plant didn't crank up until five p.m. So in order to run his printing press and linotype machine, Menninger had to buy his own generator, a diesel-powered unit.

Stuart did not have an ice plant in 1923. An ice maker in West Palm Beach sent a freight train car filled with ice to Stuart every other day, where it was parked on a railroad siding. Customers bought their ice in chunks from a bespectacled clerk.

The town had one plumber, a hotel or two, a couple of banks, a lumberyard, a movie theater, a hardware store, a grocery store, a gasoline station, and a weekly newspaper.

Menninger had made determined adjustments, learning to function without his right eye and with a mangled left hand. He'd learned to type using only his right hand, and he was able to use what remained of his left hand to operate the "shift" key of a typewriter or typesetting machine. He'd become remarkably adept at rapid typing with one hand.

Still, Menninger steadfastly refused to talk about his disabilities, and when he posed for photos, he always held his left hand behind him.

His even temperament and excellent memory for names served him well as he was trying to get a foothold in Stuart for the *South Florida Developer*. He defied the stereotype of the irascible journalist, soon becoming known as a good employer who seldom showed anger.

Menninger quickly fell under the spell of Florida, but one thing about his surroundings continually annoyed him. The only color he saw was green. The monotony of the landscape bothered him.

As part of his promotion of the *Developer*, Menninger started giving away packets of zinnia seeds to anyone who would promise to plant them. Then he held a contest to choose the best bouquets. Soon he became too busy with his growing business to continue the contests, but giving away seeds was the start of a lifelong passion for bright tropical flowers.

As summer gave way to fall in 1923, a combination of factors was aligning that would soon make Florida a national obsession. Modern advertising deployed in mass-circulation publications described Florida in florid prose as an ethereal paradise. Henry Ford's perfection of the assembly line in Detroit had steadily lowered the price of a Ford until just about anyone with a decent job could afford one.

Thanks to Carl Fisher and other visionaries, the Dixie Highway and other road construction was making it easier for more people to climb into their new Fords and chug off to Florida for a few weeks. The state's political leaders, realizing they had an opportunity to craft a more substantial image of Florida as an unusual place where ordinary rules didn't apply, passed legislation doing away with state income and inheritance taxes, and soon would raise the state's maximum speed limit to forty-five miles per hour—an unheard-of liberty at the time. Slick marketers were using large publications to paint a picture of Florida as a tropical paradise.

President Harding, who had helped to focus Americans' attention on Florida, died suddenly of a heart attack in August 1923. He would be succeeded by Vice President Calvin Coolidge, who thought that "the chief business of the American people is business."

At the time of Harding's death, enthusiastic visitors were spreading the word about Florida's playgrounds in less-conventional ways. At the base of picturesque Chimney Rock in the mountains of North Carolina, someone had turned several huge boulders into advertising. They had written, in fiery red letters, "Come to Miami Beach, Fla."; "Oh, you Miami Beach, we're waiting for you"; and "Miami Beach, the playground of the world."

But as visitors began to assemble in Miami, Miami Beach, Palm Beach, and other resort towns for the 1923–24 season, the pesky Ashley Gang was still at work. And they were plying their craft only a few miles from where young women were lounging on beaches, wealthy and influential men were playing golf and watching polo matches, and potential investors were pondering whether or not to buy some real estate.

Palm Beach County Sheriff Robert Baker and his deputies were infuriated when they heard that a man had been robbed on the Dixie Highway by John Ashley on Christmas Day of 1923. About two weeks later, Ashley and a few other gang members held up the train station at Salerno, a small town just south of Stuart. They only got $16 for their trouble, but Palm Beach County lawmen had had enough. They were determined to put an end to the gang.

Baker had finally gotten the information he needed. He'd learned the location of one of the Ashleys' hideouts in the Everglades, and he'd gotten a tip that Ashley was hiding there after the robbery of the Salerno train station.

Before daybreak on Wednesday, January 9, Baker and four deputies crept through the swamp approaching the gang's hideout. As the sun rose over the Florida Everglades on that long-ago January morning, John Ashley, Laura Upthegrove, Joe Ashley, another gang member or two, and a few of Joe Ashley's daughters were in the camp.

Their compound was a few miles back from the Dixie Highway in the Everglades, on a spot of high ground above the soggy prairie of the Glades. There were three tents. Two were used for dwellings, and the third was used for storage.

There also was a hundred-gallon moonshine still, probably one of the largest in the state.

The lawmen had finally caught Joe Ashley and his notorious family by surprise. As the sun came up on that January morning, a brief, fierce, and deadly battle was about to take place.

There are at least two versions of how that gunfight unfolded. Newspapers across the country reported one version of the battle. John Ashley, who would somehow survive the hail of bullets aimed at him, gave a slightly different account.

The *Palm Beach Post* reported that the holdup at the Salerno train station started the sequence of events that led the deputies to the Ashleys' hideout. But John Ashley, in the interview with Hix Stuart, said he'd gotten into an argument with a mechanic in Salerno who'd tried to cheat him on some repairs to a car.

"These hicks called up [Palm Beach County Sheriff] Bob Baker and told him something had to be done about me," Ashley told Stuart.

Newspapers reported that the gunfire started when a dog barked. Ashley said it started when gang member Albert Miller, who was standing outside a tent, heard a shot.

Gunfire erupted, "and in a few minutes it sounded like a war," Ashley told Stuart. Deputy Sheriff Fred Baker, nephew of the sheriff, was shot dead. Newspapers reported that Miller killed the lawman. Ashley told Stuart that he'd killed the deputy.

Miller was severely wounded in the exchange. One bullet shattered an arm; another hit him in the hip. Joe Ashley was killed as he got up from the cot where he'd been sleeping, and Laura Upthegrove was hit in the legs with a spray of buckshot.

But John Ashley was untouched.

"They poured enough lead at me to kill ten men, but fate seemed against them," he said.

The gunfire stopped after Laura Upthegrove screamed in pain. Her wounds weren't fatal, and although badly wounded, Miller managed to escape with John Ashley.

Dozens of armed volunteers spread out to chase Ashley and Miller. A mob, enraged at the death of Deputy Sheriff Fred Baker and just tired of the Ashleys' long history of crime, set fire to Joe Ashley's house in Gomez, at the edge of the Everglades, about ten miles south of Stuart. They also burned the nearby home of Miller's family, as well as a small general store belonging to the Millers.

Despite his wounds, Miller eluded the posse until after nightfall, when he finally gave up after being surrounded while hiding in a shed. John Ashley, however, got away.

The following day, the story of the deadly shoot-out in the Florida Everglades was published on the front pages of newspapers across the country.

"Murder, bank robbery, highway robbery, moonshining, piracy on the high seas, and robbery of rum runners are among the crimes credited to the Ashley gang," said the *Lima News* of Ohio.

"They are accused of every crime from murder to hijacking," the *Chicago Tribune* said.

Some of the stories undoubtedly annoyed business boosters trying to cash in on the thousands of winter visitors to Florida.

"Within a score of miles of where the wealth and society of the country are gathered in pleasure seeking, posses are scouring the Everglades . . . in an effort to capture escaped members of the gang," said the *Lincoln Star* of Nebraska.

"While the battle was in progress yesterday, society leaders and debutantes [in Palm Beach County] were dipping in the surf, dancing and playing tennis and golf, unaware of the death struggle between the law and the criminals," said the *Lincoln State Journal*.

"John Ashley, one of the two members of the notorious Ashley gang still at large, today apparently had made good his escape as small searching parties, one by one, gave up the pursuit and returned to their homes," said the *Kansas City Star*.

The gang had been dealt a stunning blow, but John Ashley wasn't through yet.

A few weeks after the battle in the Everglades, publisher William Randolph Hearst and columnist Arthur Brisbane paid a visit to William Jennings Bryan in his Miami home.

Hearst, whose newspaper circulation war in New York with publisher Joseph Pulitzer is considered a major factor in pushing the United States into war with Spain in 1898, was at the pinnacle of his publishing influence. He owned twenty-eight newspapers in 1924, as well as news services, magazines, a film company, and real estate.

But Brisbane, who had been working for Hearst since 1897, was said to be the real brains behind Hearst's success. And his boss had rewarded him. Brisbane was known as the highest-paid journalist in the United States, and he was fond of introducing himself by telling people how much Hearst paid him.

In his nationally syndicated "Today" column, Brisbane praised the "old-fashioned" beauty of Bryan's home overlooking Biscayne Bay.

"This place of mine is the most beautiful spot in Florida, and, therefore, in the world," Bryan told Brisbane.

But, Brisbane wrote, politics were "boiling and raging like lava" in Bryan's heart.

Bryan was indeed trying to insert himself once again into national politics. He'd seriously considered running for one of Florida's seats in the US Senate, and now was seeking to become part of the state's delegation to the upcoming Democratic National Convention in June.

Not all of Brisbane's travels in Florida made it into his column, however. Author Oliver Carlson wrote that railroad executives and real estate brokers wanted very much for Brisbane to see the beauty and the economic opportunities in Florida.

They knew that Brisbane was almost compulsive about real estate.

"Brisbane's enthusiasm for real estate knew no bounds," Carlson wrote. "He wrote about it in his columns. He spoke of it in his lectures. Friends, acquaintances, even strangers were urged to buy! Buy! Buy!"

Miami was in the early stages of the real estate speculation that would soon become a national mania. Solomon Davies Warfield, owner of the Seaboard Air Line Railroad, was smart enough to get Brisbane out of Miami and show him property where prices were not yet escalating. For two days, Warfield and Brisbane looked at property, including land in northern Palm Beach County near Stuart, on the St. Lucie Canal that connected Lake Okeechobee and the Atlantic Ocean.

There's no record of whether Warfield disclosed to Brisbane the fact that he was making some big plans for that area. But Warfield's plans certainly would have made the property more attractive to Brisbane, and Warfield and others who were deeply invested in southern Florida's economic growth wanted very much for Brisbane to start mentioning Florida favorably in his columns, which were read by at least twenty million people.

The best way to get Brisbane to start endorsing Florida was to sell him some property. Brisbane was very interested—and he was not alone. Many others were also becoming quite captivated.

Across the United States, readers of newspapers and large-circulation magazines were learning about the incredible profits being turned by ordinary people who had simply bought some land in Florida. In March, for example, readers of *The New Republic* read about a woman who had just sold her house in Miami for $100,000—more than $1.3 million in twenty-first-century dollars. She'd bought it for $18,000 in 1921. Another investor paid $2,500 for Florida property in 1921 and turned down an offer of $25,000.

In the past, the stream of traffic into Florida had ebbed with the traditional end of the season in April. But that didn't happen in 1924. Newcomers continued to pour in. The Dixie Highway was becoming crowded. "They come in droves, flocks, herds," *The New Republic* wrote.

And they were enchanted by what they found.

A visitor in March 1924 sent a postcard to friends back home on Washington Street in Ogdensburg, New York, describing the enchanting surroundings during one of the frequent concerts in Miami's Royal Palm Park—where even the birds seemed to join in the fun.

"Afternoons and evenings, a mockingbird sits nearby on a tree and sings beautifully along with the band and keeping in perfect tune and time," the visitor wrote.

But if the concert—and the harmonious mockingbird's accompaniment—were free, not much else was.

"There's plenty to do if one feels like spending money constantly," the Ogdensburg visitor wrote. "But there is a limit."

There was no limit on prices, however. Prices for everything—food, hotel rooms, gasoline—were steep, and getting steeper. And those who came to invest were in for a shock.

"Even swampland several miles west of Miami was selling for fantastic prices by 1924," said Miami historian Paul George.

Real estate broker J. Newton Lummus Jr. said land sales in Miami were "on fire" in 1924, and they would stay that way throughout the year instead of slowing down, as they usually did, when the tourist season ended.

It was the year, in short, that Florida starting taking on the aspects of a "modern, latter-day gold rush," George said.

As real estate prices escalated and word of fast fortunes spread, more and more people came to Florida seeking instant wealth. The gold rush mentality set in, and in such an environment, writer Gertrude Mathews Shelby would later note, thinking too much about real estate investments was a hindrance to making money.

"The people who have made real fortunes check their brains before leaving home," a real estate broker told Shelby. "Buy anywhere. You can't lose."

Handford Mobley, the daring youngest member of the Ashley Gang, was not at the Everglades hideout on the morning of the deadly shoot-out with lawmen on January 9, 1924. Some accounts say he happened to be making a run to the Bahamas when the gunfight happened. By other accounts, he was in San Francisco, and immediately started back to Florida when he read about the bloody battle in a newspaper.

By late summer 1924, however, he was back in Palm Beach County, and he and the surviving gang members were plotting another bank robbery.

On the afternoon of Friday, September 12, Mobley, John Ashley, and two occasional gang members, Joe Tracy and Ray Lynn, hijacked a motorist near Lantana, just south of West Palm Beach, and ordered him to drive south to Pompano, about halfway between West Palm Beach and Miami.

When they neared their destination, they ordered the driver to stop and Ashley tied him to a tree.

For thirteen years, John Ashley had been playing a deadly game of hide-and-seek with the law-enforcing Baker family of Palm Beach County. He was furious that Baker's posse had killed his father in the January gunfight. Before he left the driver, he gave him a bullet. Assuming that the man eventually would be talking to Palm Beach County Sheriff Robert Baker, Ashley told him to tell Baker that he had another bullet just like that one for him.

Ashley and the three other gang members drove the stolen car to the Bank of Pompano. They followed their usual plan of striking in mid-afternoon, when banks typically were less crowded.

Reports varied as to how much loot the gang got, but it was probably at least $8,000 or $9,000 in cash and about $18,000 in government bonds. Before they left, Ashley gave another bullet to a cashier and told him to keep it as a souvenir.

They drove north in the stolen car and then headed west. Lawmen found the car abandoned near the banks of the Hillsboro Canal, a drainage canal that sliced through the Everglades to Lake Okeechobee. Once again, the Glades had swallowed the Ashley Gang.

Robbing the bank at Pompano seemed to energize John Ashley and Handford Mobley. It had been a decent haul, but they wanted a spectacular take.

Ashley and Mobley had made many trips to West End to haul booze back to Florida, and they knew a huge amount of cash flowed into the liquor dealers there every day—so much money that hundreds of thousands of dollars were routinely hauled from West End to banks in Freeport and Nassau. West End was isolated from the rest of the islands. A boat fleeing West End with, say, a huge amount of money could be in trackless open water in minutes.

Mobley, Ashley, and other gang members decided that instead of holding up bootleggers on the high seas, they would aim for a fatter target. They would raid the liquor dealers at West End.

Their plan worked almost to perfection. They raided several liquor warehouses and made off with around $8,000 in cash and a boatload of booze. The only flaw in their raid was that shortly before the Ashleys arrived, a government boat had left the harbor with $250,000 in cash.

After more than a decade of chasing John Ashley through the Everglades, it was becoming clear to police that he was practically invincible in his wilderness hideout. Soon, however, a powerful natural force would drive Ashley and his gang out of the Glades, and the cops would take full advantage of that vulnerability.

On October 14, a tropical storm formed in the western Caribbean Sea and quickly morphed into an extremely powerful hurricane. On October 19, the hurricane crossed the western tip of Cuba with winds that may have reached up to 165 miles per hour.

As the storm turned to the northeast and headed toward Florida, it weakened rapidly. By the time it came ashore on the Gulf Coast, it was only a minimal hurricane. Still, it dumped almost a foot of rain as it crossed the Everglades on October 21 and went back to sea.

The drenching downpour made life miserable in the Everglades for John Ashley, Handford Mobley, and other gang members still on the lam from the recent bank robbery in Pompano. Ashley, Mobley, and two other gang members decided they'd had enough of the soggy Glades for a while. They were going north to Jacksonville, planning to perhaps knock off a bank or two along the way. They would lay low in Jacksonville until they figured out their next move.

Their plans didn't include Laura Upthegrove, and she wasn't happy about being left behind. Soon after the hurricane had crossed Florida, Palm Beach County Sheriff Robert Baker learned that Ashley, Mobley, and gang members Ray Lynn and Clarence Middleton would be leaving for Jacksonville on Saturday, November 1. They would be traveling in a Ford.

Baker saw an opportunity to catch Ashley and his remaining gang members away from their protective Everglades, but he knew his movements were constantly being watched, and that if he headed north around the same time as Ashley, his quarry likely would be warned.

Baker was running for reelection on Tuesday, November 4. While he announced that he would be campaigning in Palm Beach County on November 1, he quietly sent four of his deputies north to Fort Pierce, where they reported to St. Lucie County Sheriff J. R. Merritt.

In 1924, there was only one road into Jacksonville from southern Florida, and that route would take Ashley across a wooden bridge over the Sebastian River, about fifteen miles north of Vero Beach. Merritt decided to set up a roadblock at the bridge and grab Ashley there.

Merritt and two of his deputies joined the four Palm Beach County lawmen. Around sundown, they drove north to the bridge.

Merritt left his deputies on the south bank of the Sebastian, drove his car across the bridge, concealed it, and then walked back across the bridge.

The lawmen hung a chain across the entrance to the bridge and attached a red lantern to the chain. They hid in bushes and underbrush beside the road and waited.

Shortly before eleven p.m. a car with two men stopped at the bridge entrance. Moments later the Ford with John Ashley and his gang rolled to a stop behind the first car.

"We waited until they stopped, then came up from behind and covered them with our guns," Merritt later told the *Evening Independent* of St. Petersburg. "They were caught unawares, being interested in seeing why the car ahead had stopped.

"When we came up alongside, John Ashley saw me first and grabbed for his rifle. I pushed a shotgun in his face and Deputy Wiggins pushed a gun into his ribs at the same time, telling him to throw up his hands or we would blow his head off."

The cops disarmed the four men and ordered them to get out of the car and stand in front of the headlights.

Merritt later told reporters that he'd ordered the other lawmen to carefully search the four fugitives while he crossed the bridge to get his car, where he'd left his handcuffs. That was a lie, although the truth about what actually happened that night would not be known for more than seventy years.

The lawmen handcuffed John Ashley, Handford Mobley, Ray Lynn, and Clarence Middleton. Their hands were cuffed in front, and they were ordered to raise their hands above their heads and to not move.

Merritt then asked the men who'd arrived at the bridge just ahead of the Ashley Gang to give him a ride across the bridge to get his car to take them back to Fort Pierce. When he got to his car, he sent the men on their way and started back across the bridge in his car.

The cops guarding the gang members were edgy. After the January shoot-out in which his father was killed, John Ashley had said that he would kill any lawman who confronted him.

The deputy guarding John Ashley warned him he'd be shot if he moved. Ashley stood motionless for a few moments, but then made that sudden movement he'd been warned against. He took a quick step forward and started to drop his manacled hands. Maybe he was making a move for a concealed weapon that the cops hadn't found, or maybe the car's headlights had attracted mosquitoes—always plentiful after a hurricane has dumped heavy rains—and he'd been bitten. Whatever the reason, the deputy guarding him fired, and fired again.

Hearing the shots, and perhaps thinking that Ashley was making a move for a gun—or perhaps just waiting for an excuse to shoot—the other lawmen gunned down the other three gang members.

When Sheriff Merritt returned, he and his deputies removed the cuffs, loaded the four corpses into the Ford, and hauled them to an undertaker in Fort Pierce.

But Merritt told the *Evening Independent* a different version of how the four fugitives had died. He said they had not yet been handcuffed.

"When I returned, I stopped my car with the lights shining on the party," he said. "I got out and went to the side door of my car to get the handcuffs."

Merritt said the four men had not been searched, and that Ashley "gave a signal and all of the outlaws grabbed for their six-shooters. Then the shooting began," he said.

A few days later, Merritt told the same story to a hastily convened coroner's jury, and the jury ruled that the shooting of the four gang members had been justified. As unlikely as it would seem that an experienced lawman would not have immediately searched four notoriously dangerous criminals for weapons, or that he would have left handcuffs that he knew he would need on the other side of a long bridge, no one, other than perhaps John Ashley's grieving mother, wanted to punish the men who had finally rid South Florida of the Ashley Gang.

John Ashley, Handford Mobley, and Ray Lynn were buried near the Ashleys' modest home on November 4, 1924. *Miami Herald* reporter George L. Bradley turned the funeral into a maudlin portrait of a mother's grief.

After stifling her emotions while the coffins were carried to the open graves, Lugenia Ashley began sobbing, Bradley wrote.

"There they are—three of them," she wailed. "They killed them for not a thing in the world."

Turning her gaze to the grave of her husband who'd been killed in the January gun battle in the Everglades, she said, "He never wanted to harm a hair on anybody's head."

"It's [Sheriff] Bob Baker's work," she concluded. "We never did anything to him. I hope he's paralyzed tomorrow and they have to feed him out of a spoon for the rest of his life."

Decades later, author Ada Coats Williams interviewed the deputy who'd killed John Ashley at the Sebastian River bridge on November 1, 1924. She never identified the deputy, but she later quoted him in her 1996 book, *Florida's Ashley Gang*.

"He did not credit Sheriff Merritt with any of the shooting," Williams wrote. "He also did not apologize for his act. He made good a threat to John Ashley, and said that John had promised to kill all of them if he had a chance."

A part of the wild Florida frontier died the night that John Ashley and his gang members were gunned down on the banks of the Sebastian River. Their violent deaths, coming at the moment that a growing tide of fortune seekers was beginning to flood Florida, also marked the end of the first phase of the Florida land boom.

The people pouring into Florida would be just as eager as the Ashley Gang had been to grab all of the money they could and run; they would just use different methods to snatch their riches.

On the day after Ashley, Mobley, Lynn, and Middleton were killed, an advertisement for Coral Gables was published in the *Atlanta Constitution*.

"The tropical beauty which appears in such overflowing abundance is only one of the many attractive phases," the advertising copy read. "Certainly no state in the Union holds such unlimited opportunity for profitable investment as Florida does today."

Coral Gables developer George Merrick was an honest man trying to build something beautiful, but many of those who followed his lead had no such scruples. The new robbers coming into Florida didn't need guns to get rich; all they had to do was play on the greed of other newcomers who wanted to make a quick fortune without having to think about it too much. They would be ripe for the picking.

CHAPTER FIVE

The Stars Shine Brightest in Florida

By the winter of 1924–25, Gilda Gray had come a long, long way from the old neighborhood in the Milwaukee suburb of Cudahy, where she had been known as Marianna Michalska.

Gray came to the United States as a child with her family from what is now Poland in 1909. In January 1925, she was twenty-three years old and in her second marriage, having danced her way onto Broadway with the Ziegfeld Follies. Her sinuous dancing had even caught the attention of that darling of the Jazz Age, author F. Scott Fitzgerald, who mentioned her in a scene in his classic 1925 novel, *The Great Gatsby*.

Her journey from Milwaukee's saloons to Broadway's salons had been made possible by a trademark dance known as "the shimmy"—a shivering, shuddering, twitching dance that, combined with her striking Slavic beauty, had made her a Roaring Twenties icon of sexual allure.

She was just what the developers of Hollywood-by-the-Sea were looking for to help them sell their new planned city near Fort Lauderdale, just up the coast from Miami. Gray and her touring dance troupe were booked for a two-month appearance at the Hollywood Golf and Country Club. She would dance to music provided by one of the big-name jazz orchestras of the era, the Arnold Johnson Orchestra, whose arranger would later write the musical score for the movie *The Wizard of Oz*.

Gray's opening-night performance would be December 31, 1924, when she would ring in Florida's star-studded New Year of 1925. Hollywood-by-the-Sea's publicists blanketed Miami newspapers with ads for the lavish production. The prose walked the line between being titillating and scholarly, explaining Gray's signature dance as one she devised after "an exhaustive study of the folklore and traditions of dancing in the islands of the South Sea."

It was a tribal love dance, and Miss Gray had added her own "subtle innovations."

"How She Shivers, How She Shimmers," proclaimed a full-page ad in the *Miami Daily News* for Gray's appearance at the Hollywood Golf and Country Club.

From December until March, Gray's name would appear regularly in local newspapers, and her shows during the 1924–25 season would accomplish exactly what the developers of Hollywood-by-the-Sea had hoped—get the attention of the crowds flocking to Florida that winter, and get the name of their project into newspapers across the United States.

The terms of Gray's contract were not announced publicly. One report said she'd received a couple of choice waterfront lots in Hollywood-by-the-Sea in exchange for her services; another said she was being paid $3,500 a week—more than $46,000 in twenty-first-century dollars.

Other Miami-area businesses hired Gray to add a touch of daring glamor to their images. Burdines Department Store hired her and some of her dancers to model their new spring fashions. Burdines then partnered with a horse-racing track, and Gray wore the store's fashions to a race.

Nationally syndicated sportswriter and author Ring Lardner was at the track that day, on his way to the betting window to place a wager on a horse named Gray Gables—a hot tip, at ten-to-one odds—when photographers spotted him and persuaded him to pose with Gilda Gray. Lardner was so taken with Gray that the betting window closed before he could get his money down.

Gray Gables won. Lardner lost a chance to pocket some quick cash, but he wrote a column about his chance meeting with Gray that was read by millions in the United States and Canada.

The 1920s were becoming a golden age for sports. At the same time Gilda Gray was shimmying her way to a small fortune in Hollywood-by-the-Sea, Major League baseball players were coming to Florida to start spring training. Ten of the sixteen big league teams would get ready for the 1925 season in Miami, St. Petersburg, and other Florida cities.

"The natives, realizing the value of advertising, have catered to the ball clubs in many ways," noted a Midwestern newspaper. "There is no question but that Florida is realizing handsomely on its investment."

The New York Yankees were training in St. Petersburg, and their temperamental superstar Babe Ruth was telling reporters he was broke, despite enjoying the highest salary in the big leagues. He was so incapable of managing his huge income that the Yankees were withholding one-third of his pay to go into a savings account, and he was being sued for an unpaid horse-racing debt.

Still, he was amusing himself with many pastimes other than baseball. He was seen playing basketball at the local YMCA. And he hadn't kicked his fondness for the track.

"In Florida he would hang around a greyhound derby to late hours of the night when he should have been in bed getting his rest," said *New York Evening Telegram* sports reporter John Foster.

The Bambino also was indifferent when it came to a healthy diet. A Yankees teammate told Foster that he'd seen Ruth wolf down six hot dogs, guzzle a pint of bicarbonate of soda, and then trot onto the diamond to play baseball.

Ring Lardner noticed another distraction for players coming to Florida for spring training in 1925.

"What ball players are not crippled by accident or food down south were crippled by Florida real estate," Lardner wrote. "If the ocean rises six inches this summer and floods all of Florida, you can go to the ball grounds, not to see a ball game, but to see how many players you can count committing suicide."

Some former players were doing quite well in real estate, however. The *Helena Daily Independent* reported that Joe Tinker, who had starred as a shortstop for the Chicago Cubs, was "one of the leading citizens" of Orlando, where he'd invested his life savings in real estate.

Tinker was "one of the leading realtors" in the South, the newspaper said.

So many players for the New York Giants were dabbling in real estate that manager John McGraw told Lardner that the stability of the Florida market could be a factor in his team's performance in the 1925 season. Lardner asked McGraw if the Giants would win their third straight National League pennant in the upcoming season.

McGraw replied, "If Florida real estate holds up, there is nothing can stop us." However, if the real estate market flopped, the Giants would be doomed, he quipped.

About the same time that Gilda Gray started her extended performance at the Hollywood Golf and Country Club, developer George Merrick announced that William Jennings Bryan would be offering daily lectures at the beautiful Venetian Pool in Coral Gables. Merrick reportedly paid the Great Commoner $100,000 in cash and real estate—more than the salaries earned by Babe Ruth or President Coolidge—for his services.

The pool was an ingeniously repurposed quarry designed to resemble the Mediterranean city of Venice, Italy. Bryan's audience watched from a grandstand as he spoke to them while seated beneath a large parasol.

The contrast between the public images of the svelte, sexy shimmy queen at the Hollywood Golf and Country Club and the stern, moralistic William Jennings Bryan at Coral Gables was stark. Newspapers picked up on it and depicted it as a rivalry.

"They're here trying to see which can sell the most real estate to tourists, thereby taking their place in Miami's ranking winter industry," said William Randolph Hearst's Universal News.

Bryan did not become famous for his sense of humor, but he knew how to use self-deprecating wit to win over an audience. His topic during his lectures was real estate opportunities in Florida. He explained his own experiences, portraying himself as a guileless speculator who'd still managed to make a few bucks, because you just couldn't lose buying Florida real estate.

He acknowledged that he'd bought and sold real estate and made a little money along the way, but the people he'd sold his property to had made more money than he had, he said.

Behind the low-key humor was Bryan's clear message that Florida—and especially Coral Gables—was a can't-miss investment opportunity, a place where even an amateur investor like him could own a piece of paradise and make money in the process. His message amounted to a politician's stump speech because he repeated it often and in many different settings, with slight variations of delivery.

Florida was a "durable asset," Bryan said.

"Remember that gold mines are exhausted and that oil wells give out and even the soil is wasted by long, continued use," he said, "but God's sunshine will be here thousands of years after we are dead, and the breezes will bear healing in their wings long after our names are forgotten."

Dreamers live forever, Bryan said. "And so in the future years there will be streets, there will be towns, there will be counties, there will be localities that will bear the names of those dreamers, for their dreams are coming true in Coral Gables, in Miami, in Florida," he said.

It was exactly what the crowd wanted to hear. The people who flocked to Coral Gables and other "ideal" cities in the winter of 1924–25 were caught up in a boom within a boom. The 1920s was a time of unparalleled prosperity. Some of the people who gathered to hear Bryan speak had come to Florida with wads of cash and letters of credit, but others had little more than a few dollars and the clothes they were wearing. They came because they'd heard that anyone could make a fortune in Florida. All you had to do, Bryan told them, was take off your hat, give it a careless fling, and buy the property where it came to rest.

The implication was that soon, inevitably, someone would come along and pay you three or four or ten or fifty times more for your property than what you'd paid for it. It was that easy and that predictable.

The people looking up expectantly at Bryan were suffused with this irresistible image and overcome with the desire to own a piece it. All it would take for them to disgorge their cash was a gentle nudge from someone they trusted. And to millions of Americans, William Jennings Bryan was the epitome of trust. When this sober, old-fashioned, Bible-thumping puritan told them that Florida was the end of the rainbow, they were ready to find a salesman, throw their money at him, sign on the dotted line, and claim their slice of the good life.

One of Bryan's favorite quips when he was talking to visitors was that Florida was such an amazing place, it was impossible for a real estate salesman to tell a lie. "You can tell the biggest lie you can think of in the morning," he'd say, "and by the evening it will have come true."

Bryan denied that he was a wealthy man, noting that he'd had to sell his home, Villa Serena, because escalating real estate values had made it too expensive for his wife and him to live there. But the sharp-tongued journalist H. L. Mencken, who was not a fan of Bryan's, said he had become "a crimp for real estate speculators—the heroic foe of the unearned increment hauling it in with both hands."

A judge from Nebraska who'd visited Bryan in Miami on his sixty-fifth birthday declared that Miami's most famous citizen was indeed a millionaire.

On January 6, Bryan attended the inauguration of Florida's new governor, John Wellborn Martin, a Jacksonville businessman who'd served as that city's mayor before handily defeating his Republican opponent in the November election.

No festive occasion in 1925 would have been complete without a jazz orchestra, and George Merrick made sure the new governor would be properly serenaded by sending the Jan Garber Orchestra to Tallahassee for the occasion. The orchestra set up in the lobby of the capitol building. Among the songs it played that day was a tune the new governor had heard during a campaign tour of Florida—a sentimental ballad titled "Give Me One Rose to Remember."

Martin was introduced by outgoing governor Cary Hardee, but before Hardee handed over the reins of government, he made a few comments about conditions in Florida in January 1925.

Among Martin's duties as the state's chief executive would be confronting any problems that might arise, and in many ways, Florida's problems were no different than those of the other forty-seven states, Hardee noted.

But Florida also had some problems that were unique, the outgoing governor said. People from across the nation were pouring in, drawn by the state's wonderful climate and abundant natural resources. They were bringing wealth and new ideas.

There was, however, a downside to all of this.

"While we appreciate the great contribution other states are making, we cannot minimize the problems which rapid and varied development necessarily produce," he said. "Will our people lose themselves in a mad scramble for physical things? Will they embrace a materialism to the extent that the finer cultural things of life must be neglected?"

Hardee echoed Henry Flagler's beliefs about the responsibilities of great wealth.

"There are responsibilities in the possession of riches," Hardee said. "There is an element of danger in the sudden acquisition of wealth. Let us hold fast to the first fundamental principles, [those] of religion, of patriotism, of honor, of respect for law and constituted authority, and in doing so the possession of material things, in combination with spiritual forces, will make us a great people."

Hardee's remarks were insightful and prescient. As he spoke, thousands upon thousands of Americans were pouring into Florida. It would become one of the most remarkable migrations in the nation's history, and be likened to the gold rushes of California and Alaska.

Florida would officially become a national obsession in 1925.

Kenneth Roberts, writing for the *Saturday Evening Post*, described the traffic into Florida as "an endless serpent whose joints, composed entirely of automobiles, slipped easily over the ground in some spots and labored more violently in others, but on the whole managed to wriggle forward at a rate of about thirty miles an hour."

This "ever-flowing stream" was composed of jalopies and limousines, representing "every imaginable human combination," Roberts wrote. Some carried luggage that was neatly packed, while others "bulged with tents and bedding and mattresses and parrot cages," and containers of all sorts lashed to wherever the driver could find something to tie them to.

There were young men and women, families with children, elderly folks, mothers with kids who made faces from the rear windows at the drivers behind them, Roberts said.

Traffic from the Midwest and Northeast converged at Washington, DC, and then flowed southward through the cities and towns of Virginia, North Carolina, South Carolina, and Georgia. And it simply did not let up for an entire year.

Still more came to Florida by rail, cramming aboard the passenger trains of the Florida East Coast Railway and the Seaboard Air Line Railroad and the Atlantic Coast Line Railroad, filling the Pullman cars and coaches with humanity. At one point seventy-five to one hundred Pullman cars, each carrying dozens of passengers, were unloading every day in Miami.

British author T. H. Weigall was among the hordes who rode the train into Miami in 1925. Every few hours, he wrote, train carloads of "gullible northerners" would be unloaded into a crowd of real estate salesmen who "swarmed round the carriages like a hive of angry bees; most of them shouting, all of them sweating, all of them coatless and carrying great bundles of papers."

The scene was more or less what Weigall expected, "but also in some subtle way infinitely more repulsive and less romantic," he later wrote.

The newcomers to Florida were indeed finding more—and less—of what they expected. There seemed to be a price tag on everything, usually astonishingly high, and everyone expected to be paid. One anonymous wit wrote:

The palms, they say, of Florida
Unfold a sight bewitching
A palm you meet at every street
And every palm is itching.

But if everyone expected to be paid, it was only because there was so much money to go around for everyone—or so it seemed. Mass-circulation magazines such as the *Saturday Evening Post*, *Liberty*, *Harper's*, *Literary Digest*, and others were telling fantastic stories of instant riches in Florida.

In February, *Liberty* magazine published a story titled "Over-Night Millionaires of Florida" in which readers learned about a speculator who'd started with two quarts of gin and eight months later had parlayed that into $75,000. This was only one example of spectacular riches in a state that was "gushing gold," *Liberty* said.

An ad for the latest issue of *Liberty* asked the tantalizing question, "How many more fortunes will be made in Florida's amazing land rush?"

The stories of overnight wealth in Florida had a hypnotic effect on thousands of readers, Kenneth Roberts wrote.

"Their minds were so inflamed by tales of sudden riches that many of them lost all sense of proportion and came to believe that money could literally be plucked out of the air in Florida," Roberts wrote.

"At the bottom of the great 1925 rush to Florida was the same impelling force that has been at the bottom of all migrations—the desire to better one's condition as speedily as possible," he wrote.

So although the prices astonished some newcomers, many of them were still eager, even desperate to buy a piece of the Florida dream. A new development called Miami Shores sold $2.5 million worth of property the first day lots went on sale. George Merrick was selling around $4 million worth of property in Coral Gables every month, and had opened a sales office on Forty-Second Street in New York. On the first day of sales for a new section of his "perfect city," his salesmen raked in an astonishing $21 million.

Merrick was shaping Coral Gables into a dreamlike place of unearthly beauty that gleamed and glimmered for the winter-weary visitors from New York and Chicago and other distant, snowy cities. The dream sighed to them from the palm trees whose fronds were gently roused by the warm ocean breezes, and it glistened at them from the sparkling water that always seemed to be nearby to catch and reflect the light, and twice a day—once at sunrise, again at sunset—the dream was bathed in a soft, gorgeous glow of pink, vermilion, and ochre.

Despite the huge sums of money coming into his project, however, Merrick was being financially cautious. The money was going back into the development of Coral Gables. And in Miami Beach, Carl Fisher was tightening financial requirements for buying property even though money was being thrown about freely all around him.

A few miles up the coast, Addison Mizner, who had been shivering in a cold Long Island apartment only a few years earlier, was becoming the toast of Palm Beach society and planning his own ideal city between West Palm Beach and Miami.

The hospital for returning World War I veterans he'd designed for his wealthy friend, Paris Singer, had instead become the iconic Everglades Club in Palm Beach. Now he was planning his own perfect city, Boca Raton, a city that would be "old in romance, restful in atmosphere, poised in buildings, orderly in plan and in every feature beautiful." More succinctly, it would be "a monument to American money."

Boca Raton would be publicly advertised as a city with "every atom of beauty that human ingenuity can add to a land endowed by nature." Privately, however, Addison Mizner and his cynical, witty, and shady brother, Wilson Mizner, would refer to Boca Raton as "a platinum sucker trap." The company's marketing strategy was simple and equally cynical: "Get the big snobs, and the little snobs will follow."

Mizner's connection with Singer enabled him to recruit an impressive group of supporters for Mizner Development Corporation that included *Palm Beach Post* publisher Donald H. Conkling, who had sold the *South Florida Developer* to Edwin Menninger. Conkling's bank connections would help Mizner to secure generous loans for his projects.

Mizner's backers also included US Senator T. Coleman du Pont and Wall Street speculator Jesse Livermore, who had already made, lost, and regained a fortune when he brought his family to Palm Beach in March 1925. He stayed at the Breakers, and his presence didn't go unnoticed by some men who were determined to make a quick fortune without sinking any money into real estate.

Another guest was relaxing in a chair on the porch of the hotel when she overheard two men talking about Livermore and his family. They'd noticed that Livermore's oldest son, Jesse Jr., was an active child who rambled around the hotel alone. It would be very easy to snatch the boy, and his father had the means to pay a huge ransom for his safe return.

The woman tried to get a look at the men, but, realizing they'd been overheard, they scurried away. She told Livermore what she'd overheard, and the Wall Street multimillionaire hired a bodyguard to protect his family.

A few tourists started leaving Florida in March, and one of those who departed was Reverend R. S. Wightman, a Presbyterian minister from New Jersey. He told his congregation that it would be difficult to find a place as morally "rotten" as Florida.

"The devil is certainly in certain parts of Florida with all his hosts," the reverend said, "and if anyone wants to go to hell in a hurry, there are greased planks aplenty in Miami and Palm Beach.

"I can't see how such a condition can last. The liquor traffic is conducted in a wide-open manner, and the State authorities seem to invite the Northern people to come and spend their money with the understanding that there are no restrictions."

There was more going on that the minister did not write about, probably because he was unaware of it. Brothels operated openly with little interference from police. Jane Wood Reno, a Miami reporter whose young daughter Janet would become US attorney general, later wrote that it was "generally understood by everybody, including law enforcement folks, that they were needed to keep the tourist industry going."

The madam of a downtown Miami brothel often brought her employees to a dress shop on Flagler Street after hours for outfitting, Reno wrote.

Reverend Wightman apparently was one of the few people who saw the city's tolerance of vice as a problem, however. The usual end-of-the-season mass departure of tourists didn't happen in 1925. The crowds just kept coming. The trains were filled with passengers, the Dixie Highway was jammed with cars, and hotels were packed.

An unnamed minister who'd lived in Florida for ten years told the *New York Times* that the masses coming to the state were being drawn by "some strong force . . . or, rather, it seems as if it were the effect of unleashing a force long bound."

Now that people had discovered Florida's climate "and the other charms of this coast," they would keep coming, and the flow couldn't be stopped. "No, this is no boom," he said. "Florida is just coming into its own."

Entrepreneurs found a way to take advantage of the overcrowding. Some manufacturers of concrete blocks were taking appalling shortcuts to keep up with the demand for new housing. To save money and speed up production, smaller portions of concrete were mixed with sand to make the blocks.

"Since houses were being rushed to sell during the boom period, these blocks were frequently built into the walls of houses before they had set, and the houses were built without any thought of wind pressure," Kenneth Roberts wrote. "The people who built them had heard of hurricanes in a vague way, but probably thought of them—if at all—as something used by novelists to further the action of their stories."

The weakness of the poorly made blocks was then compounded by unskilled builders. Contractors were hiring anyone who wanted a job, regardless of whether they knew what they were doing. The shoddy concrete blocks were being improperly laid so the walls of the new buildings had almost no strength, Roberts wrote.

"When a wall like this is given a brisk kick, it trembles violently; on receiving two or three more brisk kicks in the same place, it falls down," he wrote.

The deadly danger caused by the shabbily built housing would be tragically revealed a year later.

Tourist camps for automobiles began appearing along the Dixie Highway. Instead of searching for a scarce—and probably expensive—hotel room, motorists could pull into a tourist camp and sleep in their cars. As word of these accommodations spread, some who made the trek to Florida towed homemade camping trailers to set up in the camps.

"Southern nights are cool and starlit," the *New York Times Magazine* said. "There is a delight in sleeping out of doors that no hotel room can provide, and it is not predicated on wealth or the lack of it. Often the most expensive make of car will be seen parked alongside the least expensive at one of these tourist camps."

A few people were trying—in their own ways—to hold the line against the decay of morals in Florida and elsewhere. The Ku Klux Klan was prospering amid the decadence of the 1920s, and was holding public meetings in Miami, Stuart, and other cities in Florida. Imperial Wizard Hiram Wesley Evans told a gathering of Klansmen in Kansas City that the organization's members were "the salt of the earth," and the future of civilization depended on them.

"History has proved and is proving daily that only Nordic and Anglo-Saxon people have reached a high level of intelligence," Evans said. "The undesirable hordes from other lands are driving to our sides the millions who for one reason or another have been hesitating."

William Jennings Bryan, who had been a delegate from Florida to the Democratic National Convention in 1924, had helped to defeat a motion to include a sentence denouncing the Klan in the Democrats' national campaign platform.

Speaking at a fund-raiser for a new Temple Israel in Miami in early 1925, Bryan told the gathering that religion was under attack.

"The fight today is not to defend the Christian religion nor the Jewish religion, but to defend religion," he said. "When you take away the belief in God you take away the comfort one finds in a Supreme Being, and when you take away religion you take away the belief in a living god. Religion is the one thing you can't do without."

A few months later, Bryan told a high school graduating class in Miami that while he was "an enthusiast about education," religion was more important.

"Science gives us great things, but it takes more than education to make a man or woman," he said.

Bryan's remarks to the high school seniors set the stage for the first great clash between science and religion in the classroom. Earlier in the year, Bryan had made a quick trip to Nashville to urge the Tennessee state legislature to pass a law forbidding the teaching of "any theory that denies the story of the Divine Creation of man as taught in the Bible, and to teach instead that man has descended from a lower order of animals."

Due in part to Bryan's exhortations, the bill easily passed. But the American Civil Liberties Union wanted to challenge the law, and sought someone to serve as a defendant to test it.

Some business and political leaders in Dayton calculated that having a trial there would draw a large crowd and reporters from across the nation, and be an economic boon for the little eastern Tennessee hill town. They asked John Scopes, a young science and math teacher at Rhea County High School, to be the defendant that the ACLU sought. Scopes wasn't even certain that he'd actually taught Darwin's theory in his classes, but some of his students were willing to testify that he had, and so the ACLU had its defendant.

Only a few weeks before Bryan spoke to the Miami high school graduates, Scopes had been charged with violating the law, and a trial was scheduled for July.

Bryan volunteered to join the prosecution's attorneys at the trial. It would be his last appearance as an impassioned crusader for religious certainty versus scientific inquiry.

Meanwhile, Prohibition supporters, infuriated by the free flow of booze into Florida, introduced a bill that would take the Volstead Act a dramatic step further. Proponents of the bill wanted to make it illegal to "drink liquors as a beverage" in Florida, a measure that, if enforced, probably would have put most of the state's population behind bars.

It was defeated.

Edwin Menninger was watching as trainloads of southbound paradise seekers passed through Stuart on the Florida East Coast Railway's daily trains to Miami. And he was reading about the profusion of dazzling "perfect" cities in lavish, full-page ads in the newspaper of his former employer, the *Palm Beach Post*.

The "paradise" obsession was finding its way into the pages of the *South Florida Developer*. Soon, Menninger believed, Stuart would take its rightful place as one of Florida's leading cities.

The Indian River—which actually is a long, placid lagoon separated from the Atlantic Ocean by barrier islands—was already getting attention for its natural beauty. Kenneth Roberts had seen it, and he was charmed.

"Northward from Palm Beach," Roberts wrote, "one traverses the bank of the Indian River—a broad and endless stretch of blue water on which millions of wild ducks gabble and wag their tails in contented camaraderie, from which the mullet fling themselves in playful ecstasies, and in which serious-minded pelicans pursue their dinners with admirable patience, rising with machine-like unity from the glassy surface, wheeling with military precision, and hurling themselves passionately into the middle of a school of fish with all the grand manner of a heavily laden Gladstone bag falling into a bathtub from a height of ten feet."

Ambitious developers were staking out their own versions of "perfect" cities in and around Stuart. Capitalizing on the spectacular beauty of the place where the St. Lucie River meets the Indian River and the Atlantic Ocean, developers were advertising Golden Gate. Full-page ads in the *South Florida Developer* touted the investment potential. "Millions will be made by those who buy and build at the mouth of the St. Lucie River," the ads said.

Federal engineers had started a feasibility study to determine whether the inlet could be deepened for a harbor that Golden Gate developers boasted would become "the finest south of Savannah."

"Miami's wonderful rise to greatness will be repeated here," readers were promised. "Those who profit most are those who buy today."

Sales of real estate in Stuart were steadily climbing. During the second week of January 1925, sales topped $1 million.

Despite the extravagant promises and florid prose about Stuart real estate appearing in local newspapers, perhaps the best indicator of its value and future potential was the fact that Arthur Brisbane seemed very interested in it. His tour of Florida with Solomon Davies Warfield in early 1924 apparently had done what Warfield had hoped it would do. Brisbane had returned to Florida and seemed especially interested in land near Stuart—land that he'd looked at with Warfield during his tour the previous year.

Brisbane's brief visit to Stuart in the company of two Seaboard Air Line Railroad executives on February 13 was the subject of front-page headlines in the *South Florida Developer*. The "highest-paid newspaperman in America" was "delighted" by the natural beauty around the St. Lucie River, said the *Developer*'s headlines.

"This is wonderful," Brisbane told the *Developer*. "You are given by nature in Stuart what in Miami man is seeking to build with his own hands. Stuart has a magic location which will make it one of the great cities of Florida in the coming years."

Then, accompanied by the Seaboard executives, Brisbane left Stuart to take a look at 160,000 acres that the railroad owned near Indiantown, twenty-two miles west of Stuart.

A week later, a bylined story written by Brisbane was the top story on the *Developer*'s front page.

To have a story written by the most familiar name in American journalism was a major event for Menninger's newspaper. But Brisbane wasn't simply doing a favor for a small-town editor. He had his own self-interest at heart.

Brisbane's story was actually an editorial calling on the state of Florida to spend millions of tax dollars to build two cross-state canals. One should link Stuart on the state's east coast with Fort Myers on the Gulf Coast. Part of that waterway had already been accomplished. The St. Lucie Canal linked the St. Lucie River near Stuart with Lake Okeechobee, and the Caloosahatchee River flowed from the lake to Fort Myers.

Brisbane also suggested that a second cross-state waterway was needed to connect Jacksonville and Tampa by linking the St. Johns River with a series of smaller lakes and waterways in the state's interior.

Brisbane said the state's new governor, John Martin, had told him that he intended to push for a shipping canal across the peninsula. Such a canal would cut two thousand miles off the journey of ships leaving Gulf Coast ports bound for the Atlantic, Brisbane said.

What the world's highest-paid journalist failed to mention, however, was the fact that he was on the verge of buying thousands of acres of land on the St. Lucie Canal near Indiantown. He was, in short, using his byline, fame, and prestige to lobby for public works projects that would be of enormous financial benefit to whoever happened to own nearby property.

And he was about to buy a huge chunk of that himself.

Being an insider to the plans of men of great wealth and influence was having its effect on Edwin Menninger. He was beginning to believe that anything was possible in Florida, and he was getting annoyed at those who doubted Florida's possibilities.

When R. C. Ogilvie, a physician in Superior, Wisconsin, spent three months in Florida and told his hometown newspaper that Florida was "a bubble that must soon bust," Menninger was infuriated.

"The sentimental sob stuff that Mr. Ogilvie pulls about bursting bubbles is so much bunk," the young editor wrote on the *Developer*'s editorial page. "Not having taken the pains to discover the difference between artificial and spontaneous growth of a new country, he talks as if he were a seer. . . . He does not know what he is talking about."

It was the first of many fierce rebuttals to criticism of Florida.

A few weeks after Brisbane's exclusive story for the *Developer*, Menninger published a story announcing that Warfield's Seaboard Air Line Railroad had sold the timber rights on its huge tract of land near Indiantown to lumber tycoon E. T. Roux of Bartow. The *Developer* reported that Roux planned to build a sawmill there that would employ as many as 1,500 people.

"This is the first of several industries to be located at Indiantown by the Seaboard," the *Developer* reported. "Plans are afoot to bring other manufacturing concerns to this location, with the aim of building at Indiantown a city of leading importance in South Florida."

All of the new industry and property sales were bringing new tax revenue into Palm Beach County. But residents in and around Stuart in the northern part of the county felt they were being shortchanged by county government in West Palm Beach. A county bond election in March 1925 proved it.

Northern Palm Beach County voters helped pass a $6 million proposal to provide money for new roads and other improvements in the county. But when north county residents learned that only about $250,000 of the bond money would be used in their end of the county, they were furious. A month later, business leaders in Stuart started circulating a petition to carve out a new county from portions of northern Palm Beach and southern St. Lucie counties. They formed a special committee to push for the creation of the new county, and they chose Edwin Menninger as chairman of this committee.

On April 9, they met with Representative M. S. McCracken, who represented Palm Beach County in the state legislature. McCracken told the group he'd introduce legislation to create the new county if the committee could get 2,500 signatures on the petition supporting it.

It was a tall order. McCracken had only received 1,690 votes when he was elected to office.

But led by the determined young newspaper editor, the committee collected more than 4,000 signatures. Still, the *South Florida Developer* reported stiff opposition to the new county in Tallahassee.

Then a member of the special committee had an idea: Offer to name the new county after Governor John Martin if he'd throw his political influence behind the effort.

It worked. On May 28, the state legislature passed the bill to create Martin County, and the county's namesake signed the bill the following day. Stuart was designated the county seat.

The legislature also created another new county north of Martin County. Indian River County was formed, with Vero Beach as its county seat.

Around the same time, Arthur Brisbane made yet another visit to Stuart. This time he was the guest of real estate broker E. D. Mays, and he had a long visit with Edwin Menninger.

His presence again was front-page news for the *South Florida Developer*, and he had more praise for Stuart.

"Stuart's growth in the past two years is little short of marvelous," he told Menninger.

There were rumors that the great journalist was going to buy property, but a spokesman for the land company hosting his visit denied that.

"Mr. Brisbane has not said what he intends to do," Mays said. "If he is planning to buy, I do not know of it, for he gave me no indication that that was his intention."

This was a polite fiction. Brisbane bought ten thousand acres near the St. Lucie Canal—the same waterway on which he wanted the state of Florida to spend taxpayers' money to improve. But there would not be a public comment about his purchase until 1926.

State lawmakers were also taking notice of Stuart's potential. A couple of days after Brisbane left Stuart, the lawmakers approved issuing $250,000 worth of bonds—about $3.3 million in twenty-first-century dollars—to deepen and improve the harbor.

The town's boosters dreamed of the day when deepwater oceangoing ships would be sailing through the St. Lucie Inlet.

Tourists always left Miami ahead of the steamy South Florida summer, but that didn't happen in 1925. Crowds continued to pour into the city, and the real estate mania was attracting a new type of speculator.

During the spring and summer, ambitious young men—and a few young women—from the large cities of the urban Northeast, streamed into Miami. They'd figured out a way to make a quick fortune by gaming the gullibility of the hordes of eager fortune seekers, the availability of easy credit, and Miami's overwhelmed city bureaucracy. They became known as "binder boys" because of their manipulation of the laws governing real estate transactions at the time.

In the summer of 1925, thousands of them prowled the city's streets, hawking real estate like beer vendors at a baseball game. They bought binders on a piece of property by putting up only a small portion of the cash price, usually 10 percent. This binder held the property in the name of the purchaser until the first substantial payment on the property was due, which usually was thirty days later.

But the binder boys seldom had any intention of keeping the property that long. Instead, they quickly sold their binders for a much higher price than what they'd paid for the original down payment. Whoever bought the binder then became responsible for the bigger payment due later.

The new purchaser could—and often did—resell the same binder at a higher price. By the time some documents finally made it to the overworked registrar of deeds' office, they often had changed hands many times before the first payment came due.

Wearing a sort of informal uniform of golf knickers—known as "plus fours," because they extended four inches below the knee—or white "Palm Beach" suits, the binder boys turned downtown Miami into an open-air real estate market. And the sales never stopped. At night, some of the more successful binder boys would hire a few musicians to play jazz softly as they peddled acreage on Flagler Street.

As long as real estate prices kept skyrocketing, the binder boys raked in huge profits selling what essentially were fantasies.

"The binder boys worked right on the street, holding the receipt books and pencil in hand, calling off the acreage and the amount of binder required, obtaining the deposits from people who bought lots without having any idea how far in the woods of Florida they might be," recalled A. J. Manning, who'd been a very successful real estate broker in Miami in 1925. "Lots at $5 or $10 down and so much a month sold like hotcakes, the buyer not even caring where they were or how much the total selling price. They'd have a map and make an 'X' in various places where plans were made to construct the city hall, public utilities building, and so on."

Historians have blamed the binder boys for the wild escalation of Miami real estate prices in 1925.

The potent mixture of hopes, dreams, naked greed, vast sums of easy cash, and plenty of bootleg whiskey created an intoxicating, anything-goes atmosphere.

"The people were, like, wild," Manning said. "The money went to their heads; they thought it would continue forever, and [they] became reckless and extravagant. Money galore was spent in nightclubs. Couples who were perfectly happy and contented with each other became careless in their morals, husbands holding other men's wives in their arms and vice versa."

And their eagerness to snatch a piece of the Florida dream was spiraling out of control. Later in the summer, sales of lots in the Miami Shores development nearly caused a riot. Frantic buyers literally threw money at real estate brokers. The development was sold out in three hours, and the brokers collected $33 million—more than $440 million, or almost half a billion dollars, in twenty-first-century dollars.

On June 25, Edwin Menninger traveled up the coast to Vero Beach to attend a celebration of the creation of Indian River County. The featured speaker was Florida's most famous booster, William Jennings Bryan.

The great orator sprinkled his remarks with a few references to local dignitaries and events, then launched into his familiar speech about the wonders of Florida. He told a slightly different version of his joke about Florida's marvelous growth than the one he'd used in Coral Gables, but the message was the same.

"Florida is the sanitarium for the rich and the playground for the well," Bryan told the crowd of about 3,500. "While not wishing to place one class above another, I must admit that our real estate men are less likely to lie than those of any other state. That is because truth is stranger than fiction. If a Florida real estate man should start out in the morning to lie about the country, the truth would catch up with him before night."

After Bryan's remarks, Menninger approached him and invited him to speak at a similar gathering in January to celebrate the creation of Martin County. Bryan gladly accepted.

As bright as Indian River County's future seemed, Menninger was convinced that Martin County's future would far exceed it. More new developments, backed by more men of great wealth and influence, were being planned for Martin County, and they were buying lavish advertising spreads in the *South Florida Developer*.

On the shores of Lake Okeechobee in western Martin County, Selznick Studios of Hollywood, California—owned by David O. Selznick—had bought land in a new development called Lake Okeechobee Shores. Menninger's *Developer* reported that a $6 million studio for producing motion pictures was in the works.

At the other end of the county, producer Lewis J. Selznick—David's father—had bought sixteen square miles of property that included the wilds where, less than a year earlier, the Ashley Gang had made moonshine and hid from sheriff's posses. The elder Selznick planned a development called Picture City. The *Developer* reported that Selznick intended to build a "mammoth motion picture studio" there.

A promotional brochure for Picture City described the planned development in effusive prose, saying that the Dixie Highway, which ran through the planned development, was about to become "the Fifth Avenue of Florida."

"The entire territory is ablaze with development," the brochure said. "There must be one continuous Riviera of the World between Stuart and Miami. The opening up of the territory between Stuart and Palm Beach has just begun."

The land that Picture City would be built on "is the finest in all of Florida, if not in the entire world," the brochure boasted.

William Jennings Bryan arrived in Dayton, Tennessee, for the trial of high school teacher John Scopes on July 6, 1925. He stepped from the train wearing a dark suit and bow tie, a tight-lipped smile, and an odd choice of headgear—a pith helmet typically identified with British explorers in a tropical climate.

Dayton, a mining and mill town about 140 miles east of Nashville, was sweltering in the July heat. The locals who gathered at one of the town's social centers, F. E. Robinson's Rexall Drugstore, were still debating the merits of Tennessee's anti-evolution law. The drugstore was just down Market Street—which had a twelve-mile-an-hour speed limit—from the stately Rhea County Courthouse, where the trial would be held.

One thing all the regulars at Robinson's agreed on was that the trial was shining an intense spotlight on their little town.

H. L. Mencken, the *Baltimore Sun* writer who so disliked Bryan, was there, as was W. O. McGeehan, who was covering the trial for *Harper's*.

Even more extraordinary from the locals' perspective were the newsreel cameramen who would bring the proceedings to movie theaters across the land.

And there also was the famous lawyer for the defense, Clarence Darrow, who had first met Bryan at the Democratic National Convention of 1896, when the great orator had held the delegates spellbound with his passionate praise of the common man.

Darrow also had been a staunch defender of the working man and shared many of Bryan's political beliefs. But on the question of humanity's origins, they were bitter enemies, and they knew there would be a dramatic showdown before the jury brought in its inevitable verdict that John Scopes was guilty of violating Tennessee's law against teaching Darwin's theory of evolution.

Nearly a thousand people crammed into the courtroom when the trial began on July 10, and uncounted others were able to follow the proceedings, thanks to loudspeakers set up outside the courthouse. A four-year-old boy patriotically named Thomas Jefferson Brewer was lifted up onto the judge's desk and drew the names of jurors from a hat.

Bryan, coatless, tieless, and clutching a fan advertising Robinson's Rexall Drugstore, sat grim-faced in the inferno of the courtroom as the trial proceeded. Students who'd attended Scopes's class testified that he had indeed taught that humans were descended from a single-cell organism and were mammals, just like monkeys.

The jury also heard from eminent scientists.

The man at the center of the trial was not called as a witness, however.

On July 20, Judge John T. Raulston moved the trial outside to the shade of the trees on the courthouse lawn so that more people could see and hear the trial. Finally the showdown that the nation had been awaiting occurred—Clarence Darrow and William Jennings Bryan, debating the question of how it all began.

Darrow walked Bryan through the biblical story of Creation, asking him if he believed in the literal truth of the Bible—that Jonah was swallowed by a whale, and that Eve was made from Adam's rib.

Bryan answered that he did.

"Does the statement, 'The morning and the evening were the first day,' and 'The morning and the evening were the second day,' mean anything to you?" Darrow asked.

"I do not think it necessarily means a twenty-four-hour day," Bryan answered.

Darrow got Bryan to repeat his statement—that a biblical day was not necessarily twenty-four hours—and Bryan elaborated. It would be just as easy, he said, "for the kind of God we believe in to make the earth in six days as in six years or in 6 million years or in 600 million years. I do not think it important whether we believe one or the other."

It was a puzzling answer from a man who'd spent his public life insisting that the Bible should be the only textbook used to explain how humanity came into being.

The jury took only nine minutes to convict John Scopes of violating Tennessee state law, and he was fined $100. But it was not a resounding victory for Bryan and his cause.

Bryan decided to stay on in Dayton for a few days after the trial. On July 26, he ate lunch and lay down for a nap.

He never awakened.

Thousands of mourners lined the tracks along the route of the special Southern Railway train that took his remains to Arlington National Cemetery for burial. When the train stopped briefly in Knoxville, a huge crowd gathered around the car containing Bryan's coffin.

Edwin Menninger paid tribute to Bryan in the August 4 edition of the *Developer*, recalling that he had met Bryan at Vero Beach, and that Bryan had been eager to speak at the Martin County celebration coming up in January.

"In his lifetime he was known personally by more Americans, I suspect, than any other man of our day," Menninger wrote. "Some of his notions were queer, to be sure, but so are some of yours and some of mine."

The nation's mania with Florida continued after the death of the state's most famous spokesman.

Arthur Brisbane was taking up some of the slack created by Bryan's departure. Around the climax of the Scopes trial in Tennessee, Brisbane praised Seaboard Air Line Railroad president Solomon Davies Warfield in his "Today" column for expanding his railroad in Florida. The new tracks would bring more visitors—and presumably more money—into the state, and help relieve the congestion of freight shipments that were starting to back up in rail yards and sidetracks leading into Florida.

And Edwin Menninger continued his cheerleading for the Florida miracle. In August, he took some time off for a visit to his native Kansas, but he didn't stop promoting his new home. His topic for a speech to the Kiwanis Club of Topeka was "The Wonders of Stuart, Florida." He handed out two crates of pineapples grown in Martin County and wrote a column for the *Topeka State Journal* about his new hometown.

He also noted that the Florida East Coast Railway was now running a dozen daily trains into Florida, double the number from the previous summer.

Menninger invited attention to himself during his travels in the Midwest by wearing white plus fours. The knickers had become closely identified with Florida real estate salesmen, and he was frequently approached by people who were curious about what was happening there.

Menninger admitted to his questioners that he didn't know how long Florida's remarkable growth would continue, but he thought it would be at least ten years.

Others asked him why Florida had become such an obsession.

"Florida has been there all the time," one man said to Menninger. "Why should there be a sudden panic to reach Florida?"

"So was the gold in the California hills all the time prior to 1849," he answered.

He saw unmistakable evidence of the nation's fascination as he was about to board his train back to Florida.

"I walked into Union Station in Kansas City when I started my return trip to find probably three hundred [people] jammed around the gate leading to the Florida train," Menninger said. "All the other forty gates were practically deserted."

The thousands of people coming into Florida were going to their hometown banks before they left and withdrawing millions of dollars. So much money was being withdrawn that bankers outside Florida were getting uneasy.

Withdrawals from member banks of the Massachusetts Savings Bank League had increased at an especially alarming rate, and the league's officers realized how deeply the Florida mania had penetrated their customers' psyches. People who put their money into savings banks usually couldn't afford to gamble on real estate investments. Small-time real estate speculators were withdrawing about $2,000 a day from a Boston bank, and another bank there was losing about $10,000 a week.

The manager of the league of savings banks estimated that about $20 million from his members' banks had gone into Florida real estate.

The league felt obligated to warn its depositors about the risks of such speculation. Bankers in other states were also becoming alarmed. In Ohio, bankers were so worried that they took out full-page ads in larger newspapers warning against speculating in Florida real estate. The ads' bottom-line message was that sooner or later, real estate prices would tumble.

Similar warnings were issued by the Minnesota Department of Conservation.

Edwin Menninger was one of many Florida newspaper editors who were upset by the organized advertising campaign against Florida. He continued to insist that Florida, and especially Stuart, were safe investments.

"Land is not worth a certain figure: it sells for that figure," Menninger said in the September 8 edition of the *Developer*. "Next week it sells for a bigger figure. Worth had nothing to do with the change. It is a settled conviction among us Floridians that we have established a new school of economics in which price has displaced value as a measure of a man's fortune."

A few days later, Menninger responded to a story in an Omaha, Nebraska, newspaper in which a local man warned that real estate bargains in Florida were gone and that living costs in the state were sky-high.

"The fact of the matter is that most of these people who knock Florida are unable to comprehend the size or the significance of our present development," Menninger wrote. "Seeking to bolster their stories of the 'awful' conditions in this busiest and most prosperous State in the Union, they resort to all manner of exaggeration and display astonishing ignorance of the subject they pretend to understand."

Menninger also used some reverse psychology to counteract the anti-Florida campaign.

"If these attacks succeed in slowing down the influx of tourists to Florida just a little, it would help Florida wonderfully," he wrote in the *Developer*. "We don't want as many people as we are getting because we cannot accommodate them."

Still, the momentum of Florida's stunning rise was about to shift.

The shift started when the Florida East Coast Railway had to halt freight shipments to its overcrowded yards in Miami. There simply wasn't any more room, and its equipment was nearly worn out from constant use.

Miami's harbor also was packed with ships forced to wait days to unload their cargoes.

The halt in the flow of building materials was a disaster for Florida's boomers. Without lumber, tile, nails, and concrete, they couldn't even build the shoddy housing that was allowing them to reap quick fortunes from the newcomers.

Out-of-work carpenters added to the problem by leaving town to search for work elsewhere.

The speculators—especially Miami's ubiquitous binder boys—who had made fortunes from real estate took a hit when the Bureau of Internal Revenue decided to take a closer look at the profits of some especially successful speculators. The investigators made a ruling that was disastrous for real estate speculators: Those who sold real estate would have to declare the full price of the sale as income, rather than only the amount of the down payment.

This meant that if a binder boy sold a lot valued at $10,000 but received only $1,000 as a down payment, he still had to pay taxes on the full sale price, rather than merely the deposit.

Suddenly, Florida's brisk real estate sales slowed.

And yet, people continued to pour into Miami, and they all needed a place to sleep. Enterprising residents were renting their porches as bedrooms for $25 a night—more than $330 in twenty-first-century dollars. Other newcomers were simply bedding down in public parks. As the winter of 1925 approached, the *New York Times* reported that roads into Florida were still clogged with southbound traffic, and that 600,000 people in the state were sleeping in tents.

By the fall of 1925, the country's fascination with Florida was finding its way into newspaper cartoons and comedians' punch lines. Jokes circulated about returning tourists selling the Florida sand from their tires for thousands of dollars. A service station operator in Stuart said he'd soon be selling his land for a dollar a spoonful.

Humorist Will Rogers started making Florida a regular topic in his syndicated newspaper columns. Carl Fisher, Rogers said, "took Miami away from the alligators and turned it over to the Indianans.

"He put in a jazz orchestra, and one-way excursions; advertised free heat the year around; fixed up the chug holes so the Fords could get in; rehearsed the mosquitoes till they wouldn't bite you until after you bought; shipped in California oranges and tied 'em on the trees; whispered under his breath that you were only ninety miles away from Palm Beach, with its millionaires and its scandals."

Florida as a source of humor hit the bright lights of Broadway in December when *The Cocoanuts*, starring the manic Marx Brothers, opened in New York's Lyric Theatre.

The national obsession with Florida and instant riches had caught the eye of George S. Kaufman, who made it the topic of a two-act play set in a boom-time hotel in the fictional "ideal" development of Cocoanut Beach. Groucho Marx played Hammer, the greedy, unprincipled owner of the Hotel de Cocoanut, who also is selling lots in Cocoanut Manor. Brothers Chico and Harpo played a pair of deadbeat opportunists out to steal anything they can from Hammer and the hotel guests.

The show's musical score was written by Irving Berlin, and Kaufman brought in writer Morrie Ryskind to help with the script.

The play was a biting satire of the amoral greed that had been unfolding in Florida for more than a year. After working through some rough spots with performances in Boston and Baltimore, the show opened in New York on December 8.

The show received good reviews, especially Groucho's portrayal of Mr. Hammer, the hotel owner who also is auctioning lots in the ideal city of Cocoanut Manor. The *New York Times* review noted that some of the lots were in a residential district that was so exclusive that no one lived there.

During the auction scene, Groucho delivered a spiel that could have predicted the course that Florida real estate would take in the year to come:

"You can have any kind of home you want. You can even get stucco—oh, how you can get stuck-o."

Groucho added his personal guarantee: "If these lots don't double in value in a year, I don't know what you can do about it."

CHAPTER SIX

The Bootlegger's Curse

The New York Giants did not win the 1925 National League pennant, but if their second-place finish had anything to do with Florida real estate, manager John McGraw didn't talk about it.

By the fall of 1925, however, there were some cracks appearing in the foundation of Florida's remarkable get-rich-quick market. Ads in out-of-state newspapers cautioning readers about Florida investments were causing many potential investors to hesitate and were infuriating to the state's chambers of commerce.

And some of the news stories coming out of Florida were adding to the state's image problems. In November 1925, *New York Times* readers learned that Charles Ponzi, whose name had become synonymous with fraudulent investment schemes, was in Florida trying to regain the fortune he'd lost in the infamous pyramid scam that had sent him to prison in 1920.

The embargo of freight shipments was starting to put a serious crimp in housing, and it would not be lifted until May 1926.

Still, the nation was obsessed with Florida. The US Post Office in Atlanta reported in August that it had on file 16,000 orders for forwarding mail to Florida addresses, and that was well before the usual seasonal migration had begun.

"All our gold rushes, all our oil booms, and all our free-land stampedes dwindle by comparison with the torrent of migration pouring into Florida from all parts of the country," *Literary Digest* magazine said in its edition of October 24, 1925.

Two days before Thanksgiving, US Senator T. Coleman du Pont resigned from the board of directors of Addison Mizner's company, Mizner Development Corporation. It was a staggering blow for Mizner. Du Pont was one of the marquee names on the board that was—for publicity purposes, at least—guiding the development of Boca Raton. His name provided the gravitas behind the ambitious—and at times outrageous—promises that the Mizner brothers were making for the miraculous city they were building.

Du Pont quit the board because he'd had it with the antics of Wilson Mizner and publicist Harry Reichenbach, who were making outrageous claims in newspaper advertisements for Boca Raton. Some of the ads claimed that Boca Raton could not possibly fail because the men backing it controlled more than one-third of the wealth in the United States.

Du Pont told the *New York Times* that he'd quit because of "differences of opinion" about "proper methods of business management and organization." The newspaper said the differences were so radical that the senator could not continue on the board.

Mizner tried to downplay du Pont's resignation, saying that he'd quit because of internal politics and a failed bid to add his cronies to the board of directors.

It was a foolish comment for Mizner to make. Five days later, more board members resigned in support of du Pont, including another blue-chip name in American finances, Jesse Livermore. In a statement to the *New York Times*, the former board members said their efforts "to regularize the affairs and the management of the corporation and to eliminate exaggerated publicity have been met with criticism rather than cooperation."

The gushing promises for Boca Raton and other developments would continue, but du Pont's widely publicized resignation widened the cracks in the real estate market's foundation.

Still, John McGraw moved ahead with plans to spend $3.75 million—almost $50 million in twenty-first-century dollars—to build Pennant Park, a baseball-themed subdivision in Sarasota. McGraw was urged to build the development by his friend John Ringling, the circus magnate who spent winters in Sarasota.

Full-page ads for Pennant Park were placed in Florida newspapers in December 1925 urging Florida residents to buy now rather than wait until a national advertising campaign started, when lot prices would be considerably higher. In the ads, McGraw admitted that he didn't have "maps nor plats, nor anything save Pennant Park and unbounded faith in the future.

"You, too, must have faith—faith in me—and vision," McGraw's ad said.

While McGraw was asking potential investors take his word for it that Pennant Park would be a viable moneymaking venture, the city of St. Petersburg was determined to show clear proof that Florida was a solid investment. For months, the city had been planning its reception for the fourteenth annual convention of the Investment Bankers Association of America. Hundreds of bankers who controlled immense wealth across the country would be coming to St. Petersburg—which billed itself as the "Sunshine City"—in early December 1925.

The bankers were encouraged to bring their families, and the *St. Petersburg Times* promised that the convention would be "particularly attractive to the ladies," offering dances every evening and golf and day trips to nearby attractions during the day.

The *Times* noted that the convention meant much to the city and to Florida because it would bring hundreds of bankers, who would give their presumably favorable opinions to the world. Those favorable opinions could, and likely would, mean investments.

And unlike the greedy throngs flocking to Florida looking for fast fortunes, the bankers would be men of "great vision and rare judgment in investment matters," the *Times* said.

"On their return home they will spread the news that Florida is enjoying extraordinary development and is a haven for those seeking safe investments and homes in a state whose climate is excelled by none," the *Times* predicted.

Unfortunately, just about everything that possibly could go wrong did go wrong during the bankers' visit.

St. Petersburg's claim that they were the Sunshine City was not an idle boast. The city averages about 360 days of sunshine per year, and when the *Guinness Book of World Records* started keeping track of such things, the city logged 768 consecutive sunny days.

Sunshine was so predictable and so much a part of St. Petersburg's public image that the city's afternoon newspaper, the *Evening Independent*, gave away copies on days when the sun didn't shine.

The *Independent* gave away a lot of newspapers between December 7 and December 11, 1925. Northeast winds brought a gloomy drizzle that parked itself over Tampa Bay and refused to budge. Golf tournaments and picnics were canceled. Sightseeing tours didn't get off the bus.

The city's business boosters might have salvaged some good-time jocularity if they'd been able to keep the bankers lubricated with booze. But local cops picked that time to get serious about cracking down on bootlegging. Around nine p.m. on December 10, three Pinellas County sheriff's deputies raided a room in the Soreno Hotel that had been rented by James E. Coad, the executive vice president of the St. Petersburg Chamber of Commerce.

The Soreno was the headquarters for the convention. The room had become what the bankers were calling a "reception room."

The officers seized thirty-nine quarts of various types of whiskey and three gallons of rum. Coad wasn't arrested during the raid, but police said they were going to Clearwater, the county seat, to get a warrant.

A group of bankers angrily told reporters that they'd guarantee a bond of up to $1 million if Coad was arrested. But the cops couldn't find clear evidence of who actually owned the liquor, so no one was arrested.

Pinellas County Sheriff Roy Booth later said he'd received "certain information" about the booze at the hotel and had obtained a search warrant. That "certain information" may well have come from someone still angry at Coad for derogatory public remarks he'd made about Jews in St. Petersburg a year earlier.

The bankers left the city on December 11, but instead of departing with sunny enthusiasm for the Sunshine City, they left with memories of a gloomy week and an unpleasant spat with local cops. It was a setback for the city's hopes for attracting new business and investors, and a serious blow to Florida's image. The crack in the boom's foundation opened a little wider.

Shortly after the bankers departed St. Petersburg, an eyebrow-raising warning was issued by J. H. Tregoe, an investment banker and executive manager of the National Association of Credit Men. Tregoe, who said he'd just returned from Florida, said lenders should be careful about extending credit in Florida. The state will never prosper if its only objective is to become a playground for the wealthy, he told the *New York Times*.

"Persons without means will find it difficult under these conditions to live in Florida," Tregoe said. "Only the rich can find a real welcome."

Tregoe's colleagues in Florida's banking industry were livid. The Jacksonville Association of Credit Men said Tregoe's comments were "absolutely unwarranted and unfair," and wanted him removed as the association's executive manager.

"We do not consider the man responsible or to be suitable as an executive manager of the National Association," the Jacksonville group told the *New York Times*.

Other members, however, said they supported Tregoe and would not remove him.

Edwin Menninger was continuing his staunch defense of all things Florida in the *South Florida Developer*. And he was clearly enjoying the chance to occasionally rub shoulders with some of the most famous names in American capitalism.

In October, Cornelius Vanderbilt IV, sunburned and windblown from riding in an open convertible, dropped in on Menninger at the *Developer*'s office.

Vanderbilt, who had written for the *New York Herald* and other publications under the byline of "Cornelius Vanderbilt Jr.," had unexpectedly spent some time in Stuart about a year earlier when his train was delayed by flooding. He'd chatted with Menninger then. Now, he wanted to quiz the young editor about how things were going in Stuart.

"It looks like a live place to me," Vanderbilt told Menninger.

And the town was "live," in Menninger's opinion. Soon, he told the *Developer*'s readers, Stuart's harbor would be deepened to allow oceangoing ships, and the harbor would become "the finest in the South."

"It will mark the beginning of the development on the [Florida] East Coast of a port that will rank with Tampa on the West," he wrote.

Within ten years, Menninger predicted, Martin County would have a population of 200,000, and business lots in Stuart would be selling for $10,000 a square foot. The county's interior between the Atlantic and Lake Okeechobee would be "one great fruit and vegetable farm," shipping "thousands" of train-car loads of winter produce to northern markets.

And two more great cities would be rising on the lake shores, Menninger predicted.

That same issue of the *Developer* included an advertisement offering twenty-five acres of land for sale at $1,000 an acre, and readers were advised to contact Edwin A. Menninger for more information.

As the usual post-Thanksgiving migration to Florida started, *The New York Times Magazine* reported that highways into the state were "thronged with cars, from limousines with liveried chauffeurs to flivvers with shirt-sleeved drivers, all headed for the land of De Leon and De Soto."

But the *New York Times* also reported that new residents who'd come to Florida seeking a better life were having financial problems because everything was so expensive. A head waiter at a restaurant told the paper that while he was making more money than he'd ever made, he still couldn't make ends meet because everything was so costly.

Author Theodore Dreiser was among the thousands who came to Florida in late December 1925. Dreiser and his wife made the trip to avoid reading reviews of his just-published novel, *An American Tragedy*. Dreiser wrote his off-the-cuff impressions of Florida in letters to his friend and fellow writer, H. L. Mencken, in Baltimore, and made notes in his diary. The letters and the diary notes would form the basis for articles about Florida in *Vanity Fair* magazine in the summer of 1926.

The Dreisers arrived in St. Augustine on Christmas Day, and the writer was immediately struck by "real estate schemes everywhere." As they traveled down the peninsula, Dreiser learned that booze was plentiful in Daytona at $12 a quart—before Prohibition you could buy a case of twelve quarts for that price—and he found a DeLand hotel "vile"; although it had no heat and no private bath, he still had to pay $5 a night.

As the season shifted into high gear after Christmas, famous athletes and celebrities started showing up. Babe Ruth was seen among other celebrities at a hotel opening in St. Petersburg, and newspaper sports pages announced that Stanford University football star Ernie Nevers would play in an all-star football game in Florida. Nevers would be paid $50,000—more than $657,000 in twenty-first-century dollars.

Helen Wainwright, a champion amateur swimmer, was training in Florida for her attempt to swim the English Channel later in the year. Golfer Bobby Jones—still an amateur at the time—was playing in St. Augustine, and a real estate company was offering $15,000 to tennis stars Bill Tilden and Vincent Richards if they'd play tennis at their development for a few months.

Boxers Gene Tunney and Jack Dempsey were training in Florida, and Dempsey told sportswriter Ring Lardner that he might "dabble" in real estate.

As the federal officer in charge of enforcing the Volstead Act, General Lincoln C. Andrews certainly qualified as a celebrity when he came to Miami in January 1926, but he was not there to relax and rub elbows with winter vacationers. He was there to see how well the Coast Guard was doing in its effort to keep booze out of Miami.

Notorious bootlegger Duncan "Red" Shannon picked that day to make a run from the Bahamas. As his speedy little rumrunner, the *Goose*, entered Miami Harbor, Shannon spied a small launch conveying Andrews to a Coast Guard cutter anchored at the harbor entrance.

Shannon recognized Andrews, but instead of turning away from his sworn enemies, Shannon turned toward the boat carrying the general. As he raced past Andrews's launch he thumbed his nose at the nation's top Prohibition officer before racing away in his boat, which could easily outrun the Coast Guard vessel.

Andrews was infuriated, and the Coast Guard crewmen were mortified by Shannon's ridicule. They would not forget that embarrassment.

Movie star Gloria Swanson arrived in Miami Beach around the same time of Shannon's display of contempt for Andrews. Wearing silk and mink, she appeared with an entourage at a jai alai match in Hialeah. It was, she told the *Miami Daily News*, the only place other than Havana where she could watch one of her favorite sports.

Swanson was staying at the Flamingo Hotel, as was movie star Bebe Daniels.

United News sportswriter Frank Getty reported that Major League baseball managers were concerned about how the real estate mania might affect their players during spring training.

"They have visions of a heavy hitter rounding the bases on the heels of a three-base hit suddenly shooting off at a tangent into deep left field to sell a possible prospect a choice lot or two," Getty wrote.

And there would be other "dazzling distractions," such as casinos, attractive young women in skimpy bathing suits, blue lagoons, and iced drinks, Getty wrote.

Will Rogers was back in Florida and dispatching his quips to newspapers across the country. He talked to John McGraw, noting that Sarasota was where "McGraw [had trained] his Giants every year till last year, when they sold real estate instead of training."

Rogers also reported that McGraw's good friend John Ringling was building "a little bungalow" in Sarasota that was "patterned after the Vatican in Rome, only improved on."

The managers' fears about the distractions of real estate investments were justified. As the teams finished up their preparations for the 1926 season and got ready to move north, there were news reports that several members of the Brooklyn Dodgers had lost heavily from faulty real estate investments.

The conflict baseball players experienced between focusing on the game and the lure of earning a fortune in real estate became the subject of a movie starring Thomas Meighan, one of Hollywood's best-known leading men at the time. Meighan went to Florida to film *The New Klondike*, a tale written by Ring Lardner about a baseball player forced to go into real estate sales after being fired by his jealous manager during spring training.

When real estate brokers learned that Meighan was making the rounds at spring training camps to prepare for his role, he was swarmed with requests for his endorsements of "ideal" cities being built. One company offered him 160 acres in a new development if he'd only allow the developers to use his name.

Meighan finally disconnected the phone in his hotel room.

Edwin Menninger realized that despite the dreamy advertising for the ubiquitous ideal cities, things weren't roaring along quite the way they had during the previous winter season. But he saw that as a good sign. In early January, he published a letter he'd written to a friend in New Hampshire who'd been an editor in West Palm Beach.

"Nobody here is alarmed, or even particularly distressed about the lull in real estate business in October and November," Menninger wrote. "Florida is going through a period of readjustment in which there will be less frantic trading and more sound business carried on."

Menninger said he thought 1926 would be as "spectacular" as 1925, but the real estate market would be more stable because people would be buying for themselves rather than with the idea of selling it for a huge profit.

But the lavish promises of quick profits continued, and Menninger published some of the most spectacular in the *South Florida Developer*.

In early January 1926, the *Developer* reported that a city called Port Mayaca would be built on the Martin County shore of Lake Okeechobee. Nothing like it had ever been attempted in South Florida, the *Developer* said.

"The men behind the enterprise are not giving out anything for publication," the *Developer* reported, "but others in a position to know quote figures staggering in scope when they speak of the contemplated program of city building.

"It is hinted that unlimited capital is behind the project, and when the visitor asks if it runs into millions, the answer is likely to be: 'Billions, rather,' and the remark is almost sure to follow: 'Coral Gables will be nothing to this.'"

Theodore Dreiser and his wife visited Martin County and Lake Okeechobee around the same time as the *Developer*'s story about Port Mayaca. The writer happened to stand on the shore of the giant lake around sundown, and he was impressed. In his diary, he noted "the shell-like beauty" of the lake, the sunset, and the "profusion" of waterfowl.

He also had passed through southern Martin County, where the lushly advertised Picture City was supposed to be built. "Picture City," he noted in his diary. "Nothing there."

Nor was he impressed with the crowds who were being drawn to Florida.

"All country jakedom from Wyoming East & Maine south is moving in," he wrote to H. L. Mencken.

Dreiser was critical even of Coral Gables.

"What is the matter with Coral Gables?" he wrote in his diary. "A cut and dried commercial proposition. Poetry and art manufactured to order. The mass told how and what to do."

At about the same time that Dreiser was sniffing haughtily at George Merrick's creation, the boomers and builders in Miami suffered another crippling blow.

Ambitious developers looking for a way to circumvent the severe shortage of building materials hit upon an idea to get a structure up and operating quickly. They bought an old Danish steel-hulled schooner named the *Prins Valdemar*. Their plan was to tow it into the Miami harbor and convert it into a floating hotel and casino.

The railroad embargo on freight shipping, which would be in effect for another four months, had jammed the harbor with ships waiting for a place to unload at the docks. As many as thirty ships often were waiting offshore for their turn to enter the harbor. Many of the ships carried building supplies that builders couldn't wait to get their hands on.

On January 9, the *Prins Valdemar* was being towed through the harbor channel when it ran aground and refused to be budged. The old ship blocked the entrance to the harbor like a cork in a bottle. Maritime traffic was halted, and no ship could enter or leave.

Marine engineers were trying to figure out how to move the ship when the outgoing tide caused it to suddenly capsize around noon on January 10.

More than a month would pass before the US Army Corps of Engineers could cut a new channel, and still more time before the old ship could be refloated.

Miami historian Paul George noted that the shipping tie-up caused by the capsized schooner was devastating for Miami's economy.

"The dearth of building supplies caused by the shipping impasse crippled the boom, because without the continued construction of new buildings, a collapse of boom-time speculative prices was assured," George wrote.

Five days after the *Prins Valdemar* locked up the harbor, George Merrick opened his sumptuous Miami Biltmore Hotel. Special Atlantic Coast Line and Seaboard Air Line trains brought around three hundred VIP businessmen from the Northeast for the opening.

The VIPs joined a gathering of about 1,500 guests that were part of a "formal in the extreme" splendor "rarely seen in the South," the *Miami Daily News* noted.

The Biltmore's opening dripped with opulence. In addition to the 1,500 invitees decked out in formal evening finery, dozens of beautiful young fashion models also were brought in from New York. They were dressed in an "assortment of costumes, wraps, evening gowns, and exquisite creations for every occasion," and draped with borrowed furs and jewels worth more than $200,000—more than $2.6 million in twenty-first-century dollars.

Several dining rooms were used to serve the celebrants, and stages were set up in each one. After parading across the stages to the accompaniment of orchestras, the gorgeously attired women roamed among guests on the lushly landscaped grounds outside the hotel.

It was a scene that could have been torn from the pages of *The Great Gatsby*, a lavish display of the wealth, style, and excess that epitomized the Roaring Twenties, and it would become a high-water mark of Florida's Jazz Age splendor.

Three days after the extravagant opening of the Biltmore, a large advertisement appeared in the *Miami Daily News* that likely alarmed knowledgeable readers who had grand expectations of their real estate investments. The real estate firm of Meyer & Tritton was offering lots—business property and apartment sites—in Coral Gables at 50 percent below market price.

"Here is one of those opportunities that allow you an immense return on your investment in a short time—with absolute safety," the ad copy read.

There was no explanation as to why Meyer & Tritton was making such a generous offer. But anyone who had been chasing a fortune in Florida real estate knew that prices had been going up, not down, for several years. If prices in one of Florida's blue-chip developments were going down, it must be because the simple but stern forces of the market were coming into play. Even a good product will not sell if no one wants to buy it. The implication of the ad was that Meyer & Tritton wanted to cut their losses and get rid of a product they couldn't sell.

Thursday, January 28, 1926, dawned clear and brisk in Stuart. Around 7:15 a.m., Governor John Martin arrived with his wife and entourage to celebrate the creation of the county named after him.

"The sun shone brightly, the birds sang sweetly, and everybody was happy," the *South Florida Developer* reported.

There was not an official attendance count, but the *Developer* reported that ten thousand barbecue sandwiches were served to the crowd, and Governor Martin stood on a reviewing stand for well over an hour as a two-mile-long parade that included two thousand participants marched past.

The governor, immeasurably pleased that his name would be immortalized by having a county named after him, gushed with praise for Stuart and the people who'd led the effort to form that county.

"If ever a community had a personality in her people, it is our hostess today, in this atmosphere of enterprise and solidity of growth, in this place of friendliness and hospitality, in this beautiful land where nature has given all, we meet at every corner an environment that insures a future that must make the mind marvel," Martin said to the gathering.

The festivities continued into the evening at a banquet and ball in the new Dixie-Pelican Hotel. Edwin Menninger was the master of ceremonies.

"Beautifully gowned women from all over the state, military uniforms, and the presence of the Governor and First Lady of Florida all combined to lend an air of distinction to the opening ceremonies," the *Developer* reported.

There was a fireworks show, and the partying continued long into the night. Since it was illegal to sell or possess liquor, there were no overt references to intoxicating beverages being served. But the *Developer* did mention a private party attended by fifteen or so people. Some of those attending were especially proud of their Scotch ancestry, and several times drank to the memory of eighteenth-century Scottish poet Robert Burns.

Not all of the toasts were water, the *Developer* winked.

After a couple days of celebrating, the crowds departed and the cleanup began. A rumor began circulating around town that one person who'd played a very important role in making sure the festivities were happy was himself very unhappy. According to the tale, the bootlegger who'd brought in a boatload of booze hadn't been paid, and the people who'd hired his services didn't have the cash to pay him.

He was, so the story went, furious at being stiffed. He flung angry curses at them, and said he hoped all of their brilliant plans and bright dreams would dry up and be blown away.

They laughed at him, so the story went. Everyone knew the good times would never end.

Still, ominous indications of trouble in paradise continued to appear.

About a week after the celebration in Stuart, an ad appeared in the *New York Times*. An entire subdivision in Highlands County—in the interior of the peninsula, northwest of Lake Okeechobee between Fort Pierce and Sarasota—was for sale. The property should have sold for about $2.75 million; the asking price was $750,000.

One of the development's partners had developed a "sudden illness," the ad said.

On the heels of the discount offering of Florida real estate came the news that Charles Ponzi was in trouble again. A grand jury in Jacksonville had indicted the convicted scam artist along with his wife and two partners for violating Florida laws regulating real estate sales. Ponzi, who said he was trying to repay the investors who'd lost money in the confidence scheme that had sent him to prison earlier, hadn't bothered to get a license to sell real estate in Florida.

On February 8, Solomon Davies Warfield's Seaboard Air Line Railroad continued its ambitious expansion in Florida, breaking ground for new tracks to extend its service to Naples. A few days later, Arthur Brisbane—who by now had more than a casual interest in Warfield's plans in Florida—was back in Stuart, and once again on the front page of the *South Florida Developer*.

Brisbane was accompanied once more by two Seaboard Air Line executives. He held court with some of the town's businessmen, and had more praise for Stuart.

"This is wonderful," he told the *Developer*. "You are given by nature in Stuart what in Miami man is seeking to create with his own hands. Stuart has a magic location which will make it one of the great cities of Florida in coming years."

The *New Yorker* magazine's edition of February 13 hit the newsstands the same day Brisbane was in Stuart. The magazine's cover, known for its quirky depictions of timely topics, featured a cartoon map of Florida showing palm trees, a train, and pleasure boats. It was a reminder that the nation hadn't lost its fascination with the state, despite the downturn in real estate sales.

The Miami social season was in full swing when the *New Yorker*'s Florida cover hit newsstands, and hotels were advertising entertainment by nationally known artists. The influence of African-American popular music was spreading to white orchestras, and white patrons were finding their way to previously all-black nightclubs to hear jazz. Popular music had a harmonic richness that was unique.

The hotels and nightclubs in and around Miami were full of jazz.

The Jan Garber Orchestra was playing at Tahiti Beach in Coral Gables, and Gene Fosdick and his Orchestra were playing at the Fleetwood Hotel. Elsie Janis, billed as "America's foremost comedienne," was appearing at the Hollywood Golf and Country Club. And the world-renowned Paul Whiteman Orchestra was playing for the afternoon tea dance at the Coral Gables Country Club.

The crowds attending these festive affairs were thirsty, and they'd heard that it wasn't hard to get a drink in Miami despite the presence of Coast Guard cutters trying to enforce Prohibition.

The easy availability of liquor was due in no small part to Duncan "Red" Shannon, the audacious bootlegger who had thumbed his nose, literally, at the commissioner in charge of enforcing Prohibition.

Shannon, a jovial, fun-loving daredevil who spent his ill-gotten earnings almost as quickly as he earned them, had been compared to such legendary seagoing lawbreakers as Jose "Gasparilla" Gaspar and Jean Lafitte, pirates who had operated in the waters off Florida. To the Coast Guard sailors saddled with the nearly impossible task of enforcing the Volstead Act in Florida, Shannon was known as the "king" of Miami bootleggers.

But Shannon had made enemies among other bootleggers operating in Florida. In 1925, his testimony in federal court in Pensacola had sent three rival bootleggers to prison.

Coast Guardsmen reportedly had a begrudging respect for Shannon, but when he brazenly thumbed his nose at them in front of General Lincoln Andrews, he'd crossed a line. When Coast Guard officers got a tip—perhaps from friends of the bootleggers he'd sent to jail—that Shannon would be hauling a load of booze into Biscayne Bay, they decided to use a speedy captured rumrunner to set a trap for him.

Late on the afternoon of February 24, as the sunset tinted the skies and waters with shades of pink and vermilion, an orchestra was playing foxtrots and other popular dance music for the elegantly attired guests enjoying a tea dance at the Flamingo—the hotel that had hosted a president, and was currently hosting two famous movie stars.

Red Shannon was making his run from the Bahamas. The *Goose* was loaded with whiskey.

Coast Guard Ensign Philip Shaw, commanding the converted rumrunner that was waiting for Shannon, spotted his quarry cruising across Biscayne Bay. Usually the sharp-eyed and ever-alert Shannon easily spotted his adversaries, but this time, the Coast Guard's ruse worked. Shannon had no idea Coast Guardsmen were watching him as he approached the shore.

As Shannon drew closer, Shaw gave the command to gun his boat's engine, and the Coast Guard boat leapt ahead in pursuit of Shannon. Shaw shouted for Shannon to "heave-to."

Shannon, realizing he'd been nabbed, sped for the Flamingo Hotel's yacht basin. Two men with him started throwing liquor overboard.

As the *Goose* neared the yacht basin, the Coast Guardsmen opened fire. At the sound of roaring engines and gunfire, the stylish guests at the tea dance rushed to the edge of the Flamingo's docks to watch. Others aboard anchored yachts looked up from their cocktails at the drama being played out under their noses.

Hotel owner Carl Fisher also watched.

The Coast Guard crew later said they started shooting only to try to disable Shannon's boat, but the bootlegger was gravely wounded. The *Goose* docked at the Flamingo, and Shannon staggered off the boat. Someone brought a mattress from the hotel, and Shannon collapsed onto it.

An ambulance was summoned, and Shannon was taken to Allison Hospital in Miami Beach. His companions were arrested and taken to jail.

Shannon reportedly bore no ill will toward the man who'd shot him. When he was told that he would not recover from the bullet wound that had pierced his liver, Shannon—ever the carefree sportsman—reportedly said that that was just part of the game.

He died the following day. The story of the deadly chase across Biscayne Bay made national headlines.

Witnesses—including Carl Fisher—testified at a coroner's hearing that Shannon was shot after he and his two companions on the *Goose* had raised their hands in surrender. Philip Shaw was indicted for murder, but was acquitted two years later.

As the end of the 1925–26 season approached, the torrent of visitors that had been pouring into Florida for more than a year finally slowed, and real estate sales slowed dramatically, due at least in part to warnings about Florida real estate in national newspapers and a slump in the stock market.

In Stuart, backers of a development called River Forest made a drastic attempt to lure buyers. In a series of large ads in the *South Florida Developer*, they announced that they would bury a sack of money on the property they were offering for sale, and the public would be allowed to look for it on March 13.

"Whoever finds the money owns it," the ad read.

Tampa attorney Peter Knight, whose name would soon become a lightning rod for controversy when it came to information on Florida, was given space in the *New York Evening Post* to go into great detail about Florida's wonders.

Knight avoided the gushing, florid prose used by the purveyors of paradise. He concentrated instead on statistics—bank deposits, annual yield per acre of crops, population growth, lumber production, pounds of fish, barrels of crabs, clams, and oysters. It was a dull read, but Knight wasn't aiming for starry-eyed paradise seekers. His target audience was the hard-nosed businessman who might have recently hesitated to sink money into Florida.

Knight's turgid, numbers-laden piece seemed precise, but it included one very misleading paragraph.

"Although [Florida's] development has been extraordinarily rapid, necessitating an immense expenditure of money, it has no bonded indebtedness," he wrote. "It does not owe a dollar."

That was true about Florida's state government, but Knight was a lawyer, and like any good attorney, he was presenting only the facts that supported his client's case, excluding anything that might harm that case. The "immense expenditure of money" spent during Florida's rapid development had to come from somewhere. The growing cities had not turned to the state to pay for the sewer capacity and roads and streetlights and other infrastructure needed to serve populations that were increasing by the day. Riding the crest of what seemed like endless good times, they had issued municipal bonds that were purchased by investors who expected to make money. The bonds had to be repaid with interest, however, and that repayment with interest was a debt.

Soon, towns and cities across Florida would be struggling mightily to make payments on those bonds. But, as Knight and the *Wall Street Journal* would so stridently point out, Florida's state government would remain free of such obligations. And they would fail to mention the crippling debt being carried by many of the state's municipal governments.

St. Petersburg was already beginning to see the effects of the slowing of real estate sales and a consequent slowdown in building. About six thousand mechanics and their families had left the city.

"The outskirts were filled with abandoned houses," said Walter Fuller, who only a year or so earlier was making more money than he had time to count. "People made precarious livings stealing sidewalk tile from abandoned subdivisions."

By late spring, even Edwin Menninger was acknowledging that times were changing. On May 14, he announced that the *South Florida Developer* would reduce its publication schedule from twice a week to once a week.

Menninger said he'd gone to twice-weekly publication two years earlier when he was getting more advertising than he could possibly publish in just one issue per week. But he'd never expected that the *Developer* would remain a semiweekly, and he hadn't raised subscription prices for that reason.

"We felt that a depression must come in Florida sooner or later, and the present stagnant market justifies our belief," he wrote on the *Developer*'s editorial page.

He also noted that the advertising that had paid for two issues a week wasn't there anymore. Advertisers who had believed more than a year earlier that good times would continue and had signed long contracts now couldn't afford the space they'd bought.

The advertisers who had signed those extended contracts were released from that obligation, Menninger wrote.

In the same issue of the *Developer*, Menninger also wrote a long, thoughtful, and analytical article urging readers to "put the brakes on speculation." The days of fast, easy money from fat real estate profits were gone, he said.

"The balloon is blooey," he wrote. "You have had all the soft pickings that you are going to get. In the future you can expect to get dollars only in exchange for work."

Menninger's opinion that Florida's boom days were over infuriated some people, including Stuart city commissioner Cornelius Van Anglen.

Not long after his lengthy story in the *Developer*, Menninger slipped quietly into an afternoon meeting of the board of commissioners and sat down on a stool to watch.

Van Anglen halted the meeting, announcing that there was "a traitor" in the room, and made a motion that Menninger be removed from the meeting.

Mayor Harry Dyer conferred briefly with the town attorney about the legality of such a motion, then announced that he would not allow it. Van Anglen angrily left the meeting.

Still, Arthur Brisbane certainly was doing what he could to keep things humming in Stuart. On April 4, Solomon Davies Warfield decided the time was right to announce that Brisbane had bought ten thousand acres in Florida.

Brisbane paid $800,000 for his land, adjacent to the St. Lucie Canal, where the tracks for Warfield's Seaboard Air Line Railroad crossed the canal. It also adjoined land owned by Seaboard's "Development Department."

Brisbane planned to use his land as a farm to demonstrate Florida's "extraordinary fertility" and the advantages of its climate for farming.

Because of its proximity to the canal and Seaboard's tracks, nearby Indiantown would become a divisional headquarters for the railroad, with repair and maintenance shops for its locomotives and rolling stock, Warfield said.

Brisbane was back on the front page of the *South Florida Developer* on June 11. Edwin Menninger's lead story for that edition reported that Brisbane was about to start work on his farm west of Stuart. Brisbane wrote a self-serving sidebar for the *Developer*, again urging the state to build a cross-state waterway and make improvements to the St. Lucie Canal.

Brisbane called on the collective wisdom of the people of Florida to urge the state to take on the construction projects.

Reporter Marie D. Peffer, a former employee of Brisbane's, interviewed him at the fourteenth annual Indianapolis 500 on May 31, 1926. The story was published in the *South Florida Developer*'s edition of June 18, 1926.

"You may quote me as saying that I consider Stuart to be one of the coming largest cities in Florida," Brisbane told Peffer.

Powerful hurricanes don't usually form in the Atlantic Basin in July. But occasionally the waters of the Caribbean Sea have become warm enough in the early summer to sustain a major hurricane, and that's what happened in late July 1926.

The storm began on July 22 as a tropical depression just east of the Leeward Islands near the eastern edge of the Caribbean Sea. The storm became a hurricane as it moved northwestward across the Caribbean, but it did not become an especially powerful storm until after it had crossed the Dominican Republic and entered the Bahamas.

Then it quickly intensified into a monster storm with winds of around 140 miles an hour as it approached Nassau.

The hurricane struck that city on the evening of Sunday, July 25. Nassau residents at first thought the hurricane would miss their city, but by nightfall it was clear that it was headed their way.

"There was little sleep that night for anyone on the island, just listening to this merciless crashing and tearing and roaring, and wondering what would be the outcome," the *Nassau Guardian* reported.

The outcome was very bad. The storm continued to rage at dawn, and the light "revealed a town lashed unceasingly by a pitiless wind intent on demolishing everything in its track, and driving rain as fine as smoke," the *Guardian* said.

The hurricane weakened some as it reached the northwest edge of the Bahamas, but it still had winds of perhaps 120 miles an hour, and its northwestward track put it on a course for Miami.

But the storm turned slightly more northward, and its most powerful winds stayed offshore and missed Miami. The hurricane's eye came ashore at Cape Canaveral, about 175 miles up the coast from Miami.

The worst that Miami saw was winds of 80 miles an hour. Still, the storm downed trees and power lines as it passed through the city. F. A. Lancaster, a lineman, was electrocuted while repairing power lines in Miami Beach.

It was the first hurricane for many of Miami's newcomers, and they thought they'd seen the worst that nature could throw at them.

While the hurricane of July 1926 was not powerful enough to inflict catastrophic damage in Florida, it created an image problem for the Florida Association of Real Estate Boards. In the heady, go-go days of the real estate boom, optimistic developers had erected grand entrances to their "ideal cities." In many cases, those grandiose entrances were all that was built.

Now, neglected for months, they were becoming shabby, and the hurricane's winds had been powerful enough to knock many of them askew. In abandoned developments where grandiose entrances had been built—often of nothing more than chicken wire and plaster—and streets had been laid out, the entrances were shredded, street signs were leaning, and other signs had been battered by the winds.

It was a reminder that some dreams had not materialized. The Florida Association of Real Estate Boards wanted these embarrassing eyesores removed. It wasn't good for business.

Florida was getting a lot of drive-by scrutiny from national publications, and the messages were mixed. In August, *Forbes* magazine said Florida was financially sound despite the unfair treatment it was receiving in the national press. The state's banking troubles were being exaggerated, and the problems that did exist were being caused by a weak chain of banks in Georgia.

The *Forbes* story quoted Peter Knight, who again had statistics at hand to prove that Florida was just fine. The state had had 28 banks fail in the past six years, compared to 173 banks in Montana that had failed, 160 in Oklahoma, and 153 in Iowa.

World's Work, another highly respected publication, agreed with the *Forbes* analysis of Florida, saying "it is difficult to visualize anything but further progress" in the state.

The National Park Bank of New York concurred. "What has happened in Florida has been precisely the sort of readjustment which was inevitable under the circumstances," the bank said in its regular bulletin in September.

Florida governor John Martin no doubt was aware of his state's banking situation, but on September 14, he was dealing with quite a different issue. Putnam County Sheriff R. J. Hancock and F. S. Waymer, mayor of the county seat of Palatka, had brought a chilling problem to the governor.

Palatka and Putnam County—which had so charmed journalist Edward King in 1873—was being terrorized by a mob of vigilantes determined to enforce a strict moral code in the county. The mob was dispensing its harsh justice on Saturday nights, flogging offenders for crimes such as bootlegging and prostitution. Two people had been killed, and sixty-three had been whipped in the past year, Hancock and Waymer told the governor.

The mob members were not identified as belonging to the Ku Klux Klan, but they did wear masks when they meted out their punishment.

Martin told reporters in Tallahassee that he'd received many letters from Putnam County residents, asking him to end the terrorism.

It was a serious and embarrassing problem for the chief executive of a state that was as image-conscious as Florida. The governor didn't know it, but while he was hearing pleas for help from Putnam County, a more serious problem was heading his way. Another tropical storm had formed. It would become one of the most powerful storms on record. And it would not, as the others had done, weaken and veer away from Florida at the last minute.

CHAPTER SEVEN

"Many Die; Cities Razed"

For a while, a brisk breeze coming off Biscayne Bay made the evening of Friday, September 17, 1926, more pleasant for couples dancing in the rooftop gardens of the American Legion hall that overlooked the bay. The Miami Legionnaires were in the middle of a three-day Mardi Gras–themed festival to raise money to send the post's drum and bugle team to the upcoming national convention in Philadelphia.

By eleven p.m., however, the rising wind was no longer adding to the tropical ambience. It was becoming quite a nuisance.

Someone called the local US Weather Bureau office. There was a storm offshore. The wind and rain would be increasing. The disappointed partyers decided to call it a night.

The blow wouldn't be much, they told each other. Nothing more than a windy rainstorm, like that hurricane back in July. They'd be back at the Legion hall the following day to continue their merriment.

But they were about as wrong as they could possibly be. The rising wind that chased the Legionnaires indoors was the outer edge of a fierce hurricane that had been pounding its way across the Atlantic Ocean for several days.

The Weather Bureau had been following the storm and issuing advisories since September 14. On the morning of Wednesday, September 15, as the hurricane passed just north of the Virgin Islands, the Weather Bureau advisory tersely noted, "This storm has already attained considerable intensity."

That was a calculated understatement. The hurricane unleashed that "considerable intensity" Thursday afternoon as it plowed west-northwestward across the Turks and Caicos Islands.

"At 1:55 the storm had reached such intensity as to indicate that everything would be demolished," meteorologist George Goodwin later wrote. Roofs were ripped off and hurled far from the buildings they'd once covered, and Goodwin estimated the wind speed at 150 miles per hour. And the hurricane's storm surge made it seem as though the islands were sinking into the ocean.

"The sea swell at times was well above the windowsills, and before it could recede was caught by the next swell, the sea reaching inland for about three-quarters of a mile," he wrote.

The hurricane lost little of its intensity as it moved on and gave the Bahamas a severe beating Thursday night and early Friday morning, September 17.

In Miami, Weather Bureau meteorologist Richard Gray knew a bad hurricane was closing in on Florida, but Gray and the Weather Bureau meteorologists in Washington, DC, who issued the advisories didn't know exactly where the storm was, or where it was headed. In those days before weather satellites and hurricane-hunter aircraft, pinpointing the exact position of a hurricane was largely guesswork, unless a ship at sea crossed paths with the storm's eye and radioed its position before the winds carried away its antenna.

With one tragic exception, ships were managing to avoid this storm and weren't providing Gray with much help in locating it. The unlucky ship was the British freighter, *Loyal Citizen*. Early Tuesday afternoon, the Independent Wireless Telegraph Company—a Long Island company that relayed radio traffic to and from ships at sea—picked up an SOS from the *Loyal Citizen*. The ship gave its position as "400 miles off the coast of Florida."

A few hours later, a second SOS said the ship was sinking and the crew was about to launch lifeboats. Nothing more was heard from the stricken freighter.

But the following day, a Danish tanker searching for the *Loyal Citizen* found only an overturned lifeboat floating on an empty, storm-tossed sea. The hurricane—wherever it was—had claimed the freighter and all thirty of its crew.

Although Richard Gray didn't know exactly where the storm's center was, by Friday morning he was certain that South Florida was in for a bad blow. At 10:20 a.m., he relayed the official storm advisory from Washington, saying that "destructive winds" would be raking the Florida east coast from Jupiter Inlet south to Miami—a stretch of about eighty-five miles—by Saturday morning.

And just so there could be no doubt about the danger posed by this hurricane, the official advisory included this warning: "This is a very severe storm."

The storm warning was published in the Friday-afternoon newspapers, and broadcast by radio as well. The storm warning also was telegraphed to state offices, and throughout the afternoon, Weather Bureau staff answered telephone calls from people wanting information on the storm.

Still, lots of South Florida residents didn't see any reason to worry. They recalled the July hurricane that had done little more than rustle tree limbs, and they thought that storm was the worst that nature could throw at them.

What they didn't know, however, was that they'd been very, very lucky in July. Besides rain and winds, the storm had delivered a false message—especially to newcomers—about what a hurricane could do.

One of the Weather Bureau's warning telegrams went to Fred Flanders in Moore Haven, a little town on the southwest shore of Lake Okeechobee, about ninety miles inland from Miami. Flanders, a state engineer, didn't know what to make of the warning.

"I showed it to a number of people whose reaction, like my own, was more or less negative," Flanders said. "None of us knew what to expect."

But the storm warning still made Flanders and his neighbors uneasy. They knew that a tropical storm could cause havoc in their little lakeside town.

The effect of powerful winds on Lake Okeechobee has been described as similar to a person filling a shallow saucer with water and then blowing across the water. And September 1926 was not a good time for a storm to be blowing across the giant, shallow saucer that is Lake Okeechobee. Rainfall had been unusually heavy, and the lake was brimming with water. A simple mud dike stretching for several miles along the southern rim of the lake was Moore Haven's only protection from storm-driven flooding.

As the phone continually rang at the Weather Bureau office in Miami, Gray studied the sparse information being reported by Weather Bureau offices in other Florida cities. He was especially interested in barometric pressure readings.

At sea level, a barometer's needle doesn't drop below 29.92 inches unless a bad storm such as a hurricane is nearby. As the storm approaches, the needle will begin a slow, steady descent and continue to fall as the hurricane's eye nears. The needle will not start rising until the storm center has passed and is moving away. Very intense hurricanes will cause the needle to fall very low. For example, Hurricane Camille had a barometric pressure reading of 26.84 inches when it struck Mississippi in 1969. In 1992, Hurricane Andrew had a reading of 27.23 inches when it came ashore at Homestead, Florida.

The information Gray was receiving wasn't very helpful when it came to figuring out where the center of the storm was.

Around four p.m. on Friday, Leo F. Reardon, a construction contractor in Coral Gables, left his office to play golf with a friend who was visiting from Boston. On the way to the course, the men picked up a copy of the afternoon *Miami Tribune*. A headline across the top of the front page read "Miami Warned of Tropical Storm."

Reardon and his golf partner shrugged off the *Tribune* story and headed for the first tee. Reardon lost the match to his guest, and then the men went to Reardon's home in Coral Gables, where his wife was cooking dinner for them and two other guests.

There were, however, clear indications that something awful was headed toward South Florida. At the observance of the Jewish holy holiday of Yom Kippur at Temple Israel, a white dove flew through the window, perched on the altar, and stayed there. It would not move from its perch after the services ended.

As the sun neared the horizon, a young Jane Wood Reno, who was living with her parents in a rented house in Miami Beach, walked with her mother to the beach to watch a spectacular sunset. It was "the most beautiful sunset we had ever seen," she recalled years later. "High-flying cirrus clouds and widespread cumulous floated across the sky from east to west. Everything was gold and pink and blue and calm."

It was a classic pre-hurricane sunset, as described in 1890 by Father Benito Viñes, a Jesuit priest in Cuba who was a pioneer in hurricane forecasting.

The spectacular colors linger long after sunset, Viñes wrote, "as if this dim and prophetic light tried to prolong the evil omen in the longer duration of the twilight."

At eight p.m. Friday night, Richard Gray and the Weather Bureau office in Washington, DC, got the latest weather data from other Florida cities. It still wasn't much help in locating the center of the hurricane. Key West, about 130 miles south of Miami, reported winds of twelve miles an hour and a barometric pressure reading of 29.68 inches, virtually unchanged from its reading two hours earlier.

Miami's winds were eighteen miles an hour, and its barometer was identical to Key West's reading. So the telltale dramatic drop in barometric pressure that would reveal the hurricane was moving toward one city and away from another hadn't yet become apparent.

In Moore Haven, Fred Flanders was one of many residents who went to a party Friday night to honor the town's teachers at the start of the school year. He brought the telegram from the Weather Bureau with him and showed it to other guests.

"Nobody seemed to be alarmed," he said.

Miami resident Mildred Cronin, a Dade County school board employee and a volunteer for the local Red Cross chapter, wasn't even aware of the storm until an alert Girl Scout reacted to the warning.

"A young girl who lives in the same apartment [building] as I do came running home from a Girl Scouts' meeting to put her pet dog inside," Cronin said. "This was the first time I had heard about the approaching storm."

But she wasn't concerned.

"During the evening, I went about my usual work, the reports of the storm having little effect on me," she said.

For others—especially the boomers who had come to Florida to get rich quickly and have fun—it was another Friday night in paradise, and they were determined to enjoy it. Hundreds of people crossed the causeways to Miami Beach to get a bite to eat and then dance or walk on the beach.

Most of them had no idea what a hurricane was.

But the Miami Beach cops ended the merrymaking when they went through all the restaurants and bars, telling patrons to go home because there was a storm coming. The police also chased sightseers off the beach.

Seen from high above, a hurricane resembles a spinning pinwheel as it churns across the ocean. Slender strands of clouds known as rain bands extend from the hurricane's center. As the hurricane nears land, these bands of clouds can become a sort of overture for the approaching storm. As the bands race past overhead, they can bring brief but heavy rainfall and high winds. But once they're past, the winds and rain diminish.

Around ten p.m., one of those bands passed over downtown Miami as United Press correspondent Al Reck stopped by the Dade County Sheriff's Office.

Reck, at the youthful age of twenty-eight, had already packed more death-defying adventure into his life than many older men. He'd been wounded and left for dead on a battlefield in France during World War I. He'd survived, been captured by the Germans, escaped, and been recaptured and finally released on Christmas morning of 1918, about five weeks after the fighting had stopped. He'd been discharged from the army as a lieutenant in 1919.

Reck would go on to become a legendary city editor for the *Oakland Tribune* in California. As a young reporter in 1926, he was restless, eager, and fearless—perfect attributes for a journalist about to be caught in the middle of a savage hurricane.

"I dropped over in the sheriff's office and found the county police force wondering just how bad the hurricane was going to be, or if it really was going to hit Miami," Reck later wrote.

While Reck was chatting with the deputies, an anemometer at Allison Hospital in Miami Beach—about six miles from downtown Miami—was registering winds of about thirty-five miles an hour. An hour later it was showing forty.

Shortly after eleven p.m., Weather Bureau meteorologists in Washington had enough information to justify issuing a hurricane warning. In Miami, Richard Gray's barometer was steadily and rapidly falling. The center of the storm was headed his way.

By 11:30 p.m. hurricane warning flags were flying.

The problem was that almost no one saw them, including attorney S. K. Hicks.

A few minutes before midnight, Hicks left downtown Miami to return to the Mere Grande Hotel in Miami Beach, where he lived. The rain had stopped, but as he drove across the causeway linking Miami and Miami Beach, he noticed that the wind was picking up.

At midnight, Gray's barometer read 29.54, down 0.16 inch from its eight p.m. reading. Worse, the pressure was steadily falling, a clear indication that the hurricane was getting closer to Miami. Then the rain began, and the brisk breeze that had annoyed the Legionnaires became a constantly rising wind that began to tear at Miami, Fort Lauderdale, and Miami Beach.

The party in Moore Haven began breaking up at about the same time that Hicks was arriving at his Miami Beach residence. As Fred Flanders and the other guests left, they noticed that the weather was getting worse. "The wind had increased, there were scudding clouds, and a general feeling of [an] impending storm," Flanders said.

Worried about how the dike was holding up, Flanders went to the town's lakeside waterfront. What he saw alarmed him. The winds were pushing the water higher and higher against the flimsy dike. Soon the water would top it.

Others had realized the same thing. Several men—including the mayor and the town manager—were racing through Moore Haven, knocking on doors. All able-bodied men were needed at the dike to start filling sandbags.

But it would take precious time to recruit manpower going door to door. Someone uncrated a new siren that had been purchased for the town's fire department. Wiring was hastily rigged to a generator, and the siren started blasting an ear-splitting wail. "The noise would have waked the dead," said Moore Haven resident Ed Lundy.

Soon a crowd of men was shoveling sand into bags and stacking them against the failing dike. They intended to work through the night.

In Coral Gables, Leo Reardon and his guests had gotten caught up in a conversation about whether the new motion picture industry would set up production studios in Miami. Around eleven p.m., the conversation broke up and Reardon's guests went home.

The storm was obviously getting worse, but Reardon wasn't worried. He put his two young children to bed in a closed-in sunporch and went to bed.

He drifted into sleep, but was awakened by a loud crash. He discovered that the wind had ripped an awning off his house and shoved part of the awning frame through a window.

Reardon moved his kids to an interior room and returned to the broken window. Wind-driven rain was pouring through.

"Against the lights on Ferdinand Drive, I could see the tall pines bending before the storm, and across the golf course I dimly made out the outline of the Miami-Biltmore [Hotel]," Reardon said. "Then the lights went out on the street and in all houses. We were in the blackest dark I have ever seen."

That sudden, heart-pounding awakening to terrifying crashes was being repeated across South Florida. In Miami Beach, Gertrude Rubelli—who worked for the Dade County school board and the local Red Cross chapter—and her husband were jolted awake around two a.m. when the winds blew open a hinged window on their porch.

They nailed it shut, but going back to bed was out of the question. No one could sleep in such a howling racket.

"The house rocked with every blast of wind, and at three a.m. the kitchen window was smashed by a broken awning frame, lights went out, and water was shut off," Rubelli said.

As the wind continued to rise, newcomers to Miami heard, for the first time, the ceaseless rasping moan of a powerful hurricane. The winds from the July hurricane hadn't sounded anything like this terrifying and unforgettable noise. And there were occasional eerie variations in the wind's noise that sent chills down thousands of spines.

"[I'd] never heard anything like it," Miami Beach resident Edith Royce Oakley later wrote in a letter to her brother, Herbert Royce, in Middletown, New York. "It made us all deaf, and you could not hear a single thing but the noise of the wind. One awning after another blew off the apartment, and then the French windows started blowing in and breaking off, and the glass was blown out."

Leo Reardon was wondering how much more his house could stand. The walls were trembling before the wind, and windows were crashing. Reardon was trying to decide whether to stay in his house or move his family. He went to his front door and opened it to take a look at the storm. The wind snatched him up and nearly carried him away.

"It hurled me several yards and I managed to regain the door by grabbing the awning bars that still were fastened to the side of the house," he said.

Reardon realized that he and his wife could never carry their children through such winds. He decided to move his family into the garage and put them in his car. To get to the garage, however, they had to go from the kitchen through a laundry room. "No sooner had I released the latch on the kitchen door than it shot back and was shattered against the electric range," Reardon said.

They crawled on their hands and knees into the garage and climbed into the automobile.

At 3:30 a.m., Richard Gray's barometer at the Weather Bureau office had dropped to 29.06. Thirty minutes later, his office went dark when the electric lines went down. At 4:30 a.m., Gray turned a flashlight beam on his barometer. It read 28.65. At the same time, the anemometer at Allison Hospital was showing winds exceeding one hundred miles an hour.

Out on Miami Beach, the sea was swallowing the island.

The front door of the Mere Grande Hotel was about three hundred feet—the length of a football field—from the usual high-tide mark. But as the hurricane approached, the huge breakers made a steady, thundering march up the beach until they were booming just outside the hotel's door.

"Then one giant wave battered down the door and rushed through the lobby, leaving it three feet deep in water," said S. K. Hicks, the Miami attorney who lived at the hotel.

Each successive wave made the water in the hotel lobby a little deeper. Outside, Hicks could see "many small shacks and automobiles" being carried away by the onrushing ocean."

"All night long the breakers roared," Hicks said. "Hysterical women in the hotel huddled together in little groups on the upper floors, expecting at any moment to be carried out to sea in the hotel. In order to quiet them we got a man to play the piano, and a lot of us began to sing."

Then, above the wind's roar, Hicks and the others in the Mere Grande heard awful ripping noises and a bizarre whistling sound. The storm was tearing away big chunks of the hotel's roof, and the weird whistling noise was the sound the chunks made as the wind whirled them away.

As dawn approached, the hurricane's winds had reached at least 115 miles an hour in Miami Beach. That was more than Gertrude Rubelli's house could withstand. It started coming apart.

"At five a.m. the glassed front of the house blew in, and at the same time the roof sailed off, landing several blocks away, where it was found the next day," Rubelli said.

Rubelli and her husband crawled through the wreckage of their home and fought through the winds to their car. Rubelli's husband turned the car's front into the wind, and then they got into the backseat and covered themselves with a tarp for protection in case the winds smashed the windows.

As he huddled with his family in an automobile in the garage of his disintegrating home in Coral Gables, L. F. Reardon heard for the first time the blood-curdling shriek of the wind known only by those caught in the most powerful hurricanes. Lots of people who hear that awful noise don't live to tell about it. It was a moment that Reardon never forgot.

"Above the roar of the storm there started a high wail like the sound of an ambulance siren," Reardon said. "It could not be that, for we were on the outskirts of Coral Gables, six miles from Miami. The sound rose slowly. I jumped out of the car and went to the door of the garage."

He looked out and could see nothing but sheets of rain. But he still heard that awful shriek. Somehow, his terror-stricken mind associated the noise with approaching water. *This is the end*, he thought.

He returned to the car and told his wife to prepare for the worst. But the noise died down, "leaving the dull, monotonous, deadly roar of the gale," Reardon said. "Then it came again—about ten minutes later. Never have I heard a sound that froze one's . . . blood like that."

At the Weather Bureau office, Gray's barometer was plummeting. At six a.m., it read 28.00, and the Allison Hospital anemometer showed steady winds of 104 miles an hour, with gusts up to 117. Then, at 6:10 a.m., as a dim, gray dawn crept over the battered city, the winds suddenly diminished. The hurricane's eye had arrived.

Gertrude Rubelli and her husband ventured out of their car. Their Miami Beach neighborhood was in ruins.

"We saw many of our neighbors' homes gone, or partially destroyed," Rubelli said.

They flagged down a passing car, and the driver dropped them off at a nearby church, which already had been converted to an emergency hospital. A dozen injured people were there, and more were being brought in.

"One man had a big gash across his head," Rubelli said. "Another old man had both legs badly fractured. A woman was dying from internal injuries.

"One whole family was brought in, one child dead, one possible fractured skull, the mother, father, and baby with severe lacerations of the body."

The savage winds had smashed one unlucky man in the face with a large wooden splinter, which was protruding from his cheek and nose. Rubelli was impressed with the injured man's patience as medics carefully removed pieces of wood from the ugly wound.

The bodies of three children were brought in, and then the body of a young woman. Dazed, frightened residents whose homes had collapsed around them had picked their way through the ruined neighborhood to the church, and were pleading for help.

"Families were separated and crying for their children," Rubelli said. "Some had on just nightclothes, others were wrapped in wet sheets or blankets, whatever they were able to find as their homes were blowing away. Every car that could run was out scouring the town and vicinity, bringing in injured and dead."

Once the winds had died down in Coral Gables, Reardon hustled his family back into their house, hastily cleared a path in the driveway, and set off down Ponce de Leon Boulevard in search of groceries.

"The scene of wreckage brought tears to my eyes," Reardon said. "Coral Gables' buildings, with a few exceptions, had weathered the terrific blast, but the beautiful foliage was laid low. Lights and telephone wires were strewn about in reckless abandon. The ground was covered with green grapefruit. A few weather-beaten policemen were standing about the ruins of destroyed buildings."

Remarkably, Reardon found a grocery store that was open. He hastily bought some food and threw the bags into his car. The winds were returning. He jumped into his car and raced the rising wind twenty blocks back to his home.

At the Mere Grande in Miami Beach, the frightened occupants were literally at sea.

"Dawn came, and save for the nearness of other houses, the scene was like from a ship at sea," said S. K. Hicks. "Huge rollers, as high as the hotel, came rolling in. They would crash upon the beach with a force that shook the whole structure, and, seething with foam, break about the building and go hurrying westward toward Biscayne Bay."

As the rainy, windy dawn crept over Moore Haven, the exhausted army of sandbaggers realized that they'd lost their battle with Lake Okeechobee. They couldn't hold back the lake's churning waters. The flimsy mud dike started giving way in several places.

"Water . . . was pouring over the levee and rushing across the field like a black wave, full of mud, grass, sticks, and hyacinths," Moore Haven resident Lawrence Will later wrote.

At the town's little railroad station, the agent on duty for the Atlantic Coast Line Railroad telegraphed the company's main office in Sebring, about sixty miles away, that the lowest part of the town nearest the lake was beginning to flood.

When the hurricane's eye reached Miami, reporter Al Reck ventured out of his apartment building to look around. "All I could see were wrecked and ruined homes," he recalled.

Reck didn't say whether he knew that the storm's lull was only temporary, but even had he known, it probably wouldn't have mattered to him. Like a moth drawn irresistibly to a light, Reck immediately took off for downtown Miami to chase the biggest story of his career, and as far as he was concerned, the hurricane could go to hell.

He found chaos and "a mass of debris." And the ocean, pushed across Miami Beach by the hurricane's awful winds, was surging through downtown Miami's streets.

Even worse for Reck, all telephone and telegraph wires were down, as well as radio broadcast towers. Miami was isolated. But the city needed help, and Reck felt the primal urge of any good reporter to get his story to his editors.

An idea popped into the reporter's mind. Tropical Radio Telegraph Company in nearby Hialeah had giant broadcasting towers for receiving and relaying communications to and from ships at sea. Surely those massive towers could withstand even this powerful hurricane. If those towers were intact, he could get his story—and a call for help—to the outside world.

Hialeah was less than six miles from downtown Miami, but it may as well have been a thousand miles away.

"Automobiles that had been left on the streets were either wrecked or drowned out," Reck wrote. "It was next to impossible to obtain any sort of transportation."

Next to impossible, maybe, but not *completely* impossible. Reck bumped into a taxi driver who must have been a kindred spirit. With little difficulty, Reck persuaded the cabbie to take him to Hialeah.

Not far from where Reck was climbing into the taxi, Richard Gray was appalled by the parade of people who thought the storm was over and had left their homes to gawk at the wreckage. They had no idea that the lull was only temporary and that the fierce winds would resume at any moment.

Gray ran out into the street, shouting at the sightseers to get back inside. Most of the gawkers ignored him. Many of them would pay dearly only a few minutes later.

Gray's barometer had been holding steady during the calm. But at 6:45 a.m., the needle suddenly plunged again. Now it read 27.61. In 1926, no one in the United States had ever seen a barometer reading that low in a hurricane making landfall.

Then, as though someone had flipped a switch, the winds roared to life again. In only about fifteen minutes, the wind gauge at Allison Hospital was showing a steady 109 miles an hour, with gusts of 119.

And as the winds returned, so did the awful fear.

"Saturday was the worst day I ever want to go through," Edith Royce Oakley later wrote in the letter to her brother. "The only place that we could stay where the water was not pouring in was a tiny kitchen. Briggs braced himself against the door and we sat there for hours, thinking each moment would be our last. Houses were crumbling all around us and the roofs were hurled through the air."

In the streets of Miami, Fort Lauderdale, and Miami Beach, some of the sightseeing newcomers ducked into shelter when the winds suddenly resumed.

But dozens of others couldn't find a place to hide, and they were dying because of it.

The air was filled with debris from buildings shattered during the first part of the storm. Much of the deadly debris—perhaps most of it—came from the shoddily built houses that had been slapped up by boomers obsessed with cashing in on the burgeoning rental market. Building inspectors had looked the other way while the houses were thrown together, and the fortune seekers pouring into Miami had been more than willing to rent them for exorbitant prices.

Now, the boomer shacks were mowing people down. Chunks of concrete, shards of metal, even coconuts became deadly missiles. Boards were ripped loose and became spears, skewering people who were unfortunate enough to be in their paths.

The awful dread reenveloped L. F. Reardon and his family as the winds returned.

"Never abating for an instant, the wind rose still higher until it sounded like hundreds of steamer whistles blowing at once," Reardon said. "Then came once more the terrifying siren-like moan that had made hideous the previous night."

Reardon and his wife took their children into their arms. Reardon expected to be overwhelmed by floodwaters at any moment.

"With an ear-splitting rush of raging wind the large double doors of the living room flew open and the ripping, tearing hurricane found us," Reardon said. "The wind must have been making by this time 120 miles an hour—through the living room of our home."

Reardon tried to close the door.

"A titanic gust of slashing wind picked me up bodily and hurled me against the dining-room buffet forty feet distant," he said, thinking. "The house will not stand another minute!"

With chunks of his home flying away, Reardon moved his family into the laundry room.

Despite the water covering Miami Beach, S. K. Hicks and another attorney friend ventured out of the Mere Grande when the eye arrived. They were only about a block away from the hotel when the fierce winds resumed, but with the air filled with deadly missiles, they hastily ducked into the Beach View Apartments.

"The doors at both ends of the hall on the first floor of the apartment house were ripped away and the wind swept through as though forced from a great bellows," Hicks said. "It knocked us off our feet before we could reach the stairway, and we were compelled to crawl along on our hands and knees to keep from being carried away."

Hicks and his friend climbed to the second floor. The door to one of the apartments was open. Desperate to find some safety from the wind that was howling through the hallways, they ducked into the apartment.

They found a young woman calmly sitting on a couch. She was wearing a bathing suit, and intently watching the hurricane rage outside.

"We were shivering with cold, so she got up and brought us blankets to wrap around us and also got us cigarettes," Hicks said.

Al Reck's wild taxi ride became even wilder when the winds resumed. But his luck—or maybe it was the cabbie's—held.

"That taxi driver was gifted with the luck of the gods," Reck said. "As we sped out north from Miami, past scenes of ruin and desolation on every hand, it seemed as if the wind-strained trees and telephone poles threw themselves at us but missed. The driver literally hurtled the machine over fallen trees and poles. We smashed wires by the mere strength of the heavy taxi and finally reached the radio station."

But even Tropical Radio's four sturdy towers were no match for the hurricane.

"The huge towers were flat on the ground," Reck said.

Reck and the cabbie joined other hurricane refugees in the radio station's concrete blockhouse. They were surrounded by people with broken bones and severe cuts.

"Tiny children were crying in the arms of their parents," Reck wrote. "None of the refugees were dressed except in nightclothes or clothing hastily donned. They were wet, injured, and miserable."

Combat veteran Reck did what he could to offer first aid to the injured.

In Fort Lauderdale, Peggy and Frank Pope watched in astonishment from their apartment as the raging wind lifted their car off the ground and carried it nearly a block down Condit Avenue. Before they could recover from the shock of seeing their automobile carried away, the storm sent a huge timber crashing through a window. Then the roof collapsed, jamming the doors so they couldn't be opened.

Frank Pope broke down a door, and he and his wife fled to a nearby garage apartment, where they took shelter with six other terrified families.

The winds kept increasing until they were blowing even harder than before the eye arrived. By 7:30 a.m., the winds at Allison Hospital were 123 miles an hour, and at 7:40 a.m. the anemometer was reading 132.

From a window of the Tropical Radio blockhouse, Al Reck watched the storm rage.

"Peering from the rain-clouded windows I could see houses rolling along the ground like tin cans," he wrote.

He saw someone crawling on their hands and knees toward the station. Soon a man tapped on a window. He told Reck and the others that there were nine people in a small house about a block away, including a woman with a broken leg who needed help.

Reck and the taxi driver looked at each other.

"Let's go," the cabbie said.

"There was nothing else to do," Reck said. "I went with him."

Somehow, the amazing taxi driver steered his rocking, swaying cab through the storm to the house. Reck and the driver crammed four adults and five children, plus themselves, into the vehicle. The cabbie started the return trip.

As the car pulled away, the house that had contained the refugees pulled free of its foundation and turned over.

Back at the radio station, the taxi driver and another man carried the injured woman inside. Reck picked up a toddler.

"A gust of extra heavy wind came swooping and bounding, picked my feet up, and hurled me a good twenty feet and then started me rolling," Reck said. "I held on to the child with one hand and grasped at a palmetto bush with the other. I regained my feet and crawled on my hands and knees to the station with the child."

When the refugees were safely inside the radio station, they told Reck and the others that there were people who'd sought shelter from the hurricane by hiding among nearby palmettos. The taxi driver and Reck looked at each other again.

"Let's go," the cabbie repeated.

"How many trips we made back and forth to the wireless station I do not know, but we found about thirty men, women, and children, blue and cold, in the palmettos, gripping the earth to save from getting hit by flying debris," Reck said.

As the storm worsened, Louis Slutsky was worried about Beth David Synagogue, which was less than a half-mile from the fierce winds roaring off Biscayne Bay. When Slutsky, who was the synagogue's caretaker, saw flooding and "roofs flying in the street," he decided he had to go to the synagogue to prevent the sacred Torahs from being destroyed.

Slutsky and his son pushed their way into the storm.

"It was already dangerous to walk in the street because of flying pieces from the buildings and the flood," he later told the *New York Times*. "I thought that a repetition of Noah's deluge was coming, when everything would be washed off the earth. Every second of our way was an experience, but we reached the synagogue safely."

The Beth David Synagogue was damaged, and flooding had reached the Holy Ark where the Torahs were stored. Slutsky and his son removed the holy scrolls and took them up into the gallery where women sat during services. They settled down there to wait out the rest of the hurricane.

In Moore Haven, the dike was giving way against the onslaught of the wind and waves. The first break happened just west of town. At first, the water seeped slowly and quietly into the town. Then the dike started crumbling altogether, and the water "began to come in great waves, rising over streets, over floors, and then up and still higher," Lawrence Will later wrote.

"By mid-morning the full fury of the hurricane broke upon us and the waters from the lake were rushing through the town like swift rivers, the air filled with rain, the crests of waves and flying debris," said Fred Flanders, the state engineer. "Visibility, due to the flying scud, dropped to a few hundred yards, and all signs of life disappeared. . . . It was impossible to differentiate between the torrential rain and the wind-driven spume. Looking toward town, some houses had disappeared and others were slowly floating out of sight. No dry land was visible in any direction."

A crowd of townspeople took refuge at the Mayflower Hotel, one of the town's more substantial buildings. Around 8:30 a.m., they felt the building lurch and sway. The flood had pulled it away from its foundation.

The hotel carried its terrified occupants for a brief, wild ride and then settled down in the middle of the street.

Elsewhere, dozens of Moore Haven residents were overcome by the water pouring from the giant lake. Horace Howell, one of the last men to leave the futile sandbagging effort, was swept away. He saved himself by grabbing a willow tree and holding on for dear life. Not far away, his wife fought the waters to save their four children as the water broke into their home and quickly rose above their heads.

The terrifying scene was being repeated throughout the town. Mothers and fathers grabbed children and climbed into attics, or hauled themselves onto roofs where they clung for dear life against the fierce winds. Some families managed to hold on. Others were swept away, one by one, and never seen again.

Around eleven a.m., the Atlantic Coast Line agent telegraphed the Sebring office to say that water was now flooding the train station. It was the last word that the outside world would have from Moore Haven for days. Shortly after this frantic message, all the town's telephone and telegraph wires were down.

In Sebring, Atlantic Coast Line officials decided to send a rescue train to Moore Haven, but they'd have to wait for the storm to subside some.

It was late morning in Miami, but daylight still hadn't come to the city. The hurricane had been pounding Miami and much of South Florida for almost ten hellacious hours.

Kirby Jones, who was in Miami on business for the American Bakery Company, was among about 150 refugees who were riding out the storm in a large downtown building. "The city was covered with a pall of darkness which obscured everything," Jones later told the *New York Times*.

Around nine a.m., the building where Jones and the others had taken shelter could no longer stand against the furious winds. The roof caved in. The occupants fled into the storm and made for a school building about a block away.

"It was a pitiful sight to see that crowd running through the driving rain, barely able to make headway against the terrific force of the wind," Jones said. "Women were crying hysterically and old men were whimpering that they did not want to die, their voices almost inaudible in the roar of the wind. And all the while flying timbers and glass were falling all about us."

Somehow the refugees reached the school safely.

In Coral Gables, Leo Reardon and his family were clinging to shreds of the life they'd known before the hurricane. The storm had nearly carried Reardon away a couple of times. It had rampaged through his comfortable, stylish house like an enraged but invisible beast and turned his beautiful home into soaking wreckage.

"Will this cursed storm never abate, or is it determined to decimate us and our beautiful city?" Reardon wondered as he huddled with his wife and children in the last available shelter from the winds—the laundry room.

"Hours went by—years of terror," Reardon said.

Then, around noon, although it was still dark and windy and pouring rain, the constant roar of the storm eased up. Barometers started rising. Finally, the worst part of the awful hurricane had passed over Miami and was moving away from the city.

Reardon and his family crept out of the laundry room and looked around at what had been their home.

"Nothing was left," Reardon said. "Those three words tell the story."

Numbly, Reardon loaded his family into his car and drove to the Everglades Hotel.

"Scenes of the storm's ravages were everywhere," Reardon said. "Trees, poles, and wires lay across the streets. Cuban tile dotted the scene with dull red splotches. Roofs, whole and intact, were lying blocks from their proper locations."

Entire walls of some buildings had been torn away, "disclosing semi-naked men and women moving dazedly about the ruins of their homes," Reardon said.

The wreckage of buildings—"houses, stores, and shops"—was piled and scattered everywhere. And surely, there were many corpses beneath the debris, Reardon thought.

The streets were nearly deserted.

"Are they all dead?" Reardon wondered. "Those we did see were either laughing hysterically or weeping."

Reardon heard that wailing noise again, only this time, he knew what it was.

"Ambulances rushed in every direction, their wailing sirens reminiscent of the storm," he said. He saw "a boy covered with blood running blindly across the street" and thought, "Where are his parents?"

Reardon picked his way through the wreckage of downtown Miami. Water rushed through the streets. "Third Street is strewn with twisted automobiles," Reardon said. "Along Biscayne Boulevard large yachts and barges weighing hundreds of tons have been deposited in front of the McAllister and Columbus Hotels."

The Everglades Hotel was damaged but habitable, its lobby crowded with storm refugees. Reardon and his family were shown to a damp apartment.

"We must sleep," he thought. "Or have I been dreaming a terrible dream?"

Up the coast in Stuart, the winds had raged and the rains had poured, but the blow had not been anything like what Miami had received. In the *South Florida*

Developer, Edwin Menninger later reported that, compared to Miami, Stuart had "escaped almost unscathed."

Menninger wrote: "The wind, which is said to have struck Miami with a velocity of 150 miles an hour, probably did not exceed ninety miles an hour here. The rain came down in torrents all day Saturday and far into the night, but did no greater damage than wash out a number of bridges and their approaches throughout the county, and tear up the hard-surfaced roads here and there.

"It is true, wires were down and power and light shut off at times, but little damage resulted. The city was cut off from communications with the outside world, and no trains entered Stuart for something more than thirty hours, but this was merely an inconvenience."

On Sunday afternoon, about twenty-four hours after the winds had finally died down in Miami, a northbound Florida East Coast Railway passenger train made its first stop in Stuart since before the hurricane.

The train was packed with still-terrified refugees from the awful storm. They'd had enough of Paradise, and they wanted out.

Menninger was at the Stuart station when the train chuffed to a snorting, hissing stop.

Residents in the towns north of Miami knew the hurricane down there had been bad, but the obviously shaken occupants of the train brought astonishing news from the south.

"The startled train crew and passengers announced that 'three thousand persons were dead in Miami,'" Menninger later wrote in the *Developer*. "The news spread over the city like wildfire."

"Six long passenger trains followed in quick succession, and the terror-stricken passengers corroborated the first report," Menninger wrote, although he added a newsman's natural skepticism about these tales of such a staggering catastrophe: "No real news was available, all wires being down."

That would change, however.

Soon, readers from Maine to California would be fixated on front-page stories about the Miami hurricane. The stories were emblazoned with screaming headlines such as one in an "extra" edition of the *Galveston Daily News* that was on the streets of the Texas seaport almost before the winds had stopped blowing in Miami: "Many Die: Cities Razed."

CHAPTER EIGHT

Spinning the Tempest

Leo Reardon sat down in a soggy, hurricane-battered apartment in the Everglades Hotel in downtown Miami, determined to record the experience he and his family had just endured. But his bleary mind was as blank as the paper in front of him. What day of the week was it? What was the date?

It was Saturday, September 18, 1926. The horrifying experience of riding out the worst hurricane on record had left him so dazed that he questioned his own lucidity.

"I'm not normal," he wrote. "I'm not sure that I'm perfectly sane."

Still, he continued to scribble hastily, wanting to get something on paper before he collapsed from exhaustion—or lost his mind. At the moment, both possibilities seemed likely.

Steadying himself, he continued.

"I must set this down now," he wrote, "for I'm not sure how long my reason will last. My God, but I'm tired. I'll write it now while every minute's horror of those unforgettable ten hours stands out in my brain like a year in an inferno."

Until you've been through an intense hurricane, it's impossible to really understand the unearthly power they can unleash and the primal fear they can evoke. Inexperienced human perception and anticipation inevitably tend to underestimate a hurricane's fearsome force.

After you've survived such a storm, you may never be the same again.

Meteorologists in the twenty-first century are still trying to understand these storms and calculate the immense energy they release. Today, their power sometimes is expressed in a measure that did not exist in 1926—atomic bombs. When a hurricane reaches its peak intensity, it may release energy equivalent to 500,000 Hiroshima-type atomic bombs, although that energy is spread over a vast area and is not concentrated as it would be in an atomic bomb explosion.

As Reardon gathered his wits and his strength in a damp hotel room and tried to write about a life-altering experience, thousands of dazed and terrified people crawled and pushed and wormed their way out of the wreckage in Miami and Miami Beach, Fort Lauderdale and Hialeah, and Hollywood and Coconut

Grove. Others, too seriously injured to move, lay helplessly where they'd fallen, waiting, hoping someone would find them soon.

The wail of ambulance sirens replaced the wailing screech of the hurricane's winds. Mothers searched frantically for missing children. Husbands sick with worry, exhausted but driven by dread and determination to find their loved ones, tore at piles of tangled lumber that only a few hours earlier had served as the walls and floors of their dream homes, searching frantically for family members. Children sought missing pets—or their parents.

Some survivors wept over the lifeless bodies of loved ones, or just wandered the streets, thirsty and in a state of shock, looking for water or a familiar face.

The iconic decorative touches of a tropical paradise that had existed a day earlier—Cuban tiles, stucco walls, colorful sun-bleached awnings—had been turned into mounds of twisted rubble, on top of which lay shreds of clothing, pieces of furniture, fragments of dishes, remains of cherished heirlooms . . . the deeply personal wreckage of private lives. And beneath those piles, and in floodwaters, and in wrecked cars and boats, the dead lay, awaiting discovery and identification. Some had been crushed when buildings had collapsed. Others had been speared or clubbed by debris that became deadly when it was propelled by winds that may have reached 150 miles an hour in the northeast quadrant of the eye wall. Even a coconut, that ubiquitous symbol of the tropics, could knock the life out of someone when it flew through the air at that speed.

Some victims had simply drowned when the ocean surged across Miami Beach and into the streets of downtown Miami.

The raucous, deadly sea had also flung boats and ships of all sizes out of the water. About 550 vessels—modest houseboats, barges, sturdy tugs, sleek yachts, oceangoing freighters, and small rowboats—were wrecked or sunk in the Miami River and Biscayne Bay. The bowsprit of the *Rose Mahoney*, a proud, five-masted schooner washed ashore by the storm, towered over Biscayne Boulevard.

The storm had wrecked and demolished the pleasure spots of Miami Beach. Mixed in with the other wreckage on the western shore of Biscayne Bay were chunks of polished maple boards that had been part of the dance floor of Charley's Grill. Only a few hours earlier, dancers had been doing the Charleston on those boards until cops had come in, closed the place, and told everyone to get off the island. The storm's tides and winds had carried the boards about three miles across Biscayne Bay.

Near the Flagler Street bridge, fifty-four boats had been piled up in the Miami River. An eighteen-foot pleasure boat rested on its keel near the curb at a street corner, far from any water. It looked as though the owner had left it in a choice parking space and gone shopping.

In downtown Miami, the seventeen-story Meyer-Kiser Building—also known as the Dade Commonwealth Building—was ruined. The building's opening only a few months earlier had prompted Miami's boomers to boast that their skyline of tall buildings reaching for the clouds would soon resemble New York's.

But the Meyer-Kiser's upper stories had been blasted by winds even more powerful than those that had caused so much havoc on the ground. At ground level, a hurricane's winds interact with the ground and are slowed down, but one hundred or more feet in the air, the winds are unimpeded by the ground's drag. This means that the winds that slammed into the Meyer-Kiser Building could have exceeded 160 miles an hour.

"Jack Reeves tells me he watched the antics of this seventeen-story building from the door of the Ritz Hotel," Leo Reardon wrote. "He says it waved its tail like a porpoise and did a sort of Charleston during the gale."

The building's structural steel was so twisted by the fierce winds that the building's upper floors could not be repaired. Instead, they would have to be torn down, and the Meyer-Kiser Building—which still stands in downtown Miami—would be reduced to five stories.

In the Glades northwest of Miami, an Atlantic Coast Line rescue train steamed from Sebring toward Moore Haven. No one had heard anything from the little lakeside hamlet since Saturday morning, when the town's telegraph operator reported that water was knee-deep and rising in the train station.

Around eight p.m. on Saturday, the train had to stop in Palmdale, about seventeen miles from Moore Haven, to take on water for the locomotive's boiler. Because the storm had ripped away part of the water tank's structure, the crew had to rig a trough from the tank to the locomotive to fill the boiler. It took hours to complete the task.

Around eleven p.m., the train resumed its journey. The track was surrounded by floodwaters, so crewmen ran a handcar ahead of the train to make sure the track was safe. It was slow going.

A few miles outside Palmdale, the train crew met fifteen storm refugees seeking shelter. They took them aboard and pushed on. A mile or so farther along, the track was completely underwater and impassable for the locomotive and train. So the crewmen abandoned the train, climbed onto the small handcar, and continued.

"The wind was still blowing a gale," *The Times* of Hammond, Indiana, reported. "The track was generally out of sight, and frequently at an acute angle. At other places, the fill was washed from under the track, which hung like a suspended bridge, held together only by bolts and fish plates.

"Still these five railroad men proceeded through the inky black night."

Around three a.m., the train crew reached Newhall, a tiny community about three and a half miles from Moore Haven. Here, the train tracks were just gone. The men climbed down off the handcar and started slogging through floodwaters toward Moore Haven.

The rescue party reached Moore Haven around sunup on Sunday morning. They found a nearly destroyed town covered in knee-deep water. Some of the storm survivors were crowded onto the second floors of the few buildings that had remained intact. Others had climbed into train cars that had been parked on a railroad siding.

The rescue party found usable boats and started loading survivors into them, then rowed the boats back to Newhall, where the survivors were put aboard the train and taken to safety. Meanwhile, other trains were sent to Muckway, another tiny railroad settlement near Moore Haven. Eventually, around 1,200 people were evacuated from Moore Haven.

In Miami, ambulances still sped along Biscayne Boulevard Sunday morning, and rescue workers were pulling corpses from the rubble.

Wild rumors of apocalyptic death and destruction were circulating. "Reports have it Miami Beach has been washed completely away and the dead are decomposing in piles of thousands," Leo Reardon wrote in his hotel room.

The rumor mill that follows any catastrophic event was cranking out reports that Fort Lauderdale supposedly was scrubbed clean of buildings, and thousands were dead there. Hialeah reportedly looked as though it had been shelled by the gigantic artillery the Germans had used in the Great War.

There was no reason to doubt these tales because funeral homes were filling up with corpses, and every moment more were being brought in.

Across the nation, Americans were pouring their morning coffee and opening their Sunday newspapers to screaming headlines of unimaginable catastrophe in Florida.

"Miami Wiped Out by Terrific Gale," said the *Salt Lake Tribune* in Utah.

In Florence, South Carolina, readers of an "extra" edition of the *Morning News Review* saw a headline saying that one thousand had been killed, and "Noted Resort Cities Laid Waste by Most Destructive Storm In Memory."

In Pennsylvania, subscribers to the *Clearfield Progress* read: "Beautiful Florida Coastal Cities Levelled by Hurricane / Nearly 1,000 Lives Lost."

In Texas, editors at the *Galveston County Daily News* put out an "extra" edition with a huge banner headline reading "Many Die; Cities Razed."

According to headlines in the *Chester Times* of Pennsylvania, "1,000 Dead, 50,000 Homeless / $100,000,000 Loss in Storm that Hits Florida Cities / Miami Is Devastated, with Many Buildings in Ruins in Hollywood, Coral Gables, and Nearby Places."

In Fort Lauderdale—one of the cities supposedly wiped off the map, according to headlines in other parts of the nation—the *Daily News* somehow published a Sunday edition with the headline "Hurricane Claims Heavy Toll of Life and Property."

The *New York Times* was more reserved. On Sunday morning, they reported that seventy-five were known dead in Miami and two thousand buildings had been destroyed. They noted that "scant details" were available, but said the storm was being called the "worst in history."

By late Sunday afternoon, American Red Cross officials in Florida and Washington, DC, were trying to get a handle on the hurricane's devastation. Around 5:30 p.m., a Western Union delivery boy handed a telegram to J. Arthur Jeffers, a Red Cross administrator in Washington. It was from Henry Reed in

Jacksonville, and it was alarming. Reed reported that a passenger agent for the Florida East Coast Railway had told him that more than 700 people had been killed and 38,000 were homeless.

A few minutes later, another telegram arrived from Red Cross representative Sidney Morse in Fort Pierce: "South Florida in misery and grave danger."

"Suffering terrible," Morse said. "Need food, water, doctors, nurses, and financial help immediately."

When the sun came up over the Gulf of Mexico on Monday, September 20, the hurricane's eye was just south of Pensacola at the western tip of the Florida Panhandle. And although the storm had weakened some, it was still inflicting a terrible beating on that old city. A storm surge that reached fourteen feet at some points devastated Pensacola Bay. A steady wind of 100 mph blew for five hours, and hurricane-force winds of at least 74 mph blew for twenty-four hours. Amazingly, no one was killed in Pensacola.

The storm's eye pushed inland at Gulf Shores, Alabama, just west of Pensacola, and continued westward, crossing Mississippi and finally dissipating over Louisiana.

Monday morning's newspapers continued to paint a portrait of death and devastation in South Florida, including "1,000 Perish in Florida Twister," a headline from the *Charleston Gazette* in West Virginia's capital city.

In Utah, the *Salt Lake Tribune* reported "Hurricane Levels Florida Coast Cities," killing 1,075 in the process.

The *New York Times* dropped the restraint it had used in the previous day's newspaper, reporting that a sixty-mile stretch of coastline from Miami northward had been "devastated" by the hurricane, killing one thousand. Miami was "laid waste" by the storm, and "vast damage" had been inflicted on Hollywood.

A headline in the *Chester Times* said the storm had left fifty thousand homeless.

Many of the newspaper stories cited injury and damage estimates from the American Red Cross. Some very wealthy and powerful men who were heavily invested in Florida were reading those stories. They were seething at this portrayal of slaughter and devastation, and gripped by the fear that unless they stopped it, all of the millions they'd spent turning Florida into a paradise on Earth would be wiped out.

The residents of Miami and neighboring communities were just beginning to realize the full extent of the devastation caused by the hurricane. Exactly how devastating that storm was would be debated for weeks—and years—after it struck. For the record, the official death toll has been calculated as at least 372, although about 800 people—most of them African Americans—were missing and never seen again after the storm. About 25,000 people were left homeless, and damages by the storm were calculated at about $100 million, or more than $1.3 billion in twenty-first-century dollars.

"The city is waking to the horrors of the disaster," Leo Reardon wrote on Monday, September 20, 1926. "All of yesterday there was a spirit of hysterical joking, except among those actively engaged in relief work."

The survivors were joking, perhaps, because they didn't know how badly their communities had been hit. Telephones and telegraphs were gone for the time being. Newspapers were struggling to repair damages and resume publishing.

"Details were not to be had; none yet knew the facts," Reardon said.

And one newspaper whose responsibility was to report the facts was deliberately obscuring them. In its edition of September 20, the *Miami Herald* reported that the storm had caused about $10 million in damages to that city, and that total damages in neighboring communities "will not exceed $1 million."

It was an absurdly low figure, and it started a determined effort by the city's business interests to underplay the hurricane's destruction.

Reardon drove to the causeway to see how Miami Beach had fared. The causeway had been closed. He had to show identification and a press pass, and promise police that he'd return before dark.

What he saw was stunning.

"My first view of the storm's ravages at America's Playground brought tears to my eyes," he said.

A yacht had been smashed against the causeway and ruined. Two feet of sand covered Ocean Drive. The palace-like homes of the wealthy had withstood the storm but were heavily damaged, with broken windows and water-soaked contents. Some were missing roofs.

Hotels—the Mayflower, the Boulevard, the Flamingo—were smashed open and their contents scattered for blocks. Dead fish lay decaying in the hot sun.

The storm had done its worst work at South Beach. Casinos and nightclubs simply were no more, and some of their revelers had ignored police warnings to get off the island. "They are pulling out the dead from the ruins of the casinos and shops," Reardon wrote. "The number will never be known."

Carl Fisher's famous Roney Plaza Hotel was heavily damaged by winds and storm surge. "So clean was the sweep of the torrent through the ground floor of the Roney Plaza Hotel that not a tittle of testimony remains, that only two days ago there were here dozens of smart shops, beauty parlors, and drugstores," Reardon wrote.

The Roney's roof also was gone, and most of its windows were broken.

Familiar landmarks had just disappeared. "Collins Avenue is a pathetic thoroughfare," Reardon said. "I have lived in Miami and Miami Beach three years, but had difficulty in knowing when we had arrived at the corner of Collins Avenue and Lincoln Road."

In Washington, DC, President Calvin Coolidge had heard enough about the hurricane's damage to issue a statement calling for Americans to make generous contributions to relieve the suffering in Florida.

"An overwhelming disaster has come to the people of Miami, Hollywood, and surrounding communities in Southern Florida," his statement began.

Coolidge said he would authorize federal assistance to help those hardest hit by the storm, "but realizing the great suffering which now needs relief and will need relief for days to come, I am prompted to appeal urgently to the American people . . . to contribute generously in aiding the sufferers of this disaster."

Coolidge ended his statement by urging Americans to send contributions to the Red Cross, which would use their contributions "in the most effective manner" to help those who needed it.

Immediately after the president had released his statement, Red Cross chairman John Barton Payne—who had served as secretary of the interior under President Woodrow Wilson—sent a memo to local Red Cross leaders across the country. Coolidge's statement made the Red Cross responsible for the recovery effort in South Florida, Payne said. Local Red Cross chapters should make sure Coolidge's statement was well publicized and immediately start raising money for the hurricane victims.

By late Monday afternoon, Al Reck, the determined reporter who'd braved the worst of the storm with the fearless taxi driver, had reached West Palm Beach. Along the way he'd gotten a close look at the storm's devastation and counted seventeen corpses. He sat down in a hotel room and started banging out his story. The man who had been left for dead on a battlefield in France had been awed by this hurricane.

"I never experienced anything like it and I hope I never will again," he wrote.

Hialeah and its famous dog track and kennel club were destroyed, Reck reported. Hollywood would have to be entirely rebuilt, he said.

While Reck wrote his story in West Palm Beach, A. T. Philips in Miami was composing a telegram to New York City. Philips was the manager of the Miami office of the George A. Fuller Company. The company, founded in 1882 by the architect often credited with "inventing" the skyscraper, had built a half-dozen or so prominent buildings in Miami during the boom years.

"All buildings erected by Fuller Co. came through hurricane in splendid shape structurally," Philips reported.

He described relatively minor damage to the ten-story Olympia Theater and the fifteen-story First Trust & Savings Bank in downtown Miami.

The Fuller Company had also built the famous Roney Plaza Hotel overlooking the ocean on Miami Beach. In some ways, Philips's description of the damage the hurricane had inflicted on that building didn't vary too much from Reardon's description: "Roney Plaza roof blown off and most window glass out. Water damage to furniture, sea water rushed through ground floor."

Still, to many people it would seem a bit of a stretch to describe a ten-story building that had lost its roof and most of its windows and been gutted by an eighteen-foot storm surge as being in "splendid" shape.

Reardon and Philips had different perceptions of what the hurricane had done to Miami and its surrounding communities. In the coming weeks, similar differences of perception about the destruction caused by the hurricane would erupt into a nasty national dispute between the American Red Cross and some of the country's most powerful business interests.

The public squabble between the Red Cross and businessmen who were deeply invested in Florida was perhaps the strangest saga to develop in the aftermath of the 1926 hurricane.

The American Red Cross, founded in 1881, had been sending help to the scenes of disasters for forty-five years before the 1926 hurricane. Red Cross workers had helped the survivors in Galveston, Texas, when a horrendous hurricane there killed at least nine thousand people in 1900. They had helped dazed San Francisco residents pick up the pieces of their lives after the earthquake of 1906 all but destroyed the city. And they had helped victims of countless other lesser-known disasters. Fires, tornadoes, floods—the Red Cross had dealt with them all.

To publicly challenge the Red Cross's analysis of a disaster was absurdly arrogant. But for more than two months, that's exactly what a handful of very powerful men did.

As night fell on South Florida on Monday, September 20, candles and kerosene lanterns flickered from the glassless windows of apartment buildings and homes that were still inhabitable. Elsewhere, campfires cast an eerie flickering light on the ruins of homes as their former occupants prepared to bed down again in the open air.

More than a thousand miles to the north of South Florida's hurricane-induced misery, a crowd bedecked in evening finery smiled and chuckled and howled with laughter as a leering Groucho Marx and his outrageous brothers romped through the first Washington, DC, performance of *The Cocoanuts* at the National Theater. The *Washington Post*'s drama critic gushed with praise for the performance, noting that the comedy about maniacal greed and shady land dealings in Florida "roars like a hurricane" from beginning to end.

In the days when land speculation was booming and millions of dollars were changing hands every day, developers such as George Merrick had sent their own buses to cities in the Midwest and Northeast to bring prospective buyers to Florida. The trip was free if you bought real estate, and most of the passengers got a free trip.

Late in the day of Tuesday, September 21, some of the same buses that only a year earlier had brought new dreamers and schemers to Florida were hauling bedraggled and dispirited storm refugees to the Seaboard Air Line Railroad station in West Palm Beach. Seaboard, owned by Solomon Davies Warfield, was giving free train tickets to those who'd had enough of paradise and wanted to go home.

"Gone now the spirit of adventure and excitement that marked these faces during the days of the 'great boom,'" Leo Reardon wrote. "In their stead tears, discouragement, and the wistful expression of homesickness. Tired women in bedraggled clothing alighted with puzzled children from the buses and slowly walked into the station where agents of the railroad companies and Red Cross workers distributed tickets and took down on official writing pads details of suffering and destitution in each case."

In the previous two days, more than a thousand storm-blown, soon-to-be-former residents of South Florida had made their way to West Palm Beach to board northbound trains. Most of the travelers were women, children, and older men. Younger men had stayed behind to help with the cleanup.

A locomotive pulling eleven passenger coaches slowly approached and glided to a stop at the station. The passengers who began shuffling toward the train reminded Reardon of refugees fleeing Belgium ahead of the German invasion in the early days of the Great War twelve years earlier.

"There was no rush to board the train, just a slow, steady movement of fatigued human beings, who dropped exhausted on the cushions, with a sigh and a gleam of hope in their eyes," Reardon said. "They were going [to their former] home."

An old man sitting alone at the rear of one coach began to pray aloud. Outside, the Florida sun was making its usual spectacular descent to the horizon. Someone—perhaps a local chamber of commerce—had stationed a small band at the station to play for the passengers. As the old man prayed and the train pulled slowly away, the band played "Valencia."

The song had been recorded only a few months earlier by the Paul Whiteman Orchestra, and would become one of the biggest hits of Whiteman's career. It was a familiar tune to passengers, and the doctors, nurses, and Red Cross workers who were helping them. As the song's stirring opening notes floated through the evening, its lyrics doubtless ran through the minds of some of those in the crowd. It was a song about orange blossoms and sea breezes, paradise and romance—exactly what many of them had been seeking when they had come to Florida.

Late the following day, some of the trains with Florida passengers began arriving in New York. Reporters were waiting at Penn Station. The passengers' descriptions of what they'd left behind varied some, but mostly they spoke of devastation and ruined lives.

Saul German, a former Bronx resident, told the *New York Times* that he'd lost everything he owned in the storm.

"The storm took the roof from our heads," his wife said, "and we gathered an armful of clothes, took the baby, and ran in the dark."

Burton Wilson, a student at Princeton University, had a different take. He told a *Times* reporter that most of the storm's damage had been done to buildings that were quickly and cheaply built. "Miami is not so badly off as people feared at first," he said.

But H. P. Noonan, who'd gone to Florida to open an insurance business—and presumably knew something about evaluating damage—said Miami was a "total wreck."

As the storm refugees' tales of woe were being published in newspapers, the Red Cross was getting a better idea of exactly what the hurricane had done to South Florida. By Wednesday, September 22, they knew that 135 people had been killed in Miami, 70 had died in Hollywood, and 75 in Fort Lauderdale.

At least 4,000 people had been injured in the storm, and about 1,000 of those injuries had been serious. About half of the serious injuries had been major fractures of arms and legs, as well as fractured skulls and broken necks. More than 1,300 were hospitalized.

In Fort Lauderdale, Red Cross inspectors had found twenty-two wells containing the bacteria that causes typhoid.

Five tons of lime had been shipped to Fort Lauderdale to neutralize the stench of decayed dead animals, and the Red Cross had started calculating a price tag on helping the storm survivors get back on their feet.

In Stuart, Edwin Menninger was mixing optimism and realism in his reporting of the storm in the *South Florida Developer*. He attributed a similar attitude to Governor John Martin, who had stopped in Stuart for lunch on September 22 after touring the area hit by the storm.

"It was evident [Martin] realized the gravity of the situation, but he seemed to be trying to make his remarks as optimistic as possible," the *Developer* noted. "He said he thought the Miami people had the situation well in hand."

Still, the *Developer* acknowledged that Miami had withstood a severe blow and needed outside help. Stuart's police chief and a group of businessmen had also just returned from Miami with "grave reports" of the conditions there. They were so moved by what they'd seen that they arranged for ice, medical supplies, and drinking water to be sent immediately to the stricken area and set up a committee to raise money and collect supplies.

By Thursday, September 23, letters from storm survivors still in Florida were being published in newspapers across the country. They continued to portray a grim public image of conditions in Miami and surrounding communities.

"I don't believe the papers can describe all that happened here," Henry Zimmerman wrote in a letter to his parents that was published in the *Sheboygan Press* in Wisconsin. "Everything is ruined. There is no water, light, or gas. There is little to eat and less money. Our apartment house is a total wreck, and we have no home. It is my opinion that this finishes Miami."

"Hurricane terrible," William Diesbach hastily scrawled to his friend, John Yackle, in Hamilton, Ohio. His note was published in the *Hamilton Evening Journal*. "Many lives lost. Buildings have fallen in and wrecked. Miami in terrible shape."

Helen Sweezy's letter to her parents in Middletown, New York, was published in the *Daily Herald*. "Very few of the houses have any roofs or windows left, and most of them are flat on the ground," she wrote. "Miami and Miami Beach are an awful sight."

Others, however, looked at the same damage and made very different calculations. If the newspaper headlines saying thousands had died and Miami had been leveled were greatly overstated, the responses to the tragedy from some of the plutocrats heavily invested in Florida were disturbingly understated. Their acknowledgment of the death and destruction was terse and perfunctory, and they dismissed the reports of massive damage by saying it was simply impossible for a hurricane to generate the force necessary to cause such spectacular destruction.

On September 20, the *Miami Herald* reported that the storm had done about $11 million in damages to that city. The neighboring cities of Hialeah, Coral Gables, and Miami Beach had sustained an additional $2 million.

On Wednesday, September 22, the *Wall Street Journal* published an editorial expressing sympathy for storm victims and calling for a "brave and steady eye to the future." But the newspaper's editorial board dismissed reports of the unearthly power of the hurricane, insisting that the top winds could not possibly have reached speeds above ninety-five miles an hour. The editorial characterized reports that Miami and other cities had been wiped out and would take years to rebuild as "pardonable hysterics."

"All that has been wiped out is a certain class of building, that which lacked steel construction," the *Journal* said. "It is a terrific loss, but it is measurable and can be met in months rather than years."

Solomon Davies Warfield had just spent millions expanding his Seaboard Air Line Railroad in Florida, and he had huge plans for building a great industrial city in Martin County, west of Stuart. Now his railroad was hauling dazed storm refugees out of Florida by the trainload, free of charge. Nonetheless, on September 22, Warfield issued a public statement saying the hurricane's effects on Florida were being "exaggerated to an extent far beyond actual conditions."

Although Warfield said the death toll was "unfortunate and regrettable," he added that his railroad was operating on schedule. And like the *Wall Street Journal*, he dismissed reports of the hurricane's massive power.

"I doubt if there has been as much water in the streets of these several localities as there was in the streets of Jamaica, Long Island, two weeks ago, when automobiles were floating through the streets instead of running on their tires," Warfield said.

Warfield could have been referring to any one of several severe thunderstorms that had hit New York City between early August and Labor Day. The most recent storm had struck the city on the afternoon of September 7, 1926, dumping torrential rainfall and adding to the chaos caused by thousands of people heading home after the Labor Day holiday. But Warfield's comparison of a bad thunderstorm to a monster hurricane that had pushed an eighteen-foot storm surge across Miami Beach and pounded the area with hurricane-force winds for twenty-four hours was an absurd and utterly ill-informed interpretation of reality.

Warfield's statement, published by the *New York Times* and other newspapers, and the *Wall Street Journal* editorial were the opening salvos of a publicity counterattack by those with huge financial interests in Florida. Nothing could be done to stop the stunned hurricane survivors who were leaving Florida by the thousands with no intention of ever coming back. But Warfield and others who knew nothing of huddling in terror in a disintegrating house being torn apart by 150-mile-an-hour winds were determined that those who had not actually witnessed the hurricane's unearthly power would not be dissuaded from coming to Florida and spending money. And while it was understandable that they would want to protect their investments and minimize their losses, their determined campaign of misinformation was a serious impediment to the Red Cross's efforts to raise money for the thousands of people who badly needed help.

Perhaps taking his cue from Warfield's public statements, Miami mayor Edward C. Romfh—who also was founder and president of Miami's First National Bank—issued a public statement two days later, saying news reports of the hurricane's damage were inaccurate.

"From the thousands of telegrams pouring into Miami, hundreds of which are addressed to the mayor of the city, I am convinced a very much exaggerated idea of Miami's real condition has been created," Romfh said.

His Honor acknowledged that the hurricane "was by far the most severe and destructive storm that ever touched the mainland of the United States." Far from being severely damaged, however, Miami had withstood the storm very well. Most of the damage had been done to cheaply constructed buildings and houseboats, he said.

"It is remarkable that a city of 160,000 or more people should have gone through such a severe storm with comparatively so small a number of dead and injured," Romfh continued. "That is accounted for by the fact that this city has the largest percentage of concrete buildings of any city in the United States."

Miami had made an "amazing" comeback in the six days since the hurricane struck, Romfh said. He ended with a cheery promise: "I want to give positive assurance that our friends will find Miami this winter the same enjoyable, hospitable, comfortable vacation city it has always been.

"I predict that Miami will make a world-record comeback. The people here have the enthusiasm, the will to do, an unshaken faith in the future of this great city. It is the same people who have created the fastest-growing city in America who are now turning their energies and enthusiasm to the work of reconstruction in Miami."

Edwin Menninger had doubtless read Warfield's statement in the *Wall Street Journal* before the September 24 edition of the *South Florida Developer* was published. His reporting on the storm's impact on Miami was cautious, but as accurate as he could make it.

Meanwhile, out in Moore Haven, rescue workers and survivors crazed with grief were hauling in decomposing bodies, many of them partially consumed by buzzards. Some of the bodies had been carried many miles from town by the wind and surging floodwaters.

The rescue workers begged the survivors to leave and let them deal with collecting the corpses. Shelter, dry beds, clean clothes, and food were available in nearby towns such as Sebring, where camps had been set up for storm survivors. Some gave in and left, but so many stayed that Governor John Martin finally had to order the National Guard to force them to leave.

At the end of the week, *Time* magazine's issue of September 27 hit the newsstands and mailboxes. Millions of Americans opened the magazine's pages to read a tale of irony-laden tragedy about the hurricane that had hit Miami.

"People of the 'Magic City' boasted that its indolent sun-kissed shores had never been touched by a hurricane; that Miami was, in fact, well outside the hurricane belt," the story began.

"Last week, as everyone knows, the rain and wind gods conspired with Neptune, wiped the 'Magic City' from the map."

Time's story continued, its trademark inverted, compressed sentences—stripped of conjunctions and articles—crisply implying that maybe Miami deserved the thrashing it had received: "No more would sport coats and plumed hats stroll at Hialea[h] Race [T]rack. It was gone. No more would dandies strut and women preen in Carl Fisher's fashionable Flamingo Hotel. It was wrecked. Five hundred bodies soaked in the streets, some wretchedly askew under logs, others stretched out peacefully by the Chamber of Commerce. Where had been one mammoth mansion sat a lone bathtub. And ghouls peered about, tampered with corpses.

"The [United States] was amazed, flabbergasted. It could not comprehend. Money loss was reported to be ten, twenty, fifty, one hundred millions of dollars. Thirty-eight thousand souls were homeless. There was no food; what there had been was water-soaked. People lacked water, light, clothing. Great trees, torn up like matchsticks, lay across the roads. Here sagged houses without roofs, there tilted roofs without houses. Ships nestled in once busy streets while homes floated crazily atop a panting ocean. Miami was a damned, insane region from the Ancient Mariner, and the gods were as mad as Coleridge."

Other publications were more direct in their moralizing about the harsh lessons that the Almighty had inflicted on Florida and the nation with the hurricane.

"God permitted the hurricane to strike Florida because that State's quick prosperity turned her head," the weekly *Living Church* newspaper, published in Milwaukee, editorialized. "It is the divine verdict on such lavish, quick prosperity as turns one's head. Not Florida alone, but America, is pictured vividly in the parable."

On the heels of the *Time* story, the Red Cross announced that it was mounting its greatest relief effort since the San Francisco earthquake of 1906.

Compiling the reports of dozens of Red Cross workers in Florida, a news release said 15,700 families—as many as 47,000 people—needed help.

"It is true Florida is the playground of the wealthy, but at the time of the disaster it was flooded with thousands of people of moderate means who had invested all they had in small homes," the news release said. "Through a stretch of several hundred miles centering around Miami, thousands of families have nothing today but a mass of twisted, splintered timber and wreckage."

Another Red Cross news release was aimed squarely at Miami mayor Edward Romfh's open letter saying that conditions in Miami weren't as bad as the press was portraying them.

Citing a report by Worth M. Tippy, an investigator sent to Florida by the Federal Council of Churches, the Red Cross said hurricane damage was greater than the nation realized.

"Reports which have gone out from some sources in Miami through false civic pride, [saying] that outside aid is not needed, are erroneous and should be counteracted in every possible way," Tippy said.

The investigator said he'd talked with pastors and visited many homes and aid stations. "Damage is much greater than the rest of the country thinks," Tippy said. "Five million dollars is really inadequate, and much below what the nation should do."

A few Florida newspapers were starting to pick up on the effort to downplay the damage.

"There seems to be no doubt in the minds of many that there is an organized attempt on the part of certain interests in Miami to minimize the effects of the storm for reasons probably best known to themselves," a newspaper in DeLand reported. "A letter broadcast throughout the country purporting to be from Mayor Romfh of Miami would surely lead the world to believe that practically all has been done for relief of the various districts affected."

Romfh's description was disputed by members of a National Guard unit based in DeLand that had been sent to South Florida to keep order during the relief effort, the newspaper said.

And Red Cross officials were becoming grimly aware of the task that lay before them. While they didn't dispute that well-constructed buildings, such as steel-framed office buildings and the homes of the wealthy, had, for the most part, withstood the ferocious blast of the hurricane, the vast majority of residents in and around Miami—including many of those cheery workers described by Romfh that were rebuilding the city—did not live in such structures.

"Thousands of three- and four- and five-room cottages are now only a pile of splintered wood," W. B. Taylor, a Red Cross official in Washington, said in a telegram to Douglas Griesmer in Miami. "The Red Cross has the heaviest responsibility it has ever shouldered in a disaster-relief operation in this country."

One of the greatest engineering feats of history was building a road known as the Tamiami Trail through the mysterious Florida Everglades. The 274-mile road linking Tampa and Miami took more than a decade to complete. The Tamiami Trail opened in April 1928. This photo shows a dredge in the background piling up limestone to create the roadbed. Digging the limestone formed a canal that ran alongside the road. (COURTESY STATE ARCHIVES OF FLORIDA)

In 1921, Kansas native Edwin Menninger came to Florida from New York to recover from a severe case of the flu. He worked briefly for the *Palm Beach Post,* and then bought a struggling weekly newspaper called the *South Florida Developer.* He moved the newspaper to nearby Stuart, where he reported on the Florida real estate frenzy of the 1920s. He also became a community leader and helped shape Florida's growth and development for the next half-century. (THE THURLOW COLLECTION)

Chicago gangster Al Capone, at right in the dark pinstripe suit, first visited Miami in the winter of 1927–28 under the alias of "Al Brown." He like the city and its mild climate so much that he dropped the alias and declared that he was going to stay. He formed a friendship with Parker Henderson Jr., the son of a former mayor. Henderson frequently ran errands for Capone, even buying a gun in Miami that later was used in the assassination of a rival gangster in Brooklyn. (COURTESY STATE ARCHIVES OF FLORIDA)

In September 1928, a very powerful hurricane pounded West Palm Beach, moved inland, and swept raging floodwaters out of Lake Okeechobee, devastating several small farming towns around the lake's southern shore. The storm killed at least 2,500 people, many of them black migrant workers from Haiti and the Caribbean who'd come to harvest crops. This photo shows coffins awaiting use at Belle Glade, one of the towns flooded by the hurricane. (COURTESY STATE ARCHIVES OF FLORIDA)

George Merrick was a minister's son who wrote poetry and won a prize for his writing. But he left his mark on Florida as the developer of Coral Gables, considered by many to be a masterpiece of urban planning. During the heady days of the Florida real estate frenzy in the mid-1920s, Merrick's company often brought in millions of dollars in property sales every week. Merrick put the money back into the development, and was broke when the real estate market crashed. He ended his days as postmaster of Miami. (COURTESY STATE ARCHIVES OF FLORIDA)

One of the most powerful hurricanes on record slammed into Miami in September 1926. This photo shows downtown Miami shortly after the storm. The baggy knickerbockers worn by the young man in the foreground were known as "plus-fours" because they extended four inches below the knee. In the background is the heavily damaged Meyer-Kiser Building. A witness said the seventeen-story building "waved its tail like a porpoise and did a sort of Charleston" during the storm. The top twelve stories of the building were removed, and it was rebuilt as a five-story building. (COURTESY STATE ARCHIVES OF FLORIDA)

The Dixie Highway, which ran from Montreal to Miami, became a gateway to Florida for millions of paradise seekers in the 1920s. *Saturday Evening Post* writer Kenneth Roberts wrote that at times, the line of traffic on the highway headed to Florida resembled "an endless serpent" that managed to wriggle forward at about 30 miles an hour. In this photo, tourists stop to chat on the Dixie Highway in Florida around 1925. (COURTESY STATE ARCHIVES OF FLORIDA)

Polish-born Marianna Michalski grew up dancing in the saloons of suburban Milwaukee. By the mid-1920s, she had changed her name to Gilda Gray, devised a titillating dance she called the "shimmy," and become one of Hollywood's first sex symbols. In 1925, she was paid a small fortune for an eight-week appearance in Florida at Hollywood-by-the-Sea, where her suggestive dance enticed free-spending tourists to buy real estate. (COURTESY STATE ARCHIVES OF FLORIDA)

By the 1920s, Arthur Brisbane was the nation's best-known journalist and his name had become a household word. His column, "Today," was read by at least 20 million people and he was known as the highest paid newspaper editor in the United States. His real estate investments added to his immense wealth. He made frequent trips to Stuart, Florida, between 1924 and 1926 to look at real estate there, and eventually bought 10,000 acres he intended to use as a produce farm. He used his internationally known byline and prestige to lobby state officials for public works improvements that would have greatly benefited him. (PHOTO CREDIT: PRINT COLLECTION, MIRIAM AND IRA D. WALLACH DIVISION OF ART, PRINTS AND PHOTOGRAPHS, THE NEW YORK PUBLIC LIBRARY, LENOX AND TILDEN FOUNDATIONS)

ARTHUR BRISBANE, THE TEACHER OF THE PEOPLE, TO THE "LEONARDO"

MY DEAR MR. RUOTOLO:

I congratulate you on the work that your school is doing, and I send you with great pleasure the photograph for which you ask. The best thing that has been said by anybody in my opinion was said by Dante, "Give light and the people will find their own way." You will supply the Italian version of that. If I am not mistaken it reads: — I don't speak Italian — "Date luce, ed il popolo troverà la sua via."

The next best thing said, for the inspiration of young people, was also said by Dante, "Work, as nature works, in fire". I once read that on a front page of one of D'Annunzio's books.

Yours sincerely,

ARTHUR BRISBANE

Women's fashions changed dramatically during the 1920s with shorter hemlines, sleeveless dresses and tops, and more revealing bathing suits. Carl Fisher, who developed Miami Beach, was a promotional genius who realized that photographing attractive young women on the beach could be a boost to real estate sales. He is credited with "inventing" the so-called bathing beauty. These young women are posing in the surf at Miami Beach in 1925. (COURTESY STATE ARCHIVES OF FLORIDA)

For a decade, the Ashley Gang robbed banks, made moonshine, hauled bootleg whiskey, and eluded lawmen in hideouts in the vast Everglades of southern Florida. The gang was composed of members of the family of Joe Ashley and occasional confederates. Lawmen killed Joe Ashley in January 1924. Joe's son John was killed by police in November 1924, along with gang members Ray Lynn, Handford Mobley, and Clarence Middleton. John Ashley is shown in the center of this display with his girlfriend, Laura Upthegrove. (COURTESY STATE ARCHIVES OF FLORIDA)

Indiana native Carl Fisher made millions selling automobile headlights in the early 20th century and founded the Indianapolis 500 in 1911. But his passion became building his dream city of Miami Beach, which became an icon for fun in the sun. His dream flourished and added to his wealth during the 1920s. Despite prudent money management during the boom years, however, he went broke after the Florida real estate market collapsed and the 1929 stock market crash. He died in 1939 of medical problems caused by alcoholism. (COURTESY STATE ARCHIVES OF FLORIDA)

The Volstead Act, better known as Prohibition, went into effect in 1920. The law prohibited Americans from making, selling, or transporting alcoholic beverages. But the law only succeeded in making Americans more determined to get booze, and they turned to bootleggers and moonshiners. The law was only sporadically enforced in Florida, however. In this photo, Florida lawmen have destroyed a moonshine still. (COURTESY STATE ARCHIVES OF FLORIDA)

William Jennings Bryan became the youngest man to run for president when he became the Democratic nominee at the age of 36 in 1896. He lost that race, and lost again in 1900 and 1908. He was secretary of state at the beginning of World War I in 1914, but resigned over a policy disagreement with President Woodrow Wilson in 1915. He moved to Miami in 1912 and became a passionate—and well-compensated—spokesman for Florida real estate interests during the real estate frenzy of the 1920s. His politics combined religious fundamentalism and political progressivism. He was an ardent opponent of teaching evolution in public schools. (COURTESY STATE ARCHIVES OF FLORIDA)

John Ashley, wearing an eye patch, bow tie, and white suit, is shown in this photo made at the Dade County Jail in Miami in 1915. Ashley was the central figure in the Ashley Gang, which robbed banks, made moonshine, and bootlegged whiskey in South Florida until its members were killed by lawmen in 1924. When this photo was made, Ashley was being tried in Miami for the 1911 murder of a Seminole Indian. He lost his right eye while running from police after he and other gang members robbed a bank in Stuart, Florida, in 1915. The man standing next to Ashley is another prisoner, and the third man is the jailer. The boy is the jailer's son, and the girl is the other prisoner's daughter. (ADA COATS WILLIAMS)

The war of public perception escalated on October 1, when Red Cross chairman Payne and Arthur Brisbane, the Hearst Newspapers columnist who loved being known as the world's highest-paid journalist, exchanged broadsides.

In a news release from Washington, Payne said the Red Cross's fund-raising to help 18,000 families "impoverished" by the storm was being hampered by real estate interests in Florida.

"The officials of Florida from the Governor down and the real estate operators have seriously handicapped the American National Red Cross in its efforts to provide relief for those who suffered in the hurricane that swept southern Florida on September 18 by minimizing the loss," Payne said. "The poor people who suffered are regarded as of less consequence than the hotel and tourist business in Florida."

Payne noted that the mayor of Richmond, Virginia, had heard so much about the supposedly exaggerated damage claims that he'd nearly recalled a check for $10,000 that his city had raised for the Red Cross effort.

That same day, Brisbane praised Warfield's outrageously misleading statements about hurricane damage in Florida.

Brisbane had bought ten thousand acres in Martin County, praised Warfield in an earlier column for extending his railroad in Florida, and used his prestige and fame to urge Florida officials to use public money to build a new canal that would greatly enhance the value of his holdings near Stuart. Now he praised Warfield for doing a public service by speaking the truth about what had happened in the hurricane. He urged his millions of readers not to take hurricanes too seriously, quoting the King James Version of the Bible and disparagingly referring to the powerful storm as a "tornado."

"If you are interested in Florida, do not be disturbed by that tornado any more than you would have been by the recent tornado in Denmark had you thought of moving there," he wrote. "'The wind bloweth where it [pleases],' and the earth shakes more or less everywhere. It will take more than one big wind to discourage Florida."

The war of words reached a nasty apex on Saturday, October 2, when the *Miami Tribune* accused the Red Cross of incompetency and of playing politics with its fund-raising effort.

"Through blundering officials of the American Red Cross, both locally and nationally, and because of the political ambitions and whims of certain people, a controversy criticizing Governor Martin and Mayor Romfh is raging in the newspapers," a *Tribune* editorial thundered. "The American Red Cross is being used as a tool, the sacred trust of every American to aid the distressed is being used as a political football, and Miami is being made the goat."

A national appeal for money for hurricane assistance was unnecessary and never should have been made, the *Tribune* said. "Get the money, fair or foul, rule or ruin, is the slogan of the entire nasty mess," the editorial continued.

"The public has been grossly misinformed by horrible stories, some of which this newspaper has called to the public attention," the *Tribune* concluded.

The Red Cross fired back the next day. Vice chairman James Fieser said he was deeply concerned about the "misunderstanding" regarding the need for money to help hurricane victims, noting that this was the first time a Red Cross effort to help disaster victims had been slowed by "confusion."

"As we study the situation with more care than was possible in the first days after the hurricane, we realize that Hialeah and Fort Lauderdale each present the problems of a major disaster in themselves, and that in Dade County alone there are probably families of 2,000 truck farmers in the rural sections who must have assistance," Fieser said.

That same day, Henry Baker, the Red Cross medical director in Miami, made an appeal for donations over radio station WRNY in New York City. The money was needed, he said, to help "the average man and woman and child in their communities—the small home owner, the workman, the farmer, the backbone of our civilization, who live in self-respecting self-support, but without financial reserve and bank account. The citadels of industry and business may have withstood the storm, but not so the modest homes of these people."

Baker said the hurricane "is a disaster bigger than any since the great Ohio Valley flood and the San Francisco disaster."

"America has never failed in such an emergency," he reminded listeners in closing. "Your generous gift is an important link in this bond of brotherhood."

By Tuesday, October 5, the public dispute between Florida business interests and the Red Cross had made its way onto the editorial pages of newspapers across the United States. Included in the comments was a cartoon that appeared on editorial pages of large newspapers across the nation. It showed a distraught woman standing atop a pile of rubble and calling for help, with a scolding businessman beside her, saying, "*Shhh!* Not so loud! It'll hurt business!"

On October 8, the *Wall Street Journal* jumped back into the fracas, publishing a statement by Peter O. Knight, the attorney whose clients included Warfield's Seaboard Air Line Railroad.

Knight said he "exceedingly" regretted that a controversy had arisen between the Red Cross and Florida "authorities." Because of his long residency in Florida and knowledge of the situation caused by a hurricane "in a small portion of southern Florida," Knight thought it his duty clear up the differences of opinion.

Knight then proceeded in a lawyerly fashion to essentially understate damage estimates, dispute the Red Cross's carefully compiled statistics about the number of people affected, and blame the victims for their own plight.

Knight said that as many as 18,000 people—misrepresenting the Red Cross estimate of 18,000 *families*—were homeless and needed help from the Red Cross. But, he added, their homelessness "was due to the fact that during the so-called boom thousands of people from all portions of the United States flocked to southern Florida, most of them with nothing, many of them with very little. They knew nothing about Florida conditions; purchased land indiscriminately on the installment plan; constructed thereon small cheap houses and buildings, such ones as an ordinary rainstorm would seriously damage; therefore it can be expected that with a hurricane all of them would be demolished."

Knight said the Red Cross tabulation of 18,000 families that needed assistance was "absolutely unfounded and untrue," because this would mean 90,000 people out of a state population of about 1.25 million. He added that the estimate of $100 million in damages was "simply absurd," and that the total "temporary" damage would not exceed $25 million.

A week after one of the nation's most influential newspapers allowed Knight to use its editorial page as a megaphone for what essentially was propaganda, Knight's employer, Solomon Davies Warfield, dropped a bombshell on the Red Cross effort in Florida. Warfield paid for a full-page advertisement in newspapers across the United States headlined "The Truth About Storm Damage In Florida." The ad was in the form of a personal letter to the public from Warfield as president of the Seaboard Air Line Railroad.

The letter began with Warfield's assertion that a railroad was obligated to provide information about its service area to its customers. "No agency is better qualified to gather the facts and ascertain conditions within its territory than the organization of a railroad," the letter said.

Warfield said the "good faith" of some of Florida's public officials had been questioned "by a high official of the American Red Cross because of their statements limiting the storm damage to actual conditions."

Only about 18,000 people of the "poorer classes" were left homeless by the storm, and most of these were "transients" living in flimsy campgrounds, he said.

"Polo, golf, tennis, and other amusement grounds will be ready for the coming season, including the Hialeah and other race tracks," Warfield assured readers.

Warfield closed his letter with a cheery, optimistic promise similar to the one Mayor Romfh of Miami had made earlier.

"Florida—the world's winter playground—with its unmatched climate, its fertile soil which has no superior, the length of the seasons, its freedom from the rigors of winters, all will continue to prosper and grow, and the area affected by this storm will take on a new aspect, profiting by the experience gained," he said.

The powerful blast from Warfield had a demoralizing effect on Red Cross officials trying to cope with this massive disaster. After seeing Warfield's full-page ad in the *Washington Post* on October 16, vice chairman James Fieser sat down and wrote a memo to Henry Baker, the Red Cross medical director in Miami. He was discouraged.

"The educational campaign minimizing the disaster seems to be spreading rather than diminishing," he wrote. Red Cross workers in Florida were "working in an unfriendly atmosphere," and Red Cross officials were forced to deal with "a barrage of unfavorable comment and advertising."

Fieser said he was hearing suggestions every day that the Red Cross should respond to the bad publicity, but taking the time to do so would divert them from their mission and not gain them anything.

Fieser had reached a reluctant conclusion about the Red Cross's work helping the victims of what has come to be known as the Great Miami Hurricane of 1926.

"The quicker we do our work, demobilize our staff, and get out of Florida, the better," he said.

Despite the outrageous verbal assaults on their organization, however, Red Cross workers would still be in Florida helping people who needed it well into 1927. Red Cross files in the National Archives in College Park, Maryland, show that caseworkers eventually helped 16,000 families, totaling 60,000 people. They spent about $3.45 million (more than $44 million today) on that effort. But the barrage of propaganda unleased by Romfh, Knight, and Warfield had cost the Red Cross nearly one-third of the budget they'd intended to spend on helping hurricane victims.

Like thousands of other Florida residents, Edwin Menninger was deeply invested emotionally in the belief that he was living in a paradise where prosperity was permanent. But he was unwilling to publish wild distortions about the devastation of the hurricane or scurrilous and unfounded speculation about the motives of those who were trying to help clean up the mess.

Menninger tried to buck up his readers' morale—and perhaps his own—with an editorial in the *Developer* titled "Florida Will Carry On."

Menninger cited disasters that had befallen other American cities—the hurricane that killed 9,000 people in Galveston, Texas, in 1900; a flood that had inundated Dayton, Ohio, in 1913; a fire that had destroyed downtown Baltimore in 1904; and the awful San Francisco earthquake of 1906.

As bad as these disasters were, they had led to better things for all of the cities that had been hit, Menninger said. The hurricane in Miami would do the same, he predicted.

"There will be born as there was in Baltimore and in other cities a new spirit of cooperation and initiative, and energy and will come to the front to a greater extent than in the past, and Florida will go forward in its mighty march of progress and prosperity," Menninger wrote.

CHAPTER NINE

Hope from the Swamp

In the days following the hurricane, Miami residents were dazed and edgy as they sifted through the ruins of their city, buried the dead, and tried to put their lives back together. The last thing they needed to hear was that another deadly storm was on the horizon.

But that's exactly what they heard when prankster Charles Haines went dashing through hotel lobbies shouting that another hurricane was coming.

Men panicked. Women fainted. And Charley Haines got ninety days on the chain gang.

Haines was less than a month into his sentence, however, when the real thing—another extremely powerful hurricane capable of inflicting catastrophic damage—ripped across western Cuba, turned right, and headed straight for South Florida.

The storm began on October 14, 1926, as a tropical depression off the coast of Nicaragua in the southwestern corner of the Caribbean Sea. As the windy rainstorm was slowly meandering northward and gradually gaining strength, Henry Baker, who was in charge of the Red Cross's relief effort in Miami, told the *New York Times* that, for the first time in its history, it had failed to meet its fund-raising goals to help victims of a disaster.

"Reports from all sections of the country showed that donations had practically ceased," he said.

Baker would not explain why the Red Cross had fallen short of its goals. But a memo from Red Cross national chairman John Barton Payne laid the blame at the feet of Florida governor John Martin and businessmen who had understated the losses and downplayed the damage of the September hurricane.

Meanwhile, despite the arrest of rumormongers and pranksters such as Charles Haines, hurricane panic was spreading in Miami. The word on the street was that another hurricane was going to strike Miami on Tuesday, October 19.

Hundreds of people boarded northbound trains and cranked up their tin lizzies and headed for the Dixie Highway to get out of town ahead of the storm.

"Women have been coming to my office in hysterics as the result of these rumors, and I know that many have left the city," US Weather Bureau meteorologist Richard Gray told the *New York Times*.

Gray said such reports were foolish, and he blamed "patent medicine almanacs" for publishing wildly inaccurate forecasts.

Those almanac forecasts were indeed off, but, as chance would have it, not by much.

On the evening of October 19, the tropical depression that had been browsing aimlessly across the Caribbean found a deep current of very warm water, and it did what meteorologists today refer to as "bombing out."

Feasting on the warm waters, the storm's peak winds rapidly intensified, zooming from about 90 miles an hour to 140 miles an hour in only about eighteen hours. By the morning of October 20, as its eye entered the Gulf of Batabano off the southwestern coast of Cuba, its peak winds were screaming at around 150 miles an hour.

The hurricane struck Havana around 10:45 that morning. As the vicious storm pounded its way across the ancient Cuban capital, "fishing boats floated down streets, dead cows dropped on rooftops, and houses flew overhead like birds," a survivor recalled.

Around 650 people were killed, and more than 10,000 were injured.

By early afternoon, the storm's eye had left the island. But instead of continuing its northward trek into the Gulf of Mexico, it made a sharp turn to the northeast into the Straits of Florida, the narrow waterway that separates Cuba from the Florida Keys and the Bahamas. And although the hurricane lost a little of its strength as it slowed to make its turn, its peak winds were still clocking a devastating 125 miles an hour as it settled into a northeast track. On that course, if the storm's eye wobbled even slightly to the north, its strongest winds could cross Miami. And winds of 125 miles an hour would have inflicted massive new damage on the city, undone much of what had been repaired, and been a devastating blow to boomers' efforts to rehabilitate Miami's image.

For the second time in barely a month, a pair of square black-on-red flags was raised over lighthouses, Weather Bureau offices, and post offices to signal that hurricane-force winds were expected. And again, only four days after Solomon Davies Warfield's full-page ads in newspapers across the country had assured readers that the dangers of hurricanes in Florida had been greatly exaggerated, page-one headlines in some of those same papers announced that another deadly tropical cyclone was headed for Florida.

News of the powerful storm was telegraphed to the *Miami Daily News* from Belen Observatory in Havana.

Miami mayor Edward Romfh had been among those who, only a few weeks earlier, had accused the Red Cross of overstating hurricane damage to his city. His comments had inflicted serious damage on the Red Cross's effort to raise money to help storm victims, and had contributed to the failure to meet its fund-raising goals. But with another ruinous storm at his doorstep, Romfh asked Red Cross officials to take over his city's preparations for the storm and set up shelters in the city.

The Red Cross set up aid stations throughout Miami.

The exodus from Miami escalated as hundreds of residents decided they simply could not stand the emotional strain of enduring another terrible storm. They boarded northbound trains to get as far away from the city as possible, and the Dixie Highway was clogged with northbound cars carrying women and children out of the city.

Schools and businesses closed.

"Miami Prepares to Meet Storm," headlined the afternoon *Miami Daily News* edition of Wednesday, October 20, 1926.

The evening of Wednesday, October 20, 1926, began in a frighteningly similar fashion to the awful night a month earlier. As darkness fell, winds steadily increased and rain fell in torrents.

This time, however, Miami got lucky. Although Key West, about 150 miles southwest of Miami, was lashed with 100-mile-an-hour winds as the eye passed near that city of 20,000 residents, the hurricane's eye—and its most powerful winds—stayed offshore. The outer edge of the storm still brought rain, high winds, and terrifying reminders of the earlier hurricane to Miami residents. Trees came down and fell across power lines and knocked out electricity, but fortunately, that was the worst of it.

The next day, hundreds of Miami's terrified, hurricane-weary residents gathered at the post office to watch those awful red-and-black hurricane warning flags hauled down from the flagpole. They were so delighted that they broke into a spontaneous celebration.

"The sun is shining brightly in Miami and its inhabitants, after a night of anxiety, are busily engaged in their everyday tasks," said a *Miami Daily News* editorial on Thursday afternoon, October 21. "Thursday's sunshine is emblematic of Miami's future, unmarred by threatening clouds."

Red Cross officials, however, were assembling a glum forecast as the 1926–27 tourist season approached. A few days after the October hurricane scare, Henry Baker met with other Red Cross leaders in Atlanta to discuss the progress of the agency's work in Florida.

Despite such cheery public optimism as was expressed in the *Miami Daily News*, the Red Cross leaders were skeptical about the city's immediate future. Among the topics they discussed was a prediction that tourism revenues, which had totaled about $145 million during the 1925–26 season, would drop by as much as 40 percent during the 1926–27 season, which was just around the corner. That would be devastating to small-business owners and workers who depended on tourism to pay their bills.

Unemployment was still very high, and the steep drop in tourism would mean that it would stay high during the time that it usually eased. And in the wake of the slide in real estate prices, many Florida residents were stuck with no equity in a house that was no longer worth the mortgages they were struggling to pay. In twenty-first-century parlance, their mortgages were "underwater."

Some homeowners were burdened by as many as nine mortgages. When banks stopped making loans after a third mortgage, finance companies were stepping in to provide desperately needed cash—also escalating homeowners' debts.

And even worse for the Red Cross, Baker was certain that "influential local institutions"—meaning local and state boards of real estate brokers and the Miami Chamber of Commerce—would launch a well-funded, all-out publicity campaign against the Red Cross if the agency continued to try to tell the truth about conditions in Florida.

While Red Cross leaders tried to help those who needed it and fight the headwinds of misinformation, some powerful men continued their determined effort to distort economic conditions in Florida.

The November 1926 edition of the respected journal *Review of Reviews* published essays by four business leaders who were deeply invested in Florida. The essays, collected under the heading "Florida after the Storm," were requested by the *Review of Reviews* editor, Albert Shaw, who said he'd asked the "leading men of affairs" in Florida to inform his readers of the "conditions and prospects" in the state.

The essays were written by Hamilton Holt, president of Rollins College in Orlando; Richard Hathaway Edmonds, editor of the *Manufacturers' Record*; Barron Collier, who had essentially been given his own county in 1923 by the Florida legislature after promising to complete the Tamiami Trail; and Peter O. Knight, the Tampa attorney who a few weeks earlier had taken to the pages of the *Wall Street Journal* and Arthur Brisbane's millions of readers to downplay the hurricane damage and disparage the Red Cross's efforts to raise money for storm victims.

All four writers repeated the misleading statement that the hurricane's impact on Florida had been minimal because it had affected only Miami and Moore Haven. But in reality, nearly one-third of the money driving the Florida boom was in Miami banks, and the city was leading the nation in bank clearings—that is, checks being cashed or deposited. And the city had been called "the greatest market per capita in the world today" by *Literary Digest*. So to say that Florida was fine because the hurricane had only hit Miami was like saying that since a bullet had only pierced the heart, the rest of the body was unharmed.

And the *Review of Reviews* essayists added their own touches of misdirection.

Holt, the Rollins College president, noted that "thousands of dollars" had been contributed to the Red Cross to relieve suffering in Florida, but did not mention that the Red Cross had failed to reach its fund-raising goal because of the determined campaign being waged by Warfield, Knight, and others.

Manufacturers' Record editor Edmonds said Red Cross chairman Payne had misled the nation, and accused him of disparaging "the people of Florida who went to work so vigorously, so cheerfully, and so optimistically" to rebuild after the hurricane.

Knight, the attorney who worked for Warfield, repeated his claim that damage from the storm would not exceed $25 million—even though the Miami Chamber of Commerce had publicly estimated damage at more than $100 million—and said that the only industry that had been harmed by the storm was the citrus industry. But the loss of so many citrus trees still had a silver lining because it would mean higher prices for the growers, he said.

"The tourist business . . . was not involved," Knight wrote. "There will be more tourists in Florida this winter than ever before, and by January 1 every vestige of damage, so far as the tourist business is concerned, will have disappeared."

Collier said he was moved by the "misfortune" of Miami and Moore Haven, but added: "I join Governor Martin in his just and strong condemnation of those who use the misfortunes of two cities to injure a whole commonwealth."

As 1926 drew to a close, Red Cross officials summarized their efforts in Florida, issuing on Christmas Eve a news release saying that 16,000 families totaling 60,000 people had been helped by the Red Cross effort in Florida. The Red Cross was making "an award a minute" of financial aid, and had disbursed more than $3.4 million—about $45 million in twenty-first-century dollars. Meanwhile, two of the state's largest railroads were reporting good news to their stockholders. Both the Atlantic Coast Line Railroad and the Seaboard Air Line Railroad had set records for revenue in 1926. The Atlantic Coast Line had grossed $97 million, and the Seaboard had recorded $67 million for the year.

Warfield, Seaboard's owner, was pouring money and dreams into Florida. And he'd also told Edwin Menninger's *South Florida Developer* about plans to build repair shops in Indiantown for his railroad. That would add one thousand jobs to Martin County. And in anticipation of the completion of the Tamiami Trail linking Tampa and Miami, he had inaugurated train service to Naples and other cities on the Gulf Coast.

But the crown jewel of Warfield's Florida empire was the extension of his railroad from West Palm Beach to Miami. Thanks to the new extension, the Seaboard Air Line Railroad now would offer direct connections from New York to Miami.

At 6:25 p.m. on the evening of January 5, 1927, Warfield and hundreds of businessmen and bankers boarded a southbound Seaboard Air Line train at New York's Pennsylvania Station. It was the inaugural run of a train featuring amenities that would quickly make it a legend—the Orange Blossom Special.

Additional trains—also part of the Orange Blossom Special's inaugural run—joined the New York group in Philadelphia and Baltimore. The trains chuffed southward into the night through Virginia, the Carolinas, and Georgia, carrying around six hundred well-heeled passengers who controlled millions of dollars' worth of potential investments.

Florida governor John Martin and a group of Florida dignitaries that included Tampa attorney Knight joined the celebratory caravan. They were accompanied by dozens of reporters from Florida and national news services, such as the *New York Times*, the *Philadelphia Record*, the *Atlanta Constitution*, and others.

Once the Special reached Florida, it stopped at every town and hamlet along the way. Much of Florida dropped its daily routine and turned out to welcome the train.

"School children in white summer clothes were there, singing and waving flags; farmers came from miles around, traveling in motor cars or on foot, to greet Mr. Warfield and Governor Martin," wrote a reporter for the *New York Times*. "At Fort Myers, the citizens arranged an elaborate reception, with brass bands and an automobile parade through decorated streets. There was a similar reception in Naples, which was welcoming a railroad for the first time in its history."

The celebration continued on the state's east coast. Parades, local dignitaries, and attractive young women greeted the Special at every stop. Warfield, Martin, and Knight vied to see who could kiss the most girls at each station, and a reporter for the *Miami Daily News* declared Knight the winner.

As the four trains comprising the Special neared Miami, the celebrations became more complex. At Opa-locka, developed around an Arabian theme by aviator Glenn Curtiss, the festivities included men dressed as Arabian warriors on horseback and women in harem costumes.

During the stop at Hollywood, the earthy, acerbic Knight entertained the crowd and reporters with pithy comments about the passengers from the large northern cities.

"I'm tired of that bunch of millionaires from the north who make up the first section of this train having all the glory at these receptions," Knight said. "We of the third section are just Florida crackers, but we're proud of it, and if it hadn't been for us, the financiers up ahead would never have come to Florida at all.

"One thing is certain. Those hard-boiled, cold-blooded capitalists didn't come here just because they like us or wanted to be nice. It takes fourteen cocktails to make any one of that bunch germinate the first spark of sentiment."

Reporters didn't ask Knight how he had managed to count the number of cocktails necessary to soften up a Yankee banker on a train supposedly prohibited from selling liquor.

The Orange Blossom Special arrived in Miami at dusk on January 8, hours late because of all of the celebrations along the way. Fireworks exploded as the trains rolled to a stop at a temporary Seaboard Air Line station at Seventh Street and Twentieth Avenue. At Royal Palm Park on the waterfront, the crowd was entertained by Arthur Pryor's Band. The band included more than two dozen musicians led by virtuoso trombonist Arthur Pryor, who had once so dazzled an audience of German soldiers that they had insisted on taking apart his instrument to see if it was real. The band had recorded the novelty song "The Whistler and His Dog" in late 1925, and the catchy, lilting tune was still being hummed and whistled across the nation.

The Orange Blossom Special's arrival in Miami brought a renewed sense of optimism to the city's boosters, which included the *Miami Daily News*.

"Today Miami enters upon another era of progress," the *Daily News* said in a front-page editorial on January 9, 1927.

The new Seaboard Air Line service to Miami was an indication that the erratic boom-based economy of 1925–26 was being replaced by stable growth. "Booms frequently follow railroad expansion; but railroads do not follow booms," the editorial continued.

Warfield's decision to invest heavily in South Florida was based on a careful cost-benefit analysis. And the Seaboard's benefit from its Miami extension would be income from shipping fruits and vegetables grown on land reclaimed from the Everglades, the *Daily News* said. The *South Florida Developer* predicted that the farms also would be needed to feed the thousands of workers coming to Indiantown to work at the new sawmill and train repair shop.

"When expansion of the character Miami now witnesses is consummated, we may rest assured it is only after all the risks have been carefully weighed," the *Miami Daily News* editorial said. ". . . Railroads open up undeveloped lands and create markets at the same time. That is Warfield's mission in Florida. It will be fulfilled."

Despite the new optimism among Miami boosters, however, there were stubborn signs of problems in Paradise. A few weeks after the Orange Blossom Special merrymaking, Henry Baker, the chairman of the Red Cross's relief effort in Miami, reported to the agency's national headquarters that unemployment was becoming "more acute daily."

In a January 27 report, Baker noted that families who had not needed help in the weeks immediately after the September hurricane now needed financial assistance.

"No one would expect that unemployment would be a serious problem here at this time of year," Baker wrote.

A few days later, the *Miami Herald*—one of the early deniers of serious hurricane damage—published an editorial acknowledging that there was "a great deal of actual destitution in Miami."

"Little children are actually suffering on account of lack of food," the *Herald* editorial said. "Delicate women, scores of them, have insufficient food. Men are actually going hungry, looking for any small jobs that may turn up from the proceeds of which they may help their families."

The *Herald* noted that the county's welfare board—which was responsible for providing help for those in need—had "almost ceased to function" because the county had not had the money to keep the board funded. The *Herald* editors asked "generous-minded people of Miami" to make donations to the welfare board.

Around the time that the *Herald* was seeking donations to help the city's needy, an innocuous businessman rented a bungalow for a winter vacation in Miami Beach. He said his name was Al Brown, and his business card said he was a dealer in secondhand furniture.

Brown was a beefy, jowly man with thinning black hair who might have been regarded as just another businessman who'd done well enough to afford to take several months off in the sun. But a long, nasty-looking scar on his left cheek belied his bland-sounding name and set him apart from the typical vacationers. Clearly, Brown had incurred some risks on his path to success.

In the coming months, Brown would provide a small stimulus to the ailing South Florida economy. And his presence would not go unnoticed by local officials or the national press.

By mid-February, the Red Cross was ready to fold up its tent and get out of Miami. On February 14, vice chairman James Fieser sent a special-delivery letter from Miami to Red Cross National Headquarters saying the Red Cross's mission did not include staying in Florida to help those unable to find work. Besides, they couldn't stay if they wanted to. They were out of money.

Solomon Davies Warfield was known as an autocratic business leader who could be very charming when it suited his purposes. As February turned to March and word spread that the Red Cross was pulling out of Miami, Warfield and other prominent Miami business leaders decided it was time to bury the hatchet.

On March 1, 1927, Henry Baker, the director of the Red Cross relief effort in Miami, was the guest of honor at a testimonial luncheon at the Columbus Hotel. The gathering was hosted by James Gilman, the former chairman of a citizens' committee formed to help with Miami's post-hurricane recovery.

Among the speakers who praised Baker and the Red Cross's relief effort was Miami mayor Edward Romfh, whose actions had helped to cripple the Red Cross's fund-raising effort.

Romfh said the Red Cross effort had been "magnificent," and that the city had been very lucky that Baker had been in charge.

Baker was equally magnanimous, saying that he'd been in charge of 147 disaster-relief efforts across the United States, and had never seen such a "vigorous and intelligent" local relief effort.

"There is an elusive but definite something here which I can only define as the Miami spirit," Baker said. "It is a spirit of cooperation, understanding, and vigorous determination to overcome all problems."

The following day, Baker was invited to a smaller gathering with a few of Miami's high rollers. This gathering was held at the First National Bank in the private dining room of the bank's president—Miami mayor Edward Romfh.

Warfield, the charmer, had an ulterior motive for meeting with Baker in a more private setting. He wanted to coax information from the Red Cross official. Joining Baker, Warfield, and Romfh at the lunch were *Miami Herald* publisher Frank Shutts and Glenn Curtiss, the aviator turned developer.

Baker sent a letter the following day about the meeting to Fieser, who had returned to Red Cross headquarters in Washington, DC, "The luncheon did not have to do with our disaster relief except in a rather indirect way," Baker wrote.

Baker said that the reason Warfield and the others had invited him to lunch was to ask him what he'd learned during his Red Cross work about the "financial matters of Miami and the East Coast of Florida," adding that "Mr. Warfield was quite interested in this phase of post-hurricane developments."

Baker said Warfield had asked him and the others to keep their conversation confidential, and went so far as to ask Baker not to say anything to his supervisors in Washington. Baker honored that request in his letter, but he did say that the conversation was related to "a big reclamation project" in the Everglades. He promised Fieser that he would fill in the details in a private conversation when he returned to Washington.

Baker added that Warfield had nothing but praise for the Red Cross's efforts in Florida, and invited Baker to visit his office in Washington sometime. Apparently, Warfield's determined effort to discredit the Red Cross's integrity wasn't mentioned.

Baker's private comments to his colleagues when he returned to Washington are lost to history because there's no record in the National Archives of what he said about his private meeting in Miami with Warfield, Romfh, and the others about the 1926 hurricane in the Red Cross files. But it's likely that completing the construction of the Tamiami Trail was one of the Everglades "reclamation" projects they discussed.

And another tycoon was pouring money into that project.

Barron Collier had persuaded the Florida legislature to essentially give him his own county—a county larger than the state of Delaware—in 1923 in exchange for promising to complete the Tamiami Trail through the Everglades and his namesake county. If Collier hadn't realized how difficult it would be to keep that promise when he made it, he certainly realized it three years later. And he may have been wondering if he'd have been better off promising to build a road to the moon instead.

Today, the Tamiami Trail, 274 miles between Tampa and Miami, is part of US 41. Much of the Trail is lined with strip malls, shopping centers, franchise restaurants, convenience stores, and gated communities. And even along the stretches where development is restricted and the Everglades are relatively undisturbed, a motorist speeding along the wide asphalt highway at sixty miles an hour is not likely to notice much of what makes that stretch of road so unusual.

But it is unusual—in fact, it's one of the most unique stretches of highway in the world.

"It leaps like a flung lance, blue-black in the blazing distance, shimmering with a mirage, clear and clean across the whole of South Florida," author Marjory Stoneman Douglas said of the Tamiami Trail in her classic work, *The Everglades: River of Grass*. "Along it buses thunder between Miami and Fort Myers and Tampa, and automobiles and huge trucks. The road roars with their passing, but after that the silence flows back again, the ancient inviolable silence of the Everglades."

The Trail "reaches and vanishes from sky to sky; from dawns of pale silver and tangerine over the grape-colored ramparts of Gulf Stream clouds to sunsets in the blue winters like explosions of orange and bronze and brass," Douglas wrote.

"People rushing across it look and see nothing," she continued. "'But there's nothing,' they say. They see neither the Everglades nor the Trail's drama."

For all of the exotic wildlife in the Everglades, it is indeed surprisingly quiet. Silence and stillness are mandatory for a first-time visitor to even begin to comprehend this strange and wonderful place.

There's a twenty-four-mile remnant of a branch of the original Tamiami Trail just off the modern US 41, about forty miles west of Miami. The road was rebuilt in places after Hurricane Wilma sent floodwaters across it and washed out some sections in 2005. The road remains unpaved and still resembles the Tamiami Trail as it was when it was opened nearly a century ago.

A canal, created when the limestone underlying the Everglades muck was used to build the original roadbed, runs parallel to the Trail.

It's not unusual to see an alligator sunning on the far bank of the canal. If you get out of your car to take a photo of the gator, you begin to absorb the silence. And if you remain quiet and still and allow your eyes and your consciousness to adjust to the surroundings, sometimes you see the wildlife.

Of course, it takes no adjustment to see the small, jet-black mosquitoes that immediately surround you. After a few moments of stillness, perhaps you'll see turtles on a log; or a huge frog whose natural camouflage makes it nearly invisible in its surroundings; or several otters somberly watching you from the canal in the near distance; or a motionless anhinga perched on a limb, its wings spread to dry; or a thick, dark water moccasin gliding through the black water.

You don't see these things when you're in a hurry.

Suddenly a splash will break the silence. A turtle or a frog has dropped into the water, and instantly alligators you had no idea were so near rush from the grass and flora and hit the water in frenzied pursuit of whatever made the splash. That's the drama Douglas alluded to.

You hurry back to your car a bit shaken as you realize unseen deadly predators were watching you the entire time you were standing there.

The wilderness seems endless and impenetrable and untamable. And Barron Collier promised to build a road through the wildest part of it.

By September 1926, work on the Trail had been starting and stopping for ten years, and many people doubted it would ever be completed. Collier's work crews still had thirty-one miles to go to reach the Dade County line.

The national publicity about the September 1926 hurricane's devastation in Miami may have spurred Collier to push to finish the trail as quickly as possible.

Collier had made his fortune in advertising, and he understood how a public image affects business. With Miami on the ropes after the storm, Collier and other Florida boosters knew something was needed to boost morale and redirect the nation's perception of Florida away from images of death and destruction.

Otto Neal, who worked on the Tamiami Trail construction project, recalled that in late September 1926—when newspapers were full of stories about the hurricane's devastation—he was told to report to the office of David Copeland, a former US Navy engineer that Collier had hired to supervise the work.

Copeland asked Neal if they could push the road to the Dade County line by April 1, 1927. "He said that it HAD to be done," Neal told the *Collier County News* shortly before the Tamiami Trail opened in late April 1928.

Neal told Copeland that he thought they could make the deadline, but suggested that another piece of heavy equipment known as a "walking dredge" should be put on the job.

Within a month, Collier had tracked down one of the remarkable contraptions, bought it, and shipped it to the job site.

At first glance, the walking dredge, built in Bay City, Michigan, looked immovable. Seen in profile, the machine, made of steel beams, could be said to vaguely resemble a giant praying mantis. It was essentially a large scoop attached to a steel frame. The machine, which now sits at Collier-Seminole State Park near Naples, was so ingeniously designed that in 1993 it was designated a National Historic Mechanical Engineering Landmark by the American Society of Mechanical Engineers.

That designation gave the walking dredge the same historic significance as the *Saturn V* rocket that carried men into space between 1967 and 1972.

The engine that powered the dredge sat on a large wooden platform on the steel frame, which was about forty feet wide by about thirty feet long. The operator's controls were in front of the engine, and the engine and operator were protected by a shedlike wooden shelter with a tin roof.

The platform and frame were supported by four wooden "shoes" at each corner of the machine. Two more shoes were at the center of the frame. Using a system of cables and pulleys, the operator could lift the four corner shoes off the ground so that the weight was temporarily supported by the middle shoes, and thus move the frame and platform forward about ten feet.

A long boom in front of the platform supported a one-cubic-yard steel bucket with manganese teeth. The bucket could scoop up about 2,800 pounds of rock with each bite.

But it was a long, grueling, and dangerous process to reach the point where the dredge could scoop up chunks of limestone and pile up the rock to be used for the roadbed. And it took a special kind of construction worker to plunge into the Everglades to build a road.

Accounts vary about how many men died building the Tamiami Trail. Meece Ellis, who worked on the construction project for eight years, told the *Orlando*

Sentinel in 1998 that only one man was killed. That man died when he fell off the platform of the dredge and hit his head on the bucket, Ellis said.

But other other accounts say that men died from construction accidents, alligator attacks, and snakebites.

Many men who hired on with the construction project were former farmhands from Georgia. The state's cotton crop had been devastated by the boll weevil in the mid-1920s, and the south Georgia farm boys had heard that workers were needed to build the Trail. They were willing to work and live in horrendous conditions for a few dollars a day, plus room and board.

The men had to literally take on the Everglades with just a few tools and their bare hands. And they surely saw the sights that had prompted Dr. Jacob Motte to describe the Glades as "a most hideous region" in 1837.

"First a crew went forward through sawgrass and water and rocky hammocks with axes and machetes, cutting a trail," Douglas wrote. "They worked up to the armpits in water, tormented with mosquitoes in the season, always watchful for rattlesnakes and the uncounted dark heads of moccasins. They lived, ate, and slept in muck and water."

The men lived in rolling sheds that were moved along as the work progressed. It took men of unusual toughness and determination to stick with this type of construction and see it through to the end.

At one point, Collier was asked how many shifts he had at work building the Tamiami Trail.

Three, he replied—one shift on the road down from Tampa looking for work, one shift working on the construction project, and one shift who'd quit the project and were going back to Tampa.

"The men on the job were wonderful," Otto Neal told the *Collier County News* in 1928. "Many would work all night Saturday and Sunday to get their machines in perfect order for the new attack Monday. The men seemed to realize the proportion of the work and the benefits that would be derived by the travelling public and wanted to see the thing through. They did their part—and they did it exceptionally well."

Undoubtedly there was some truth to Neal's glowing recollection of his fellow workers. But the men who built the Tamiami Trail were not saints.

Ray Crews, who would become the father of Harry Crews, a legendary writer and instructor at the University of Florida, followed a childhood friend from Georgia to join a Tamiami Trail construction crew. He was seventeen years old.

"They were not violent men, but their lives were full of violence," Harry Crews later wrote about his father's experience. "When Daddy first went down to the Everglades, he started on a gang that cut the advance right-of-way and, consequently, was out of the main camp for days, at times for more than a week."

During one of their expeditions away from the camp, Ray Crews was nearly killed when a steel cable broke. It looked like an accident, but the teenager was certain that it was deliberate.

"When he almost got killed working out there on the gang, [his friend] Cecil almost killed a man because of it," Harry Crews wrote. "Daddy's foreman was an old man, grizzled, stinking always of chewing tobacco and sweat and whiskey, and known through the construction company as a man mean as a bee-stung dog. He didn't have to dislike you to hurt you, even cripple you."

There were few comforts for the construction gang, most of them rough young men with no outlet for their hormones. Since Ray Crews could not have what he wanted, he tried to want what he could have, his son wrote.

Ray Crews worked at that job for six years, and one of the few times he left the swamp was to seek treatment in the town of Arcadia for a case of gonorrhea after an ill-considered tryst with a woman—whose name he never learned—who'd snuck into the work camp.

"He had not wanted her, but they had been in the swamp for three years," Harry Crews wrote. "They worked around the clock, and if they weren't working or sleeping, their time was pretty much spent drinking or fighting or shooting gators."

Someone had a camera, and when they had a few moments, Ray Crews and his friends shot photos of their adventures deep in the swamp.

Moonshine was another source of diversion for the construction gangs. And it wasn't hard to find. The late Ashley Gang had not operated the only stills in the Everglades.

Ellis, the former dredge operator, admitted seventy years later that he kept a jug of moonshine at hand on his machine.

Roan Johnson was another young Georgian who worked on the Trail. He left his home in Quitman, a few miles north of the Florida border, in 1926 to join a cousin working on the construction crew. He was eighteen.

Like all new hires, Johnson started out working on the crew that hacked through the woods and swamp to lay out the right-of-way for the Trail.

"I remember the water was everywhere . . . clear, clear water, just everywhere," he told the *Miami Herald* in 2003.

The men constantly had to pull off their boots and dump water out of them, Johnson said.

Johnson also remembered the insects—hordes of horseflies and mosquitoes so thick that it was like the construction workers "had stumbled into a biblical plague."

At night, mosquito netting protected the men's bunks. The nights were "dark as only a swamp can be dark," Crews wrote.

Johnson said the construction workers didn't worry too much about the presence of alligators.

"You knew they were there, but they didn't bother you," he told the *Herald*.

Still, foremen slung high-powered rifles across their shoulders and constantly scanned the woods and swamps for danger while their men worked.

The men were fed in the work camps, but Meece Ellis said the workers often didn't eat the meat that was provided because by the time it reached the camp, it had gone bad. So the workers bought wild game such as turkeys, wild hogs, and deer from Seminole Indians who lived in the Everglades.

Occasionally, the scent of fresh meat enticed Florida panthers—a smaller subspecies of the American cougar that lives only in South Florida—to prowl around the camp.

The work gang that followed the crew clearing the right-of-way laid down a crude sort of railroad, using cypress logs for crossties and rails. A drilling machine had been rigged up to ride this cypress railroad. The wheels were automobile tire rims, which fitted over the logs so the drill could be pulled across the wet, soggy muck.

"Sometimes the drills stuck in the mud and there would be days of back-breaking man-labor, with heavy hand jacks, to set them up again," Marjory Stoneman Douglas wrote.

It's hard to imagine that the soggy Everglades has a base of solid rock beneath the black water and muck, but it does. And engineers eventually realized that the only way to build a road through that swamp was to clear away the muck and build the road on top of the limestone that lay beneath the water, muck, and saw grass.

So the drilling crew dug holes every one hundred feet—thousands of holes. The men who worked behind the drill crew led ox teams pulling wagons of dynamite on the cypress railroad. They dropped dynamite into those holes. Every so often, the workers backed well away from the recently drilled holes, and the dynamite was ignited.

From late 1926 until the Tamiami Trail was completed in 1928, more than two million sticks of dynamite were used to break up Everglades limestone. In its November 1928 issue, *Explosives Engineer* magazine reported that the Tamiami Trail construction crew was using about twenty tons of dynamite per mile.

After each blast, the walking dredge was brought up, and the operator scooped up the limestone fragments, 2,800 pounds at a time, and piled them alongside the canal that was formed by the explosions.

The limestone was crushed and compacted and eventually became a surprisingly smooth road. Working under these awful conditions, the construction crews built a mile or two of road each month.

On April 10, 1927, Collier's construction gang achieved a milestone—they reached the Dade County line.

"Just ten days behind the schedule that we set for ourselves, and I tell you, that isn't so bad," Otto Neal proudly told the *Collier County News*. "After that we dug our way four miles on through the other side of the Dade County line to meet the dredges coming from the east coast, and the most difficult rock of all was found in this four-mile stretch in Dade County."

It was around this time that Ray Crews and his friend Cecil quit their jobs with the Tamiami Trail construction crew and headed back to Georgia.

They had money in their pockets, and each had a gold watch engraved with their name and "Pioneer Builder of the Tamiami Trail."

With a bottle of whiskey on the floorboard of a Model T Ford, Crews and his friend took nearly three weeks to amble up the Dixie Highway from Miami to Jacksonville.

"In the car with him as they drove, there was a shoebox full of pictures of my daddy with five or six of his buddies, all of them holding whiskey bottles and pistols and rifles and coons and leashed alligators out here in the rugged dug-out sea of sawgrass and mangrove swamp through which they had built the Tamiami Trail," Harry Crews wrote. "His is the gun that is always drawn; his is the head that is turned back under the whiskey bottle."

They had been deep in the swamp while the real estate speculation mania had swept across Florida and crested, and it had started to ebb by the time they finally came out of the Everglades. And while Florida's economic conditions probably held little interest for two young men with money in their pockets, time on their hands, a bottle of booze, and years of pent-up libido, there were deepening signs of trouble all around them.

About the same time that Ray Crews and his friend Cecil started their leisurely trip up the Florida coast, a heavily guarded armored car left Miami, bound for West Palm Beach. It was carrying $2 million in cash.

Miami banks were sending the money to prevent three West Palm Beach banks from failing.

The *New York Times* of March 8, 1927, reported that banks in Palm Beach County had been struggling since shortly before the hurricanes of September and October 1926. Bankers in Miami feared a domino effect that would drag down more banks if they didn't step in and help.

Three banks in Palm Beach County had failed in June 1926, the *Times* reported. The continued slump in real estate, an upheaval in local politics, and the recent failure of another bank "have created a feeling of unrest and lack of confidence resulting in persistent and continual withdrawals on the part of depositors," the *Times* said.

The First American Bank and Trust Company, one of the banks teetering on the brink of failure in March 1927, had been hemorrhaging deposits, losing more than $10.5 million in withdrawals in less than a year.

"Consistent withdrawals averaging $1 million a month brought deposits in The First American Bank and Trust Company from $13.5 million down to less than $3 million in ten months' time and was responsible for its failure to open this morning," the *Times* reported.

The slumping real estate market also caused problems for smaller investors, including a star Major League baseball player.

On March 16 at the Boston Braves' spring training camp in St. Petersburg, first baseman Jacques Fournier—who had a reputation for being as quick with his fists as he was with his bat—punched out a man who tried to talk to him after an exhibition game against the New York Giants. Unfortunately for Fournier, the man he clipped on the jaw was a deputy sheriff trying to serve him with a court summons.

"The version I got was that [the man] didn't announce himself nor his intentions but proceeded to get in an argument with Fournier," Braves manager Dave Bancroft told reporters. "My first baseman resented his manner and punched him."

Fournier was being sued for $5,000 by a real estate firm in Sarasota. Fournier had put down a binder on some real estate in Sarasota, Bancroft said. "Later he decided to call the deal off, and my understanding is that both parties agreed," he said. "I suppose the other party figured he could hold him to the contract."

"Fournier did not know he was socking an officer, and furthermore, he thought the whole matter was settled long ago," Bancroft said. "A hearing on the charges has been set for next week in Sarasota, but we hope to fix it up before that."

Bancroft kept his slugger out of jail by posting a $1,000 bond and guaranteeing that Fournier would show up in court.

One Florida commodity whose demand and prices had not been affected by the real estate downturn was whiskey. Fierce—and sometimes deadly—battles still were being fought between bootleggers and the Coast Guard off the Florida coast.

On August 7, 1927, Horace Alderman and his partner Robert Weech took on a load of booze at Bimini, the westernmost island of the Bahamas, and headed back to Florida in broad daylight. They were spotted by a Coast Guard patrol about thirty-four miles off Fort Lauderdale. The two bootleggers were captured, but three Coast Guard crewmen were killed in a struggle with Alderman.

Alderman would be convicted of murder and, in keeping with the maritime tradition of execution, hanged, but the jury that convicted him also rebuked the Coast Guard for the tactics it was using against rumrunners.

Florida boosters, including Edwin Menninger, were looking for ways to reassure themselves about their stumbling economy. In late September 1927, Menninger met briefly with Solomon Davies Warfield in New York, and on October 3 he had a longer meeting with Warfield in Baltimore. Warfield told Menninger he'd try to stop by Stuart during a trip to Florida he'd planned for mid-October.

But Warfield had to cancel his trip. He was feeling a lot of discomfort because of a double hernia, and on October 12 he was admitted to Union Hospital in Baltimore for surgery.

On October 21, while Warfield was still in the hospital, Menninger's *South Florida Developer* reported that the Seaboard Air Line Railroad's plans were going to be a major boost to Martin County and Florida. Warfield's railroad had moved its Florida headquarters from West Palm Beach to Indiantown. The company also transferred its maintenance and repair crews from Wildwood to Indiantown.

The *Developer* said that Eugene Kifer, vice president of the Land Company of Florida and a land agent for Seaboard, told an audience in nearby West Palm

Beach that Stuart and other cities would "reap great benefits from the development of Indiantown and its farm lands."

Kifer said that Seaboard had already spent about $1.9 million—more than $25 million in twenty-first-century dollars—on its plans for Indiantown, and they were just getting started. Seaboard's work in and around Indiantown already had prompted construction of housing, a school, and a hotel, the *Developer* said.

Seaboard also sent agents to large cities in the Northeast and Midwest to speak to audiences about the company's plans for Florida, and those lectures had prompted hundreds of people to move to Indiantown, Kifer said. The company would spend $500,000—about $6.6 million today—advertising its efforts in a national advertising campaign, he said.

"Mr. Kifer urged the abandonment of any doubt as to the successful future of the state," the *Developer* said.

Only a week after the *Developer*'s confident prediction of prosperity in Martin County and Florida, however, came stunning news. Solomon Davies Warfield was dead.

Warfield's doctor told the *New York Times* that Warfield's recovery from hernia surgery had been "uneventful," and that around 6:30 p.m. on October 24, he'd been sitting up in bed, chatting with a nurse and a vice president of Seaboard.

Suddenly, Warfield lost consciousness. Physicians rushed to his bedside, but there was nothing they could do. A blood clot had formed in Warfield's heart, and he was dead.

Edwin Menninger looked for optimism in the face of what he realized could be a disaster for Martin County.

"Stuart as a community will feel this blow, coming as it does when it was known to be Mr. Warfield's policy to extend the Seaboard into this city," Menninger wrote on the *South Florida Developer*'s editorial page on October 28. "But doubtless the policies already outlined will be carried out and other men will be raised up to continue the great work of this mastermind in railroad building."

The Seaboard Air Line Railroad had sunk too much money into its plans for Florida and Martin County to walk away after Warfield's death, Menninger wrote.

CHAPTER TEN

Mr. Brown in Paradise

Sunsets are routinely spectacular in the Everglades.

As the sun descends, its slanting rays splash colors across the western horizon that span the visible spectrum, from reds and yellows and oranges and pinks nearest the horizon to greens and shades of blue higher in the sky. The departing sun's rays also touch the clouds, lighting their undersides with flaming reds.

There's usually an expanse of water somewhere that reflects the sky, so that heaven and Earth become, for a few minutes, a riot of color.

Maybe the Everglades sunset lifted the spirits of the Boston Braves on March 27, 1928. The Braves had absorbed an 11–2 drubbing from the Philadelphia Athletics in a spring-training exhibition game in Fort Myers. After the game, the Braves players boarded a bus for a historic trip to Miami, where they would play an exhibition game the following day against the Brooklyn Dodgers.

Their bus would be one of the first vehicles to make the trip over the Tamiami Trail through the Everglades from Florida's Gulf Coast to its Atlantic coast. The general public wouldn't be able to use the Trail until late April, so the Braves' management had to get special permission.

Although the Tamiami Trail supposedly was going to open in less than a month, it was far from completed. In some places, large boulders still lay on the road. Potholes and rough spots were a problem. Still, the Braves arrived in Miami late that night and squared off against the Dodgers at three p.m. the following day at Miami's Tatum Field.

The Boston-Brooklyn matchup was only an exhibition game, but Miami's boosters were confident that a large crowd at the ballpark might prompt the Braves and the Dodgers to move their spring-training camp from Florida's west coast to Miami or a nearby city on the peninsula's east coast.

"The attendance at the exhibition games is a big item toward defraying the expenses, and the ball club owners realize that in the well-populated east coast the crowds will be better, because of the fact that this coast is a drawing card for the sporting element of the nation," the *Miami Daily News* said on the day of the game. "It is here that the vacationists flock, and it is here that the big leaguers receive the proper attention from the sporting element."

Brooklyn won the game, 9–0, but intermittent rain held down attendance.

Despite the untimely death of Solomon Davies Warfield a few months earlier, Edwin Menninger was still bullish on Florida's future. Menninger and many other Florida boosters were convinced that the good times would return when the Tamiami Trail opened.

"If Adam and Eve could have seen Florida, they might not have mourned the loss of Eden," Menninger wrote in the January 13, 1928, edition of the *South Florida Developer*.

Menninger said he'd been registering at a hotel in Philadelphia recently when a woman standing near him overheard that he was from Florida. "Oh, I am so sorry for you folks down there in Florida," the woman said to him. "You are having such a hard time. People are selling their automobiles to get money to come back north."

Menninger told the woman he had no idea what she was talking about.

"Florida people are not so 'hard up' as many northern people seem to think they are," he wrote in the *Developer*. "There has been a depression, to be sure, but not anything like the extent that is imagined over the country."

Menninger said Florida residents probably lived better than residents of any other state. "This is a wonderfully good country for moneymaking—more so than outsiders yet realize—and the majority of the people here are accustomed to good incomes," he wrote. "What would be called hard times here would be called good times in some other sections of the country."

And better times were coming for Stuart, Martin County, and Florida. Menninger also reported that the Brown-Cummer Company, a bond house in Wichita, Kansas, had agreed to buy $1 million worth of bonds from the St. Lucie Inlet Commission to pay for deepening the channel of the St. Lucie Inlet. Deepening the channel to allow oceangoing ships would be a major step in Stuart's ambitions to surpass Miami and Savannah as a deepwater port. The contract for the work was awarded to United Dredging Company of New York City in January 1928. Plans called for the channel to be two hundred feet wide and twenty feet deep.

But bad news came on the heels of the announcement about the dredging work. The great industrial city in western Martin County would not happen. The Seaboard Air Line Railroad closed its offices and railroad shops in Indiantown on February 3 and moved its operations to Tampa.

Still, the 1927–28 tourist season was getting off to a roaring start. The *Stuart Daily News* reported on January 5, 1928, that about ninety thousand visitors had entered Florida since November, and two months later Edwin Menninger reported in the *South Florida Developer* that a tourist camp in Stuart was doing a booming business. "There are more tourists in Stuart this winter than ever before," he noted.

Shrewd observers outside Florida also thought they perceived a return to better times.

In January 1928, humorist Will Rogers said he'd been avoiding jokes at Florida's expense for more than two years because of the state's difficulties.

"But I have just seen the state and noticed conditions down here now, and my sympathy is getting back to the old envy again," he wrote in his nationally syndicated column. "With this climate Florida needs the sympathy of no one, and the jokes of no one can hurt it."

Those improving conditions had drawn a shady but charismatic winter visitor to Miami, and he was becoming pals with the son of a former mayor of Miami. Their friendship would cause quite a stir in the city during the 1927–28 season.

Parker Henderson, who was mayor of Miami in 1917, probably had high hopes for his teenage son's future when he enrolled young Parker Jr. at Georgia Military Academy. The school advertised itself as "The South's Most Splendidly Equipped Prep School" where "careful, individual attention is given to each student."

The school, in the Blue Ridge foothills just outside Atlanta, boasted that it could prepare young men for careers in business, engineering, and other professions. And it offered "an ideal social and moral atmosphere" to shape the character of its students.

But a few years after Parker Henderson Jr. finished his studies, there were indications that maybe he hadn't fully absorbed the benefits of the academy's salubrious environment.

In August 1927, shortly after his father's death, the junior Henderson, at the age of twenty-four, signed a five-year lease to operate the Ponce de Leon Hotel in downtown Miami.

Henderson told the *Miami Daily News* that the hotel would open under his management in time for the 1927–28 tourist season, and that he intended to run a "first-class commercial house."

Henderson pledged "not to rob the public." But he said nothing about not deceiving them.

Not long after Henderson took over management of the Ponce de Leon, a businessman who'd apparently done very well selling secondhand furniture came to him to negotiate a deal for renting a suite of rooms on the top floor of the hotel. Henderson was fascinated by the swarthy, affable tenant who loved wearing colorful suits and was known to hand out $100 bills like they were after-dinner mints.

When he first arrived in Miami, the so-called furniture dealer had said his name was Al Brown, but by January 1928 he'd decided to drop the alias. His name was Al Capone, known in some circles as "Scarface," and his business was, as he put it, providing the public with what it wanted.

What the public wanted—what they still wanted after eight years of Prohibition—was booze, and lots of it. Capone provided it for them, and he was rewarded handsomely. In 1928 he was making money like he had a license to print it.

Only a handful of people in the United States could dole out cash like Capone. His income in 1927 alone has been estimated at $105 million—nearly $1.4 billion in twenty-first-century dollars. He did have a sizable overhead—everyone from truck drivers and warehouse workers to cops and judges were on his payroll—but his income was, after all, tax-free.

Capone boldly dropped his alias on the morning of January 10. Accompanied by a friend that the *Miami Daily News* couldn't or wouldn't identify, Capone walked into the lobby of the Miami Police Department and asked to see police chief Leslie Quigg. After he was shown into Quigg's office, word raced around the neighborhood that Al Capone was having a sit-down with the cops. When Capone came out of Quigg's office a few minutes later, he was surrounded by reporters and police officers.

Capone "stuffed his hands deep into the pockets of his neatly creased blue serge trousers and beamed affectionately at the welcoming committee of bluecoats and newspapermen," the *Daily News* reported. He was at his genial best as he talked to the crowd.

He sidestepped questions about whether he'd left Chicago because gangland warfare had erupted in that city. "I'm down here for a rest and here I'm going to stay," he said.

He was asked about a recent quick trip to—and hasty exit from—Los Angeles.

"When I got in, a bunch of the boys met me at the train," Capone said. "Some of them must have had guns on their hips and the police didn't like that, so they thought I was a bad moral influence or something. They had me all wrong there, and I'm glad to say my reception here has been quite different."

Noting that Miami's climate was "more healthful than Chicago's and warmer than California," Capone said he'd sought a meeting with Quigg to assure the city's top cop that he was in town only for a vacation and had no intention of setting up shop.

He also threw a bouquet to the city's cash-starved real estate brokers.

"I like Miami so well that I'm going to vacation here all winter," Capone said. "In fact, I expect my wife, mother, and child in on the train this afternoon, and we plan to buy a home either in Coral Gables or Miami Beach."

Capone had been studying the Florida real estate market, and he let it be known that he intended to make a few investments.

"I believe now is the time to buy down here, and I'm thinking of going into the market rather heavily," he said. "I don't believe there will be any sensational climb in values for five years, but I'm contented to wait that long."

Police chief Quigg told reporters he saw no reason why Capone should not be treated the same as any other winter visitor, the *Daily News* said.

Eyeing the large crowd that had gathered outside the police station, Capone and his friend slipped quietly out a side door and left.

Capone made quite an impression on Miami. But his presence there stirred deeply mixed feelings among the city's business and tourism boosters.

His name had become a household word, and the fact that a man as famous as Al Capone was spending the winter in Miami would be an indicator that maybe things were getting a little better in Florida. And his declaration that he intended to invest heavily in Florida real estate undoubtedly sent a surge of joy through some of the city's businessmen.

But Capone also linked Miami with Chicago's notorious organized crime syndicate. In 1928, Chicago's gangsters—including those who worked for Capone—were getting mentioned in newspapers quite often because the lives of so many of them were being suddenly and violently ended in gangland warfare. And when the newspapers wrote about the violence in Chicago, they inevitably noted that Capone had left the city and was spending the winter in Miami.

To some readers, that may have added to Miami's mystique. To others, it only confirmed their conviction that Miami was the capital of sin and corruption.

There was, of course, obvious irony and no small amount of hypocrisy in Miami's indignity over Capone's winter residence. He was, hands down, the nation's most famous bootlegger. He had made his immense wealth by flaunting laws and tapping into the bottomless market for booze created by Prohibition.

Florida's tourism boosters made a selling point of the fact that the state's law enforcement officials—especially in Miami—didn't trouble themselves too much with enforcing Prohibition. That was the Coast Guard's worry. Coast Guard patrol boats made occasional arrests on the high seas, and occasionally a bootlegger trying to come ashore up the coast from Miami was unlucky enough to be spotted by a local sheriff who was eyeing the next election. And there had been the Coast Guard's spectacular sundown shoot-out with bootlegger Red Shannon during a Flamingo Hotel tea dance two years earlier.

But it was obvious that bootleggers making runs from the Bahamas to Florida almost always got through.

Capone's presence in Miami marked a turning point in South Florida's criminal element and was a milestone in its growth and the public image it was projecting. In the early days of the wild real estate speculation and remarkable population growth, when an unprecedented amount of money was flowing into South Florida, the criminals—such as the ill-fated Ashley Gang—were homegrown crackers who used their resourcefulness, skills, and knowledge of the local terrain to outwit and outrun local cops.

Those criminals were daring opportunists who often acted on the spur of the moment, robbing a bank, running a still, and selling moonshine whiskey, or hijacking a bootlegger on the high seas making a run from the Bahamas back to Florida. When the cops chased them, they melted into the Everglades.

And while their crimes netted them impressive profits by the standards of the day, they were pickpockets compared to Al Capone and his ruthless, highly organized, and efficient criminal machine. Miami police undoubtedly realized that when Al Capone showed up, their days of chasing clever moonshiners and rowdy stickup artists were over. Now they were facing a shrewd, sophisticated, and tough opponent who had more resources, more weapons, and more manpower at his command than they could ever squeeze out of a harried city council always worried about property tax rates and the next election. And the new criminal also was represented by skillful, well-paid attorneys.

Despite Miami's pride in its reputation as a city untroubled by the annoying rules that restricted the rest of the country, much of Miami's officialdom was piqued that Al Capone was enjoying their wonderful winter weather. And Parker Henderson Jr., educated in old-fashioned morals and manners at Georgia Military Academy, was enthralled by the dapper gangster's blend of magnetic personal charm and ice-cold calculation. He loved being on the periphery of Capone's dark, violent world and perhaps being allowed to call Capone by the nickname "Snorky," a reference to his stylish, expensive wardrobe and a privilege reserved for only his closest friends. Since Capone wanted to maintain a low profile in Miami, Henderson was glad to help him avoid public scrutiny by doing small favors, such as running errands and some occasional shopping.

When Capone's associates in Chicago wired money to him, Henderson went to the Western Union office in Miami Beach. There, he would accept a money transfer for "Albert Costa," disguising his handwriting to sign for the telegram.

Henderson made a lot of trips to the Western Union office in the winter of 1927–28. During Capone's six-month stay, he received wire transfers from Chicago totaling $73,800, or just under $1 million in twenty-first-century dollars. Henderson duly collected Capone's walking-around money and delivered it to him.

Around mid-January, Capone called Henderson to his room and asked him to do a favor. He handed him a wad of cash and asked him to buy a dozen guns and bring them to his room. Henderson dutifully trotted off to a hardware store, bought a dozen pistols, and brought them back to Capone's room. But the room was empty.

Henderson put the guns on the bed and left. When he checked back a little later, the guns were gone. Concerned, he mentioned it to Capone later, but Capone told him not to worry about it.

Capone's presence in the Ponce de Leon turned into a financial bonanza for Henderson and his staff. Every night, Capone would order the hotel dining room to prepare enough food for a banquet.

"He would order food for about fifty people, and probably there would be only about seven or eight at the table," Henderson said later. "When we would present the check, Capone would refuse to pay it unless we doubled it. When we would abide by his wishes, he would pull out a large bill and the waiters would keep the change."

The dining room had been losing money until Capone moved in. During his stay, it became highly profitable.

There were other benefits for Henderson. The *New York Times* later noted that Henderson had "a liking for the company of celebrities and . . . was keen for racing or other sports with a percentage of uncertainty in them." His new friendship with Capone gave him plenty of opportunities to indulge in those interests.

Capone showed his appreciation for Henderson's friendship with lavish presents, including a diamond-studded belt buckle.

Henderson was also occasionally called upon to host Capone's friends from Chicago and show them the town.

Around the same time of Capone's lavish spending at the Ponce de Leon, the US Coast Guard began assembling patrol craft at nearby Fort Lauderdale and tightened its blockade of bootleggers trying to slip into Miami with whiskey from the Bahamas. The enforcement was so effective that no booze entered Miami during the week of January 9 through January 13, and prices of bootlegged whiskey skyrocketed.

"Since the first patrol craft of the coast guard forces departed from the concentration base at Fort Lauderdale for duty along the coast, no rum runners have been able to slip by the line of the dry navy, according to information," the *Miami Daily News* reported. "Six liquor boats were known to have started away from Bimini in the Bahamas Tuesday night with cargoes for delivery in and around Biscayne Bay. Five of those craft are said to have been captured."

But the crackdown had nothing to do with any renewed, long-term commitment to stopping the flow of alcohol into Miami. The Coast Guard was cracking the whip because President Calvin Coolidge's train was going to stop in Miami for an hour or so on Friday, January 14. The president was en route to Key West, where he would board a US warship to sail to Cuba for the Pan-American Conference in Havana. The Coast Guard didn't want any rumrunners dashing across Biscayne Bay while the president of the United States was watching.

About one hundred thousand spectators had gathered along the eight-mile route followed by Coolidge's motorcade. For a taciturn man sometimes called "Silent Cal," Coolidge was effusive in his praise of Miami.

A reporter duly jotted down the president's comments as Coolidge noted that Miami's skyline "greatly resembles the Battery of New York." The president was impressed by the city's many fine hotels, and amazed that the luxuriant foliage in Bayfront Park had been grown in less than eighteen months since the 1926 hurricane had denuded the park. He also commented on the many steamships and speedboats in Biscayne Bay.

"And Miami is only thirty-one years old!" he exclaimed near the end of his brief tour. "I understand why you call it the 'Magic City.' I cannot imagine a more beautiful climate than we have enjoyed this afternoon."

Not long after Coolidge's train headed south for Key West, the bootleggers' business was back to normal.

On January 17, Al Capone moved from the Ponce de Leon Hotel to a rented villa on North Pine Tree Drive in Miami Beach. About that same time, Hearst columnist Arthur Brisbane was on an eastbound train that had just left Chicago. Brisbane had learned of the gangland war in that city.

As the train rattled through rain near Elkhart, Indiana, Brisbane worked on his "Today" column.

"This morning attention turns to the Chicago gangster war, going on while 'Scarface Al' Capone is resting in Florida," Brisbane wrote.

Brisbane told the story of Harry Fuller, a foolish young man who tried to take advantage of Capone's absence by organizing a robbery of one of Capone's trucks carrying illegal booze. Capone's crew retaliated by kidnapping and killing Fuller and two of his assistants.

The grim story of gangland killings was seen by Brisbane's readers—estimated to be at least twenty million—on January 19, 1928. Those same readers also learned that the powerful man heading the crime syndicate that committed those murders was vacationing in Florida.

Miami-area residents and leaders—at least some of them—were aghast that, thanks to Brisbane, their city was seen as harboring the nation's most notorious criminal. It was one thing to have Capone's name mentioned occasionally in local newspapers. It was quite another thing when the man considered by many to be the leading journalist of that era mentioned Florida, Chicago gangland violence, and Al Capone in the same sentence.

Two days after Brisbane's column, J. Newton Lummus Jr., the real estate agent who was now mayor of Miami Beach, and city manager C. A. Renshaw met with Capone at city hall to discuss how Capone's presence was harming the public image of their fair city.

After the brief meeting, Capone brushed past reporters, went straight to his car, and left. But His Honor, the mayor, had a few words for the scribes.

"Mr. Capone was one of the fairest men I have ever been in conference with," Lummus said. "He was not ordered to leave Miami Beach, but after our conference we decided it would be to the best interests of all concerned if he left."

The following day, Capone told reporters that he would indeed leave Miami Beach, but he didn't say where he intended to go. A spokesman for the Chicago Police Department said the cops in his city were very concerned about how the bitter Chicago winter might affect Capone's "frail health," and they hoped that, for his own good, he would stay in the warm, sunny South.

Capone left town briefly. A few days later, Capone and his brother Ralph—also known as "Bottles"—were registered at a hotel in New Orleans under the names of James Brown and Albert Ross. But police in the Crescent City got a tip about the real identities of Brown and Ross and arrested the brothers "under suspicion of being dangerous characters."

They were kept in custody briefly, then New Orleans police released them and told them to move on.

By early March, Al Capone was back in Florida. This time he had no intention of leaving, and he launched a new publicity campaign to try to become a part of the community.

Capone was fond of telling people that he'd served in the US Army in World War I and that the scar on his left cheek was from an injury he'd sustained fighting the Germans in France. There's no record of Capone serving in the military, but he tried to join the Coral Gables post of the American Legion anyway, even though military service is a requirement for membership. Legion officials dutifully sent a letter to Chicago police asking if Capone had ever been convicted of a felony, which would disqualify him from joining. On March 8, newspapers around the nation reported that Chicago police lieutenant William Rohan told the Coral Gables Legionnaires that Capone had been arrested many times, but had never been convicted of anything.

Miami Beach's most infamous resident also was maneuvering behind the scenes to buy a house there. And his eager gopher, Parker Henderson, was helping him conduct the purchase in such a way as to keep the gangster's name off public records.

On March 27, James and Modesta Popham sold their 10,000-square-foot waterfront mansion on Palm Island in Biscayne Bay to Henderson for $40,000—around $550,000 in twenty-first-century dollars. The transaction took place in the office of the real estate firm of Lummus & Young, and the deed transfer was witnessed by one of the firm's partners, Miami Beach mayor J. Newton Lummus Jr., who had asked Capone to leave town only two months earlier.

Henderson, in turn, quietly sold the property to Mae Capone, Al's wife. The intricate maneuvering kept the transaction out of the newspapers—for a few months, at least.

Soon I'm gonna leave all my cares behind
For I've made, yes, I've made up my mind
Soon I'll wander down the Tamiami Trail
Where it leads down to the sea.

By the spring of 1928, Gene Austin's recording of the pop song "Tamiami Trail," written by Cliff Friend and Joseph Santly, had been in music stores for almost two years, and so the road had achieved a measure of fame well before it opened.

With the opening of the Trail only days away, the Reo Motor Car Company of Lansing, Michigan, saw an opportunity to link the name of one of its most popular automobiles with the event.

The Reo Wolverine was advertised as "A Car for the Ends of the Roads." What better way to demonstrate that advertising slogan than for a Wolverine to be the first passenger car to drive through the Everglades—the wild, mysterious Everglades—on the Tamiami Trail.

As the manufacturers of the Wolverine hoped, the stunt got into the newspapers.

The big sedan made the trip with only a few scratches and a dent from hitting a rock, the *Capital Times* of Madison, Wisconsin, reported on April 1, 1928.

"At times, large boulders that blocked progress had to be removed, and many other obstacles overcome, but the Wolverine fought its way through, much after the manner of the wolverine of the woods from which the Reo Wolverine gets its name—the strongest and most fearless animal of its size known to man," said the *Capital Times* news story, which probably was written by an advertising agency.

Not only did the publicity gimmick get the name of the Wolverine into the public's consciousness, but it also was a reminder that the Tamiami Trail was about to open.

Edwin Menninger described the Trail as "one of the world's most notable achievements." He also was bullishly optimistic about Florida's future, and said the downturn of real estate prices during the past two years was merely a "readjustment period."

"Indications are not wanting that Florida is to have an unusually good summer," he wrote in the *South Florida Developer* on April 13. "All in all, Florida's outlook for the coming summer is very bright. And this will be only the beginning of a great, new outlook of prosperity which will presage not only a return to normalcy, but better times than Florida has ever yet enjoyed."

Predictions that the opening of the Tamiami Trail would mark the return of good times for Florida had spread beyond the state.

"This magnificent Tamiami Trail will open millions of acres of land to cultivation and settlement," said an editorial in the *San Antonio Light*. "It will make it easy for children to reach their schools. It will provide fertile acres for good workers. And, you may be sure, it will not be made a pretext for more reckless real estate booming and misrepresentation."

On April 24, 1928, Governor John Martin—who was campaigning for the June Democratic primary nomination for one of Florida's seats in the US Senate—looked out over a crowd of thousands gathered in Tampa and proclaimed that the Tamiami Trail was open to traffic.

Florida newspapers were ecstatic. The *Fort Myers Tropical News* said the Trail was "the great highway of our dreams," and the *Sarasota Herald* said the opening of the Trail marked the dawn of "a new era of prosperity for the west coast of Florida.

"The tremendous influx of visitors, who will travel the route, will stimulate the building of fine hotels on the west coast, particularly in view of the fact that the west coast has bathing beaches more superior to those of the east coast and enjoys a more salubrious climate," the *Herald* said.

Meanwhile, a caravan that eventually would include more than one thousand cars assembled in Lake City, about 170 miles north of Tampa. The caravan, carrying thousands of people, would drive to Tampa, join others, and make the 274-mile trek over the Tamiami Trail from Tampa to Miami.

The caravan reached Fort Myers on the evening of April 25. The opening of the Trail was such a momentous event that even the famously busy Thomas Edison opened the grounds of his winter home in Fort Myers to the public. But not his lab. Visitors were warned in advance that the brilliant inventor wouldn't have time to chat.

From Fort Myers, the procession passed through Naples and entered the newest segment of the road that pierced the heart of the Everglades.

Years later author Florence Fritz described the scene as the caravan of noisy revelers penetrated the unique solemnity of the Everglades.

"Approaching autos caused countless flocks of egrets, wood ibis, blue herons, and gray herons to rise in clouds and settle down again as the flag-flying cortege passed on through the Everglades for the first time in history," Fritz wrote.

From that moment forward, the perception of the Everglades was forever changed.

"No longer was it the unconquerable domain of blistering sun and bloodthirsty mosquitoes," Jeffrey Kahn wrote for the *Palm Beach Post* in 1981. "It had become Florida real estate."

Bob DeGross, chief of interpretation and public affairs for the Big Cypress National Preserve near Miami, said the Tamiami Trail was "an amazing engineering feat" that changed South Florida forever.

"The Tamiami Trail and the Lincoln Highway opened up the whole country to the average person," DeGross said. "Today we think nothing of doing a long road trip, but back then it was a life-changing experience."

The day after the Trail opened, as if on cue from a natural force furious at the violation of the Glades, an unusually violent thunderstorm tore across the state from St. Augustine to Bartow, killing four people, drenching the area with rain, and ripping off roofs with winds approaching hurricane force.

Al Capone returned to Chicago while Parker Henderson quietly dealt with the negotiations and paperwork needed to buy the house on Palm Island. Capone had important business to attend to in the Windy City. It was election season, and Capone had a slate of candidates that he was determined would win. He needed to be at his battle station while the campaign was waged.

And the Chicago Republican primary campaign of 1928 would be a battle in the truest sense of the word.

The campaign leading up to election day on April 10, 1928, included the usual pledges from candidates to throw out the incompetent incumbents and set the city onto a new course of prosperity for all. But the outcome of the election also would determine how strictly Prohibition laws would be enforced.

Capone backed candidates who were part of Mayor William "Big Bill" Thompson's political machine. Thompson had won the mayor's office a year earlier by campaigning on a platform that essentially promised to ignore Prohibition. Capone reportedly contributed $250,000—more than $3.4 million in twenty-first-century dollars, a staggering amount of money in 1927—to Thompson's campaign.

The Republican primary campaign of 1928 would go down in infamy as the "Pineapple Primary." The nickname was derived from the appearance of a US Army hand grenade, which soldiers often referred to as a "pineapple." Capone wasn't willing to rely on the persuasive appeal of candidates' stump speeches to make up voters' minds. Instead, he decided that lobbing explosives at candidates and various underworld figures would be more effective in determining the outcome of the election.

More than sixty politically related bombings happened in the months before Election Day, and there were several murders as well. Capone lost some of his aides, and he eliminated some of his enemies.

The campaign was so violent that a Chicago journalist parodied "The Star-Spangled Banner" to describe it: "And the rockets' red glare, the bombs bursting in air, gave proof through the night that Chicago's still there."

The violence leading up to the Chicago election received national attention, and Al Capone's name was frequently mentioned in those stories.

The candidates backed by Capone won the election. With politics behind him for a while, Capone turned his mind to other projects.

As the summer of 1928 approached, George Merrick, the genius behind Coral Gables, was having both financial and health problems. He had also been elected to the town's governing body, the Coral Gables Board of Commissioners. He had been recuperating for some time in Atlanta and was unable to attend meetings. But Merrick had tabulated more votes than any other candidate in the last election, and it was clear that Coral Gables voters wanted him on the board of commissioners.

Still, Merrick had enemies on the board, and on June 5 the other commissioners voted to expel him. The move set off a controversy in the town that Merrick built.

In early July, three creditor companies asked that the Coral Gables Corporation be placed in receivership. George Merrick owed an estimated $29 million, and he had no assets available. Only a few years earlier, Merrick had sometimes brought in that much money in just a few days.

By mid-June, Al Capone was back in Miami Beach. And he was annoyed. His toady Parker Henderson had a message for him from Dade County solicitor Robert Taylor: Stay out of Dade County.

On Monday, June 18, accompanied by three bodyguards, Capone walked into the headquarters of the Miami Police Department and insisted on meeting with the new police chief, Guy C. Reeve.

Capone made his usual show of disarming affability. But the *Miami Daily News* reported that the reception Capone received was quite different from his meeting a few months earlier with then-chief Leslie Quigg.

Capone told Reeve he was in town "for an indefinite stay," and that he had no intention of leaving until he was ready.

"Coldly impersonal, Chief Reeve advised Capone that if he had returned 'for his health,' as reported, he probably would find Miami 'very unhealthful,'" the *Daily News* reported.

"I informed Capone that he was considered an undesirable character by a majority of the citizens, and that many thought he was here to gain control of the liquor and gambling activities," Reeve told the *Daily News*. "He denied this, stating that his business was in Chicago."

Later that day, county solicitor Robert Taylor told Capone to come to his office in the Dade County Courthouse. Around 5:30 p.m., accompanied by an attorney and a bodyguard, Capone sat down with Taylor, Miami city manager Welton Snow, public safety director H. H. Arnold, police chief Reeve, and state's attorney Vernon Hawthorne.

The meeting didn't last long. Capone was asked to leave Miami and not come back. Capone said he hadn't done anything wrong, didn't intend to do anything wrong, and wasn't going anywhere. And he'd fight all the way to the US Supreme Court before he'd allow himself to be forced out of town. Capone and his entourage left the building around six p.m.

The day after the terse meeting, the *Daily News* sent a reporter to try to pry a statement out of county solicitor Taylor about what he intended to do about Capone's unwanted presence.

Taylor told the reporter he wasn't planning on doing anything.

There followed an increasingly acrimonious conversation between Taylor and the *Daily News* reporter, who had to chase the county attorney up and down an elevator to talk to him.

The reporter reminded Taylor that during his recent campaign in the Democratic primary, he'd said that he was determined that Capone would not live in

Miami as long as he was in office, and had written a letter to the editor of the *Daily News* saying Capone "cannot and will not live, operate, or make his headquarters in Dade County."

A half-dozen times the reporter asked Taylor if he'd changed his mind about Capone's residency in Dade County. Each time, with increasing vehemence, Taylor denied that he'd changed his mind but said he did not want to make a statement.

The following day, the *Miami Daily News* escalated its campaign against the gangster's presence in the city.

"Capone in Summer 'White House'" blared the front page of the *Daily News* on Wednesday, June 20. A subhead read, "Miami Is Made Gang Capital for Chicagoan."

The *Daily News* also reported on an "indignation meeting" of prominent Miami residents who wanted Capone banished.

"The gangster chief, who has established himself in a walled estate at Palm Island and never leaves without a bodyguard, appeared unperturbed Wednesday by threats to move him," the *Daily News* said. "He was quoted as having adopted the famous Coolidge phrase that he does not 'choose to run,' and to have suggested nothing less than the Supreme Court of the United States can change that decision. Apparently his chief concern was centered in the latest dispatches from Chicago, where a new outbreak of gang warfare had taken three lives."

Miami Beach mayor J. Newton Lummus Jr. did not attend any of the meetings with Capone, nor did he attend the so-called "indignation meeting." But he did issue a statement to the *Daily News* saying that he didn't know of any legal method to force Capone to leave town.

"If Al Capone does anything to warrant his arrest, he will be prosecuted to the fullest extent of the law," Lummus said in his statement. "This matter has been brought up several times and I have given it serious consideration. I believe that if Capone attempts to establish himself in an illegal business here, or becomes a public nuisance in any way, it will be my privilege and pleasure to see that he is prosecuted. As long as he resides here as a respectable citizen, however, I don't believe we have any right to question his constitutional right as an American citizen to live wherever he chooses."

The *Daily News* kept digging. The following day, the newspaper lowered the boom on Lummus.

"Capone Deal Involves Lummus," was the headline for the *Daily News* of Friday, June 22.

The story reminded readers that Lummus had asked Capone to leave town in January, and then asked the mayor why, after asking the gangster to leave, he'd sold him a house two months later.

Lummus did not answer that question.

"I don't think Capone is half as bad as some people picture him, not half as bad as some other characters who have been at the Beach for a long time unmolested," Lummus said. "I am acting on the advice of attorneys, and I do not see how I can legally do anything about his living at the Beach."

Lummus noted that, unlike some other local government officials, he hadn't bragged about what he'd do if Capone returned to Miami, and he didn't think it was up to him to do anything.

"I'm not afraid of Capone," Lummus said. "He's a better citizen than a lot we have down here now."

That same day, Parker Henderson gave up the lease to operate the Ponce de Leon Hotel. Knowing that he would be taking heat from local newspapers—because his participation in the complicated transaction that conveyed the Palm Island house to Al Capone's wife would soon be discovered—Henderson decided it would be a good time to take a long vacation in the cool mountains of North Carolina. He immediately left for Asheville.

The hotel's owners didn't explain why he'd given up the lease. When reporters tried to contact Henderson for an explanation, friends told the newspaper that he'd left town and they didn't know where he was or when he'd return.

On Thursday, June 28, the Miami Beach City Council called a special meeting to discuss Al Capone. It was a stormy session. The council members vented their anger at Mayor Lummus for condoning the presence of the nation's most notorious gangster. They also passed a resolution calling on every cop in the county to arrest Capone for the slightest infraction.

While Al Capone was tussling with local leaders in Dade County, four of his most trusted associates boarded a southbound train in Chicago for a long trip. When they arrived in Miami they slipped across the causeway to Capone's walled estate. While they were in town, two of them—dark, well-dressed, immaculately groomed young men with impeccable manners—hit the Miami Beach nightlife scene with two young women they'd met when they had visited town a few months earlier. The young men, who called themselves "Mike" and "George," had been introduced to the women by Parker Henderson. But Mike and George didn't see Henderson on this trip.

On June 29, Capone's four friends went to the Miami train station and bought tickets back to Chicago. As they were about to board the train, the men made an excessive show of pointing out to bystanders and the train crew that they were headed for Chicago.

Only they weren't. The train made a scheduled stop in Atlanta, and when it left the four men weren't aboard. With much less fanfare, they had quietly boarded a different train for a short trip to Knoxville, Tennessee.

In Knoxville, two of the men went to a Nash car dealership. They found a big, roomy, low-mileage black sedan, and one of the men, who said his name was Charles Cox, peeled off $1,035 from a roll of cash. They put a Tennessee license plate on the car and drove away.

On Sunday, July 1, around three p.m., Frank Uale was having a drink at a speakeasy in Brooklyn. Uale, known on the street as "Frankie Yale," had once been a friend and business partner of Al Capone's, but he and Capone had had a disagreement about how profits should be divided, and their partnership was dissolved. Even worse, Uale had formed a partnership with Capone's enemies in New York.

Exactly one year earlier, on July 1, 1927, gunmen had tried to assassinate Frankie Yale on the street in Brooklyn, but missed. Uale's forces retaliated by killing Capone ally James DeAmoto. Capone swore vengeance.

Uale did a good business running a speakeasy cabaret on Coney Island known as the Harvard Inn, where Al Capone got his start in the business. It was here that Capone, only eighteen at the time, had made an insulting remark to a mobster's girlfriend and the thug had pulled a razor, sliced his face, and left the scars that prompted his nickname.

Like his former friend, Uale loved to dress well and display his success. On that Sunday, he was wearing a light-gray, summer-weight suit and a Panama hat. He also was flashing a diamond stickpin, two diamond rings, and a diamond-studded belt buckle.

Uale tried to spread his wealth around the neighborhood. He had given thousands of dollars to a Catholic church in Flatbush, and he was willing to help the less fortunate with cash. That included loans to cops.

The phone rang, and the bartender called Uale to the receiver. Whatever he heard sent him running to his car. A few minutes later, he was cruising slowly down Forty-Fourth Street, a residential street in Brooklyn, in his Lincoln.

A big, black Nash sedan pulled in behind Uale's Lincoln. For a few moments, the Nash followed at a distance of about 150 feet. Then the driver of the Nash gunned the engine, and the big car overtook Uale.

Suddenly gunfire erupted from the Nash, shattering the quiet of the Sunday afternoon. The rear window of Uale's Lincoln exploded. He pushed the accelerator to the floor, trying to escape, but the Nash had drawn abreast of him and was forcing him toward the curb. And guns were blazing. Bullets narrowly missed a seven-year-old girl who was sitting in her father's car parked at the curb.

But most of the bullets found their mark, and Uale was dead before his car stopped rolling. It lurched onto the sidewalk. Terrified mothers snatched their children from its path as it pushed through a hedge and slammed into the stone steps of an apartment building at 923 Forty-Fourth Street.

The big black Nash sped away and disappeared. Police found it the next day. The killers hadn't driven far, abandoning the car near the Green-Wood Cemetery, only a few blocks from where Uale was killed.

The cops found a few clues in the car. One of the most ominous was a Thompson submachine gun. It was the first time the weapon had been used in a gangland assassination in New York. At that time, there was only one place where this expensive, rapid-fire weapon was used by gangsters—Chicago.

They also found a pistol. It was less exotic than the tommy gun, but it would reveal even more about who was behind Uale's murder.

Slowly, New York cops began to piece together the plot to kill Frankie Yale.

Meanwhile, the gang war continued. On July 4, the body of a bookie was found in a sand pit in Brooklyn's Greenpoint neighborhood. His head had nearly been blown off by gunfire. Police suspected he'd been shot with a Thompson.

Two days later, the *Miami Daily News* reported that Uale had been laid to rest in a $15,000 coffin trimmed with silver, and that New York gunmen might be coming to Miami to avenge his death.

On July 8, New York police announced that they'd linked the Uale murder to Al Capone. The *New York Times* reported that Frankie Yale's death was part of Capone's plot to create an "alcohol empire" that stretched from New York to Chicago and from Canada to Florida.

It turned out that Capone had been quite busy when he left Miami earlier in the year.

"His campaign called for the smuggling of liquors of all varieties, not only through New York, but through Detroit, Miami, and New Orleans," the *Times* said.

After printing the stories linking Capone to Uale's death and explaining his plans for a massive expansion of his bootlegging operation, the newspapers became quiet for a few days. But police in Miami and New York were very busy.

A week or so later, Parker Henderson boarded a train in Asheville. Police in Miami wanted to talk to him.

It's a long train ride from the mountains of western North Carolina to the southern tip of the Florida peninsula. Henderson had a lot of time to stare out a window and think about what he was going to tell the cops when he got to Miami.

Henderson met first with Miami police chief Guy Reeve, and then with New York police detective Tom Daly and Dade County solicitor Robert Taylor. At first, Henderson said he didn't know anything about Uale's death or whether Al Capone was involved in some way. But New York police had traced one of the pistols found in the big black Nash to Miami. It was unquestionably one of the guns that Henderson had bought for Capone six months earlier.

Finally, Henderson signed an affidavit saying that he had bought the gun and delivered it to Capone's hotel room. Detective Daly asked him to come to New York to talk to police there. Henderson didn't like that suggestion, but he talked it over with some friends and agreed to do it.

On Saturday, July 29, Henderson boarded a train in Miami, bound for New York. By this time, his name had been in newspapers across the country linking him to Al Capone and one of the weapons used to kill Frank Uale. So Henderson had a traveling companion—Miami police chief Guy Reeve.

Henderson stayed out of sight between meetings with police and the Kings County District Attorney's Office in Brooklyn. On August 7, he appeared before a grand jury in Brooklyn. The jurors had already heard testimony from the two young women—described as "cabaret performers" in newspapers—that Henderson had introduced to "George" and "Mike" in Miami.

Henderson explained his relationship with Al Capone for the jurors. He admitted that he'd bought a dozen guns for Capone as a favor. He hadn't asked Capone why he wanted the guns.

The grand jury and district attorney were satisfied with Henderson's story. He would not have to testify before the grand jury again, nor would he be charged with anything. He was free to return to Miami.

Late in the evening of August 7, Miami police chief Reeve and a greatly relieved Parker Henderson got aboard the southbound Havana Special at Pennsylvania Station. As the train chugged southward through the Carolinas and into Georgia, it ran into heavy rains and gusting winds.

The 1928 hurricane season had been quiet through July. But on August 3, a tropical storm formed at the northeast edge of the Caribbean Sea. It didn't amount to much as it moved northwestward across the Bahamas, but as it was about to leave the islands, it suddenly intensified. As it neared landfall, its strongest winds were blowing at about 105 miles an hour.

The storm was coming ashore as the train carrying Henderson and Reeve crossed into Florida. The train had to stop several times and wait for workers to remove downed trees and debris from the tracks. It rolled into Miami about three hours late.

The storm's eye made landfall just before dawn between Fort Pierce and Vero Beach. Reporter Cecil Warren of the *Miami Daily News* said at least two-thirds of the buildings in Fort Pierce had their roofs ripped off. The hurricane then tore into the ripening citrus groves of the famous Indian River region. No fatalities were reported, however.

But the hurricane of August 8, 1928, was just a warm-up. The worst—far worse—was yet to come.

CHAPTER ELEVEN

Blown Away

THE EYE OF THE HURRICANE THAT DELAYED PARKER HENDERSON JR.'S RETURN to Miami tore into Stuart and Fort Pierce with surprising fierceness on the morning of August 8, 1928. Electric wires and telegraph lines went down almost immediately, so newspapers from West Palm Beach to Vero Beach could not run their presses.

But Edwin Menninger, now publisher of both the *South Florida Developer* and the *Stuart Daily News*, was determined to get the story of the hurricane's fury to the outside world—even if it meant risking his life.

As the storm still raged, Menninger got into his car and started a perilous journey north. Buffeted and rocked by high winds and slammed by driving rain, he pushed through the storm seeking a town where he could get his story to the Associated Press.

Along the way, he took note of the storm's damage.

Menninger found electricity and phone service in Melbourne, about seventy miles up the coast from Stuart. He filed his story to the AP there.

The winds in the hurricane's eye wall were around 90 miles an hour when it made landfall, Menninger said. Around midnight, the storm's calm eye arrived, and all was quiet for an hour or so. But then the back side of the eye wall arrived, and the winds resumed with greater fury than before. Menninger later reported that the winds reached about 110 miles an hour after the eye passed. On the modern Saffir-Simpson scale—which rates hurricanes by wind speed and destructive potential—a hurricane with peak winds of 111 miles an hour is considered major.

Hundreds of homes and businesses from Stuart to Vero Beach were heavily damaged, and many had their roofs blown off, Menninger said. "Signboards, awnings, timbers, and parts of buildings lay all over the streets," he wrote. "Broken tile, plate glass, and strips of felt and metal roofing covered the sidewalks."

The winds had denuded tens of thousands of citrus trees and covered the ground with ripening grapefruit and oranges. "Citrus groves along the East coast [of Florida] looked like a winter scene in the North," Menninger said.

Even in the middle of a story about destruction, however, Menninger found an opportunity for promotion. When he mentioned the storm's damage to Stuart, he noted that the town was "famed for its fishing and great natural harbor."

No deaths were reported from the storm. Still, one sad death during the storm was discovered later. The body of the thirty-five-year-old, unmarried postmaster at Olympia was found on August 9. He was sitting in a chair in his home. Police learned that he'd been deeply disappointed when a recent love affair had been broken off. So as the hurricane raged around him, the postmaster sat down in an easy chair, pondered his unhappiness, put a pistol to his head, and pulled the trigger.

In his story for the Associated Press, Menninger reported that the storm had inflicted several million dollars' worth of damage from Stuart to Vero Beach. But the hurricane's worst effects wouldn't become evident for a while. The storm dumped more than a foot of rain in some places in South Florida, and most of that water soon made its way to Lake Okeechobee.

Florida boosters are fond of pointing out that the lake is the nation's second largest, if you exclude the four Great Lakes with shorelines that touch both the United States and Canada. The lake covers about 750 square miles and is about half the size of the state of Rhode Island.

The deepest part of Lake Okeechobee is at sea level. The shallow saucer-like lake's average depth is about nine feet, so the saucer is pretty much filled when the surface of the water is fourteen or fifteen feet above sea level. Because the lake is so shallow, winds blowing across it can pile up water against shorelines and dikes.

In the days following the hurricane, water poured into Lake Okeechobee. Most of it was dumped into the lake by the Kissimmee River, which drains about 3,000 square miles as it flows southeasterly for about 130 miles down the center of the Florida peninsula to the lake's northern shore. Two smaller creeks—Taylor Creek and Fisheating Creek—also emptied more water into the lake.

There was more water than the Kissimmee could handle, and it spilled over the river's banks and spread out miles on both sides of the river. On August 14, the *Palm Beach Post* reported that the Kissimmee had reached the highest level since record-keeping had started.

And Lake Okeechobee was steadily rising. By mid-August it exceeded seventeen feet above sea level, approaching the eighteen-foot level that was considered dangerous. People living near the lake nervously watched the dikes and recalled what had happened only two years earlier when the hurricane that devastated Miami also sent water spilling over a dike, flooded Moore Haven, and killed hundreds of people.

One of those dikes near the town of Okeechobee on the lake's northern shore gave way on August 14, flooding about 1,200 acres. It was a reminder to Glades residents that state politicians seemed incapable of solving a problem that had long bedeviled them.

Controlling the lake's water level and eliminating flooding had been discussed in Tallahassee for decades, but the discussions had always broken down over how such a program would be administered. South Florida residents wanted to control how decisions would be made about a drainage program in their region. But opponents didn't want to give up control of a program funded by residents of the entire state that would benefit only residents of one region.

When John W. Martin ran for governor in 1924, he had promised voters that if they elected him, he would do all he could to improve drainage around Lake Okeechobee and stop the frequent flooding.

But in early July 1928, near the end of his four-year term as governor and now running for the US Senate, Martin had thrown up his hands in frustration after Florida commissioner of agriculture Nathan Mayo refused to sign a bond issue that had been overwhelmingly approved by the state legislature. The bond would have provided $20 million—about $270 million in twenty-first-century dollars—for drainage improvements around Lake Okeechobee.

Mayo, whose signature was required along with those of the state treasurer, the state comptroller, and the state attorney general, said he wouldn't sign the documents because a lawsuit challenging the constitutionality of the bond issue hadn't been decided by the US Supreme Court. It didn't matter to Mayo that the Florida Supreme Court had upheld the constitutionality of the plan that the legislature had approved.

State engineers did what they could to lower the lake level after the August 1928 hurricane. Thousands of gallons of water per second were pouring through the gates of the St. Lucie Canal, and a state engineer charged with monitoring the lake level said there was no danger that the dikes would give way. But William Griffis, editor of the *Okeechobee News*, disputed him. The Kissimmee and the two creeks were pouring water into the lake faster than the canal could drain it off, Griffis said.

By August 16, however, the Kissimmee had crested and the water level was falling, and Lake Okeechobee's rise had stopped. Residents living near the lake relaxed a little and waited for the ground to dry out so they could return to tending their crops.

Many of the people who lived in those little lakeside farming towns—Clewiston, Belle Glade, Pahokee, Moore Haven, Canal Point, and South Bay—were drawn there by the prospect of working the dark, fertile soil around Lake Okeechobee. But they were a very different breed than the newcomers who had flocked to the stylish beach towns during the peak of the real estate speculation a few years earlier. Davida Gates, who grew up in Belle Glade in the 1920s and had become a schoolteacher, later wrote in her autobiography that the Glades people were "rough, tough, domineering, good-hearted men with uncomplaining, God-fearing wives and graceless, half-civilized, hardy children."

They were joined by thousands of migrant workers, most of them black, many of them Haitians and other natives of the Caribbean who spoke little or no English. They came to plant and harvest green beans, sugarcane, and other crops.

In her classic novel, *Their Eyes Were Watching God*, author Zora Neale Hurston described the scene around Lake Okeechobee during the waning days of the summer of 1928. Every day, "hordes of workers poured in," she wrote.

"They came in wagons from way up in Georgia, and they came in truck loads from east, west, north and south," Hurston wrote. "Permanent transients with no attachments and tired looking men with their families and dogs in flivvers. All night, all day, hurrying in to pick beans. Skillets, beds, patched up spare inner tubes all hanging and dangling from the ancient cars on the outside and hopeful humanity, herded and hovered on the inside, chugging on to the muck. People ugly from ignorance and broken from being poor."

So many migrants were coming to the towns around Lake Okeechobee in the late summer of 1928 that there was no place for them to sleep. Landowners started building nightly bonfires, and men slept on the ground near the fires. "But they had to pay the man whose land they slept on," Hurston wrote. "He ran the fire just like his boarding place—for pay."

Money had not poured into the Glades towns the way it had in Miami, Stuart, West Palm Beach, St. Petersburg, and other towns on the coast. Still, as the autumn of 1928 approached, community leaders in the lakeside towns were echoing the optimism that Herbert Hoover voiced when he accepted the Republican nomination for president on August 11 in California.

Hoover, a taciturn engineer who'd become a politician, told a crowd of 75,000 in the Stanford University football stadium that the United States was on the verge of accomplishing one of the most noble of human aspirations.

"We in America today are nearer to the final triumph over poverty than ever before in the history of any land," Hoover said. "The poorhouse is vanishing from among us."

Glades residents weren't expecting to eliminate poverty, but better times did seem to be at hand.

"Almost as great a boom as the east coast of Florida had in 1925 is the development that is now under way in the upper Everglades," the *Canal Point News* said in early September 1928. The weekly newspaper noted that two railroads were laying new track near the lake and new highways were being built by the state. Florida Power and Light Company was putting up new electrical lines from Pahokee to South Bay, a big new sugar mill was being built in Clewiston, and hundreds of acres of land were being cleared to plant sugarcane.

On September 10, an Associated Press story predicted that the same coastal towns that had been roughed up by the August hurricane were preparing for "the best winter season ever experienced" in Florida. The story even found a silver lining to the hurricane. Its destruction had been a stimulant to business because of all the building and repair that followed it.

The story closed on a reassuring note. "Meteorologists say the storm season virtually closes in September," the story concluded.

There was no doubt in Edwin Menninger's mind that happy days were about to return to Florida. His *South Florida Developer* of Friday, September 14, was brimming with optimism.

"Florida looks forward today to one of the best and most prosperous winters that the state has ever known," the *Developer* predicted. "Every sign points to a banner season. The number of advance tourists, indicated by the foreign license tags you see daily on the streets now, foreshadows an influx a month or two months from now that will tax our resources of accommodation."

"One thing is certain, the situation in Florida is improving," the *Developer* said. "We have been on bedrock, and the next change will be upward and for the better."

When events don't unfold as expected, that's irony. German philosopher Friedrich Nietzsche noted that while irony's purpose is to humble and shame, it can be useful when it is applied to teach a lesson that leads to a good resolution and teaches people to show honor and gratitude.

When irony is not used for that purpose, it is rude and vulgar, Nietzsche said.

As Florida's hopeful businessmen found reasons to be optimistic about the return of good times, a massive dose of irony was headed their way. But it would not lead to a good resolution.

Hurricanes draw their power from warm seawater, and by the first week of September, a stretch of the Atlantic Ocean between the Cape Verde Islands off the west coast of Africa and the Caribbean Sea had been heated by the summer sun until it had become a prime spawning ground for hurricanes. The windy thunderstorms—known as tropical depressions—that roll off Africa's west coast at this time of year often pick up a counterclockwise circulation imparted by the spin of the earth, draw power from this warm seawater, and become tropical storms.

For all of their power, however, hurricanes are delicate, and even small changes in conditions—cooler water or upper-level winds that impede their circulation and disrupt their momentum—can cause a storm to weaken and even dissipate.

Every so often, though, one of these late-summer storms encounters exactly perfect conditions as it rumbles past the Cape Verdes and continues westward across the Atlantic. Sometimes, there is nothing to impede its development. Some of history's worst hurricanes have been born from these conditions at this time of year. Those storms became so infamous that meteorologists gave them a special designation—Cape Verde hurricanes.

On September 6, a tropical depression found those perfect conditions just off the African west coast and quickly strengthened into a tropical storm as it moved south of the Cape Verde Islands. By September 10—when the Associated Press was predicting the greatest tourist season in Florida's history and telling readers that hurricane season "virtually closes in September"—the storm had grown into a hurricane with maximum winds of about seventy-five miles an hour.

That same morning the SS *Commack*, an American freighter bound from Brazil to Philadelphia with a load of bananas, ran into a surprisingly strong storm about 1,600 miles west of the Cape Verde Islands. The ship's captain, Samuel Kruppe, radioed the hurricane's position.

It was the farthest east that a hurricane had ever been documented. Clearly, there was something sinister about this storm.

About 280 miles southwest of the *Commack*, the captain of the SS *Clearwater* was encountering the same rough weather. A rapidly falling barometer indicates that a bad storm is nearby. The captain of the *Clearwater* had been closely watching his barometer for about two hours. During that time, the reading had dropped one-tenth of an inch. That doesn't sound like much of a change to a landlubber, but it's an alarming drop to a sailor whose ship is being pounded by a bad storm thousands of miles from the nearest land.

By September 12, the storm had traveled 2,500 miles across warm summer seawater. As the hurricane approached the ring of islands marking the eastern boundary of the Caribbean, it was a bona fide monster, with maximum winds of around 145 miles an hour. It tore into the Caribbean island of Guadeloupe with savage fury. And it started killing people.

When a hurricane's barometric pressure falls below 28 inches, it's a very intense storm. Hurricane Charley, which carved a path of destruction across the Florida peninsula in 2004, had a barometric pressure reading of 27.79 just before it made landfall near Port Charlotte on Florida's Gulf Coast. That storm's maximum sustained winds reached at least 145 miles per hour.

A meteorologist in Pointe-à-Pitre, Guadeloupe, recorded a reading of 27.76 inches on September 12, 1928, as the hurricane passed over the island.

Alexander Hamilton, who was born in the British West Indies and later became the first US secretary of the treasury, was about fifteen years old and living on Guadeloupe in August 1772 when a very powerful hurricane crossed the island. He was astonished and deeply moved by the power he witnessed.

"It seemed as if a total dissolution of nature was taking place," he later wrote in a letter to his father. "The roaring of the sea and wind—fiery meteors flying about in the air—the prodigious glare of almost perpetual lightning—the crash of the falling houses—and the ear-piercing shrieks of the distressed, were sufficient to strike astonishment into Angels."

The hurricane that crossed Guadeloupe in September 1928 was similar in power to the 1772 storm, and the island had been caught unprepared. As many as 1,200 people may have died as the hurricane thrashed across the island and entered the northeastern Caribbean Sea. The storm turned slightly to the northwest and gathered even more strength as it bore down on Puerto Rico.

Other islands in the hurricane's path had a little more warning than Guadeloupe. At ten p.m. on September 12, a cannon boomed from the ramparts of Fort Christiansvaern on St. Croix. It was a warning to residents that they should come immediately to the ancient eighteenth-century citadel for protection from the approaching storm.

In Puerto Rico, ships were weighing anchor and leaving ports to avoid the storm. Police went door-to-door, warning residents to prepare for a very bad blow. The hurricane's winds began to tear at Puerto Rico's southeastern coast around four a.m. on September 13, 1928.

During its short, 320-mile run from Guadeloupe to Puerto Rico, the storm had feasted on the warm Caribbean waters. The hurricane's eye reached Guayama on the southeast coast of the island around 2:30 p.m. The storm's arrival happened to coincide with the Catholic Church's celebration of the feast of Saint Philip, or San Felipe. It was the second time in Puerto Rico's history that a hurricane had struck the island on that saint's feast day. So the hurricane that pounded Puerto Rico on Thursday, September 13, 1928, came to be known as San Felipe Segundo, or Saint Philip the Second.

As the eye passed over Guayama, winds in San Juan, about 30 miles to the north, reached 160 miles an hour before the instruments measuring wind speed were blown away.

The *San Lorenzo*, a Puerto Rican passenger liner with British passengers aboard, was riding out the hurricane in the San Juan harbor.

"We could see whole houses hurtle past, and tall trees swept along by the wind," passenger Estelle Rice later told *The Times* of London.

The noise from the storm was so loud that the passengers aboard the *San Lorenzo* did not hear an ammonia plant blow up during the hurricane, even though it was only a few hundred feet from where they were anchored.

And it may have been worse at Guayama, which was closer to the eye. Meteorologists with the US Weather Bureau thought winds there may have reached 200 miles per hour.

Despite the ferocity of the storm, the advance warnings saved lives in Puerto Rico. In Coamo, only about eighteen miles northwest of where the storm came ashore, Felicia Cartegena, a telephone operator, stayed at her switchboard while the hurricane roared around her. She sent warnings to other parts of the islands and dispatched help for those who'd been injured.

She paid for her bravery with her life.

In Cayey, ten miles north of Guayama, a mother tucked a child under each arm and tried desperately to find shelter. She and her children were nearly cut in two when the storm sent pieces of a roof whirling through the air. Not far away, a merchant who opened his door to admit a man seeking shelter battled the winds to try to close the door. Suddenly the wind snatched him up, hurled him through a window, and into a river, where he drowned.

And there was one more unusual death. Franz Romer, a twenty-nine-year-old German-born veteran of World War I, had launched a sail-powered kayak into the Atlantic at Lisbon, Portugal, on March 31, 1928, planning to sail the tiny craft, just over twenty-one feet long, across the Atlantic to Miami.

By early September, an exhausted Romer had reached Puerto Rico. After recuperating for several days in San Juan, he set out again. About an hour after he left, the first hurricane warning reached San Juan.

Romer was never seen again, and no trace of him or his tiny boat was found.

More than 300 people were killed in Puerto Rico before San Felipe was finished with its deadly work. Red Cross officials later estimated that the hurricane had left half of the island's population—perhaps 600,000 people—homeless.

The *Palm Beach Post* of Friday, September 14, 1928, had a front-page story saying that Florida was not threatened by the hurricane that had devastated Puerto Rico.

"While weather bureau officials emphasized there is no cause for alarm on the Florida coast, as the hurricane may deviate from its present course or dissipate itself at sea, they said it was undoubtedly the worst this year, and may be of the proportions of the hurricane which swept Miami in 1926," the *Post* story said.

Actually, San Felipe was a little more powerful than the 1926 hurricane. And it was approaching Florida at a very bad time. Heavy rain had resumed again in late August and early September, and Lake Okeechobee had begun to rise again.

The rains continued during the first two weeks of September, when as much as another foot fell in some places. By mid-month, Lake Okeechobee was frighteningly high, and once again lakeside residents were nervously eyeing the water lapping at the low mud dikes.

On Saturday, September 15, the front page of the *Palm Beach Post* was dominated by a blaring headline: "Florida May Feel Storm's Wrath." It must have been jarring to *Post* readers who just the day before had been told there was "no cause for alarm" about the hurricane.

"Giving ironclad forecasts upon the hurricane is practically impossible," the *Post* story admitted. "Possibilities were apparent last night that the storm might veer to the right and travel northward, which would head it again to sea," the story continued. "Again, it may continue to the Florida coast and strike at a point which it is now too early to determine."

San Felipe had lost some of its fierceness since it had devastated Puerto Rico, but it was still a very powerful, dangerous, and deadly storm. Around three p.m. Saturday, the eye of the storm passed over the German steamer *August Leonhardt* near the southeastern tip of the Bahamas, about 450 miles east-southeast of West Palm Beach.

A ship's officer on the *August Leonhardt* struggled to describe San Felipe's power.

"The force of the wind, if more or less, could only be judged by the noise made by the storm, which reminded me of the New York subway going full speed passing switches," the officer later wrote.

At eleven p.m. Saturday night, the US Weather Bureau in Washington, DC, issued a statement saying that winds on the southern Florida peninsula could exceed fifty miles an hour. "There was no indication last night that Miami or vicinity will be in the path of dangerous winds," the statement said. "Indications were that when the storm reaches a position due east of Miami Sunday morning it will be 170 miles to sea and winds during the day should shift to the north and diminish as the storm moves up the coast."

The Weather Bureau's forecast wasn't entirely wrong. Miami would get little more than a windy rainstorm from the hurricane. And Arthur Brisbane apparently was keeping an eye on the forecasts. The *Palm Beach Post*'s edition for Sunday, September 16, published the optimistic forecast and Brisbane's "Today" column on the front page.

Brisbane was detached and flippant about the powerful storm that was bearing down on Florida, noting that at about the same time the hurricane was devastating Puerto Rico, a tornado was killing eleven people in South Dakota and Nebraska.

"But science can foresee a day when high winds will be under man's control," Brisbane wrote. One day, "in the days far off, perhaps 50,000 years or 500,000 years hence," humans would control the earth's temperature and transfer "surplus heat" from the equator to the poles. The winds that caused such destruction today would blow "where man says it shall blow, and at a speed prescribed by him," he wrote. "There is nothing fanciful about that."

That same morning, American Red Cross vice chairman James Fieser read the forecasts for Florida and had a very different reaction than Brisbane. He was alarmed. He picked up his phone and ordered experienced disaster workers to go to Jacksonville and wait for the storm to pass. He called local Red Cross chapters in southern Florida counties and told them to prepare for a disaster. And he sent a telegram to Florida governor John Martin, advising him that the Red Cross was alerting its relief workers to prepare to deal with a tragedy.

On his small farm near Belle Glade, Jack Zuber was getting ready for "a hard wind."

"I nailed boards over the windows and reinforced my garage doors with heavy timbers," Zuber said. "We felt comparatively safe after that."

Zuber was optimistic. He had ridden out the hurricane two years earlier in the same house. The water had only gotten a couple of feet deep and his house had withstood the blow, so he figured it would withstand this storm.

It seemed like a safe assumption.

At 10:30 Sunday morning, the US Weather Bureau in Washington, DC, ordered hurricane warnings to be hoisted from Miami to Daytona Beach. "This hurricane is of wide extent and great severity," the Weather Bureau advisory read. "Every precaution should be taken against destructive winds and high tides on Florida east coast, especially West Palm Beach to Daytona."

By early Sunday afternoon, San Felipe's outer winds were raking the Florida coast. Attorney Everett Muskoff Jr. and his wife were driving north from Miami and reached West Palm Beach shortly after noon.

"A brisk wind was blowing," Muskoff recalled. "We were looking at the skies when suddenly a roof of a building went hurtling by. We went to the first hotel we could find. When we got out of the car we could hardly walk, so strong was the wind."

The hotel lobby was already crowded. "The crowd stood about, looking out the doors," Muskoff said. "By this time a drenching rain had set in. There could be heard crashes and rumblings. The tiles of the hotel roof clanked off to the pavement at irregular intervals. It sort of got on one's nerves."

Around the same time, Frances Ball left the Hotel Pennsylvania in West Palm Beach with a friend named Jimmy to get some lunch. Then they went to visit a friend whose office was in the Harvey Building, a fourteen-story skyscraper that was the tallest building in downtown West Palm Beach. It was around 1:30 p.m.

"The gale was blowing so strong at the time that we could just barely make headway against it," she later wrote in a letter to her parents. "Half the time we [were] just pawing the air."

The electricity to the Harvey Building had already been cut, so Ball and her friend had to walk up fourteen stories to their friend's office. "The whole top was swaying enough to make you seasick," Ball told her parents. "We left immediately for the ground floor but in that short time the wind and rain had increased so that you couldn't stand up. Naturally we stayed in that building."

About forty miles inland from West Palm Beach, fifteen-year-old Vernon Boots and his young friends were enjoying the windy day. The winds weren't yet as fierce as those that were already slashing at West Palm Beach.

"Us boys, we were having a big time," Boots recalled in 1988.

Boots and his friends were making propellers by nailing a piece of a shingle to a stick and holding it up to the wind.

"And actually, the wind got to blowing so hard, the prop would turn so fast, it would burn a hole right through [the propeller]," Boots said.

Boots and his family lived on a farm on the southern shore of Lake Okeechobee, where they grew beans, potatoes, tomatoes, and other produce. Vernon's father, William Boots, also worked for the state highway department.

They had no idea that the wind was a harbinger of disaster. "Of course, we were enjoying it, you know, not having sense enough to know something bad was about to take place."

Around 2:30 p.m., downtown West Palm Beach was being drenched by rain and raked by steadily increasing winds when Margaret Best started writing her thoughts into a letter to her sister in Lowell, Massachusetts. She and her husband, Amos, were riding out the storm in the downtown cafeteria they operated. With them were their son and two of their daughters.

Amos Best and his family had spent the day trying to prepare for the hurricane, bracing doors, protecting plate-glass windows, gathering candles. Now all they could do was wait and listen to San Felipe's howling arrival.

"The wind is blowing a mile a minute, believe me, and overhead there is a rumble like thunder," Margaret Best wrote. "The rain is sweeping the street in sheets."

Margaret was already wondering whether their building would withstand the storm, and she and her husband were discussing whether to move to the cellar of a friend who lived nearby.

"We have candles all ready," she wrote. "The lights are all out and there is no power in the store. Dave came by about an hour ago with the latest reports of this being the worst storm ever here. . . . It is only 2:30 now and it is not expected to strike until 7 o'clock. It will be a wonder if there is anything left of us by then, it is so bad now."

Contemplating the roaring hurricane outside and the uncertainty of her fate, Margaret jotted a note on the back of the envelope containing the letter to her sister. "Someone Please Mail," she wrote.

At the Harvey Building, Frances Ball and her friend Jimmy were riding out the storm with other refugees.

"There were about 12 of us shut up in there," Ball wrote. "The water was pouring in through the doors and windows. All of a sudden, crack—then a second of silence—then a deafening, crashing, splintering of plate-glass windows! You should have heard the air scream through the transoms and around the corners."

Among the businesses in the building was a pharmacy on the ground floor, "all glass, too, and lighted by skylights," Ball said.

"The first thing we know one of the skylights came crashing down and it was pandemonium let loose inside there," she said. "The owner had some expensive stuff that must not get wet so he and two others dashed in to get it."

Moments later came another deafening crash, and the three terrified men raced out of the pharmacy. The roof and shelves lining the walls had collapsed. The stench of spilled chemicals followed the fleeing men.

"By that time the entire building was swaying and trembling in a manner to strike terror to your heart," Ball wrote.

And the worst part of the hurricane was still several hours away.

By five p.m. Margaret and Amos Best and their children had moved to the neighbor's cellar.

Margaret added a few hasty notes to her letter: "Storm terrific. One awning on store blown away. House rocking. Have our bags packed and blankets ready to leave if possible. Big piece of roofing blown off house. Wires down all around."

And nightfall was coming early.

"It is getting dark which adds to our fear," Best wrote. "Part of house blown away. We are going to try to be brave. Love."

The residents of the farming communities around Lake Okeechobee also were getting pummeled by the hurricane. By five p.m., the winds were just starting to arrive. At Canal Point, the wind was clocked at about forty miles an hour.

Nineteen people had gathered at the home of Pat Burke near the southern shore of the big lake. Burke's small one-story house was in the tiny farming community of Chosen, just outside Belle Glade. Residents had taken the name from biblical references to "a chosen place."

Burke's stepdaughter, Helen McCormick, was among the group that had assembled to ride out the storm. Her mother had discussed leaving the lake area with her husband, but they'd decided against it because it was a fifty-mile drive to the town of Okeechobee on the northern shore of the lake.

"We all had a big day with a big dinner, and the children playing and all," McCormick recalled, "and that night we was gathered in the front room and everyone was talking about where they'd go if they had to leave the house."

In Belle Glade, seventeen-year-old Jabo Tryon was tired and hungry. He'd gotten up at four o'clock that morning to go to work at his job at the local ice plant, and had worked more than twelve hours delivering ice with only a cup of coffee for sustenance. Storm or no storm, he was determined to get something to eat. He went to a restaurant in Belle Glade's small business district.

"So I went in there and ordered me a cup of coffee and a piece of pie," Tryon recalled in 1988. "She had some mighty fine pie."

Shortly before six p.m. the eye of San Felipe was just offshore from the oceanfront mansions of Palm Beach, and its winds were ripping away at downtown West Palm Beach on the other side of Lake Worth. Forty miles away on the southern shore of Lake Okeechobee, the intensifying winds were piling up water against the flimsy mud dikes.

Jack Zuber noticed that the water in a nearby canal had been steadily rising since around four p.m., and that made his wife Celia nervous.

"So was I," Zuber admitted. But they had two children: a son, Robert, and an infant. They were trying not to show their nervousness because of their kids.

San Felipe's eye touched land at Palm Beach around seven p.m. Its barometric pressure reading was 27.43 inches—even more intense than the hurricane that had hit Miami only two years earlier. At the time, it was the most intense hurricane on record to make landfall in the United States.

And then, suddenly, stillness. The eye of the storm had reached West Palm Beach.

"A little after seven the lull came and it was just about as terrifying as the storm," Frances Ball wrote in the letter to her parents. "Several people went reconnoitering but we stayed put."

As the winds died to a whisper, more storm refugees scurried into the Harvey Building seeking shelter.

"Mothers with tiny new babies," Ball wrote. "Women with canaries and dogs, fathers and youngsters—oh! It was pitiful. The lobby was jam full of women and children."

And then, after about a thirty-minute lull, bedlam returned.

"All of a sudden the wind changed," Ball said. "The lull was over and back she came in full fury. And one of the men had the bright idea that the glass might blow in because the wind had changed. So he had everybody move up to the second story and on up to the fifth.

"Now I'm not exaggerating one little bit when I say that he had no more got everybody out of the lobby, off the first stairway, when there came the most bloodcurdling *bang crash*! The steel girders were bent and twisted, and the lobby and stairway one mass of wall, tile, brick, and timber. Jimmy and I had been sitting on the next-to-the-bottom stair.

"We hadn't been gone five minutes before that whole thing caved in," Ball said. "It was pitch dark, and you should have heard the women and children scream! There simply are no words adequate to describe the terror of those few minutes. The air was full of chipped walls, plaster, sand, and glass."

The *Miami Daily News* later reported that the destruction had been caused when a heavy chimney gave way to the winds and crashed through the entire fourteen floors of the Harvey Building.

Ball and her friend Jimmy sat down on a stairwell on the third floor and leaned against a wall.

"As we were leaning there we could hear things go thudding down behind the walls of the stairway," Ball wrote. "It sounded awful and nearly petrified me, but we never breathed a word for fear of creating a panic."

But the winds seemed to be easing a bit.

"A little lull would come, then a new rush of wind and a series of crashes and dull thuds," Ball said. "The whole stairway would quiver and sway. Lord! It was awful."

Forty miles inland, the counterclockwise circulation of San Felipe's outer winds were starting to work on Lake Okeechobee, piling water higher and higher along the dikes on the southern shore.

"So it was just a little bit before dark that the water began to get right to the top of the dike, which was simply a muck dike, probably four, five feet high," said Vernon Boots. "So the water elevation was a good bit higher than the houses."

A hurricane's powerful winds move water even when it's far out to sea, crossing deep ocean waters. But in deep water, the effect is reduced because the deep water absorbs the wind's energy, and not as much water is piled up by the winds.

When a hurricane blows across shallow water, however, the wind's effects are far greater because the water's depth cannot absorb the wind's energy. So the water piles up.

Zora Neale Hurston eloquently described how the 1928 hurricane affected the lake.

"It woke up old Okeechobee and the monster began to roll in his bed," she wrote in *Their Eyes Were Watching God*. "Began to roll and complain like a peevish world on the grumble."

The lake became steadily more raucous as the hurricane moved inland and its eye passed West Palm Beach and started across the Everglades.

Hurricanes inevitably lose their power when they move over land. The land disrupts the storm's circulation, slows its momentum, and diminishes its winds. The deterioration usually happens quickly.

It's about forty miles from West Palm Beach to the southern shore of Lake Okeechobee. Usually, a hurricane has lost at least some of its intensity after traveling that far inland, but during the wet summer of 1928, the downpour from the August hurricane and the rains that had fallen almost continuously since early September had made the Everglades wetter than usual. San Felipe, in effect, was still over water as it roared inland toward Lake Okeechobee. And that probably allowed it to retain most of its monstrous power.

In Belle Glade, Jabo Tryon was digging into his pie. Outside, the winds were steadily increasing.

"And I'm setting there, when she set my coffee down and the pie, I took a bite of pie," Tryon recalled. "But the building was rocking so that my coffee was slopping out of the cup."

Tryon and another man sitting beside him at the counter were the only customers in the restaurant at the time. Tryon looked at the man and said, "This building ain't going to stand much of this. Look at my coffee cup, how it's rocking."

The winds began to claw away pieces of the building. "I guess I took one sip of my coffee, and the plaster began to fall out of the ceiling, into my pie and coffee," Tryon said.

Chunks of a false front over the entrance of the building began to tumble into the street. Two women who worked in the restaurant screamed and ran for the door, but Tryon and the other man persuaded them to wait until the pieces of the false front had stopped falling.

When the shower of debris ended, Tryon and the other man helped the women cross the alley to the Tedder Hotel, where other refugees had gathered. They joined the crowd in the hotel.

The winds increased with stunning quickness. A few minutes before eight p.m., the barometric pressure reading in nearby Canal Point was 28.54, and winds were blowing at sixty miles per hour. Only fifteen minutes later, the pressure had dropped to 28.25 and the winds were clocked at seventy-five.

Jack Zuber walked into the kitchen of his house and looked through a window in the back door. "It was jet dark, but every once in a while lightning gave me a glimpse of things."

Zuber guessed that he stood at the door staring into the storm for at least an hour.

At nine p.m., the barometer at Canal Point was reading 27.97, and winds were blowing at 150 miles an hour or more. And the barometer was still falling, which meant that the worst of the hurricane was still to come.

"Water was lapping up over the porch, I remember, when an exceptionally hard gust of wind came," Zuber said. "It just seemed that the house was going to pieces."

Zuber checked on his family. His wife was restraining her fear as she held their children.

"I went back into the kitchen again and as I looked through the window, lightning flashed just in time to show me the garage as it went over on its side, balanced there for a second, then crashed into a tree and was demolished," he said.

Celia cried out in terror. Zuber sat down beside her and took her hand. "I could feel that she was shaking all over," he said.

In the Tedder Hotel in Belle Glade, Jabo Tryon realized something bad had happened. Water was rushing under the hotel door.

"Well," Tryon said to a man standing next to him, "the dike's broke."

"Hush," the man said. "You want to start people screamin' and hollerin,' make 'em have fits?" the man said.

"You ain't gonna keep that a secret," the teenager retorted. "It's coming."

Soon the water was knee-deep in the hotel. "I could feel the muck come down my breeches leg, the muck that was floating in that rushing water. And that was muck that come off the plowed fields."

In the labor camps where migrant workers were huddling in their shacks for protection from the storm, chaos had been unleashed when the dikes gave way.

At Jack Zuber's farm, the water had risen to more than a foot deep in his living room.

"Suddenly there seemed to come a kind of wave, and the water must have risen about a foot all at once," Zuber said. "Celia jumped up, still holding both children. I took Robert from her."

"Things happened fast after that," Zuber said.

The building lurched, nearly throwing them off their feet. Another lurch sent Celia to the floor and Jack flying across the room. He decided he had to get his family out of the house. But then the house started coming apart.

"It seemed to me I was being washed miles and miles, then I felt the weight off and found myself on top of the water," he said.

Zuber was floating atop a wall that had been part of his house. "I looked around for Celia, and I just glimpsed her as she passed out of sight," he said. "She just kind of faded away in the water."

Zuber's raft of wreckage was swept on by the storm for what seemed an endless time. Finally the wall lodged firmly between two trees. Then Zuber passed out.

San Felipe's winds had driven more and more water against the dikes until they finally gave way and freed the beast of Lake Okeechobee, Hurston wrote. The raging water was pushing the disintegrating dikes ahead of it, and the muddy wall slammed into the migrants' shacks and "uprooted them like grass," Hurston wrote.

The workers fled for their lives, dodging flying debris as they went.

"They had to fight to keep from being pushed the wrong way and to hold together," Hurston wrote. "They saw other people like themselves struggling along. A house down, here and there, frightened cattle. But above all the drive of the wind and the water. And the lake. Under its multiplied roar could be heard a mighty sound of grinding rock and timber and a wail. They looked back. Saw people trying to run in raging waters and screaming when they found they couldn't. A huge barrier of the makings of the dike to which the cabins had been added was rolling and tumbling forward. Ten feet higher than and as far as they could see the muttering wall advanced before the braced-up waters like a road crusher on a cosmic scale."

All along the southern shore, water was tumbling out of Lake Okeechobee and driving everything before it. It was slamming into cottages, filling ground-floor living rooms, tearing infants from their mothers' arms, pushing still-occupied homes off their foundations, and carrying their occupants on a horrifying, deadly ride.

Water began filling the house where nineteen people, including Helen McCormick, had enjoyed a wonderful Sunday lunch only a few hours before.

"Everyone wanted to go to the roof, so they cut a hole through the roof," McCormick recalled. "When they got it cut through, the water was up around my waist."

A piano became a stairway through the hole to the roof. Once they were on the roof, McCormick's mother was holding her baby brother, and an older brother kept calling to their mother to make sure she was safe. For a while, McCormick heard her mother answering the calls. Then the answering voice went silent. The wind and water were capsizing the house.

"The next thing I knew I was in the water," McCormick said. "I felt myself slipping and I was under the water with things falling around me. My stepfather had told us earlier that if we was underwater it wouldn't hurt us as bad as if we was above it, so I just stayed submerged."

McCormick stayed underwater as long as she could, then surfaced. She struggled through the water to get back to her house, which was now upside down. She found her stepfather—the only other person alive. McCormick and her stepfather clung to the house, hoping the water would recede.

Elsewhere, terrified people ran blindly screaming into the night. Some of them were near the fields of sugarcane, where the ripening stalks, towering ten or twelve feet above them, were being whipped into a wild, flailing frenzy by the roaring winds that may have briefly reached 160 miles an hour.

The wind hurled some of the luckless refugees into the cane fields. Others were swept into the cane by the surging, relentless water. The stalks closed around them, weaving a lattice-like trap, pinning arms and legs, holding them helpless. Then more water followed, deeper and deeper until it covered them.

There was no escape.

As the storm started rising, Vernon Boots and his family decided to go to the house of a game warden. Eventually, more than sixty people, both African-American and white, had gathered there. It was one of the few places where both blacks and whites gathered to ride out the storm.

As the water started rising, they climbed into the attic.

"After a bit the black folks are praying, and singing and praying," Boots recalled. "The white folks were, I don't know why, very quiet, never said a word."

But the winds and surging waters pushed the house off its foundation. The house floated a short distance and then started breaking up, spilling its occupants into the water.

The wind and water scattered everyone and carried Boots and his brothers miles into the Everglades. They clung to a section of roof.

Back in Belle Glade, rain and water were pouring through the Tedder Hotel, but the building was somehow withstanding the pounding. Jabo Tryon was exhausted. He climbed the stairs to the hotel's upper floor, found a dry corner, and soon was fast asleep. He spent the rest of the night there undisturbed.

In Martin County, vicious winds were whipping off the eastern shore of the lake. In Indiantown, a blast of wind lifted a small building and dropped it on Ki Wilson, an African-American man who worked for L. L. Mayo, a logging contractor.

Both of Wilson's legs were broken. Mayo was afraid to move Wilson, but he realized the man had to have medical attention as quickly as possible. So the white contractor and four other men, all black, piled into Wilson's car and set out into the storm to fetch a doctor from Stuart.

The four men with Mayo rode along to remove downed trees and debris that might be blocking the road between Indiantown and Stuart. Mayo sped along until he came to a section of the road that had been washed out. Mayo slammed on the brakes, but his car skidded and overturned in water about fifteen feet deep.

Two men managed to escape the wreck, but Mayo and three others were trapped and drowned.

In West Palm Beach, the hurricane's winds started to diminish shortly after midnight. Frances Ball and her companions picked their way down debris-strewn stairs to stand at the smashed-in front door of the Harvey Building. Outside, the wind was still shrieking.

A group of American Legionnaires appeared and offered to guide the refugees in the Harvey Building to a hotel that had thrown open its doors. They left the building and followed the Legionnaires down windswept Datura Street.

"The wind was so driving and the rain so strong that in three blocks I managed to catch my breath three times," Ball wrote to her parents.

"And such a sight as met our eyes!" she continued. "The street was piled full of cars heaped up on each other. Wires were down across the way and a building [was] sitting in the street. Of course all these things were just dim shapes and we didn't see the wires.

"A huge gust of wind whipped me down the street and a tight wire cut me a mean clip under the chin that sent me back about five feet."

Ball regained her balance and the group continued. "We scrambled around in the mud and wire until we finally got clear and then started for an alley," Ball wrote. "We climbed over a roof or two, some mashed-in walls, and missed a couple of wrecked cars and fell into the cellar of this hotel, where a bunch of Negro porters got us started up the stairs."

They joined dozens of others who had taken shelter in the Pennsylvania Hotel.

"It was going on one a.m. when we got here and the halls were lined with refugees rolled up in blankets—just like the war scenes in movies!" Ball wrote.

Ball and her group were given blankets. "There I spent the night with four men!" Ball told her parents. "I lay awake and prayed while the walls quivered and shook from the impact of the storm."

At about the same time Frances Ball went to bed, Margaret Best finished her letter to her sister in Massachusetts.

When the eye reached West Palm Beach, Best and her family had taken refuge in a neighbor's cellar with more than two dozen other people.

"I'll write again tomorrow," Best concluded. "We sure are weary."

Frances Ball, still picking bits of plaster and glass from her hair, finished her letter to her parents the following day.

"The ambulances have been tearing about all day," she wrote. "The dining room here is an impromptu operating room and the lobby is the hospital. Two babies were born here during the nite [*sic*] to add to all the rest of the confusion."

"PS," she concluded, "my hair isn't even gray yet! But I sure hate to hear people drop things with a thud. I wonder which wall has gone now!"

As gray daylight crept into the Everglades on Monday, September 17, low, dark clouds to the north marked San Felipe's departure. The storm quickly lost its ferocious intensity after its eye moved north of the lake, but it was still packing destructive winds and heavy rainfall.

Vernon Boots and his brothers began slogging through the Everglades, hoping to find their way back to where they had last seen their family.

"We were back in undeveloped land," Boots recalled. "The woods [were] full of snakes and turtles and alligators and anything, birds and all type of life, where the animals had died in the bushes."

The brothers hadn't gone far when they heard someone shouting. It was one of their friends, a young boy named Mutt Thomas, who also had survived being swept into the Glades. The youngster joined the older boys, and they continued their journey across the ruined watery landscape.

It looked as though a giant hand had upended Lake Okeechobee and spilled its water across miles of the southern shore.

"Water, knee-deep, covered all the land," wrote author Lawrence Will, who survived the awful storm and later wrote about it in his book, *Okeechobee Hurricane: Killer Storms in the Everglades.* "Projecting dismally above the flood were fragments of roofs and floors, bed posts, and trunks, uprooted custard apple trees, wrecked automobiles. From limbs and snags high above the ground hung festoons of hyacinths, and rags that had been clothing. The eye searched in vain for familiar buildings. Instead it was confused by strange houses, leaning crazily, where none had been before."

And there were corpses, flung into trees, floating in the water, or simply lying cold and stiff and still on the higher ground that occasionally rose above the floodwater.

In Belle Glade, "tight-packed wreckage filled the streets," Will wrote. "Figures of men began to appear, staring about in amazement. I joined them," he said.

The men splashed through the water, stunned at what they were seeing. They found the bodies of a young boy and his little sister. A poolroom that was still partially standing became a morgue, and they laid the children's bodies on a pool table.

Jack Zuber, still unconscious on the raft that had been a side of his house, felt something warm in his mouth and slowly roused himself to consciousness. He had been found, and someone was trying to force warm coffee into his mouth.

Eight days later, Zuber still had no word about the fate of his wife and children.

Other than the unlucky people around the lake, the public didn't have any idea what had happened on the southern shore of Lake Okeechobee. But the Red Cross was getting alarming reports early Monday morning from J. Denham Bird, its local chairman in the town of Okeechobee on the lake's northern shore.

"Conditions serious here," Bird telegraphed Red Cross headquarters in Washington, DC, "We would appreciate help. Imperative. Reported many drowned and homeless."

Red Cross officials also were getting their first reports about conditions in West Palm Beach. In Jacksonville, Red Cross officials received a message from an amateur radio operator. Three-fourths of the homes in West Palm Beach were damaged, and nearly every business was heavily damaged, he said.

But somehow, Florida governor John Martin wasn't yet in the loop about hurricane damage. He could be forgiven for not being aware of the horror in the little towns on the southern shore of Lake Okeechobee. Cut off by flooded roads and isolated by downed telegraph and electrical lines, it would be days before the gruesome details of San Felipe's slaughter emerged. But Martin seemed to dismiss the severe damage the storm had done to West Palm Beach, one of the state's larger and better-known cities. When the commander of Florida's National Guard asked Martin to send troops to the area where the hurricane had done its worst, the governor hesitated.

"If necessary, of course, I will act on the request," Martin said.

Around eight a.m. on Monday, September 17, the storm's eye made its closest approach to Tampa, coming to about thirty miles east-southeast of the city.

But the hurricane had weakened considerably since wreaking havoc from West Palm Beach to Lake Okeechobee. Its strongest winds, blowing at about 100 miles an hour, were well to the east of Tampa, where peak winds reached only about 30 mph.

Still, that was all the irrepressible Tampa attorney Peter Knight needed to make up his mind about the effects of this hurricane.

Without waiting for details of the Lake Okeechobee horror to emerge, and taking it upon himself to speak for the entire state of Florida, Knight dispatched a telegram to Arthur Brisbane.

"News dispatches sent out from Florida concerning so-called hurricane positively malicious and criminal," Knight seethed. "The velocity of wind in Tampa has not exceeded thirty miles per hour. No damage here. Damage to entire state negligible. Please give this publicity."

Negligible.

In Knight's estimation, the most powerful hurricane in US history at that time had been nothing more than a windy, rainy day in Florida. Knight's irresponsible and wildly inaccurate telegram to Brisbane was the first shot in another publicity duel between Florida business interests and the American Red Cross.

As the storm spun northward, an announcer on WDBO radio in Orlando was summarizing the hurricane's effects on that city. Speaking from the station's broadcast studios in the Fort Gatlin Hotel, the announcer told his listeners that "little, if any damage" had been done in Orlando.

Outside, the storm's winds whipped through the hotel's street-level arcade. Unlike Tampa, however, Orlando was on the strong side of the hurricane and the winds were considerably stronger.

A few minutes after telling listeners that Orlando had suffered little damage, the WDBO announcer was back. The radio station would be off the air for a while, he said. The hurricane had just ripped the ceramic tile roof off the chic, Spanish Mission–style hotel.

As soon as the winds had died down enough to allow people to emerge from their shelters, Florida's larger newspapers in Miami, St. Petersburg, and West Palm Beach sent out reporters to try to find their way to Lake Okeechobee. But it was slow going. Roads were flooded and piled high with debris and downed trees.

On Tuesday, September 18, a few details of the death and damage caused by the hurricane were published in newspapers. The *Palm Beach Post* said the Red

Cross was estimating that fifty people had been killed in Palm Beach County. The *Post* also reported that dikes along Lake Okeechobee's southern shore had broken, and there had been some flooding in Belle Glade.

Telephone service was restored to parts of the lake area Tuesday night, and a few more details were reported. Those details were published in newspapers on Wednesday, September 19.

The *St. Petersburg Times* reported that thirty bodies, most of them African Americans, lay in an improvised morgue in Belle Glade. The *Palm Beach Post* reported that N. B. Jones, a *Post* employee, had been among the rescue workers who had left West Palm Beach late Monday night. He returned the following day driving an ambulance with the bodies of thirteen African Americans.

Arthur Brisbane's "Today" column for Tuesday, September 18, 1928, included a breezy comment on the hurricane.

"If you have made any winter plans about Florida, don't let any news reports, accurate or exaggerated, influence you," he wrote. "There are no tornadoes in Florida in winter. Information about 'terrible tornado in Florida' comes in this dispatch from Peter O. Knight, one of the ablest lawyers in Florida."

Brisbane then reprinted Knight's telegram of the previous day, dismissing the hurricane's damage as "negligible."

But President Calvin Coolidge was getting a different perception of the hurricane's wrath in Florida and Puerto Rico from the Red Cross and the US Weather Bureau. Coolidge, far better informed than Brisbane and Knight, understood the magnitude of the catastrophe and wanted the federal government to do whatever it could to help.

In Tallahassee, Governor John Martin also was following the scraps of news about the hurricane's impact. He later told the *Stuart News* that he got the first indication of the seriousness of the hurricane's damage in messages he received from several wireless radio operators.

On September 18 Martin began preparing for a long drive from Tallahassee to West Palm Beach with Florida attorney general Fred Davis. Before he left Tallahassee, he contacted US secretary of war Dwight Davis and asked for immediate help from the federal government for West Palm Beach. The secretary immediately granted Martin's request, and Florida's governor and attorney general set out on their long trek eastward across the Florida Panhandle and then down the peninsula.

Around 1:45 a.m. on Tuesday, September 19, Red Cross vice chairman James Fieser received a radio message from the National Guard troops that had been dispatched to the hurricane area. There were at least 400 dead in Palm Beach County, and the situation around Lake Okeechobee was "very serious." Around 6,000 people were in refugee camps. In keeping with the Jim Crow practices of the day, whites were gathered in a camp in Miami, while African Americans were sent to a camp in Pompano Beach.

Property damage in Palm Beach County was estimated at $30 million, or more than $403 million in twenty-first-century dollars.

But the editorial page in that day's edition of the *Tampa Morning Tribune*—whose board of directors included Peter Knight—downplayed the hurricane's damage.

An editorial briefly acknowledged that people were killed—to be fair, no one had any idea yet of the true death toll—but suggested that the greatest loss caused by the storm seemed to be in the state's citrus crop.

"Compared with the wholesale destruction in Porto Rico [*sic*] and other islands, the storm seems to have become moderate before touching Florida," the *Tribune* said. "There have been more terrific storms in many other parts of the country this summer, and there will be worse blizzards next winter."

That same day, the *Wall Street Journal* echoed Knight's sentiments and the *Tribune* editorial. Just as it had done after Miami had been wrecked by a hurricane two years earlier, the *Journal* scorned any talk of an unmeasurable catastrophe in Florida and dismissed the storm's damage as superficial.

"Cyclone or hurricane damage is essentially surface damage," the *Journal* said. "It has every element of the spectacular and it always looks several times as bad as it really is."

The *Journal* called the hurricane deaths "deplorable," but added that death "happens any day of the year from causes other than hurricanes."

"When the Florida winter season opens at Christmas there will be no evidence of wreckage that the Northern tourist can recognize," the *Journal* predicted.

Miami Daily News readers got a jarring look at San Felipe's work on Wednesday, September 20, when the newspaper published photos from Belle Glade taken by reporter Cecil Warren. In addition to wrecked buildings and flooded landscapes, Warren photographed corpses. Among them was a shot of four rescue workers, hands on hips, helplessly looking at the bodies of three or four victims about to be loaded onto a truck for removal to West Palm Beach.

"This may seem like it is exaggerated to those who have not visited the drowned lands, where bodies lie lodged against palmetto bushes, caught in drifts and prone by highways, exposed to plain view," Warren later wrote. But, he said, the photos did not exaggerate conditions in and around Belle Glade.

Warren said an unnamed deputy sheriff told him that photos were forbidden in Belle Glade. Warren, the skeptical newsman, asked National Guard officers if photography was prohibited. Other men gathered around Warren and the Guardsmen as they talked. The officers said photography was not forbidden.

One of the men who'd overheard the conversation spoke to Warren in a steely tone.

"Boy," the man said, "you take all the pictures you want, of whatever you want. Snapshot these bodies and homes, show the world in full what has happened. We want everyone to know the truth."

By now, a small crowd had assembled around the *Daily News* reporter. If anyone tried to stop Warren from taking photos, the man assured the reporter, he and others "[would] attend to that little matter."

"Show me the man who tried to keep you from it," the man said.

The man told Warren that he'd lost his home but had been lucky enough not to lose his family. Nonetheless, he understood the grief of those who'd lost loved ones.

"If I was one of those standing here on the bank of this canal and saw the body of my wife and three children brought up, when I saw them the first thing I would do would be to grab my shotgun and go to Tallahassee after the man who is responsible," he said.

"I will say that he named the man he thought was responsible," Warren wrote, "but I will not, because there is no man who, in full knowledge of the consequences, would have brought about such destruction as exists in the Everglades—one vast, rotting pool, filled with the bodies of men, women, and little children, their hopes and belongings."

Other larger Florida newspapers published stories about conditions at Lake Okeechobee on Thursday, September 21.

Cecelia Copeland, a reporter for the *St. Petersburg Times*, described her trip into the Glades with a rescue crew. She filed her story from Clewiston, where storm damage had been less severe and a refugee camp had been established.

"Families have been cruelly separated," Copeland wrote. "Crying but lovable little tots are harbored here but are totally unidentified. Rapidly graying mothers ply through the crowds of refugees, eagerly scanning their faces in hope of finding relatives."

Being surrounded by misery and destruction was having an effect on Copeland.

"I have seen sights in this section that I hope never to see again," she wrote. "This is no place for sightseers and curious people."

That same day, Red Cross officials and others started responding to charges that storm damage was being exaggerated.

Howard Selby, the Red Cross chairman for Palm Beach County, sent a telegram to Peter Knight telling him that he'd acted irresponsibly in claiming to speak for the entire state and saying the hurricane's damage had been "negligible."

Citing the growing death toll and the thousands that were homeless, Selby urged Knight to retract his comments.

"Known dead over 700; homeless 15,000; without clothing 8,000; property damage $20 million," Selby said in the telegram. "These facts are given after deliberate and careful survey, and other authorities have stated these estimates [as] too conservative."

Selby ended with a challenge to Knight: "If you are to serve as spokesman for [an] entire state, won't you kindly make personal visit here? We are distressed and need the help of the nation."

By nightfall Thursday, Florida governor Martin and attorney general Davis had reached Stuart in the governor's namesake county. The two high-ranking state officials stopped there and talked with Edwin Menninger's *South Florida Developer*.

"I could not see my own county suffer," Martin said. "I think more of Martin County than any other county in the state. . . . I will not let the people of Martin County suffer."

Martin had not yet seen the devastation on the southern shore of Lake Okeechobee.

In Tampa, Peter Knight tried to deflect harsh criticism of his earlier comments and spin his hasty assessment that hurricane damage had been "negligible." The *St. Petersburg Times* of Friday, September 21, printed a follow-up letter that Knight had written to Arthur Brisbane.

Knight acknowledged that the storm had caused "great damage at Palm Beach and immediate vicinity," and "some damage" to the north and south of West Palm Beach, but said his "negligible" comment had referred to the entire state.

He made a passing acknowledgment of the deaths, but added "no reference can be made to the loss of life. That is too sacred. It cannot be measured in dollars and cents. We have to deal simply with the monetary loss."

And then he dismissed even the monetary loss in the small farming towns that had been nearly wiped out by the hurricane.

"The little settlements around Lake Okeechobee were composed of houses of a very cheap character, ranging all the way from tents up," Knight wrote. Those losses "could not exceed $100,000," he said.

Knight said he'd sent the telegram to Brisbane "for the protection of the state."

"I was correct when I stated that the damage to the entire state was negligible, because such is the case," he said.

The *Tampa Morning Tribune*, Knight's hometown newspaper, tried to straddle the fence about the controversy surrounding one of its directors.

"The storm did serious damage to a small section of the peninsula, and thus indirectly hurt the whole state . . . ," the *Tribune* said on its editorial page.

But the newspaper also scolded Brisbane for his cavalier ignorance. "This was a severe hurricane," the *Tribune* said. "Brisbane and others should learn that it was not a tornado any more than it was a waterspout."

And the *Tribune* indirectly criticized Knight. "The fact that the storm effects were confined to a comparatively small section of Florida does not mean that it was by any means negligible," the editorial said. "It was heartbreaking to thousands."

That night, A. L. Shafer, who was directing Red Cross relief operations in Florida, sent a telegram to his headquarters in Washington, updating his bosses. His note included a horrifying preliminary estimate of the death toll.

"Conditions Lake Okeechobee region simply terrible," Shafer wrote. "Many bodies not recovered and sanitary conditions bad. We have received reports that 1,500 are dead in this region but will hold my estimate to 450 until such numbers are confirmed."

There were more grim statistics: 15,000 families registered for Red Cross assistance; 95 percent of homes destroyed in West Palm Beach; 5,500 being fed in West Palm Beach every day.

To make matters worse, sanitary conditions around the lake were getting worse. Bodies were surfacing in the lake every day and, of necessity, were being buried without identification as quickly as possible. There was talk of moving every single person, including rescue workers, away from the lake and using airplanes to spray the entire area with lime to prevent the growth of bacteria on the corpses and to reduce the awful odor of decaying bodies.

"General condition absolute destitution," Shafer tersely concluded.

Paul Hoxie, commander of the American Legion post in St. Petersburg, explained how those conditions were affecting rescue workers in a report to the Red Cross on September 24. Nearly one thousand Legionnaires were working between Pahokee and South Bay, looking for corpses.

The grim work was taking such an emotional toll on the men that Hoxie resorted to the drastic measures used by a Civil War commander to steel his soldiers for the grisly task of gathering and burying the dead after the Battle of Antietam. He issued whiskey to them before sending them out to perform their awful chore.

"It boils down to this," he said. "If you send men out on a 'dead detail,' they have to be half-drunk before they can go. If fifty men go on this detail today, only about twenty-five of them will be fit to go tomorrow."

Hoxie said local doctors who "deem it necessary" were providing whiskey to fortify the Legionnaires for this ghastly work.

That same day, Governor John Martin had finally gotten a firsthand look at the worst of the storm damage, and he was appalled.

Around midnight, a weary and stunned Martin invited reporters into his room at the Hotel Monterey in downtown West Palm Beach. He sat down on his bed and for an hour he described what he'd seen.

"Today, in traveling six miles on the road between Pahokee and Belle Glade, I counted twenty-seven corpses floating in the water adjacent to the road or lying in the road," the governor said.

At least one million acres around Lake Okeechobee had been flooded, and the skies were filled with carrion birds feasting on corpses, he said.

"It was the most horrible thing I ever saw," Martin said.

That night, Martin sent a telegram to the mayors of all of the state's cities, asking them to urge residents to contribute to the Red Cross relief fund.

Still, despite the increasing clarity of the monumental disaster that had taken place in Florida, the *Wall Street Journal*'s editorial page again insisted on Saturday, September 22, that the storm's effects were exaggerated, and any opinion to the contrary was hysteria.

The editorial followed the same formula as earlier ones had done: briefly acknowledge the tragedy in the opening paragraph, genuflect to the deaths, then dispute any facts that contradicted the *Journal*'s contention that the storm damage was exaggerated, and insult any and all who challenged the accuracy of the *Journal*'s depiction of the event.

Newspapers other than the *Wall Street Journal* "are practically instructed to send sensational figures rather than properly sifted facts," the editorial said. "In captions such a figure as a thousand deaths looks more impressive than 271 and is much less trouble to collect."

Late Sunday evening, September 23, John Martin stopped again in Stuart. The *South Florida Developer* said the governor, still reeling from what he'd seen in the lakeside towns, "staggered into the Red Cross headquarters" in Stuart.

After spending two days in the "vast, rotting pool" of death and devastation around Lake Okeechobee, the governor apparently needed to unburden himself, and he decided that he was among friends in Martin County. He assembled the Red Cross workers and started talking.

"Just a few hours ago I saw the bodies of thirty-two colored men stacked up on the canal bank, and this I mention only because it was the last horror upon which I have gazed," Martin said. "I have seen death and suffering everywhere. But no human tongue or pen can describe it."

He mentioned the awful discovery of bodies hopelessly ensnared in the sugarcane fields. Some of the corpses were so tightly entangled that, after nearly a week, rescue workers still hadn't figured out how to remove them.

But even a clearly stunned governor's eyewitness account of the horror didn't alter the *Wall Street Journal*'s relentless condescending and disparaging narrative on the hurricane's effect and Red Cross efforts to deal with the aftermath. On Monday, September 24, the *Journal* published its most sarcastic and cynical commentary yet on the catastrophe.

"There is a political reason for the apparently senseless exaggeration of any disaster which happens to the State of Florida," a *Journal* editorial began. "That exaggeration has been repeated over and over again, and only a few newspapers like *The Wall Street Journal*, whose readers demand accuracy and know when they are getting it, have treated the recent hurricane on a sane basis."

The *Journal* made the obligatory acknowledgment that people had been killed, but added that most of the deaths had been among "small [N]egro cultivators with minor casualties in the white population of the few towns in the immediate track of the storm." The estimate of property damage by the storm was "absurdly exaggerated," the editorial said.

The whole thing amounted to class warfare against the wealthy, the *Journal* said. The people who were portraying Florida's condition in such dire terms were furious that the state did not impose most of the taxes that were so common in other states. And Florida's enemies couldn't stand it that the state was fiscally sound without these taxes.

"The State does not owe a dollar; it has no indebtedness, bonded or otherwise, and it has $4 million cash in the treasury," the *Journal* said. "The State is on a cash basis and commits the crime against other States of attracting wealthy residents who nevertheless object to being robbed."

The *Journal* then identified New York governor Al Smith—the Democratic nominee for president in the upcoming election—as a villain in the plot against Florida. Smith, the editorial said, was in favor of maintaining the federal tax on estates transferred at the owner's death.

"Here is the true basis of a misrepresentation which may well be called hysterical, with, however, the proviso that there is method in such madness," the *Journal* concluded.

Many Americans disagreed with the *Journal*'s reasoning about the hurricane relief. An editorial in the *Grand Rapids Herald* said the *Journal*'s editorial was "sick," and sounded as though it had been "edited in a padded cell by a victim of delirium tremens."

But the *Journal*'s editorials, coupled with misunderstanding and ignorance about the area where the hurricane had struck, were once again creating confusion and making it difficult for the Red Cross to reach its fund-raising goal of $5 million. Even some of the Red Cross's own local leaders in other parts of the United States thought the damage reports were exaggerated.

J. B. Ellis, chairman of the Lincoln County chapter of the American Red Cross in Elsberry, Missouri, sent a clipping of a *Wall Street Journal* editorial to Red Cross officials in Washington, DC.

Referring to the editorial, Ellis said he thought the Red Cross should forget about spending money to help people in Florida and instead use it to help hurricane victims in the Caribbean. Florida didn't need the Red Cross's money, Ellis said.

"Is it not a fact that Palm Beach is practically owned by millionaires?" he asked.

Newspaper headlines such as one that appeared in the *Montreal Gazette* didn't help either. A headline in the Canadian newspaper read "250 Dead In Tampa," which had barely been touched by the hurricane.

Red Cross officials and Palm Beach County leaders decided to confront the problem directly. On September 28, a delegation from Palm Beach County met with newspaper reporters in New York City to explain what the hurricane had done. The Florida group included Howard Selby, chairman of the Palm Beach County Red Cross chapter; former Palm Beach mayor Cooper Lightbown; and W. A. Payne, business manager of the *Palm Beach Post*.

Wall Street Journal editors begrudgingly changed the tone of their editorials after the meeting.

On Monday, October 1, the *Journal*'s editorial page insisted the newspaper had done the right thing by telling readers that the hurricane had not been a disaster for the entire state of Florida, and repeated its absurd claim from two years earlier that damage reports of the 1926 Miami hurricane had been "preposterous."

"But the damage to Palm Beach County is a matter so serious as to call for the generous assistance of the whole country," the paper said.

Ten days after the editorial was published, the Red Cross announced that it had reached its $5 million fund-raising goal.

The *Journal* also acknowledged, for the first time, that the death toll from the storm had been very high, adding, however, that "about three-fourths were [N]egroes."

The Journal's backhanded acknowledgment of African-American deaths was only a hint of the suffering that the hurricane had inflicted on them in the Jim Crow–era South.

In the late summer of 1928, thousands of black migrant workers were coming to Lake Okeechobee from across the South, as well as from the Bahamas and the Caribbean. They lived in labor camps, shacks, and tents. Some simply slept in the open. They weren't required to register. They were paid in cash and they moved on. There was no documentation of any sort to record their names or track their movements.

There was simply no way of knowing how many were killed because there is no way of knowing how many were there before the storm.

More than six hundred black victims of the storm were buried in a mass grave in downtown West Palm Beach and forgotten until 2002.

After the hurricane, blacks and whites were sent to separate refugee camps. Red Cross officials insisted that they did not treat black refugees any differently than white refugees in the segregated camps, and inspections by committees of prominent African-American advisors verified the Red Cross's contention.

But it was a different story outside the Red Cross camps.

Red Cross documents in the National Archives in College Park, Maryland, describe several ugly racial incidents in the days following the hurricane.

The worst incident happened on September 23, when Knowlton Crosby, a white twenty-year-old National Guard soldier, shot and killed Cootie Simpson, a thirty-five-year-old African American who was a World War I veteran with a wife and two children in West Palm Beach.

Accounts vary on exactly what happened, but what is certain is that it happened while National Guard troops were rounding up men to clear hurricane damage and bury the dead.

Public officials in hurricane-ravaged towns had imposed some harsh emergency regulations in the wake of the storm. In West Palm Beach and Stuart, men of both races who weren't employed and working their normal jobs could be legally forced to work on hurricane cleanup and burial crews.

Crosby ordered Simpson to join a work detail and Simpson refused. Some accounts say he'd been working on such a detail for several days and was leaving to go home to his wife when Crosby shot him. Another account says Simpson said he would ask his boss for permission to join the work detail and walked away, and Crosby shot him. A third account said Simpson started to attack Crosby and the Guardsman killed him in self-defense.

Simpson's wife, Juanita, asked the Red Cross for money to ship his body to Surrency, Georgia, where they'd lived before coming to Florida.

A coroner's inquest on September 24 found that Crosby had been justified in shooting Simpson. A single sentence concluded that Simpson met his death "[b]y a rifle wound inflicted by Knowlton Crosby, a member of Company C, 114th Infantry, Florida National Guard, while in the lawful discharge of his duty."

A few days after Simpson's death, an organization called the Negro Workers Relief Committee in New York City announced that it had launched an "emergency" fund-raising effort to help African-American victims of the hurricane.

In a story published in black-owned newspapers across the United States, the committee said it had started the effort because black refugees were being discriminated against by the Red Cross and other relief agencies.

The Negro Workers Relief Committee claimed many prominent African Americans among its advisors, including famed author and editor W. E. B. Du Bois.

But Du Bois, educator Mary McLeod Bethune, and other African-American leaders disavowed any connection with the Negro Workers Relief Committee. Bethune visited the hurricane area and said she "detected no discrimination whatever" in the Red Cross's relief effort, "but rather an enthusiastic desire" to help everyone who needed help.

Du Bois wrote a letter to the Negro Workers Relief Committee telling them he did not support their fund-raising effort, and not to use his name for that effort. The Associated Negro Press later said the Negro Workers Relief Committee was affiliated with the American Communist Party.

In mid-October 1928, the Red Cross compiled statistics outlining the hurricane's effect on Florida. More than 2,000 people had been killed by the hurricane, "with no possibility of accurate count," the Red Cross concluded. The death toll was still being calculated seventy-five years later. In 2003, the National Weather Service raised the official number of deaths in the 1928 hurricane to "at least 2,500." Still, NWS meteorologist Rusty Pfost said, "We all know we really don't know what the answer is."

There were other grim numbers: 95 percent of the buildings in Palm Beach County had been damaged, and 25 percent destroyed; the homes of 690 farmers had been destroyed; 15,000 people had been left homeless by the hurricane, which had "seriously" affected seven counties; 17,500 people were receiving help from the Red Cross, and 5,000 people were living in Red Cross refugee camps.

The year had begun with optimistic predictions for Florida's future—the Tamiami Trail would open, real estate prices would stabilize, investors and money would return, and good times would resume.

But 1928 was drawing to a decidedly depressing close.

CHAPTER TWELVE
Dreamland After All

A few weeks before his March 4, 1929, inauguration, President-elect Herbert Hoover took a quick look at the small towns around Lake Okeechobee that had been ravaged by the hurricane five months earlier. It wasn't the first time Hoover had seen the aftermath of a disaster. In the spring of 1927, he had coordinated the effort of local, state, and federal agencies to help victims after massive flooding along the Mississippi River had left 600,000 people homeless.

Preventing another flooding tragedy around Lake Okeechobee was a winning campaign issue in Florida in the 1928 election. Hoover, a Republican and a former engineer who had campaigned on improved flood control, easily carried Florida, with about 56 percent of the vote. In the governor's race, Democrat Doyle Carlton made flood control part of his campaign, and he won more than 60 percent of the vote.

By contrast, former governor John Martin, who had tried and failed to enact a flood-control program, was soundly defeated by incumbent Park Trammell in the Democratic primary for one of Florida's seats in the US Senate.

Although much of the area around the lake's southern shore that had been hardest hit by the storm had made a remarkable recovery by the time Hoover toured the area in February 1929, there were grim reminders. A house remained in a canal, and a large pile of storm-driven debris remained by the road between Belle Glade and Pahokee. Many residents were still living in tents or hastily constructed shacks.

Many miles of road washed out by the flooding had been only partially repaired, and Hoover's motorcade had to slow to a crawl in places.

Remains of storm victims still were being found, and that would continue for years.

The storm debris provided a stark contrast to the thriving crops of cabbages, beans, tomatoes, and sugarcane that had been replanted as soon as the floodwaters had drained off and evaporated.

Hoover made only one stop during his five-hour drive around Lake Okeechobee. In South Bay, where dozens of bodies had once been piled in the town's main street after the storm, the president-elect was presented with a bouquet of flowers, and he posed for cameramen for a few moments.

Crowds awaited him in other towns, but his procession didn't stop, only slowing down so he could wave at the disappointed onlookers.

Hoover attended a banquet in Clewiston that night, and the crowd made it clear that they wanted the federal government to pay the tab for almost $11 million—more than $157 million in twenty-first-century dollars—worth of draining and flood-control improvements to prevent a recurrence of the 1928 disaster.

But the president-elect stayed mum while other speakers addressed the crowd, and he slipped out of the gathering and went to bed early.

Still, work eventually started on a more substantial structure to protect the small lakeside towns. A sixty-six-mile levee, 175 feet thick at its base and 34 feet high, was completed on the lake's southern shore in 1935. By the 1950s, the massive levee had been extended another eighty miles so that it encircled the lake. The structure was named after Hoover.

While Hoover toured the storm area, Miami newspapers were boasting of a booming tourist trade for the 1928–29 season.

"Facts and figures give indisputable evidence that even the most skeptical must accept as evidence that Greater Miami has returned to prosperity," the *Miami Daily News* crowed in its edition of February 17, 1929. The city's winter population was at least 15 percent higher than it had been during the 1927–28 season.

But the city also was looking over its shoulder, hoping to avoid a return of the "be-knickered tribe of speculators" that had descended on the city in 1925, the *News* said.

And the city would have preferred that some winter visitors had stayed away, especially when *The New Yorker* magazine noted in its edition of March 2, 1929, that Al Capone was spending another winter in Florida.

Miami Beach leaders had continued their determined effort to force Capone to leave town. The company insuring the Palm Island mansion had canceled the policy when they learned Capone lived at the property, but Capone had dug in for a legal battle to hold on to the house.

Organized-crime operatives, many of them drawn by Capone's presence, were coming south to enjoy the state's gentle winters and swank amenities. The rowdy, backwoods bootleggers and bank robbers of the Ashley Gang era were being replaced by a different type of criminal—clever, well-groomed, sophisticated, and often armed with attorneys instead of guns.

On March 7, 1929, gangland violence from New York and Chicago spilled over into Miami with deadly results. On that date, about twenty people were playing cards in a two-room suite on the fourteenth floor of the posh Miami Biltmore Hotel. Among the group of stylishly dressed men and women was Thomas "Fatty" Walsh, who enjoyed telling people that he'd been a bodyguard for the late kingpin of underworld gambling, Arnold Rothstein, who many thought had fixed the 1919 World Series.

Walsh had been questioned by police after Rothstein was mortally wounded three months earlier in New York's Park Central Hotel.

Suddenly a door opened and a man stepped into the doorway and began shooting. Moments later, Walsh lay dead on the floor. Mobster Arthur Clark, who said he'd come to Miami to recover from the flu, was wounded.

Clark, who was willing to talk to detectives investigating the crime, said he didn't think he was the target of the killer's bullets and had been hit accidentally. But he was guarded by police while he recovered in a Miami hospital.

Miami cops who investigated the Biltmore shooting unraveled a thread that went all the way back to the slaying of gangster Frank Uale eight months earlier—the murder that had been linked to Al Capone and his Miami pal, Parker Henderson Jr., who had bought guns for the bootlegging king.

Police also found evidence that Walsh had been in Chicago a few weeks earlier when a slaughter that horrified the nation took place—the infamous St. Valentine's Day Massacre, in which seven men were lined up against a wall and machine-gunned to death.

Walsh apparently had come to Miami to meet with Capone, police learned.

The afternoon after the shooting, Miami police rounded up fifteen men known to be connected with organized crime in New York and Chicago.

The gangland shooting in Miami's most opulent hotel and subsequent roundup of underworld thugs was a reminder of how Capone's presence was affecting the city's image. It was also starting to affect property values and real estate sales. Potential buyers were having second thoughts about Miami Beach property because of Capone's presence.

Still, Capone clung to the mansion, even after he was convicted of tax evasion and sentenced to prison in 1931. He eventually died there after having a stroke in 1947.

In his "Today" column of March 1, 1929, Arthur Brisbane—who was now the largest individual taxpayer in Martin County—was still bullish about Florida's future. He noted that the state had shipped 38,000 train carloads of winter fruits and vegetables north, and that this represented less than half of the season's crop.

He also noted that Carl Fisher had reported the tourist crowds in Miami were the largest in the state's history.

But up the coast, Martin County was facing serious problems.

The spectacular "ideal" developments that had been advertised with such grandeur in the *South Florida Developer*—Picture City, Port Mayaca, Okeechobee Shores—never materialized, nor did the deepwater harbor that would have been "the best south of Savannah."

Instead of becoming an ideal city that exceeded even Coral Gables, Port Mayaca became better known for being the final resting place for about 1,600 victims of the 1928 hurricane buried in a mass grave.

Indiantown's dreams of becoming a thriving industrial giant—and perhaps being renamed to honor its benefactor—evaporated when Solomon Davies Warfield died. And Arthur Brisbane's 10,000-acre "demonstration" farm was never built.

Had the Ashley Gang still been around, they would've had to go someplace other than Stuart to find a bank to rob. By March 1929, both of the town's banks had closed their doors, and the money deposited there—representing income from businesses, government funds, and the life savings of hundreds of people—were gone forever.

The banks' closings were only one of many economic problems for Martin County.

On March 19, the *Stuart Daily News*—now owned by Menninger—reported that the town was facing a financial crisis. Only about 34 percent of the tax payments due had been paid. And in less than sixty days, the town would have to come up with $40,000—more than $546,000 in twenty-first-century dollars—in payments due on bonds and other debt obligations.

Nor could the town pay its electric bill, and the streetlights were turned off.

Things were no better for the county government. County finances were so strapped that employees were laid off or had their pay drastically cut. The county's agricultural extension agent took a pay cut, from $250 per month to $85 per month.

"People of larger financial resources were just recovering from the storms when the Seminole Bank closed in late February, and the Stuart Bank in early March," Leora Field, executive secretary of the Martin County chapter of the Red Cross, wrote in one of her reports.

The Red Cross had even loaned the county money to pay one employee to make road repairs.

"Martin County is still suffering and mentally panic stricken by the financial depression," Field wrote in April 1929.

"Our community is discouraged and is not normal because of it," Field said. "However, the causes of discouragement are real. Our gasoline station man, with sternly set face, talks to us of the loss of his entire year's earnings in the bank."

Taxes weren't being paid, schools closed early because the county couldn't afford to keep them open, and many residents were eating almost nothing but fish, Field wrote.

And there were other problems elsewhere.

Addison Mizner's ambitious and overhyped Boca Raton was in deep trouble in 1926, and he eventually was bankrupt. Infuriated investors hurled lawsuits at Addison, his brother Wilson, and the former members of the corporation's all-star board of directors. Wilson Mizner, always quick with a quip, said he could hardly open the door without a lawsuit blowing in.

That sense of humor didn't desert him when he was being grilled by attorneys. During his testimony in one suit brought by an unhappy investor, the plaintiff's attorney asked him, "Did you, or did you not, tell my client he could grow nuts on this land?"

"I certainly did not," Wilson snapped. "I told him he could *go* nuts on it."

In April 1929, the Mizner brothers, T. Coleman du Pont, Jesse Livermore, and other former directors of the Mizner Development Corporation were sued for $1.45 million by ninety-three plaintiffs who'd invested in Boca Raton. The defendants were accused of "conspiring to sell by fraudulent representations unimproved Florida real estate of little value."

The lawsuit noted that Mizner Development Corporation had taken in more than $9 million from the sale of real estate, but when the company's assets were sold at bankruptcy, those assets brought only $56,000.

St. Petersburg, which had so hopefully hosted the Investment Bankers Association of America convention a few years earlier, was struggling under the debt of bonds issued to pay for municipal services during the peak of the boom.

Walter Fuller, who'd sold millions of dollars' worth of real estate in St. Petersburg, wryly noted that the lesson learned from the boom years "is that of the drunk who opens a bleary eye the next morning, defends his hilarity of the night before by claiming, 'But look at all the nice new empty bottles I got.'"

Fuller had a pithy explanation for the failure of Florida's real estate market: "We just ran out of suckers."

Even Coral Gables was drowning in red ink, with $35 million in debts.

In a letter to the editor of the *South Florida Developer*, author Robert Ranson of St. Augustine said that while much was being made of the fact that the state government was debt-free, Florida's local governments were drowning in red ink.

"Though what we owe in bonds could only be properly estimated by a county-to-county, and town-to-town canvass, I might tell you that as near as I can get it from various sources, it is somewhere between $400 million and $538 million, and increasing," Ranson wrote.

Stated more bluntly, while the per capita debt of the population of the United States was $16.61, the per capita debt of Florida was about $508, he said.

Those figures never appeared in the *Wall Street Journal* or the columns of Arthur Brisbane.

If the mountain of debt wasn't enough for Florida to deal with, a dangerous natural pest appeared to cause still more trouble. On April 6, citrus growers discovered Mediterranean fruit flies in groves near Orlando. These flies are considered one of the world's most destructive pests. Their larvae feed on the pulp of fruits, and can eventually destroy an entire crop.

There was speculation that the pest had been brought into Florida on straw used to wrap bootleg whiskey. If there was an upside to the pest's presence in Florida, it was that twenty thousand men were hired to eradicate the flies. The state's citrus industry was nearly destroyed before the pest was eliminated in November 1930.

Still, the good times and easy money kept rolling elsewhere in the country. Wall Street continued spewing paper profits to millions of new investors, and no one expected it to end.

But the market showed signs of shakiness in March after Michael Meehan and other stock manipulators drove up the price of RCA shares—the high-tech stock of the 1920s—for a week and then sold their holdings for gigantic profits on March 18, 1929. Others began to sell stock, and on March 25, the market started tumbling.

Many investors had bought their stocks on margin. Like Florida real estate speculators four years earlier, snapping up binders for down payments of 10 percent, they had put up perhaps 10 percent in cash of the actual cost of the stocks. The rapid decline in the market caused a credit crunch. Investors who'd bought on margin had to come up with more cash for their brokers when the value of their stocks fell below the amount of cash they'd actually put up when they bought those stocks. Interest rates soared when investors had to borrow more money to hold on to their portfolios.

The slide was halted when Charles Mitchell of National City Bank said he'd make $25 million available for lending so investors wouldn't lose their investments. The market stabilized, the fear abated, and the return of good times seemed assured.

But in Florida, where giddy land speculators had seen their wealth evaporate almost overnight, more seasoned observers looked at the stock market stumble and recovery with some skepticism. On March 27, the *Stuart Daily News* published an editorial comparing the Wall Street edginess of a few days earlier to the rise and fall of the Florida land boom. The editorial warned that like Florida's real estate market, the stock market could eventually tumble.

The editorial was not signed, but it read like Menninger's work.

"We can recall what happened to us, and we can also remember how very sure we were in 1925 that nothing could check our excitement and prosperity," the editorial said.

"Good old Wall Street!" the editorial continued. "You are having a glorious time right now, just as we had a few years ago. Have a good swig of it while it lasts, boys, because the reckoning day is coming for you, just as it did for us. The bottom drops out of every overburdened basket."

The editorial even scolded Martin County's famous patron, Arthur Brisbane, for talking so optimistically about Florida in his column and making his readers think that prosperity was just beginning.

"That is what we Floridians thought in 1925," the editorial continued. "Today we are sadder and wiser. We have seen plenty of days when first class, improved, income-producing real estate could not be sold at any price. And Wall Street will see the day when its highest grade stocks will be a drag on the market. Laugh all you want to now, but watch for the doldrums. They come!"

It was a prescient comment, although no one would realize it for six or seven months. Groucho Marx, who, with his brothers, was making a movie of the Florida satire *The Cocoanuts*, recalled that everyone was buying stock in 1929.

"The plumber, the iceman, the butcher, the baker, all of them panting to get rich, were tossing their puny salaries—and in many cases, their life's savings—into Wall Street," Marx wrote in his autobiography, *Groucho and Me*. "Occasionally the market would falter, but then it would shake itself free from the resistance of the bears and common sense and resume its steady upward climb."

On September 3, 1929, the Dow Jones Average climbed to its highest point in history—381.17. RCA had reached $505 a share, and AT&T was at $304. General Electric was at $396, and US Steel at $262.

Beneath the roaring prosperity, however, investors' fears were volatile, and it took only a small spark to ignite a panic. That came on September 5, only two days after the market's historic peak, when economist Roger Babson spoke at a conference of businessmen in Massachusetts.

He was unmoved by the stock market's latest surge, and he warned that terrible times were ahead. Babson used the spectacular collapse of real estate prices in Florida as an example of what would eventually happen to the stock market. "Sooner or later a crash is coming," Babson said, "and it may be terrific."

The market dropped the following day. It stabilized briefly and then began fluctuating wildly, like an electrocardiogram tracing for a patient with a failing heart. Brief rallies were followed by long slumps.

Still, as the end of summer approached, great things again were predicted for Florida's winter tourism season. George Morse, executive manager of Florida Motor Lines, told reporters in Orlando that all transportation providers who served the state—railroads, steamship lines, and bus lines—were expecting a banner season. Morse said the predictions were based on his conversations with executives of transportation companies in New York, Atlantic City, Philadelphia, and other larger cities in the urban Northeast.

As the peak of the hurricane season arrived in September, Florida again was very lucky. On the whole it was a quiet season, but on September 19, a tropical depression formed about nine hundred miles east of Nassau and began slowly meandering toward the islands.

First it drifted westward, then turned to the northwest, slowing strengthening into a minimal hurricane. On September 24, however, the storm encountered very favorable conditions and began rapidly strengthening, continuing its slow, indecisive movement.

By September 25, its strongest winds had increased from 85 to 120 miles an hour, and it started a sharp but slow turn to the southwest. Hurricanes often lose some of their power when they make sharp turns, but this storm's intensity mushroomed. In eighteen hours, its peak winds were blowing at 155 miles an hour.

The storm moved slowly across the Bahamas, gradually weakening but doing major damage and killing forty-eight people. It then turned to the northwest, weakened some more, and crossed the then sparsely populated Florida Keys, with peak winds of around 115 miles an hour. It continued to weaken as it crossed the Gulf of Mexico and made another landfall near Pensacola as a minimal hurricane.

The storm had been at its roaring peak when it crossed the Bahamas, and even though it had hit the Florida Keys with powerful winds, its odd, meandering path had kept even those winds away from much more densely populated Miami and southern Florida.

Arthur Brisbane advised his readers not to get too upset about reports of the storm's intensity. "The newspapers will tell of a 'tropical storm of great intensity leaping toward the Florida coast, taking in a region between Jupiter and Miami,'" he wrote in "Today."

"But like eastern stories of western earthquakes, Florida's tornado stories often resemble the report of Mark Twain's death, which he described as 'greatly exaggerated.'"

It was an irresponsible and callous comment to make about a storm that had blasted the Bahamas with winds exceeding 150 miles an hour, killing dozens of people there.

An editorial in the *Schenectady Union Star* was much more accurate about the hurricane's damage and unpredictability.

"The trouble with this particular hurricane was that it took a fancy to remain stationary over the Bahamas, Nassau suffering long and heavily from its violence," the *Union Star* said. "Which way the storm would spring when it did decide to move, no one could predict with certainty. Meteorology has still much to learn about the life habits of hurricanes. Let us hope that it has learned some secret from this one. Suspense of the kind Florida has been experiencing is too much of a strain even for her steady nerves."

Edwin Menninger, the determined and analytical optimist, kept his readers informed and entertained during the edgy fall of 1929. Stuart's streetlights were turned back on in early October. And he peppered his editorial page comments with humor and cornball jokes

In the September 20 edition of the *Developer*, Menninger noted that a reader had dropped by his office recently to give him a bar of soap as a present.

"So many dirty things appear in the paper from time to time that I was not surprised to receive a contribution of this kind," he quipped.

Menninger said he'd keep the soap "for an emergency." If he was ever on a boat that sank, he said, "I can always get out this bar and wash ashore."

The *Developer* also reported that, once again, a record-breaking number of tourists were forecast for Florida. The prediction was based on numbers tabulated at inspection stations set up at the state's borders, with Georgia and Alabama as part of the effort to eradicate the Mediterranean fruit fly. The *Developer* reported that careful records were being kept of all automobiles entering the state. During the first week of October, 6,222 vehicles entered Florida. Every state except South Dakota was represented, the *Developer* said.

The arrhythmias in the stock market continued, however, and the underlying edginess that had characterized the market for months was about to erupt into full-scale panic.

"There came a Wednesday, October 23, when the market was a little shaky," economist John Kenneth Galbraith said. "Weak. And whether this caused some spread of pessimism, one doesn't know. It certainly led a lot of people to think that they should get out. So on Thursday, October 24—the first 'Black Thursday'—the market, beginning in the morning, took a terrific tumble."

Once again, prominent bankers stepped in with offers of millions of dollars in cash and credit, and the panic eased. But something happened between Friday night, October 25, and Sunday night, October 27. During that weekend, investors had time to think about the previous week's frightening drop.

When the market opened on Monday, October 28, people started unloading their stocks.

The real panic set in on Tuesday, October 29. Everyone was selling. No one was buying.

"It was just like a nightmare," said Horace Silverstone, who was a telephone clerk at the New York Stock Exchange. "I couldn't believe what was going on here. Every 'Buy' order was written on a black pad, and every 'Sell' order was on a red pad. All I saw was members running around with a fistful of red orders, just like chickens with their heads cut off. They didn't know which way to run. They were panicking. Screaming. Everybody was bumping into everybody else."

When the market closed, anyone who wanted RCA stock could've bought it for $26 a share, but no one was touching it. At the end of the awful day, about $10 billion in stock values—more than twice the amount of money in circulation in the United States at the time—had vanished.

"Some of the people I knew lost millions," said Groucho Marx. "I was luckier. All I lost was $240,000. I would have lost more, but that was all the money I had."

On the day of the crash, Marx got a phone call from his friend Max Gordon, who had also lost a fortune that day. "All he said was 'Marx, the jig is up!' Before I could even answer, the phone was dead," Marx said.

The United States and the rest of the world were headed for the worst economic depression in anyone's memory.

In the immediate aftermath of the crash, Edwin Menninger still thought he saw a reason to be optimistic about the future.

"I believe that 1929 will go down in Florida history as our worst year," he wrote in the *South Florida Developer*. "There are unmistakable signs on every hand of an improvement in fundamental conditions, and the first real estate activity in years is in evidence in Florida."

Winter visitors were bringing new money to Florida, and the season promised to be "bigger and better than ever before," Menninger wrote. "You are going to see more smiles in Florida from now on and fewer long faces."

And people were coming to Florida despite the stock market crash. In its issue of January 1930, *National Geographic* magazine reported that tourists in Florida would spend about $200 million—more than $2.7 billion in twenty-first-century dollars—between December 1929 and March 1930.

But a return to prosperity for Florida was not just around the corner, and Edwin Menninger was among the first to publicly acknowledge that reality.

An editorial published in the July 30, 1930, edition of Menninger's *Stuart Daily News* was an epitaph for both the Florida land boom and the wild decade of unfettered hope, profound upheaval, unbridled foolishness, and crushing disappointment that had just ended with a crash.

"They once tasted excitement, and the dregs of routine are bitter," the editorial said. "We are only cheating ourselves when we dream about the rising of a magic metropolis here overnight."

Menninger kept the *South Florida Developer* going for a while, but stopped publishing it in 1931.

But he kept the *Stuart Daily News* going even as the Great Depression strangled the US economy. He reduced the newspaper's publication schedule from daily to once a week, and changed the name to the *Stuart News*. And he showed the same resourcefulness and thrift that had allowed him to skillfully manage and expand his newspaper routes as a boy in Kansas. When cash became almost impossible to come by in the depths of the Depression, he set up a barter system. Advertisers who couldn't pay cash for an ad gave Menninger vouchers for goods or services. On paydays, employees received the vouchers as part of their pay.

Florida didn't recover from the collapse of the boom until after World War II, when the state's sunshine and temperate climate—coupled with air-conditioning and effective mosquito-control programs—once again attracted newcomers with pockets stuffed full of cash from America's post–World War II prosperity. There was no mad, colorful land speculation boom such as what occurred in the 1920s, but developers and tourism boosters still sold Florida as a fantasyland.

Edwin Menninger became a community pillar as he helped Martin County become one of the nation's most prosperous counties. He also wrote a series of books about tropical flowering trees that made him a world-renowned expert on the topic. By the time of his ninetieth birthday in 1986, he was a beloved and respected figure in Martin County.

The collapse of the Florida land boom left a bitter aftertaste for Martin County residents who rode out the tough times after the crash. When newcomers and ambitious developers started returning in the 1950s, a new generation of local leaders would have none of the wild, grandiose growth plans that had made their parents so starry-eyed.

In the coming decades, the county enacted some of the most restrictive development regulations in the state. The result is that Martin County has retained much of its subtropical splendor while attracting some of the world's wealthiest retirees.

Menninger died on February 17, 1995. The ailing young journalist who'd come to Florida in 1922 to shake the flu had lived to be nearly one hundred years old. He'd also helped to transform Stuart into a beautiful, prosperous little city, and shape Florida into the nation's tropical paradise.

If you head south on Interstate 95 or Interstate 75 on the Sunday following Thanksgiving, you will become part of a migration that is as predictable as any seasonal cycle of nature.

On that day, thousands of people pile into their automobiles and head south to Florida. Whether they've left from upstate New York, from Kentucky, or from Ontario, by the time they reach the Georgia-Florida border, this sunshine-bound caravan has formed into phalanxes of motor vehicles, many miles long, often moving at eighty miles an hour.

They aren't going to Florida to seek the ordinary. They're going there in search of things that don't exist anywhere else—a winter suntan, a respite from the discomforts of old age, a stylish escape into luxury and fantasy. And they'll probably find what they're seeking.

In the following weeks, thousands more will follow. Multimillion-dollar yachts escaping icy northern waters will arrive at Palm Beach, Sarasota, Jupiter Island, Ocean Reef, and other exclusive Florida harbors. Drawbridges will be going up and down and cars will be backed up, and year-round residents caught in the snarled traffic will look at each other wryly and say, "They're back!"

But they never really left. Despite continued challenges in the decades that followed the insanity of the 1920s—more terrible hurricanes, more ups and downs in the state's real estate and housing markets, and a steady succession of bizarre and sometimes macabre news stories coming out of Florida—the crowds kept coming. "Visit Florida," the state's official Department of Tourism website, said that almost ninety-seven million visitors came to Florida in 2014, and spent more than $82 billion. More than one million workers have jobs that are related to tourism, and the industry produces 23 percent of the state's revenue from sales tax.

Florida, more than any other state, is associated with a healthful life in the sun and the fulfillment of dreams and fantasies. Even the vision that drove Hamilton Disston to suicide has been realized. The land where he once planned a "magic" city is now home to Walt Disney World's "Magic Kingdom," where fantasies are a serious and lucrative business.

The state offers something for everyone, regardless of age, income, personal interests, or sexual orientation.

Upscale families and singles are lured to places such as Sanibel and Captiva Islands, and other destinations that are well beyond the reach of all but the wealthiest. College students on spring break cram into the bars of Panama City Beach and Key West.

In the sports world, a winter trip to Florida becomes a symbol of the pinnacle of success for hundreds of thousands of fans. Backers of successful college football teams go to Jacksonville, Orlando, Miami, or Tampa to see their favorites play in a postseason bowl game. And the Super Bowl is regularly played in one of those cities as well.

In October, gays and lesbians look forward to the annual Fantasy Fest, a colorful, stylish, and always outrageous weeklong street party in Key West.

The enticement of Florida can be permanent instead of seasonal. Couples reaching retirement age leave behind the cares of a lifetime and, as Homer Simpson once phrased it, "run out the clock in Florida." The well-heeled buy multimillion-dollar homes at Ocean Reef and Jupiter Island, or in oceanfront gated communities all along the state's nearly 2,300-mile coastline. Others go to affordable retirement towns such as Port St. Lucie, Winter Haven, and Port Charlotte, where, after decades of planning and saving, they settle into their 2,000-square-foot houses on their 10,000-square-foot lots.

The lure is so intense that desperate Cubans have risked their lives aboard flimsy rafts, hoping that fate and the whims of the winds and tides will push them across the Straits of Florida to a land of opportunity where they can have a better life.

But Florida has not escaped the cycles of fiscal boom and bust and earthly natural disasters.

There have been other economic peaks and valleys, albeit none as colorful and outrageous as those of the 1920s. The wave of foreclosures and struggling condominium associations in Miami and other Florida cities that followed the collapse of the subprime mortgage market in 2008 are eerily similar to the collapse of the state's real estate market nearly ninety years ago.

And there have been other spectacular natural disasters. In 1992, Hurricane Andrew terrified South Florida and came within a few miles of inflicting a repeat of the devastating 1926 storm that wrecked Miami. In 2004 and 2005, a series of powerful hurricanes swept across Florida and drove many discouraged residents from the state.

Americans have short memories, however, and those who seek a better life will always be drawn to Florida. It's still a land of perpetual sunshine and sea breezes, and savvy observers of Florida's real estate market think the state will recover again. In the wake of the subprime mortgage debacle, Karen Procell, a former real estate attorney in Orlando, said she thought the real estate market would stabilize, and her reasoning had a very familiar ring to it.

"The year-round sunshine motivates tons of people, especially up North," Procell said. "The proximity to beaches on either coast, the sand, sun, and beautiful people of Miami Beach, the theme parks in Orlando—that's an appealing lifestyle, especially if you're out shoveling snow and it's ten below zero.

"These things don't go away. The beaches aren't going to go away; the sunshine is not going to go away. People want that. That will continue to be attractive to them."

The next round of feverish real estate speculation could begin around the centennial of the Florida land boom of the 1920s. And when the new generation of boomers arrives, all of the earlier hopes and dreams that have been dashed to pieces amid the palm trees and wading birds and pink-and-vermilion sunsets won't matter to these new seekers. They'll see the gorgeous twilight reflected in the water that seems to be everywhere, and they'll watch the breakers roll onto a beach, and feel the sun warming their bones. And like the paradise seekers who've been coming to Florida for centuries, they'll have no earthly idea how powerful a hurricane can be.

Instead, they'll see all of the promise that Florida offers, and like Theodore Dreiser—standing on the shores of Lake Okeechobee, deeply moved by the fragile beauty of it all—they'll convince themselves that by coming to Florida they can achieve the American dream of perpetual happiness in the sun.

Acknowledgments

This book would not have happened without the tireless efforts of my agent, Jeanne Fredericks, of the Jeanne Fredericks Literary Agency in New Canaan, Connecticut. I owe her a tremendous debt of gratitude. Every writer should be so lucky to find an agent like her—diligent, loyal, and tenacious.

Marissa Walsh of Gotham Writers' Workshop in New York City was invaluable as a marketing consultant and was instrumental in getting the book proposal ready to pitch to publishers.

I'm very grateful to Lyons Press for their commitment to this project, and I was so very lucky that they assigned Tom McCarthy as my editor. He was a patient, unflappable veteran with a steady hand. His support of this project and faith in me were inspiring and deeply appreciated.

I'd also like to thank senior acquisitions editor Holly Rubino and production editor Lauren Brancato at Lyons for their guidance. Copyeditor Melissa Hayes had a light but deft touch on the manuscript.

Miami historian Paul George encouraged me to take on this project and helped me with his own deep expertise on the history of the Florida land boom. Historian Robert Alicea at the University of South Florida in Tampa also provided guidance and research sources.

My old friend, novelist and screenwriter John Miglis, helped me shape the narrative and offered additional advice and commentary during discussions at various watering holes in St. Augustine. He and his lovely wife, Diane—who bakes an amazing shepherd's pie—gave me warm hospitality and provided a base of operations during many research trips to Florida.

Paul Dickson, author of dozens of books about everything from history to baseball, was always willing to share his wisdom.

Meteorology instructor Greg Nordstrom at Mississippi State University in Starkville and cinematographer and storm-chaser Michael Laca of Tropmet.com in Miami reviewed some of the sections about hurricanes. Meteorologist Rob Jones of Pembroke Pines provided a treasure trove of information about Florida in the 1920s.

Virginia Menninger of Jensen Beach told me about her late father-in-law and former employer, Edwin Menninger. Mabel Witham of Stuart shared useful documents and helped me find other sources of information. Stuart author Sandra Thurlow generously shared photos from her collection for the book.

Bob DeGross, chief of interpretation and public affairs at Big Cypress National Preserve in Ochopee, was kind enough to review and critique my narrative of the construction of the Tamiami Trail.

Librarians and archivists—those diligent and unsung caretakers of our accumulated knowledge—made huge contributions to this book. I'm grateful to the staffs at the George A. Smathers Libraries at the University of Florida in Gainesville, the Richter Library at the University of Miami, and the Collier County Public Library in Naples, and to the archivists at the National Archives and Records Administration in College Park, Maryland, and the State Archives of Florida in Tallahassee.

Jim Misenheimer, my friend since childhood, and his wife, Cindy, allowed me unrestricted use of their cabin in the Uwharrie Mountains back home in Stanly County, North Carolina, where I could work in undisturbed privacy anytime I wanted. My brother-in-law, Bob Morrow, and his wife, Ann Marie, let me set up shop in their home in Glen Ridge, New Jersey, when I needed to attend meetings in New York City. I'm also grateful to Pat Huber of Roseville, Minnesota, for the use of her house at Fort Myers Beach during a lengthy research trip to Florida.

And of course, there's my wife, Dr. Jane Morrow, who served as a story consultant and first-draft editor and allowed me to get away with the quirks and annoying habits for which writers are notorious.

Willie Drye
Plymouth, North Carolina
May 7, 2015

A Note about Sources

This book describes events that took place almost a century ago.

In some cases, the documentation for these events is plentiful and specific. In other cases, however, the documentation is scarce, and sometimes the documentation that does exist is conflicting or fragmentary or the events described do not align with other well-documented events that were taking place at the same time.

This is especially true about the career of the Ashley Gang, where I found differing accounts of several events.

For example, newspaper stories written while John Ashley was on trial for the murder of Desoto Tiger repeatedly wrote that he'd been paid $584 for the otter hides he stole from the Seminole Indian. Later accounts, however, said he'd received $1,200 for the hides. Because $584 was, without exception, consistently reported by all of the journalists covering the trial as it unfolded, I used that amount.

Tiger's first name also was spelled Desoto, DeSoto, and De Soto. I used the spelling I found most often in news stories.

The *New Smyrna News*, citing the *Miami Daily News*, reported that after Ashley escaped from prison in July 1918, he served several months in the US Navy aboard the battleship USS *Maryland* and then deserted. But the battleship was being built when Ashley escaped. The *Maryland* was launched in March 1920, but it was not completed and commissioned for service by the navy until July 1921—more than a month after Ashley was recaptured and returned to prison.

I was not able to determine whether Ashley might have been aboard the battleship briefly before it was commissioned. So I did not mention Ashley's possible military service.

There were similar uncertainties about John Ashley's nephew, Handford—or Hanford—Mobley, starting with the spelling of his first name. Newspaper stories of the day consistently spelled his name Hanford. Author Hix Stuart, who claimed to have the only interview ever granted by John Ashley, also used this spelling.

But Mobley's tombstone spells his first name Handford, and this is the spelling I've used.

There also are uncertainties about some of Mobley's crimes and adventures. The *Miami Herald* reported on November 9, 1924, that it was Mobley who had served in the navy. I also found frequent mention in books and magazine stories about Mobley and other gang members robbing liquor distributors in the Bahamas sometime before his death in late 1924. But the only account of this robbery that was written fairly soon after Mobley's death was by Stuart, whose book about the gang was published in 1928. Stuart mentions the robbery but does not give a date.

The *New Smyrna News* of November 21, 1924, mentions that Mobley was wanted for piracy for stealing $15,000, but this story says he stole the money on the high seas between Florida and the Bahamas and does not mention a robbery of liquor distributors. Other accounts of Mobley's crimes were written many years after his death, and these stories gave conflicting information about the robbery.

Stories about the gang's bank robberies also were inconsistent, especially about the amount of money they stole in each robbery.

There were similar discrepancies in the newspaper stories about the gangland murder of Al Capone's enemy, Frank Uale.

In writing about these and other events, I pieced together the stories as best I could from the documentation that was available. Where there were inconsistencies, I used the version that seemed to me to be the most plausible or matched with other events that happened simultaneously.

Notes

Chapter One: An Old Man's Memories

1. "I tried to talk them out of it": *Miami Herald*, March 16, 1986; *Daily Capital* of Topeka, Kansas, March 2, 1915

2. The look was becoming so popular that Macy's: *Time* magazine, September 16, 1985

2. The wind off the ocean made the early summer heat bearable: *Vero Beach Press*, July 2, 1925

2. As the acerbic journalist H.L. Mencken had noted: Andrist, Ralph K., chief editor, *The American Heritage History of the 1920s & 1930s* (New York, American Heritage/Bonanza Books, 1970) p. 33

3. Their spree had ended only six months earlier: *Nevada State Journal*, February 22, 1924

3. Rumor had it that John Ashley had hidden more than $110,000: *Sarasota Herald-Tribune*, August 5, 1926

3. Every day trains were bringing as many as seventy-five Pullman cars: George, Paul, "Brokers, Binders, And Builders," *Florida Historical Quarterly*, vol. 65, no. 1, July 1986, p. 35

4. "It was easy to lie to a prospect in those days": Fuller, Walter P., *This Was Florida's Boom* (St. Petersburg, Florida, Times Publishing Co., 1954) p. 39

4. Jesse Livermore, the legendary stock market manipulator: Paige, Emeline K., editor, Untitled promotional booklet about the history of Martin County (Stuart, Florida, Southeastern Printing Co. and First National Bank and Trust Co. of Stuart, Florida, 1973) from the P.K. Yonge Library of Florida History, University of Florida

4. In neighboring Palm Beach County, architect Addison Mizner: Promotional brochure, *Boca Raton Mizner Development Corporation*, from the collections of the Boca Raton Historical Society and Museums, Boca Raton, Florida (Philadelphia, J.H. Cross Company, 1925) p. 21

4. He'd moved from Nebraska to Miami in 1912: US Department of the Interior, National Parks Service, National Register of Historic Places Registration Form, William Jennings Bryan House, Miami, Florida, December 9, 2011

4. Miami developer George Merrick was paying Bryan $100,000 a year: Nolan, David, *Fifty Feet in Paradise: The Booming of Florida* (New York, Harcourt Brace Jovanovich Publishers, 1984) p. 177

5. In the summer of 1925, sales of property in Coral Gables: George, Paul, "Brokers, Binders, And Builders," *Florida Historical Quarterly*, vol. 65, no. 1, July 1986, p. 38

5. . . . when Merrick started selling lots in the new Sylvania Heights section of Coral Gables: George, Paul, "Brokers, Binders, And Builders," *Florida Historical Quarterly*, vol. 65, no. 1, July 1986, p. 42

5. "I never see a crowd of people": *The New York Times*, September 27, 1896

5. When he finished, the twenty thousand delegates didn't simply applaud: *The Newark* (Ohio) *Daily Advocate*, July 11, 1896

6. But the canny old political warhorse also had seriously contemplated: Flynt, Wayne, "Florida's 1926 Senatorial Primary," *The Florida Historical Quarterly*, vol. 42, no. 2, October 1963, pp. 142–143

6. "He can smell the battle afar off": *Nevada State Journal* of Reno, February 22, 1924

6. The dresses they wore—thin, revealing, with hemlines at the knee: Allen, Frederick Lewis, *Only Yesterday: An Informal History of the 1920s* (New York, Perennial Classics, an imprint of Harper Collins, 2000) pp. 79–80; *Palm Beach Post*, May 25, 1925

7. In the mid-1920s, however, the fashion dictated a stark contrast: "Historically Accurate 1920s Makeup Tutorial," produced by Zabrena, available at https://www.youtube.com/watch?v=P_iMr-yOUbo

7. Some of the women even dared to light up cigarettes: Allen, Frederick Lewis, *Only Yesterday: An Informal History of the 1920s* (New York, Perennial Classics, an imprint of Harper Collins, 2000) p. 78

7. He had recently introduced a bill in Tallahassee: *Palm Beach Post*, May 25, 1925

7. The proposal was defeated: *Palm Beach Post*, June 7, 1925

8. He started with a self-deprecating quip: *Vero Beach Press*, July 2, 1925

9. "I would feel lost if I were not there on that occasion": *South Florida Developer*, August 4, 1925

Chapter Two: Railroad to Dreamland

10. The immortal Greek warrior Alexander the Great: Delumeau, Jean, *History of Paradise: The Garden of Eden in Myth and Tradition* (Urbana and Chicago, University of Illinois Press, 2000) p. 46

10. Tales of a fountain in a land somewhere to the north: Delumeau, Jean, *History of Paradise: The Garden of Eden in Myth and Tradition* (Urbana and Chicago, University of Illinois Press, 2000) p. 76

11. So to honor the season, Ponce de León named: Delumeau, Jean, *History of Paradise: The Garden of Eden in Myth and Tradition* (Urbana and Chicago, University of Illinois Press, 2000) p. 136

11. In the summer of 1559, Spain sent another expedition to Florida: Hudson, Charles; Smith, Marvin T.; DePratter, Chester B.; and Kelley, Emilia, "The Tristan De Luna Expedition, 1559–1561," *Southeastern Archaeology*, vol. 8, no. 1, Summer 1989, p. 34

12. A hurricane would deposit more visitors on a Florida beach in 1696: Dickinson, Jonathan (edited by Evangeline Walker Andrews and Charles McLean Andrews), *Jonathan Dickinson's Journal, or God's Protecting Providence* (Port Salerno, Florida, Florida Classics Library, 1985) p. 5

13. Florida, Motte wrote, "is certainly the poorest country": Motte: Jacob R., *Journey into Wilderness* (Gainesville, University Press of Florida, 1953) p. 199

13. . . . Motte saw "picturesque clumps of cypress trees": Motte: Jacob R., *Journey into Wilderness* (Gainesville, University Press of Florida, 1953) pp. 191–192

14. Colonel William Chase, a West Point–educated army engineer: Bearss, Edwin C., "Civil War Operations In and Around Pensacola Part II," *Florida Historical Quarterly*, vol. XXXVI, 1957–58, p. 128

14. . . . President Grant "ushered in that hustling period": Carlson, Oliver, *Brisbane: A Candid Biography* (New York, Stackpole Sons, 1937) pp. 80–81

15. "No dreamland on earth: Stowe, Harriet Beecher (edited by Abbie H. Fairfield), *Flowers and Fruit from the Writings of Harriet Beecher Stowe* (Boston and New York, Houghton Mifflin and Company, 1888) p. 18

15. But she also was aware of Florida's faults: Stowe, Harriet Beecher, *Palmetto-Leaves* (Boston, James R. Osgood and Company, 1873) pp. 29–39

15. "Undoubtedly the finest winter climate": Brinton, Daniel G., *A Guide-Book of Florida and the South for Tourists, Invalids and Emigrants* (Philadelphia, George MacLean, 1869), pp. 127–128

16. "In the winter months, soft breezes": King, Edward, *The Great South: A Record of Journeys in Louisiana, Texas, the Indian Territory, Missouri, Arkansas, Mississippi, Alabama, Georgia, Florida, South Carolina, North Carolina, Kentucky, Tennessee, Virginia, West Virginia and Maryland* (Hartford, Connecticut, American Publishing Company, 1875) p. 379

16. King noted that Florida's Silver Spring: King, Edward, *The Great South: A Record of Journeys in Louisiana, Texas, the Indian Territory, Missouri, Arkansas, Mississippi, Alabama, Georgia, Florida, South Carolina, North Carolina, Kentucky, Tennessee, Virginia, West Virginia and Maryland* (Hartford, Connecticut, American Publishing Company, 1875) p. 401

16. Colby claimed to have been led there: Cassadaga Spiritualist Camp website, "A Brief History," available at http://www.cassadaga.org/history.htm

17. "I am very much pleased with Florida": Jones, James P. (editor), "Grant Forecasts the Future of Florida," Ulysses S. Grant and Florida, *Florida Historical Quarterly*, vol. 39, no. 1, July 1960, p. 53

17. Florida's leaders thought they could pull the state out of the postwar wreckage and political chaos: Garrison, Webb, *A Treasury of Florida Tales* (Nashville, Tennessee, Rutledge Hill Press, 1989) pp. 96–98; Gannon, Michael, *Florida: A Short History* (Gainesville, University Press of Florida, 1993) p. 53

18. After Flagler was gone: "Humanity At Palm Beach," by W.L. George, *Harper's*, January 1925, p. 214

18. Flagler, the son of a poor Presbyterian minister: *Norwalk* (Ohio) *Reflector*, January 8, 1907

19. Remembering the charms of St. Augustine: Tindall, George B., "The Bubble In The Sun," *American Heritage*, vol. 1, no. 5, August 1965

19. That same year, young Thomas Edison: *New York Times*, June 24, 1990; Garrison, Webb, *A Treasury of Florida Tales* (Nashville, Tennessee, Rutledge Hill Press, 1989) pp. 102–103

19. Teed said that the angel: McIver, Stuart B., *Dreamers, Schemers and Scalawags: The Florida Chronicles, Vol. 1* (Sarasota, Florida, The Pineapple Press, 1995) pp. 219–22; *The Daily News* of Perth, Western Australia, March 20, 1909; *The Maitland* (New South Wales, Australia) *Weekly Mercury*, February 20, 1897

20. On Christmas Day, the temperature climbed into the 80s in Orlando: *Orlando Sentinel*, December 25, 1994

20. A few days after Christmas, citrus growers gathered in Orlando's San Juan Hotel: *Orlando Sentinel*, December 25, 1994; *Monthly Weather Review*, February 1895; *The Daily News* of Portsmouth, Ohio, February 9, 1895; *The New York Times*, February 9, 1895

20. But on February 7, 1895, an even colder icy blast: Bangs, Outram, "The Present Standing of the Florida Manatee, Trichechus Latirostris (Harlan) in the Indian River Waters"; *The American Naturalist*, vol. XXIX, September 1895, pp. 783–784

21. Before the freezes, eight banks operated in Orlando: *Orlando Sentinel*, December 25, 1994

21. While orange and grapefruit trees in Florida were being killed by icy weather: *The Daily News*, Portsmouth, Ohio, February 9, 1895; *New York Times*, February 9, 1895

21. But while the rest of the nation was shivering and cursing the cold: Allman, T.D., *Miami: City of the Future* (New York: The Atlantic Monthly Press, 1987) pp. 119–120

21. His young son George: "Miami on the Eve of the Boom: 1923," by Frank B. Sessa, *Tequesta*, vol. XI, (1951), p. 21

21. By April 1896, Flagler had extended: Standiford, Les, *Last Train to Paradise: Henry Flagler and the Spectacular Rise and Fall of the Railroad that Crossed an Ocean* (New York, Crown Publishers, 2002) p. 66

21–22. And in January 1897, the sumptuous hotel: Buchanan, James E., *Miami: A Chronological & Documentary History 1513–1977* (Dobbs Ferry, New York, 1978) p. 6

22. Flagler bought land from Julia Tuttle and the Brickell family: George, Paul, "Bootleggers, Prohibitionists and Police: The Temperance Movement in Miami, 1896–1920," *Tequesta: The Journal of the Historical Association of Southern Florida*, vol. 39, 1979, p. 34

22. In Chicago, Democrats were divided about their nominee: Baker, Kevin, "Political Speech," *American Heritage*, vol. 51, Issue 3, May/June 2000; *Newark* (Ohio) *Daily Advocate*, July 11, 1896

23. Bryan paid his first visit to Florida in 1898, when unrest in Cuba: Koenig, Louis W., *Bryan: A Political Biography of William Jennings Bryan* (New York, G.P. Putnam's Sons, 1971) p. 278

23. In January 1898, rioting erupted in Havana: O'Toole, G.J.A: *The Spanish War: An American Epic—1898* (New York and London, W.W. Norton & Company, 1984) p. 12

23. On the evening of February 15, about half an hour after a US Marine bugler: O'Toole, G.J.A: *The Spanish War: An American Epic—1898* (New York and London, W.W. Norton & Company, 1984) pp. 28–29

23. Goaded on by sensationalistic newspaper stories about the explosion of the *Maine* and Spanish atrocities in Cuba: *New York Journal and Advertiser*, February 17, 1898; O'Toole, G.J.A: *The Spanish War: An American Epic—1898* (New York and London, W.W. Norton & Company, 1984) p. 81

24. And because of Florida's proximity to Cuba, it was a logical place for the army: O'Toole, G.J.A: *The Spanish War: An American Epic—1898* (New York and London, W.W. Norton & Company, 1984) p. 197

24. An army inspector filed two reports saying that Miami was not a good place: Buchanan, James E., *Miami: A Chronological & Documentary History 1513–1977* (Dobbs Ferry, New York, 1978) p. 7

24. . . . a Louisiana soldier described Miami as "a waste wilderness as can be conceived only in rare nightmares.": Standiford, Les, *Last Train to Paradise: Henry Flagler and the Spectacular Rise and Fall of the Railroad That Crossed an Ocean* (New York, Crown Publishers, 2002) p. 68

24. American military leaders thought Tampa would be the perfect site to assemble: O'Toole, G.J.A: *The Spanish War: An American Epic—1898* (New York and London, W.W. Norton & Company, 1984) p. 209

24. Commanding General of the Army Nelson Miles was dismayed by the conditions: O'Toole, G.J.A: *The Spanish War: An American Epic—1898* (New York and London, W.W. Norton & Company, 1984) p. 229

24. William Jennings Bryan volunteered his services to the US Army: Koenig, Louis W., *Bryan: A Political Biography of William Jennings Bryan* (New York, G.P. Putnam's Sons, 1971) p. 277

24. The executor of her will, Harry Tuttle: George, Paul, "Bootleggers, Prohibitionists and Police: The Temperance Movement in Miami, 1896–1920," *Tequesta*, vol. 39, 1979, p. 35

24. The railroads continued to bring wealthy visitors to Florida: Sessa, Frank, "Miami on the Eve of the Boom: 1923," *Tequesta*, vol. 11, 1951

24. In those long-ago days before labor unions, the Occupational Safety and Health Administration, he was extending his railroad: Standiford, Less, *Last Train to Paradise: Henry Flagler and the Spectacular Rise and Fall of the Railroad That Crossed an Ocean* (New York, Crown Publishers, 2002) pp. 150–151

25. "I carried a lunch in my pocket": *Norwalk Reflector*, January 8, 1907, reprinted in *History Talk from the Upper Florida Keys*, edited by Jerry Wilkinson, Spring 2004

26. Joe Ashley brought his family from the state's Gulf Coast: Stuart, Hix C., *The Notorious Ashley Gang: A Saga of the King and Queen of the Everglades* (Stuart, Florida, St. Lucie Printing Co., Inc., 1928) p. 8

26. In 1905, Flagler's work crews began clearing the right-of-way to lay rails to the tip of the Florida peninsula: Standiford, Less, *Last Train to Paradise: Henry Flagler and the Spectacular Rise and Fall of the Railroad That Crossed an Ocean* (New York, Crown Publishers, 2002) p. 18

26. "It is indeed a wonder that when cold weather comes": Gifford, John, "The Florida Keys," *National Geographic* magazine, January 1906, pp. 8–9

Chapter Three: Dreamers and Thieves

27. Ashley went to work on one of the crews: Stuart, Hix C., *The Notorious Ashley Gang: A Saga of the King and Queen of the Everglades* (Stuart, Florida, St. Lucie Printing Co., Inc., 1928) p. 8; *Stuart News*, January 9, 1964

27. . . . opponent had sworn revenge when he recovered: Hanna, Alfred Jackson and Hanna, Kathryn, *Lake Okeechobee: Wellspring of the Everglades* (Indianapolis and New York, The Bobbs-Merrill Company, 1948) pp. 204–205

27. It was said that John could lay a whiskey bottle on its side: *Stuart News*, January 9, 1964

28. On December 19, Ashley stopped at the encampment of Homer Tindall: *Weekly Miami Metropolis*, April 9, 1915

28. . . . Ashley wondered if the Indians had had better luck with their traps than he'd had with his: *Daily Tropical Sun*, June 4, 1915

28. The Seminoles had indeed had better luck, accumulating a pile of eighty-four pelts: *The Daily Tropical Sun*, June 4, 1915

28. He spoke perfect English and was married with two small children: *Weekly Miami Metropolis*, January 12, 1912

29. The crew of the *Caloosahatchee* shut down to take a Christmas holiday: *Weekly Miami Metropolis*, January 12, 1912

29. After an evening of boozing, Ashley showed up at the Seminoles' camp: *Weekly Miami Metropolis*, April 9, 1915

29. Later that day, another Seminole took his tribesman who'd been injured: *Weekly Miami Metropolis*, January 12, 1912

30. One bullet had struck him between the eyes and exited the back of his head: *Weekly Miami Metropolis*, April 2, 1915

30. It was a .38-55 caliber slug: *Weekly Miami Metropolis*, January 12, 1912

30. Girtman made Ashley an offer: *Miami Daily Metropolis*, January 8, 1912

30. . . . gave $500 to Ashley: *Weekly Miami Metropolis*, April 2, 1915

30. Flush with cash, Ashley went into a whorehouse: Stuart, Hix C., *The Notorious Ashley Gang: A Saga of the King and Queen of the Everglades* (Stuart, Florida, St. Lucie Printing Co., Inc., 1928) p. 9

30. . . . where he hired on with a logging crew out of Seattle: *Weekly Miami Metropolis*, April 9, 1915

30. . . . a dignified and well-spoken Sioux Indian from Muskogee, Oklahoma: *Weekly Miami Metropolis*, January 12, 1912

31. . . . request Florida governor Park Trammell to offer a reward, and they were willing to do that: *Weekly Miami Metropolis*, January 12, 1912

31. . . . he met with a multimillionaire businessman who'd recently arrived in Miami: *Miami Metropolis*, January 18, 1912

31. In 1910 he bought a mansion on a stretch of Brickell Avenue: "Mr. Miami Beach: Meet Carl Fisher," *The American Experience* episode, 1998, from PBS website, http://www.pbs.org/wgbh/amex/miami/filmmore/transcript/index.html

32. . . . he was going to build a city here—"a city like magic": Fisher, Jane, *Fabulous Hoosier: A Story of American Achievement* (Chicago, Harry Coleman & Company, 1953) p. 82

32. So Fisher became a driving force behind two major arteries: Fisher, Jane, *Fabulous Hoosier: A Story of American Achievement* (Chicago, Harry Coleman & Company, 1953) p. 80

32. . . . forbade cemeteries on the island: Roberts, Kenneth L., *Florida* (New York and London, Harper & Brothers Publishers, 1926) pp. 75–89

32. . . . voters narrowly approved a referendum banning the sale of alcoholic beverages: Buchannan, James E. (editor), *Miami: A Chronological and Documentary History 1513–1977* (Dobbs Ferry, New York, Ocean Publications, Inc., 1978) p. 12

33. He took a quick look at the Everglades: *Miami Daily Metropolis*, January 22, 1912

33. "As soon as I breathed the balmy air of Miami": *Miami Metropolis*, December 24, 1909; US Department of the Interior, National Parks Service, National Register of Historic Places Registration Form, William Jennings Bryan House, Miami, Florida, December 9, 2011; *Miami Daily Metropolis*, January 22, 1912; Kauffman, Kathleen S., and Uguccioni, Ellen J., "Designation Report: The William Jennings Bryan Residence," City of Miami Preservation office, December 4, 2007

33. He liked it so much he bought it: *Naples Daily News*, April 1, 2012

34. "... a trifle too loquacious": Station Inspection Reports 1871–1930; Records Group 27, Records of the US Weather Bureau, National Archives and Records Administration, College Park, Maryland

34. Solomon Merrick, the minister who had left behind New England's bitter winters: "A History of Coral Gables: A Look into the Past," by Stacey Steig, produced by the Coral Gables Chamber of Commerce, available at http://coralgableschamber.org/visit/a_history_of_coral_gables.aspx

34. On January 27, 1914, Floyd Chaffin, a civil engineer: *Weekly Miami Metropolis*, April 9, 1915

35. Tell Sheriff Baker not to send any more "chicken-hearted men": Stuart, Hix C., *The Notorious Ashley Gang: A Saga of the King and Queen of the Everglades* (Stuart, Florida, St. Lucie Printing Co., Inc., 1928) pp. 10–11

35. Finally, the family made a cynical calculation: *Weekly Miami Metropolis*, April 9, 1915

35. But three had dared to vote to convict John Ashley of murder: *Miami Daily Metropolis*, July 1, 1914

36. "All this madness, all this rage, all this flaming death": Russell, Bertrand, edited by Ray Perkins Jr., *Yours Faithfully, Bertrand Russell: A Lifelong Fight for Peace, Justice and Truth in Letters to the Editor* (Peru, Illinois, Open Court Publishing Company, a division of Carus Publishing Company, 2002) p. 35

36. ... the newspaper's editors misspelled "Serb" and "Serbian": *Miami Daily Metropolis*, June 29, 1914

37. Bryan submitted his resignation: Kazin, Michael, *A Godly Hero: The Life of William Jennings Bryan* (New York, Alfred A. Knopf, 2006) pp. 232–242

37. ... so he was never handcuffed, and he was allowed to receive home-cooked suppers: Stuart, Hix C., *The Notorious Ashley Gang: A Saga of the King and Queen of the Everglades* (Stuart, Florida, St. Lucie Printing Co., Inc., 1928) pp. 10–11; *Daily Tropical Sun*, November 16, 1914

37–38. ... then told the 150 potential jurors that any of them who were sick: *Stuart Times*, November 11, 1914

38. As usual, Ashley was not in handcuffs when he got into an automobile: *Daily Tropical Sun*, November 16, 1914

39. ... seagulls learned that when a passenger train crossed the bridge: Work Projects Administration, *Florida: A Guide to the Southernmost State* (New York, Oxford University Press, 1939) p. 312

40. "They were young fellows, and they looked like farmers": *The New York Times*, February 8, 1915

40. But the men turned out to be drifters: *New York Sun*, February 9, 1915

40. It so happened that silent film director George Terwilliger: *Evening Ledger* of Philadelphia, February 26, 1915

41. . . . C. C. Myers and a boatload of tourist hunters: *Miami Daily Metropolis*, February 16, 1915

41. On Tuesday, February 23, the Ashleys committed the crime: *Miami Daily Metropolis*, February 23, 1915

42. Somehow, John Ashley was shot in the head: *New York Times*, February 24, 1915; Stuart, Hix C., *The Notorious Ashley Gang: A Saga of the King and Queen of the Everglades* (Stuart, Florida, St. Lucie Printing Co., Inc., 1928), pp. 13–15; *Stuart News*, January 9, 1964; *Daily Tropical Sun*, February 27, 1915

43. In 1915, Edwin Menninger was a senior at Washburn: Winslow, Walker, *The Menninger Story* (Garden City, New York, Doubleday & Company, Inc., 1956) pp. 158–161

43. On March 22, Ashley was in court in West Palm Beach: *Daily Tropical Sun*, March 10, 1915; *Daily Tropical Sun*, March 11, 1915

44. In 1909, L. D. Reagin, publisher of the *Sarasota Times*: *Sarasota Herald*, April 24, 1928

44. Still, a few dreamers were willing to try: Perry, Francis W., and Jaudon, James F., *History of the Tamiami Trail* (Miami, Florida, Tamiami Trail Commissioners and Dade County Board of Commissioners, 1928) pp. 4–7

45. Judge Pierre Branning issued some special instructions: *Weekly Miami Metropolis*, April 2, 1915; *Weekly Miami Metropolis*, April 9, 1915; *Stuart News*, January 9, 1964; Stuart, Hix C., *The Notorious Ashley Gang: A Saga of the King and Queen of the Everglades* (Stuart, Florida, St. Lucie Printing Co., Inc., 1928) pp. 18–19; *Daily Tropical Sun* of West Palm Beach, June 4, 1915; *The De Soto County News*, June 3, 1915

47. Some people who were acquainted with Joe Ashley: *Stuart News*, January 9, 1964

47. The Ashleys' jailbreak attempt came in a sudden: *Daily Tropical Sun*, June 4, 1915; *De Soto County News*, June 3, 1915; Stuart, Hix C., *The Notorious Ashley Gang: A Saga of the King and Queen of the Everglades* (Stuart, Florida, St. Lucie Printing Co., Inc., 1928) pp. 18–19

49–50. Among the discussion items on their agenda was the proposed highway: Perry, Francis W., and Jaudon, James F., *History of the Tamiami Trail* (Miami, Florida, Tamiami Trail Commissioners and Dade County Board of Commissioners, 1928) pp. 4–16

50. . . . met in Chattanooga, Tennessee, to discuss the road's route: Perry, Francis W., and Jaudon, James F., *History of the Tamiami Trail* (Miami, Florida, Tamiami Trail Commissioners and Dade County Board of Commissioners, 1928) p. 7

50. ". . . a splendid road from this city to Tampa": *Miami Herald*, October 15, 1915

51. On August 4, A. J. Rose, Ashley's court-appointed attorney: *Weekly Miami Metropolis*, August 4, 1916

51. Ashley left the jail handcuffed: *Weekly Miami Metropolis*, September 15, 1916

51. "Hands up, gentlemen,": *Miami Daily Metropolis*, September 15, 1916

51. For the next two weeks, the robbers fought a running gun battle: *Miami Daily Metropolis*, September 19, 1916; *Miami Daily Metropolis*, September 21, 1916

51. . . . about forty miles north of Gainesville: *Evening Independent*, November 15, 1916; Stuart, Hix C., *The Notorious Ashley Gang: A Saga of the King and Queen of the Everglades* (Stuart, Florida, St. Lucie Printing Co., Inc., 1928), p. 20

51–52. On February 10, Miami engineer John W. King: Perry, Francis W., and Jaudon, James F., *History of the Tamiami Trail* (Miami, Florida, Tamiami Trail Commissioners and Dade County Board of Commissioners, 1928) p. 25; Larned, W. Livingston, "Lost in the Everglades," *Forest and Stream* (eight-part series), February 1918 and May 1918 p. 278

53. John Ashley was back to his old tricks: Stuart, Hix C., *The Notorious Ashley Gang: A Saga of the King and Queen of the Everglades* (Stuart, Florida, St. Lucie Printing Co., Inc., 1928) p. 20; *Palm Beach Post*, July 11, 1918

54. . . . world events were inexorably dragging the United States: Koenig, Louis W., *Bryan: A Political Biography of William Jennings Bryan* (New York, G.P. Putnam's Sons, 1971) pp. 568–569: Rice, Arnold S., and Krout, John A., *United States History from 1865*, (New York, Harper Perennial, 20th Edition, 1991) pp. 168–172

55. Suffering from a leg injury that wouldn't heal: Seebohm, Caroline, *Boca Rococo: How Addison Mizner Invented Florida's Gold Coast* (New York, Clarkson Potter/Publishers, 2001) pp. 151–156; Tindall, George B., "Bubble in the Sun," *American Heritage*, August 1965; Boulton, Alexander O., "The Tropical Twenties," *American Heritage*, May/June 1990

Chapter Four: Leave Your Brain at Home

56. "There was an immense, all-pervading disillusionment": Catton, Bruce, "The Restless Decade," *American Heritage*, August 1965

56. ". . . into the easy-going life and beauty of the European past": Allen, Frederick Lewis, *Only Yesterday: An Informal History of the 1920s* (New York, Perennial Classics/ Harper Collins, 2000) p. 237

58. "I would like to acclaim an era of good feeling": *Gettysburg Times*, March 4, 1921

58. "We are not doing anything to combat this propaganda": *Miami Daily Metropolis*, November 23, 1921

58. In November 1921, Merrick had added several thousand acres: Tindall, George B., "Bubble in the Sun," *American Heritage*, August 1965

58. . . . sold his first lots for $600 each: *Evening Independent*, December 2, 1974

58. . . . knowledgeable people thought Merrick's plans were doomed: Roberts, Kenneth L., *Florida* (New York and London, Harper & Brothers Publishers, 1926) pp. 75–89

59. ". . . practically down to his last dollar": Fisher, Jane, *Fabulous Hoosier: A Story of American Achievement* (Chicago, Harry Coleman & Company, 1953) pp. 135–137

60. Fisher installed Harding in one of the luxurious villas: *Miami Daily Metropolis*, January 31, 1921; *Miami Daily Metropolis*, February 2, 1921

60. . . . John Ashley and his felonious family had been operating three moonshine stills: Stuart, Hix C., *The Notorious Ashley Gang: A Saga of the King and Queen of the Everglades* (Stuart, Florida, St. Lucie Printing Co., Inc., 1928) p. 20

61. Selling booze to Florida bootleggers was such an economic boon to the Bahamas: Buchanan, Patricia, "Miami's Bootleg Boom," *Tequesta*, vol. 30, 1979, p. 18

61. When Poucher and a deputy arrived: Stuart, Hix C., *The Notorious Ashley Gang: A Saga of the King and Queen of the Everglades* (Stuart, Florida, St. Lucie Printing Co., Inc., 1928), p. 20

62. Three days later, Ashley was behind bars again: *Palm Beach Post,* June 5, 1921

62. Just after dark on Wednesday, October 19, 1921, Ed and Frank Ashley: Stuart, Hix C., *The Notorious Ashley Gang: A Saga of the King and Queen of the Everglades* (Stuart, Florida, St. Lucie Printing Co., Inc., 1928) pp. 24–25; *Palm Beach Post*, November 14, 1921

63. . . . prices for bootleg liquor in Miami were low: Roberts, Kenneth L., *Florida* (New York and London, Harper & Brothers Publishers, 1926) pp. 75–89; *Miami Daily Metropolis*, January 31, 1921; *Davenport Democrat*, March 21, 1922

64. Business was usually quiet in the mid-afternoons: *The Lima News*, January 10, 1925; *Miami Daily Metropolis*, May 13, 1922; *Palm Beach Post*, May 13, 1922; *Ocala Star-Banner*, November 7, 1954

65. . . . and signed an order allowing Mobley, Matthews, and Middleton to be temporarily transferred: *Ocala Star-Banner*, November 7, 1954; *Miami Daily Metropolis*, December 15, 1922

66. In February 1923, Collier bought a dredge: *Collier County News* of Naples, Florida, April 26, 1928

66. In Fort Myers, civic and business leaders decided that something had to be done to revive public interest: McIver, Stuart, *True Tales of the Everglades* (Boynton Beach, Florida, Florida Flair Books, 1989) pp. 23–24; Kay, Russell, "Tamiami Trail Blazers: A Personal Memoir," *Florida Historical Quarterly*, vol. 49, no. 3, January 1971, p. 281

67. "The outside world had no knowledge": Kay, Russell, "Tamiami Trail Blazers: A Personal Memoir," *Florida Historical Quarterly*, vol. 49, no. 3, January 1971, p. 281

67. On April 11, the *Miami Herald* sent a reporter aloft: *Logansport* (Indiana) *Pharos-Tribune*, April 13, 1923; *San Antonio Express*, April 12, 1923; *The Eau Claire* (Wisconsin) *Leader*, April 12, 1923; *Miami Herald*, April 19, 1923

68. main group was still several days behind them: *Miami Herald*, April 22, 1923

68. In Fort Myers, people were furious: *Fort Myers Press*, April 18, April 19, April 23–28, April 30, May 1–2, 1923

69. The *Miami Herald* said that the Trailblazers: *Miami Herald*, April 19, 1923

69. . . . had attracted cameramen from Warner-Pathé News and Fox Movietone News: *Fort Myers Press*, April 24, 1923

69. Back on the Gulf Coast, the fracas about whether to create a county: *Tampa Times*, reprinted in the *Fort Myers Press*, April 23, 1923

69. On April 21, a state House of Representatives subcommittee: *Fort Myers Press*, April 25, 1923

69. Legislator S. Watt Lawler Jr. telegraphed Collier opponents: *Fort Myers Press*, April 26, 1923

69. On Friday, April 27, the *Press* was practically foaming: *Fort Myers Press*, April 27, 1923

70. The fight dragged on into May, when two giants of American industry: Albion, Michele Wehrwein, *The Florida Life of Thomas Edison* (Gainesville, Florida, University Press of Florida, 2008) p. 111

70. "I do not blame the people of Fort Myers and the rest of Lee County": *Fort Myers Press*, July 7, 1923

71. Menninger went to West Palm Beach: *Stuart News*, January 9, 1964; Winslow, Walker, *The Menninger Story* (Garden City, New York, Doubleday & Company, Inc., 1956) pp. 160–161; *The Stuart News*, February 21, 1995; Thurlow, Sandy, *Stuart on the St. Lucie: A Pictorial History* (Stuart, Florida, Southeastern Printing Company, 2001) p. 30; Author's interview with Virginia Menninger, Jensen Beach, Florida, November 27, 2013

72. On September 27, 1923, Ashley and another convict: *Miami Herald*, September 29, 1923

72. . . . the state's prison system was engulfed in scandal: *The Evening Independent*, June 4, 1923

72. "Automobiles were stolen, burglaries committed": Stuart, Hix C., *The Notorious Ashley Gang: A Saga of the King and Queen of the Everglades* (Stuart, Florida, St. Lucie Printing Co., Inc., 1928) p. 34

73. Beginning in November 1922 and continuing into the winter months of 1923–24: *Moberly Monitor Index*, November 21, 1922; *Fort Wayne News Sentinel*, November 25, 1922; *Waukesha Daily Freeman*, January 1, 1923

73. often were regarded as "addicts to the potent loco-weed.": Roberts, Kenneth L., *Florida* (New York and London, Harper & Brothers Publishers, 1926) pp. 52–54

73. Still, construction statistics for four Florida cities in early 1923: Sessa, Frank, "Miami on the Eve of the Boom 1923," *Tequesta: The Journal of the Historical Association of Southern Florida*, no. 11, 1951, pp. 24–25

74. In late January and early February 1923, sophisticated and skilled jewel thieves: *Miami Daily Metropolis*, February 2, 1923; *Miami Daily Metropolis*, February 3, 1923

75. But on April 23, a jury decided that Phelps was not guilty: *Miami Daily Metropolis*, April 24, 1923

75. The *Chicago Daily News* reported that booze purchases: *Chicago Daily News*, reprinted in the *Cumberland Evening Times*, July 10, 1923

75. "Any Prohibition enforcement agent that didn't have lead": Sessa, Frank, "Miami on the Eve of the Boom, 1923," *Tequesta: The Journal of the Historical Association of Southern Florida*, no. 11, 1951, pp. 13–14

75. Crime or no crime, President Harding: *Miami Daily Metropolis*, March 15, 1923

76. Edwin Menninger—who moved from West Palm Beach to Stuart in August 1923: *Stuart News*, January 1, 1964

77. At the base of picturesque Chimney Rock: Sessa, Frank, "Miami on the Eve of the Boom, 1923," *Tequesta: The Journal of the Historical Association of Southern Florida*, no. 11, 1951, pp. 20–21

77. Palm Beach County Sheriff Robert Baker and his deputies: *Palm Beach Post*, January 10, 1924

78. But John Ashley, in the interview with Hix Stuart: Stuart, Hix C., *The Notorious Ashley Gang: A Saga of the King and Queen of the Everglades* (Stuart, Florida, St. Lucie Printing Co., Inc., 1928) pp. 52–53

78. Newspapers reported that the gunfire started: *Nevada State Journal* of Reno, January 10, 1924; *The Lima* (Ohio) *News*, January 10, 1924; *Appleton* (Wisconsin) *Post-Crescent*, January 10, 1924; *Lincoln* (Nebraska) *Star*, January 10, 1924; *The Daily Star* of Oneonta, New York, January 10, 1924; *Lincoln* (Nebraska) *State Journal*, January 11, 1924

79. "This place of mine is the most beautiful": *Nevada State Journal* of Reno, February 22, 1924

79. ". . . boiling and raging like lava": *Hamilton* (Ohio) *Evening Journal*, February 23, 1924

80. "Brisbane's enthusiasm for real estate knew no bounds": Carlson, Oliver, *Brisbane: A Candid Biography* (New York, Stackpole Sons, 1937) p. 180, p. 273

80. In March, for example, readers of *The New Republic:* Sisto Benedicte, "Miami's Land Gambling Fever," *Tequesta: The Journal of the Historical Association of Southern Florida*, vol. 59, 1999, p. 56

80. A visitor in March 1924 sent a postcard to friends: Postcard, postmarked March 4, 1924, describing concert at Royal Palm Park, Miami; from the collection of Rob Jones, New Port Richey, Florida, photocopied November 14, 2013

81. "Even swampland several miles west of Miami: George, Paul, "Brokers, Binders and Builders," *Florida Historical Quarterly*, vol. 65, no. 1, July 1986, p. 30

81. "The people who have made real fortunes": Shelby, Gertrude Mathews, "Florida Frenzy," *Harper's Monthly Magazine*, January 1926, p. 180

81. By other accounts, he was in San Francisco: *Ocala* (Florida) *Star-Banner*, November 7, 1954

81. On the afternoon of Friday, September 12: *Miami Daily News*, September 13, 1924; *Miami Daily News*, September 16, 1924

82. Ashley and Mobley had made many trips to West End: Stuart, Hix C., *The Notorious Ashley Gang: A Saga of the King and Queen of the Everglades* (Stuart, Florida, St. Lucie Printing Co., Inc., 1928) pp. 47–50

82. On October 14, a tropical storm formed in the western Caribbean: *Monthly Weather Review*, December 1924, p. 589

82. The drenching downpour made life miserable in the Everglades for John Ashley, Handford Mobley: *Decatur* (Illinois) *Sunday Review*, November 2, 1924; *Ocala* (Florida) *Star-Banner*, November 7, 1924; *The Evening Independent* of St. Petersburg, November 3, 1924; *The Evening Independent* of St. Petersburg, September 28, 1925; *The Ledger* of Lakeland, Florida, October 12, 1975

84. "There they are – three of them": *Miami Herald*, November 9, 1924

85. Decades later, author Ada Coats Williams: Sonne, Warren J., "The Ashley Gang: What Really Happened," *Indian River Magazine*, October 2007.

Chapter Five: The Stars Shine Brightest in Florida

86. By the winter of 1924–25, Gilda Gray: *Miami Daily News*, December 20, 1924; *Miami Herald*, December 22, 1924

86. "How She Shivers, How She Shimmers": *Miami Daily News*, January 3, 1925

87. The terms of Gray's contract: *Fitchburg Sentinel*, reprinted in *Lowell Courier-Citizen*, January 9, 1925

87. Burdines Department Store hired her: *Miami Herald*, January 2, 1925

87. Nationally syndicated sportswriter and author Ring Lardner: *Free Press* of Winnipeg, Ontario, March 14, 1925; *The Davenport Democrat and Leader* of Davenport, Iowa, March 15, 1925

87. . . . Babe Ruth was telling reporters he was broke: *Kingston Daily Freeman*, March 11, 1925

87. He was seen playing basketball: *Fitchburg Sentinel*, January 9, 1925

87. "In Florida he would hang around a greyhound derby": *Syracuse Herald*, April 10, 1925

88. Ring Lardner noticed another distraction: *Lincoln Sunday Star*, April 26, 1925

88. The *Helena Daily Independent* reported that Joe Tinker: *Helena Daily Independent*, March 24, 1925

88. . . . manager John McGraw told Lardner that the stability of the Florida market: *Lincoln Sunday Star*, April 26, 1925

88. Merrick reportedly paid the Great Commoner $100,000: Nolan, David, *Fifty Feet in Paradise: The Booming of Florida* (New York, Harcourt Brace Jovanovich, 1984) p. 177

88. "They're here trying to see which can sell": *The Bee*, Danville, Virginia, January 15, 1925

89. Florida was a "durable asset": *Miami Herald*, January 16, 1925

89. "You can tell the biggest lie you can think of": Nolan, David, *Fifty Feet in Paradise: The Booming of Florida* (New York, Harcourt Brace Jovanovich, 1984) p. 179

89. ". . . he had become "a crimp for real estate speculators": Nolan, David, *Fifty Feet in Paradise: The Booming of Florida* (New York, Harcourt Brace Jovanovich, 1984) p. 177

90. A judge from Nebraska who'd visited Bryan: *Miami Herald*, January 21, 1925

90. On January 6, Bryan attended the inauguration: *Miami Herald*, January 7, 1925

90. ". . . an endless serpent whose joints, composed entirely of automobiles": Roberts, Kenneth L., *Florida* (New York and London, Harper & Brothers Publishers, 1926) pp. 8–13

91. British author T. H. Weigall was among the hordes: Weigall, T.H., *Boom in Florida* (London, John Lane The Bodley Head Limited, 1931) pp. 27–28

91. The palms, they say, of Florida: Rainbolt, Victor, *The Town that Climate Built: The Story of the Rise of a City in the American Tropics* (Miami, Parker Art Printing Association, 1925) p. 76

91. Over-Night Millionaires of Florida: *St. Petersburg Times*, February 17, 1925

92. "Their minds were so inflamed: Roberts, Kenneth L., *Florida* (New York and London, Harper & Brothers Publishers, 1926) pp. 28–31

92. A new development called Miami Shores sold $2.5 million: "Brokers, Binders and Builders," by Paul George; *Florida Historical Quarterly*, vol. 65, no. 1, July 1986, p. 35

92. . . . his salesmen raked in an astonishing $21 million: Roberts, Kenneth L., *Florida* (New York and London, Harper & Brothers Publishers, 1926), p. 42

92. . . . Merrick was being financially cautious: Roberts, Kenneth L., *Florida* (New York and London, Harper & Brothers Publishers, 1926) p. 86

92. Carl Fisher was tightening financial requirements: "Brokers, Binders and Builders," by Paul George; *Florida Historical Quarterly*, vol. 65, no. 1, July 1986, p. 41

92. The hospital for returning World War I veterans: Tindall, George B., "Bubble in the Sun," *American Heritage*, vol. 16, no. 5, August 1965

92. ". . . every atom of beauty that human ingenuity can add": Promotional brochure, *Boca Raton Mizner Development Corporation*, from the collections of the Boca Raton Historical Society and Museums, Boca Raton, Florida (Philadelphia, J.H. Cross Company, 1925) p. 21

93. "Get the big snobs": Vickers, Raymond B., "Addison Mizner: Promoter in Paradise," *Florida Historical Quarterly*, vol. 75, no. 4, p. 384

93. . . . that included *Palm Beach Post* publisher Donald H. Conkling: Vickers, Raymond B., "Addison Mizner: Promoter in Paradise," *Florida Historical Quarterly*, vol. 75, no. 4, p. 387

93. Mizner's backers also included US Senator T. Coleman du Pont: Vickers, Raymond B., "Addison Mizner: Promoter in Paradise," *Florida Historical Quarterly*, vol. 75, no. 4, p. 384

93. . . . she overheard two men talking about Livermore and his family: *New York Times*, March 9 and March 16, 1925; *The Evening Independent* of St. Petersburg, November 29, 1940; *Milwaukee Journal*, January 6, 1939

93. . . . one of those who departed was Reverend R. S. Wightman: *New York Times*, March 9, 1925

93. Brothels operated openly with little interference: Reno, Jane Wood, and Hurchalla, George (editor), *The Hell with Politics: The Life and Writings of Jane Wood Reno* (Atlanta, Peachtree Publishers, Ltd., 1994) pp. 34–35

93. . . . the masses coming to the state were being drawn: *New York Times*, March 22, 1925

94. "Since houses were being rushed to sell": Roberts, Kenneth, "In the Wake of the Hurricane," *Saturday Evening Post*, November 27, 1926

94. "Southern nights are cool and starlit": *New York Times Magazine*, December 6, 1925

94. Imperial Wizard Hiram Wesley Evans told a gathering: *Miami Daily News*, September 24, 1924

95. . . . had helped to defeat a motion to include a sentence denouncing the Klan: Kazin, Michael, *A Godly Hero: The Life of William Jennings Bryan* (New York, Alfred A. Knopf, 2006) p. 284; *Miami Daily News*, September 24, 1924

95. "The fight today is not to defend the Christian religion": *Miami Herald*, March 28, 1926

95. "Science gives us great things": *Miami Herald*, June 12, 1925

95. Earlier in the year, Bryan had made a quick trip to Nashville: Author's visit to Scopes Trial Museum, Dayton, Tennessee, February 4, 2013

95–96. . . . illegal to "drink liquors as a beverage" in Florida: *Palm Beach Post*, June 7, 1925

96. ". . . "one traverses the bank of the Indian River": Roberts, Kenneth L., *Florida* (New York and London, Harper & Brothers Publishers, 1926) p. 129

96. "Millions will be made": *South Florida Developer*, January 27, 1925

96. Federal engineers had started a feasibility study: *South Florida Developer*, January 20, 1925

96. "the finest south of Savannah": *South Florida Developer*, January 27, 1925

96. During the second week of January 1925: *South Florida Developer*, January 20, 1925

97. Brisbane's brief visit to Stuart: *South Florida Developer*, February 13, 1925

97. A week later, a bylined story written by Brisbane: *South Florida Developer*, February 20, 1925

97. When R. C. Ogilvie, a physician in Superior, Wisconsin: *South Florida Developer*, April 21, 1925

98. Warfield's Seaboard Air Line Railroad had sold the timber rights: *South Florida Developer*, March 27, 1925

98. Northern Palm Beach County voters helped pass a $6 million proposal: *Stuart News*, January 9, 1964

98. On April 9, they met with Representative M. S. McCracken: *South Florida Developer*, April 14, 1925

98. Offer to name the new county after Governor John Martin: *South Florida Developer*, September 13, 1929

98. On May 28, the state legislature passed the bill: *South Florida Developer*, May 28, 1925

99. Around the same time, Arthur Brisbane made yet another visit: *South Florida Developer*, May 1, 1925

99. . . . the lawmakers approved issuing $250,000 worth of bonds: *South Florida Developer*, May 1, 1925

99. Crowds continued to pour into the city: Tindall, George B., "The Bubble In The Sun," *American Heritage*, vol. 1, no. 5, August 1965

99. During the spring and summer, ambitious young men: George, Paul, "Brokers, Binders, And Builders," *Florida Historical Quarterly*, vol. 65, no. 1, July 1986, pp. 35–37

100. "The binder boys worked right on the street": Burnell, Elvira S., "A.J. Manning's Reminiscences: Boom of the 20s," Library of Congress, American Life Histories: Manuscripts from the Federal Writers' Project, 1936 to 1940, available online at http://www.loc.gov/item/wpalh000381/

100. Historians have blamed the binder boys: George, Paul, "Brokers, Binders and Builders: Greater Miami's Boom of the mid-1920s"; *Florida Historical Quarterly*, vol. 65, no. 1, July 1986, p. 1, July 1986, p. 35

100. The development was sold out in three hours: George, Paul, "Brokers, Binders and Builders," *Florida Historical Quarterly*, vol. 65, no. 1, July 1986, p. 41

100. On June 25, Edwin Menninger traveled up the coast to Vero Beach: *Vero Beach Press*, July 2, 1925; *South Florida Developer*, August 4, 1925

101. "Florida is the sanitarium for the rich": *Vero Beach Press*, July 2, 1925

101. On the shores of Lake Okeechobee in western Martin County: *South Florida Developer*, July 7, 1925

101. "the Fifth Avenue of Florida.": "History of Olympia-Picture City," Collection M74-13, State Archives of Florida, Tallahassee, Florida

101. William Jennings Bryan arrived in Dayton, Tennessee: Author's visit to Scopes Trial Museum, Dayton, Tennessee, February 4, 2013

102. Darrow walked Bryan through the biblical story of Creation: Linder, Douglas O., "Famous Trials" webpage, University of Missouri-Kansas City School of Law; Bryan's testimony online at: http://law2.umkc.edu/faculty/projects/ftrials/scopes/day7.htm

103. . . . recalling that he had met Bryan at Vero Beach: *South Florida Developer*, August 4, 1925

103. . . . Brisbane praised Seaboard Air Line Railroad: *South Florida Developer*, July 24, 1925

103. And Edwin Menninger continued his cheerleading: *South Florida Developer*, August 21, 1925

104. Withdrawals from member banks of the Massachusetts Savings Bank: Frazer, William, and Guthrie, John J., Jr., *The Florida Land Boom: Speculation, Money and the Banks* (Westport, Connecticut, Quorum Books, 1995) p. 119

104. Similar warnings were issued by the Minnesota Department of Conservation: George, Paul, "Brokers, Binders and Builders," *Florida Historical Quarterly*, vol. 65, no. 1, July 1986, p. 48

104. "Land is not worth a certain figure": *South Florida Developer*, September 8, 1925

105. "The fact of the matter is": *South Florida Developer*, September 11, 1925

105. "If these attacks succeed in slowing down": *South Florida Developer*, October 13, 1925

105. The shift started when the Florida East Coast Railway: George, Paul, "Brokers, Binders and Builders," *Florida Historical Quarterly*, vol. 65, no. 1, July 1986, p. 46

105. Out-of-work carpenters added to the problem: *South Florida Developer*, October 9, 1925

105. The speculators—especially Miami's ubiquitous binder boys: George, Paul, "Brokers, Binders and Builders," *Florida Historical Quarterly*, vol. 65, no. 1, July 1986, p. 46

105. Enterprising residents were renting their porches: George, Paul, "Brokers, Binders and Builders," *Florida Historical Quarterly*, vol. 65, no. 1, July 1986, p. 43

105. As the winter of 1925 approached: *New York Times*, December 5, 1925

105–6. Jokes circulated about returning tourists selling the Florida sand: *Syracuse Herald*, October 18, 1925

106. A service station operator in Stuart said he'd soon be selling his land for a dollar a spoonful: *South Florida Developer*, October 20, 1925

106. Humorist Will Rogers: *Fresno Bee*, October 11, 1925

106. Florida as a source of humor hit the bright lights of Broadway: Meredith, Scott, *George S. Kaufman and His Friends* (Garden City, New York, Doubleday & Co., Inc., 1974) p. 274; *New York Times*, December 9, 1925

Chapter Six: The Bootlegger's Curse

107. In November, *New York Times* readers learned that Charles Ponzi: *New York Times*, November 17, 1925

107. The US Post Office in Atlanta reported in August: *South Florida Developer*, October 9, 1925

107. "All our gold rushes, all our oil booms": *Literary Digest*, October 24, 1924

107. Two days before Thanksgiving, US Senator T. Coleman du Pont: *New York Times*, November 25, 1925

108. Mizner tried to downplay du Pont's resignation: Vickers, Raymond B., "Addison Mizner: Promoter in Paradise," *Florida Historical Quarterly*, vol. LXXV, 19XX, pp. 389–390; *New York Times*, November 25, 1925

108. Still, John McGraw moved ahead with plans to spend $3.75 million: *Palm Beach Post*, December 6, 1925; *St. Petersburg Times*, February 24, 1965; *Sunday Times-Signal*, December 6, 1925

108. While McGraw was asking potential investors to take his word: *St. Petersburg Times*, December 8, 1925

109. Northeast winds brought a gloomy drizzle that parked itself over Tampa Bay: *St. Petersburg Times*, December 29, 2011

109. But local cops picked that time to get serious about cracking down on bootlegging: *The Evening Independent*, December 10, 1925; *Wisconsin Rapids Daily Tribune*, December 10, 1925; *Kingsport Times*, December 10, 1925; *Decatur Review*, December 10, 1925

109. That "certain information" may well have come from someone: *Evening Independent*, August 6, 1924

110. Shortly after the bankers departed St. Petersburg, an eyebrow-raising warning: *New York Times*, January 10, 1926

110. Tregoe's colleagues in Florida's banking industry: *New York Times*, January 24, 1926

110. In October, Cornelius Vanderbilt IV, sunburned and windblown: *South Florida Developer*, October 10, 1925

110. Soon, he told the *Developer*'s readers, Stuart's harbor would be deepened: *South Florida Developer*, September 22, 1925

111. As the usual post-Thanksgiving migration to Florida started: *New York Times Magazine*, December 6, 1925

111. Author Theodore Dreiser was among the thousands who came to Florida: Riggio, Thomas P.; West III, James L.W.; Westlake, Neda M.; and Lohmann, Christoph K.,

Theodore Dreiser: American Diaries, 1902–1926 (Philadelphia, University of Pennsylvania Press, 1982) p. 430

111. Babe Ruth was seen among other celebrities at a hotel opening in St. Petersburg: Hatton, Hap, *Tropical Splendor: An Architectural History of Florida* (New York, Alfred A. Knopf, 1987) p. 75

111. . . . Stanford University football star Ernie Nevers would play in an all-star football game in Florida: *Davenport Democrat and Leader*, January 1, 1926; *Lincoln Sunday Star*, January 17, 1926

111. Helen Wainwright, a champion amateur swimmer: *Davenport Democrat and Leader*, January 1, 1926

111. Golfer Bobby Jones—still an amateur at the time: *Helena Daily Independent*, December 19, 1925

111. . . . and a real estate company was offering $15,000 to tennis stars Bill Tilden and Vincent Richards: *Zanesville Signal*, December 17, 1925

111. Boxers Gene Tunney and Jack Dempsey were training in Florida: *Helena Daily Independent*, January 18, 1926

111. As the federal officer in charge of enforcing the Volstead Act: *Lima News*, March 8, 1926; *The Star*, Wilmington, Delaware, December 7, 1926

112. Movie star Gloria Swanson arrived in Miami Beach: *Miami Daily News*, January 16, 1926

112. . . . as was movie star Bebe Daniels: *Miami Herald*, February 26, 1926

112. United News sportswriter Frank Grey reported that Major League baseball managers: *Cedar Rapids Republican*, January 8, 1926

112. Will Rogers was back in Florida and dispatching his quips: *Lincoln Sunday Star*, February 14, 1926

112. The managers' fears about the distractions of real estate investments: *Cedar Rapids Republican*, March 26, 1926

112. The conflict baseball players experienced between focusing on the game: *Lincoln Sunday Star*, January 10, 1926

113. "Nobody here is alarmed": *South Florida Developer*, January 5, 1926

113. Theodore Dreiser and his wife visited Martin County: Riggio, Thomas P.; West III, James L.W.; Westlake, Neda M.; and Lohmann, Christoph K., *Theodore Dreiser: American Diaries, 1902–1926* (Philadelphia, University of Pennsylvania Press, 1982) p. 440

114. "What is the matter with Coral Gables?": Riggio, Thomas P.; West III, James L.W.; Westlake, Neda M.; and Lohmann, Christoph K., *Theodore Dreiser: American Diaries, 1902–1926* (Philadelphia, University of Pennsylvania Press, 1982) p. 439

114. Their plan was to tow it into the Miami harbor and convert it into a floating hotel and casino: Boulton, Alexander J., "The Tropical Twenties," *American Heritage*, May/June

1990; George, Paul, "Brokers, Binders and Builders," *Florida Historical Quarterly*, vol. 65, no. 1, July 1986, p. 47

114. On January 9, the *Prins Valdemar* was being towed: *The Evening Independent*, January 11, 1926

114. "The dearth of building supplies": George, Paul, "Brokers, Binders and Builders," *Florida Historical Quarterly*, vol. 65, no. 1, July 1986, p. 47

114. The VIPs joined a gathering of about 1,500 guests: *New York Times*, January 15, 1926; *Miami Daily News*, January 16, 1926

115. Three days after the extravagant opening of the Biltmore, a large advertisement appeared: Mackle, Elliott, "Two-Way Stretch: Some Dichotomies in the Advertising of Florida as the Boom Collapsed," *Tequesta: The Journal of the Historical Association of Southern Florida*, vol. 33, 1973, pp. 20, 28; *Miami Daily News*, January 18, 1926

115. Thursday, January 28, 1926, dawned clear and brisk in Stuart: *South Florida Developer*, January 29, 1926

115. . . . but the *Developer* reported that ten thousand barbecue sandwiches: *South Florida Developer*, February 2, 1926

116. According to the tale, the bootlegger who'd brought in a boatload of booze: Paige, Emeline K. (editor), Untitled promotional booklet about history of Martin County (Stuart, Florida, Southeastern Printing Company and First National Bank and Trust Company of Stuart, 1973); from the P.K. Yonge Library of Florida History, University of Florida, Gainesville

116. About a week after the celebration in Stuart: Mackle, Elliott, "Two-Way Stretch: Some Dichotomies in the Advertising of Florida as the Boom Collapsed," *Tequesta: The Journal of the Historical Association of Southern Florida*, vol. 33, 1973, p. 28

116. On the heels of the discount offering of Florida real estate: *New York Times*, February 9, 1926

116. On February 8, Solomon Davies Warfield's Seaboard Air Line Railroad: Turner, Greg M., *A Journey Into Florida's Railroad History* (Gainesville, University Press of Florida, 2008) p. 202

116. A few days later, Arthur Brisbane: *South Florida Developer*, February 13, 1926

117. The *New Yorker* magazine's edition of February 13 hit the newsstands: *New Yorker*, February 13, 1926

117. The influence of African-American popular music: Author's interview with Stephen Anderson, PhD, Associate Professor of Music, University of North Carolina, December 19, 2014

117. The hotels and nightclubs in and around Miami were full of jazz: *Miami Daily News*, March 1, 1926

117. Shannon, a jovial, fun-loving daredevil who spent his ill-gotten earnings: *Miami Herald*, February 25, 1926; *Miami Herald*, February 26, 1926; *The Star* of Wilmington, Delaware, March 7, 1926; *Lima* (Ohio) *News*, March 8, 1926

118. As the end of the 1925–26 season approached, the torrent of visitors: George, Paul, "Brokers, Binders and Builders," *Florida Historical Quarterly*, vol. 65, no. 1, July 1986, p. 49

118. In Stuart, backers of a development called River Forest: *South Florida Developer*, March 5, 1926

119. Tampa attorney Peter Knight, whose name would soon become a lightning rod: *New York Evening Post*, reprinted in the *South Florida Developer*, March 16, 1926

119. St. Petersburg was already beginning to see the effects of slowing real estate sales: Fuller, Walter P. *This Was Florida's Boom* (St. Petersburg, Florida, Times Publishing Co., 1954) p. 62

119. By late spring, even Edwin Menninger was acknowledging: *South Florida Developer*, May 14, 1926

120. Menninger's opinion that Florida's boom days were over infuriated some people: Hutchinson, Janet, and Page, Emeline, *History of Martin County* (Stuart, Florida, Historical Society of Martin County, 1998) p. 390

120. On April 4, Solomon Davies Warfield decided the time was right: *South Florida Developer*, April 4, 1926

120. Brisbane was back on the front page of the *South Florida Developer* on June 11: *South Florida Developer*, June 11, 1926

121. Then it quickly intensified into a monster storm: *Nassau Guardian*, July 28, 1926

121. F.A. Lancaster, a lineman, was electrocuted: *The Evening Independent*, July 29, 1926

122. The Florida Association of Real Estate Boards wanted these embarrassing eyesores: *The Evening Independent*, July 29, 1926

122. In August, *Forbes* magazine said Florida: *Forbes* magazine, August 1926, reprinted in *Sarasota Herald-Tribune*, August 18, 1926

122. *World's Work*, another highly respected publication: *World's Work*, reprinted in *Lancaster Daily Eagle*, August 31, 1926

122. Putnam County Sheriff R.J. Hancock and F.S. Waymer, mayor of the county seat of Palatka: *Stuart Daily News*, September 14, 1926

Chapter Seven: "Many Die; Cities Razed"

123. For a while, a brisk breeze coming off Biscayne Bay: *Florida Cracker Legionnaire*, October 11, 1926

123. The Weather Bureau had been following the storm and issuing advisories: *Monthly Weather Review*, October 1926, p. 414

123. "At 1:55 the storm had reached such intensity as to indicate that everything would be demolished": *Monthly Weather Review*, October 1926, p. 414

124. With one tragic exception, ships were managing to avoid this storm: *New York Times*, September 15, 1926

124. But the following day, a Danish tanker searching for the *Loyal Citizen*: *New York Times*, September 16, 1926

124. At 10:20 a.m., he relayed the official storm advisory from Washington: *Miami Daily News*, September 17, 1926

124. One of the Weather Bureau's warning telegrams went to Fred Flanders: Will, Lawrence, *Okeechobee Hurricane: Killer Storms in the Everglades* (Belle Glade, Florida, The Glades Historical Society, 1990) p. 14

125. Around four p.m. on Friday, Leo F. Reardon, a construction contractor: Reardon, Leo, *The Florida Hurricane & Disaster 1926* (Coral Gables, Florida; Arva Parks & Company, 1986) p.4

125. There were, however, clear indications that something awful: "We Went Through Quite an Ordeal," by Helen Frank; *Update*, vol. 10, no. 2, May 1983, p. 3

125. As the sun neared the horizon, a young Jane Wood Reno: Reno, Janet Wood, *The Hell With Politics: The Life and Writings of Jane Wood Reno* (Atlanta, Peachtree Publishers, 1994) pp. 34–35

126. The spectacular colors linger long after sunset: Garriott, E.B., "West Indian Hurricanes" (Washington, U.S. Weather Bureau, 1900)

126. At eight p.m. Friday night, Richard Gray and the Weather Bureau office: *Monthly Weather Review*, October 1926, p. 409

126. In Moore Haven, Fred Flanders was one of many residents who went to a party: Will, Lawrence E., *Okeechobee Hurricane: Killer Storms in the Everglades* (Belle Glade, Florida, The Glades Historical Society, 1990) p. 14

126. Miami resident Mildred Cronin, a Dade County school board employee: "The Florida Hurricane, September 18, 1926: Official Report of the Relief Activities," by American National Red Cross; Folder DR-207, Florida hurricane of 9-18-1926: Donated Records Collection (formerly Records Group 200), Records of the American Red Cross 1917–1934, National Archives and Records Administration, College Park, Maryland

127. Around ten p.m., one of those bands passed over downtown Miami: Reardon, Leo, *The Florida Hurricane & Disaster 1926* (Coral Gables, Florida; Arva Parks & Company, 1986) pp. 20–21

127. While Reck was chatting with the deputies, an anemometer at Allison Hospital: *Monthly Weather Review*, October 1926, p. 415

127. A few minutes before midnight, Hicks left downtown Miami: *New York Times*, September 22, 1926

127. At midnight, Gray's barometer read 29.54, down 0.16 inch: *Monthly Weather Review*, October 1926, p. 412

127. The party in Moore Haven began breaking up at about the same time: Will, Lawrence E., *Okeechobee Hurricane: Killer Storms in the Everglades* (Belle Glade, Florida, The Glades Historical Society, 1990) p. 14

128. In Coral Gables, Leo Reardon and his guests: Reardon, Leo, *The Florida Hurricane & Disaster 1926* (Coral Gables, Florida; Arva Parks & Company, 1986) p. 5

129. At 3:30 a.m., Richard Gray's barometer in the Weather Bureau office had dropped to 29.06: *Miami Daily News*, September 18, 1926

129. Out on Miami Beach, the sea was swallowing the island: *New York Times*, September 22, 1926

129. As dawn approached, the hurricane's winds had reached at least 115 miles an hour: *Monthly Weather Review*, September 1926, p. 410

129. That was more than Gertrude Rubelli's house could withstand: "Report of Mrs. Gertrude Rubelli employed by Dade County School Board and Red Cross Chapter"; Folder DR-207, Florida hurricane of 9-18-1926: Donated Records Collection (formerly Records Group 200), Records of the American Red Cross 1917–1934, National Archives and Records Administration, College Park, Maryland

130. As he huddled with his family in an automobile in the garage: Reardon, Leo, *The Florida Hurricane & Disaster 1926* (Coral Gables, Florida; Arva Parks & Company, 1986) p. 7

130. At the Weather Bureau office, Gray's barometer was plummeting: "Facts on Tropical Hurricane Whose Centre Passed over Miami, Florida September 18, 1926: Folder DR-207, Florida Hurricane 9-18-1926: Donated Records Collection (formerly Records Group 200), Records of the American Red Cross 1917–1934, National Archives and Records Administration, College Park, Maryland

130. Gertrude Rubelli and her husband ventured out of their car: "Report of Mrs. Gertrude Rubelli employed by Dade County School Board and Red Cross Chapter"; Folder 207, Florida hurricane 9-18-1926: Donated Records Collection (formerly Records Group 200), Records of the American Red Cross 1917–1934, National Archives and Records Administration, College Park, Maryland

131. Once the winds had died down in Coral Gables: Reardon, Leo, *The Florida Hurricane & Disaster 1926* (Coral Gables, Florida; Arva Parks & Company, 1986) p. 8

131. "Dawn came, and save for the nearness of other houses": *New York Times*, September 22, 1926

131. As the rainy, windy dawn crept over Moore Haven: Will, Lawrence E., *Okeechobee Hurricane: Killer Storms in the Everglades* (Belle Glade, Florida, The Glades Historical Society, 1990) p. 23

131. At the town's little railroad station, the agent on duty: *The Times*, Hammond, Indiana, 10-13-1926

131. When the hurricane's eye reached Miami, reporter Al Reck: Reardon, Leo, *The Florida Hurricane & Disaster 1926* (Coral Gables, Florida; Arva Parks & Company, 1986) pp. 21–22

132. Not far from where Reck was climbing into the taxi, Richard Gray was appalled: *Monthly Weather Review*, September 1926, p. 410

132. "Saturday was the worst day I ever want to go through": *The Daily Herald*, Middletown, New York, September 23, 1926

133. "Never abating for an instant, the wind rose still higher": Reardon, Leo, *The Florida Hurricane & Disaster 1926* (Coral Gables, Florida; Arva Parks & Company, 1986) p. 9

133. Despite the water covering Miami Beach, S.K. Hicks and another attorney friend: *New York Times*, September 21, 1926

134. Al Reck's wild taxi ride became even wilder: Reardon, Leo, *The Florida Hurricane & Disaster 1926* (Coral Gables, Florida; Arva Parks & Company, 1986) p. 22

134. In Fort Lauderdale, Peggy and Frank Pope watched in astonishment: *New York Times*, September 22, 1926

134. The winds kept increasing until they were blowing even harder: *Monthly Weather Review*, October 1926, p. 415

134. "Peering from the rain-clouded windows I could see": Reardon, Leo, *The Florida Hurricane & Disaster 1926* (Coral Gables, Florida; Arva Parks & Company, 1986) p. 22

135. As the storm worsened, Louis Slutsky was worried: *New York Times*, September 24, 1926

135. In Moore Haven, the dike was giving way: Will, Lawrence E., *Okeechobee Hurricane: Killer Storms in the Everglades* (Belle Glade, Florida, The Glades Historical Society, 1990) p. 15

136. In Sebring, Atlantic Coast Line officials decided: Reardon, Leo, *The Florida Hurricane & Disaster 1926* (Coral Gables, Florida; Arva Parks & Company, 1986) p. 32

136. It was late morning in Miami, but daylight still hadn't come: *New York Times*, September 21, 1926

136. In Coral Gables, Leo Reardon and his family were clinging to shreds of the life: Reardon, Leo, *The Florida Hurricane & Disaster 1926* (Coral Gables, Florida; Arva Parks & Company, 1986) p. 10

137. Up the coast in Stuart, the winds had raged and the rains had poured: *South Florida Developer*, September 24, 1926

138. The stories were emblazoned with screaming headlines: *Galveston Daily News*, September 19, 1926

Chapter Eight: Spinning the Tempest

139. Leo Reardon sat down in a soggy, hurricane-battered apartment: Reardon, Leo, *The Florida Hurricane & Disaster 1926* (Coral Gables, Florida; Arva Parks & Company, 1986) p. 11

140. The bowsprit of the *Rose Mahoney*: Florida State Archives, photo RC08696, "Scene along Bay Shore Drive after the 1926 hurricane—Miami, Florida," available at https://www.floridamemory.com/items/show/31638

140. The storm had wrecked and destroyed the pleasure spots of Miami Beach: *Manitoba Free Press*, September 24, 1926

140. An eighteen-foot pleasure boat rested on its keel: Florida Photographic Collection, Image #N031900, "Maxwell Arcade after hurricane of 1926, available at https://www.floridamemory.com/solr-search/results/?q=%28n031900%20OR%20tt%3An031900%5E10%29&query=n031900

140. In downtown Miami, the seventeen-story Meyer-Kiser Building: Reardon, Leo, *The Florida Hurricane & Disaster 1926* (Coral Gables, Florida; Arva Parks & Company, 1986) p. 17

XX. In the Glades northwest of Miami, an Atlantic Coast Line rescue train: *The Times* of Hammond, Indiana, October 13, 1926

142. "Miami Wiped Out by Terrific Gale": *Salt Lake Tribune*, September 20, 1926

142. In Florence, South Carolina: *The Morning News Review* of Florence, South Carolina, September 19, 1926, noted resort cities laid waste

142. In Pennsylvania, subscribers to the *Clearfield Progress* read: *The Progress* of Clearfield, Pennsylvania, September 19, 1926

142. In Texas, editors at the *Galveston Daily News*: *Galveston Daily News* extra, September 19, 1926 "Many Die; Cities Razed"

142. According to the headlines in the *Chester Times*: *Chester* (Pennsylvania) *Times*, September 19, 1926 1,000 Dead

142. In Fort Lauderdale—one of the cities supposedly wiped off the map: *Fort Lauderdale Daily News*, September 19, 1926

XX. The *New York Times* was more reserved: *New York Times*, September 19, 1926

142. By late Sunday afternoon, American Red Cross officials in Florida and Washington, DC, were trying to get a handle: Box 732, Folder 207, Donated Records Collection, formerly Records Group 200, Records of the American National Red Cross 1917–1934, Florida hurricane 9-18-1926, National Archives and Records Administration, College Park, Maryland

143. When the sun came up over the Gulf of Mexico on Monday, September 20: Barnes, Jay, *Florida's Hurricane History* (Chapel Hill, The University of North Carolina Press, 1998) pp. 123–124

143. "1,000 Perish in Florida Twister": *Charleston Gazette*, September 20, 1926

143. "Hurricane Levels Florida Coast Cities": *Salt Lake Tribune*, September 20, 1926

143. The *New York Times* dropped the restraint it had used: *New York Times*, September 20, 1926

143. A headline in the *Chester Times*, said the storm had left: *Chester* (Pennsylvania) *Times*, September 19, 1926

143. For the record, the official death toll has been calculated: Barnes, Jay, *Florida's Hurricane History* (Chapel Hill, The University of North Carolina Press, 1998) p.126

144. "The city is waking to the horrors of the disaster": Reardon, Leo, *The Florida Hurricane & Disaster 1926* (Coral Gables, Florida; Arva Parks & Company, 1986) p. 32

144. And one newspaper whose responsibility was to report the facts: *Miami Herald*, September 20, 1926

144. Reardon drove to the causeway to see how Miami Beach had fared: Reardon, Leo, *The Florida Hurricane & Disaster 1926* (Coral Gables, Florida; Arva Parks & Company, 1986) pp. 33–38

144. In Washington, DC, President Calvin Coolidge had heard enough about the hurricane: Memo from John Barton Payne to All Chapter Chairmen, September 20, 1926; Box 732, Folder 207, Florida hurricane 9-18-1926: Donated Records Collection, formerly Records Group 200, Records of the American National Red Cross 1917–1934, National Archives and Records Administration, College Park, Maryland

145. By late Monday afternoon, Al Reck, the determined reporter who'd braved the worst of the storm: *The Athens* (Ohio) *Messenger*, September 20, 1926

145. "All buildings erected by Fuller Co. came through hurricane: *Wall Street Journal*, September 23, 1926

146. As night fell on South Florida on Monday, September 20: Reardon, Leo, *The Florida Hurricane & Disaster 1926* (Coral Gables, Florida; Arva Parks & Company, 1986) p. 5

146. More than a thousand miles to the north of South Florida's hurricane-induced misery: *Washington Post*, September 21, 1926

146. Late in the day of Tuesday, September 21, some of the same buses: Reardon, Leo, *The Florida Hurricane & Disaster 1926* (Coral Gables, Florida; Arva Parks & Company, 1986) p. 72

147. Saul German, a former Bronx resident: *New York Times*, September 22, 1926

148. As the storm refugees' tales of woe were being published in newspapers: Telegram from Sidney Morse to American Red Cross Headquarters, Washington D.C., September 19, 1926; Telegram, Henry T. Reed to American Red Cross Headquarters, Washington, D.C., September 19, 1926; Box 732, Folder 207, Florida Hurricane 9-18-1926: Donated Records Collection, formerly Records Group 200, Records of the American National Red Cross, 1917–1934, National Archives and Records Administration, College Park, Maryland

148. In Stuart, Edwin Menninger was mixing optimism and realism: *South Florida Developer*, September 24, 1926

148. "I don't believe the papers can describe all that happened here": *The Sheboygan* (Wisconsin) *Press*, September 22, 1926

148. "Hurricane terrible," William Diesbach hastily scrawled to his friend: *Hamilton* (Ohio) *Evening Journal*, September 22, 1926

148. Helen Sweezy's letter to her parents in Middletown, New York: *Daily Herald* of Middletown, New York, September 23, 1926

149. On September 20, the *Miami Herald* reported that the storm: *Miami Herald*, September 20, 1926

149. On Wednesday, September 22, the *Wall Street Journal* published an editorial: *The Wall Street Journal*, September 22, 1926

149. Nonetheless, on September 22, Warfield issued a public statement: *New York Times*, September 23, 1926

150. Perhaps taking his cue from Warfield's public statements, Miami mayor Edward C. Romf: Buchannan, James E. *Miami: A Chronological & Documentary History 1513–1977* (Dobbs Ferry, New York, Oceana Publications, Inc., 1978) p. 98

151. Meanwhile, out in Moore Haven, rescue workers and survivors crazed with grief: *The Portsmouth* (Ohio) *Daily Times*, September 25, 1926; *New Smyrna* (Florida) *Daily News*, September 24, 1926

151. At the end of the week, *Time* magazine's issue of September 27: *Time* magazine, September 27, 1926

151. "God permitted the hurricane to strike Florida": *Living Church*, reprinted in the *New York Times*, September 25, 1926

152. "It is true Florida is the playground of the wealthy": American Red Cross News Release, September 29, 1926; Box 732, Folder DR-207.72, Florida hurricane 9-18-1926; Donated Records Collection, formerly Records Group 200, Records of the American National Red Cross 1917–1934, Florida hurricane 9-18-1926, National Archives and Records Administration, College Park, Maryland

152. Citing a report by Worth M. Tippy, an investigator sent to Florida: American Red Cross News Release, September 29, 1926; Box 732, Folder DR-207.72, Florida hurricane 9-18-1926, News releases Donated Records Collection, formerly Records Group 200, Records of the American National Red Cross 1917–1934, Florida hurricane 9-18-1926, National Archives and Records Administration, College Park, Maryland

152. A few Florida newspapers were starting to pick up on the effort: Newspaper clipping, undated, "Experience Of Local Unit In Storm Area Convinces Of Necessity For Relief," no byline; Box 732, Folder DR-207, Florida hurricane 9-18-1926; Donated Records Collection, formerly Records Group 200, Records of the American National Red Cross 1917–1934, National Archives and Records Administration, College Park, Maryland

152. "Thousands of three- and four- and five-room cottages are now only a pile: Telegram, William B. Taylor, American Red Cross Headquarters, to Douglas Griesmer, Miami, Florida, September 30, 1926; Folder DR-207, Florida hurricane 9-18-1926, Reports and statistics, Donated Records Collection, formerly Records Group 200, Records of the American National Red Cross 1917–1934, Florida hurricane 9-18-1926, National Archives and Records Administration, College Park, Maryland

153. In a news release from Washington, Payne said the Red Cross's fund-raising: American Red Cross News Release, October 1, 1926; Box 732, Folder 207, Florida hurricane 1917–1934; Donated Records Collection, formerly Records Group 200, Records of the American National Red Cross 1917–1934, National Archives and Records Administration, College Park, Maryland

153. That same day, Brisbane praised Warfield's outrageously misleading statements: *The Bee* of Danville, Virginia, October 1, 1926

153. The war of words reached a nasty apex on Saturday, October 2: *Miami Tribune*, September 18, 1926

154. The Red Cross fired back the next day: American Red Cross News Release, October 3, 1926; Box 732, Folder 207, Florida hurricane 9-18-1926; Donated Records Collection, formerly Records Group 200, Records of the American National Red Cross 1917–1934, National Archives and Records Administration, College Park, Maryland

154. That same day, Henry Baker, the Red Cross medical director in Miami, made an appeal: Radio script for Henry M. Baker for WRNY Radio; Box 732, Folder 207, Florida hurricane 9-18-1926; Donated Records Collection, formerly Records Group 200, Records of the American National Red Cross 1917–1934, National Archives and Records Administration, College Park, Maryland

154. Included in the comments was a cartoon that appeared on editorial pages of large newspapers: *The World-Herald* of Omaha, Nebraska, October 5, 1926

154. On October 8, the *Wall Street Journal* jumped back into the fracas: *Wall Street Journal*, October 8, 1926

155. A week after one of the nation's most influential newspapers allowed Knight: *Washington Post*, October 16, 1926

155. "The educational campaign minimizing the disaster": Memo, James Fieser to Henry Baker; Box 732, Folder 207, Florida hurricane 1917–1934; Donated Records Collection, formerly Records Group 200, Records of the American National Red Cross 1917–1934, National Archives and Records Administration, College Park, Maryland

156. Despite the outrageous verbal assaults on their organization: American Red Cross news release, December 24, 1926; Box 732, Folder 207, Florida hurricane 9-18-1926; Donated Records Collection, formerly Records Group 200, Records of the American National Red Cross 1917–1934, National Archives and Records Administration, College Park, Maryland

156. Like thousands of other Florida residents, Edwin Menninger: *South Florida Developer*, September 24, 1926

Chapter Nine: Hope from the Swamp

157. But that's exactly what they heard when prankster Charles Haines: *Manitoba* (Ontario) *Free Press*, September 24, 1926

157. "Reports from all sections of the country showed that donations": *New York Times*, October 15, 1926

158. The hurricane struck Havana around 10:45 that morning: Perez, Louis A. Jr., *Winds of Change: Hurricanes and the Transformation of 19th-Century Cuba* (Chapel Hill, University of North Carolina Press, 2001) p. 6

159. "The sun is shining brightly in Miami": *Miami Daily News*, October 20, 1926

159. Red Cross officials, however, were assembling a glum forecast: Memo, "Confidential Notes of Conference in Atlanta, October 23, 1926; Box 732, Folder 270, Florida hurricane 9-18-1926; Donated Records Collection, formerly Records Group 200, Records of the American National Red Cross 1917–1934, National Archives and Records Administration, College Park, Maryland

160. The November 1926 edition of the respected journal *Review of Reviews: Review of Reviews*, vol. LXXIV, no. 442, pp. 483–485

161. As 1926 drew to a close, Red Cross officials summarized their efforts: American Red Cross news release, December 24, 1925; Box 732, Folder 270, Florida hurricane 9-18-1926; Donated Records Collection, formerly Records Group 200, Records of the American National Red Cross 1917–1934, National Archives and Records Administration, College Park, Maryland

161. At 6:25 p.m. on the evening of January 5, 1927, Warfield: Turner, Greg M., *A Journey Into Florida's Railroad History* (Gainesville, Florida, University Press of Florida, 2008) p. 204; *New York Times*, January 6, 1927; *New York Times*, January 8, 1927; *Miami Daily News*, January 8, 1927; *Miami Daily News*, January 9, 1927

163. Despite the new optimism among Miami boosters: Box 732, Folder 270, Donated Records Collection, formerly Records Group 200, Records of the American National Red Cross 1917–1934, Florida hurricane 9-18-1926, National Archives and Records Administration, College Park, Maryland

164. By mid-February, the Red Cross was ready: Box 732, Folder 270, Donated Records Collection, formerly Records Group 200, Records of the American National Red Cross 1917–1934, Florida hurricane 9-18-1934, Florida hurricane 9-18-1926, National Archives and Records Administration, College Park, Maryland

164. Solomon Davies Warfield was known as an autocratic business leader: Turner, Gregg M., *A Journey Into Florida Railroad History* (Gainesville, University Press of Florida, 2008) p. 199

164. On March 1, 1927, Henry Baker, the director of the Red Cross relief effort in Miami: *Miami Herald*, March 2, 1926

164. The following day, Baker was invited to a smaller gathering: Letter, Henry Baker to James Fieser, March 3, 1927; Box 732, Folder 270, Florida hurricane 9-18-1926;

Donated Records Collection, formerly Records Group 200, Records of the American National Red Cross 1917–1934, National Archives and Records Administration, College Park, Maryland

165. "It leaps like a flung lance": Douglas, Marjory Stoneman, *The Everglades: River of Grass* (Sarasota, Florida, Pineapple Press, 1997) pp. 342–343

166. For all of the exotic wildlife in the Everglades: Author's visits to Everglades, 1993–97, 2000, and 2013

167. Otto Neal, who worked on the Tamiami Trail: *The Collier County* (Naples, Florida) *News*, April 26, 1928

167. At first glance, the walking dredge: Author's visit to Collier-Seminole State Park, Naples, Florida, November 20, 2013

167. Meece Ellis, who worked on the construction project: *Orlando Sentinel*, March 1, 1998

168. But other accounts say that men died: Douglas, Marjory Stoneman, *The Everglades: River of Grass* (Sarasota, Florida, Pineapple Press, 1997) p. 344

168. Many men who hired on with the construction project: Haney, P.B; Lewis, W.J.; and Lambert, W.R., *Cotton Production and the Boll Weevil in Georgia: History, Cost of Control, and Benefits of Eradication* (Athens, GA: College of Agricultural and Environmental Sciences, The University of Georgia, 2012) p. 14

168. "First a crew went forward through sawgrass": Douglas, Marjory Stoneman, *The Everglades: River of Grass* (Sarasota, Florida, Pineapple Press, 1997) p. 344

168. At one point, Collier was asked how many shifts: *Naples* (Florida) *Daily News*, July 4, 1976

168. "The men on the job were wonderful": *The Collier County* (Naples, Florida) *News*, April 26, 1928

168. "They were not violent men, but their lives were full of violence": Crews, Harry, *Classic Crews: A Harry Crews Reader* (New York, Touchstone Books, 1995) p. 24

169. "He had not wanted her": Crews, Harry, *Classic Crews: A Harry Crews Reader* (New York, Touchstone Books, 1995) p. 20

169. Moonshine was another source of diversion: *The Davenport* (Iowa) *Democrat*, August 26, 1926

169. Ellis, the former dredge operator: *The Orlando Sentinel*, March 1, 1998

169. Roan Johnson was another young Georgian: *The Miami Herald*, August 31, 2003

169. The nights were "dark as only a swamp": Crews, Harry, *Classic Crews: A Harry Crews Reader* (New York, Touchstone Books, 1995) p. 19

169. The men were fed in the work camps: *The Orlando Sentinel*, March 1, 1998

170. The work gang that followed the crew clearing: Author's telephone interview with Bob DeGross, Chief of Interpretation and Public Affairs, Big Cypress National Preserve, Ochopee, Florida, May 28, 2014

170. "Sometimes the drills stuck in the mud: Douglas, Marjory Stoneman, *The Everglades: River of Grass* (Sarasota, Florida, Pineapple Press, Inc., 1997) p. 344

170. In its November 1928 issue: *Explosives Engineer* magazine, November 1927, reprinted in *History of the Tamiami Trail*, published by The Tamiami Trail Commissioners and the County Commissioners of Dade County, Florida, 1928, p. 22

170. The limestone was crushed: Author's telephone interview with Bob DeGross, Chief of Interpretation and Public Affairs, Big Cypress National Preserve, Ochopee, Florida, May 28, 2014

170. "Just ten days behind the schedule": *The Collier County* (Naples, Florida) *News*, April 26, 1928

171. With a bottle of whiskey on the floorboard: Crews, Harry, *Classic Crews: A Harry Crews Reader* (New York, Touchstone, 1995) pp. 22–23.

171. . . . a heavily guarded armored car left Miami: *New York Times*, March 9, 1927

171. On March 16 at the Boston Braves' spring training camp: *The Evening Independent* of St. Petersburg, Florida, May 16, 1927; *Modesto* (California) *News-Herald*, March 17, 1927

172. On August 7, 1927, Horace Alderman and his partner: Buchanan, Patricia, "Miami's Bootleg Boom," *Tequesta*, vol. 30, 1979, pp. 25–26

172. In late September 1927, Menninger met briefly: *South Florida Developer*, October 28, 1927

173. Warfield's doctor told the *New York Times: New York Times,* October 25, 1927

173. "Stuart as a community will feel this blow": *South Florida Developer*, October 28, 1927; *Kingsport* (Tennessee) *Times*, October 25, 1927; *The Gettysburg* (Pennsylvania) *Times*, November 23, 1927

Chapter Ten: Mr. Brown in Paradise

174. Maybe the Everglades sunset lifted the spirits of the Boston Braves: *Miami Daily News*, March 27, 1928; *Miami Daily News*, March 28, 1928

174. Their bus would be one of the first vehicles: *Lincoln* (Nebraska) *State Journal*, March 28, 1928

174. . . . Miami's boosters were confident that a large crowd: *Miami Daily News*, March 28, 1928

175. Brooklyn won the game, 9–0: *Evening Independent*, 3-30-1928

175. "If Adam and Eve could have seen Florida": *South Florida Developer*, January 13, 1928

175. "Oh, I am so sorry for you folks": *South Florida Developer*, January 13, 1928

175. Menninger also reported that the Brown-Cummer Company: *South Florida Developer*, January 27, 1928

175. The Seaboard Air Line Railroad closed its offices and railroad shops: *South Florida Developer*, February 3, 1928

175. Still, the 1927–28 tourist season: *Stuart Daily News*, January 5, 1928

176. "There are more tourists in Stuart": *South Florida Developer*, March 23, 1928

176. "But I have just seen the state": *South Florida Developer*, January 22, 1928

176. Parker Henderson, who was mayor of Miami in 1917: *Miami Metropolis*, November 20, 1916

176. The school, in the Blue Ridge foothills: *Miami Metropolis*, July 26, 1919

176. In August 1927, shortly after his father's death: *Miami Daily News*, August 28, 1927

176. . . . a businessman who'd apparently done very well: *Tuscaloosa News*, May 6, 1986

177. Capone boldly dropped his alias: *Miami Daily News*, July 1, 1928

177. "When I got in, a bunch of the boys met me at the train": *Miami Daily News*, January 10, 1928

177. Noting that Miami's climate was "more healthful than Chicago's": *Miami Daily News*, January 10, 1928

177. "I like Miami so well": *Miami Daily News*, January 10, 1928

177. "I believe now is the time to buy down here": *Miami Daily News*, January 10, 1928

178. . . . spotted by a local sheriff who was eyeing the next election: *Stuart Daily News*, January 3, 1928

179. When Capone's associates in Chicago wired money to him: Kobler, John, *Capone: The Life and World of Al Capone* (New York, G.P. Putnam's Sons, 1971) p. 220; *Pittsburgh Press*, October 9, 1931

179. Around mid-January, Capone called Henderson to his room: *Newark Advocate and American Tribune*, July 31, 1928; *New York Times*, August 1, 1928

179. "He would order food for about fifty people": *Miami Daily News*, July 13, 1928

180. Capone showed his appreciation: *New York Times*, August 1, 1928

180. . . . the US Coast Guard began assembling patrol craft: *Miami Daily News*, January 13, 1928

180. A reporter duly jotted down the president's comments: *Miami Daily News*, January 15, 1928

181. On January 17, Al Capone moved from the Ponce de Leon Hotel: *Miami Daily News*, January 17, 1928

181. "This morning attention turns": *The Capital Times*, Madison Wisconsin, January 20, 1928

181. Two days after Brisbane's column: *Miami Daily News*, January 21, 1928

182. A few days later, Capone and his brother Ralph: *Galveston Daily News,* January 31, 1928

182. Capone was fond of telling people that he'd served: *Miami Daily News*, June 20, 1928

182. . . . he tried to join the Coral Gables post of the American Legion: *Charleston Gazette*, March 9, 1928

182. On March 27, James and Modesta Popham sold: *Miami Daily News*, June 22, 1928

182. Henderson, in turn, quietly sold the property to Mae Capone: *Pittsburgh Press*, October 9, 1931

183. With the opening of the Trail only days away: *The Capital Times* of Madison, Wis., April 1, 1928

183. Edwin Menninger described the Trail: *South Florida Developer*, April 6, 1928

183. "This magnificent Tamiami Trail will open": *San Antonio Light,* April 5, 1928

184. "The tremendous influx of visitors": *Sarasota Herald*, April 24, 1928

184. . . . even the famously busy Thomas Edison: Albion, Michele Wehrwein, *The Florida Life of Thomas Edison* (Gainesville, The University Press of Florida, 2008) p. 136

184. "Approaching autos caused countless flocks of egrets": Fritz, Florence, *Unknown Florida* (Coral Gables, Florida, University of Miami Press, 1963) p. 146

184. "No longer was it the unconquerable domain": *Palm Beach Post*, November 30, 1981

184. ". . . an amazing engineering feat": Author's interview with Bob DeGross, May 28, 2014

184. The day after the Trail opened: *Fort Myers Tropical News*, April 28, 1928

185. The Republican primary campaign of 1928 would go down in infamy: Tuohy, John W., *The Chicago Mob. A History. 1900–2000* (Bad Guys and Bullets Press.Com, 2010) available online at http://gunsandglamourthechicagomobahistory.blogspot.com/2012/12/pineapple-primary.html

186. George Merrick owed an estimated $29 million: *Lewiston Daily Sun*, July 6, 1928

186. On Monday, June 18, accompanied by three bodyguards: *Miami Daily News*, June 19, 1928

186. The day after the terse meetings: *Miami Daily News*, June 20, 1928

187. The following day, the *Miami Daily News* escalated: *Miami Daily News*, June 20, 1928

187. "Capone Deal Involves Lummus": *Miami Daily News*, June 22, 1928

188. That same day, Parker Henderson gave up the lease: *Miami Daily News*, July 31, 1928

188. On Thursday, June 28, the Miami Beach City Council: *Evening Independent*, June 28, 1928

188. While Al Capone was tussling with local leaders in Dade County: *Miami Daily News*, August 5, 1928

188. In Knoxville, two of the men went to a Nash car dealership: *New York Times*, July 4, 1928; *New York Times*, July 5, 1928

189. On Sunday, July 1, around three p.m., Frank Uale was having a drink: *New York Times*, July 2, 1928; *New York Times*, July 4, 1928

190. . . . Uale had been laid to rest in a $15,000 coffin: *Miami Daily News*, July 6, 1928

190. . . . Capone's plot to create an "alcohol empire": *New York Times*, July 9, 1928

190. Henderson met first with Miami police chief Guy Reeve: *Miami Daily News*, July 31, 1928

190. Henderson stayed out of sight between meetings: *Miami Daily News,* August 7, 1928

191. The storm's eye made landfall just before dawn: *Miami Daily News*, August 8, 1928

Chapter Eleven: Blown Away

192. But Edwin Menninger, now publisher of both the *South Florida Developer* and the *Stuart Daily News*: *The Evening Independent*, August 9, 1928

193. Still, one sad death during the storm was discovered later: *Miami Daily News*, August 9, 1928

193. In his story for the Associated Press: *The Evening Independent*, August 9, 1928

193. The storm had dumped more than a foot of rain in some places: *Palm Beach Post*, August 14–17, 1928; *South Florida Developer*, August 17, 1928

193. One of those dikes near the town of Okeechobee on the lake's northern shore: *Palm Beach Post*, August 14, 1928

194. But in early July 1928, near the end of his four-year term as governor: *Miami Daily News*, July 6, 1928

194. William Griffis, editor of the Okeechobee News, disputed him: *South Florida Developer*, August 17, 1928

194. Davida Gates, who grew up in Belle Glade in the 1920s: Gates, Davida, *Growing Up Ain't Easy!: A South Florida Depression Chronicle* (Livingston, Texas, Pale Horse Publishing, 2008) p. 35

194. They were joined by thousands of migrant workers, most of them black: Hurston, Zora Neale, *Their Eyes Were Watching God* (New York, Harper Perennial Modern Classics, p. 2006) pp. 131–132

195. Money had not poured into the Glades towns the way it had in Miami: *Canal Point News*, reprinted in the *South Florida Developer*, September 14, 1928

195. "We in America today are nearer to the final triumph over poverty": *Miami Daily News*, August 12, 1928

195. "Almost as great a boom as the east coast of Florida had in 1925 is the development that is now under way in the upper Everglades": *Canal Point News*, reprinted in the *South Florida Developer*, September 14, 1928

195. On September 10, an Associated Press story predicted that the same coastal towns that had been roughed up: *South Florida Developer*, September 14, 1928

196. "Florida looks forward today to one of the best and most prosperous winters": *South Florida Developer*, September 14, 1928

196. German philosopher Friedrich Nietzsche noted that while irony's purpose is to humble and shame: Gemes, Ken, and Richardson, John, editors, *The Oxford Handbook of Nietzsche* (Oxford, Oxford University Press, 2013) p. 112

197. That same morning the SS *Commack*, an American freighter bound from Brazil: *Monthly Weather Review*, September 1928, p. 347

197. About 280 miles southwest of the *Commack*, the captain of the SS *Clearwater*: "Beating the Hurricane," by William G. Shepherd, *Collier's* magazine, November 17, 1928, pp. 8–9, p. 40

197. Hurricane Charley, which carved a path of destruction across the Florida peninsula in 2004: Barnes, Jay, *Florida's Hurricane History* (Chapel Hill, University of North Carolina Press, 2007) p. 16

197. That storm's maximum sustained winds reached at least 145 miles per hour: Pasch, Richard J., Brown, Daniel P. and Blake, Eric S., "Tropical Cyclone Report/Hurricane Charley/9-14 August 2004, published by the National Hurricane Center, p. 2

197. A meteorologist in Pointe-à-Pitre: *Monthly Weather Review*, September 1928, p. 347

197. Alexander Hamilton, who was born in the British West Indies: Hamilton, Alexander, letter to the *Royal Danish American Gazette*, September 6, 1772; available online at http://founders.archives.gov/documents/Hamilton/01-01-02-0042

197. The hurricane that crossed Guadeloupe in September 1928: *Monthly Weather Review*, September 1928, p. 347

198. At ten p.m. on September 12, a cannon boomed: "The West Indies Hurricane Disaster September 1928/Official Report of Relief Work in Porto Rico, the Virgin Islands and Florida," by the American National Red Cross, p. 5; Box 750, Folder 284, West Indies Hurricane 9-13-28, Donated Records Collection (Formerly Records Group 200), Records of the American National Red Cross 1917–1934, National Archives and Records Administration, College Park, Maryland

198. The storm's arrival happened to coincide: Emanuel, Kerry, *Divine Wind: The History and Science of Hurricanes* (Oxford, Oxford University Press, 2005), p. 118; Kleinberg,

Eliot, *Black Cloud: The Great Florida Hurricane of 1928* (New York, Carroll & Graf, Publishers, 2003) p. 47

198. As the eye passed over Guayama: *Monthly Weather Review*, September 1928, p. 349

198. The *San Lorenzo*, a Puerto Rican passenger liner: *The Times* of London, September 19, 1928

198. And it may have been worse at Guayama: *Monthly Weather Review*, September 1928, p. 351

198. In Coamo, only about eighteen miles northwest of where the storm came ashore, Felicia Cartegena: "The Hurricane's Tragic Toll," no byline, *The Literary Digest*, October 6, 1928, p. 14

199. And there was one more unusual death: *Palm Beach Post*, September 14, 1928

199. Red Cross officials later estimated that the hurricane had left: American Red Cross news release, September 16, 1928; Box 750, Folder 284, West Indies Hurricane 9-13-28, Donated Records Collection (Formerly Records Group 200), Records of the American National Red Cross 1917–1934, National Archives and Records Administration, College Park, Maryland

199. The *Palm Beach Post* of Friday, September 14: *Palm Beach Post*, September 14, 1928

199. By mid-month, Lake Okeechobee was frighteningly high: *Monthly Weather Review*, August 1928, p. 77; *Monthly Weather Review*, September 1928, p. 89; Will, Lawrence E., *Okeechobee Hurricane: Killer Storms in the Everglades* (Belle Glade, Florida, The Glades Historical Society, 1990) p. 49

199. "Florida May Feel Storm's Wrath": *Palm Beach Post*, September 15, 1928

199. Around three p.m. Saturday, the eye of the storm passed over the German steamer *August Leonhardt*: *Monthly Weather Review*, September 1928, p. 347

200. At eleven p.m. Saturday night, the U.S. Weather Bureau in Washington, DC, issued statement: *Miami Daily News*, September 16, 1928

200. Brisbane was detached and flippant about the powerful storm: *Palm Beach Post*, September 16, 1928

200. That same morning, American Red Cross vice chairman James Fieser: American Red Cross news release, September 16, 1928; Box 750, Folder 284, West Indies Hurricane 9-13-28, Donated Records Collection (Formerly Records Group 200), Records of the American National Red Cross 1917–1934, National Archives and Records Administration, College Park, Maryland

200. On his small farm near Belle Glade, Jack Zuber: *Miami Daily News*, September 24, 1928

201. "This hurricane is of wide extent and great severity": *Monthly Weather Review*, September 1928, p. 348

201. Attorney Everett Muskoff Jr. and his wife: *The Evening Independent*, September 18, 1928

201. Around the same time, Frances Ball left the Hotel Pennsylvania: Frances Ball, letter to parents, September 17, 1928, from the collection of Palm Beach County Public Library, Belle Glade, Florida

201. About forty miles inland from West Palm Beach: "The Night 2,000 Died," produced by Glades-area students in the Gifted and Talented Program, 1988; from the collection of the Palm Beach County Public Library, Belle Glade, Florida

202. Around 2:30 p.m., downtown West Palm Beach was being drenched: *Lowell Sun*, September 25, 1928

202. At the Harvey Building, Frances Ball and her friend: Frances Ball, letter to parents, September 17, 1928, from the collection of Palm Beach County Public Library, Belle Glade, Florida

202. By five p.m., Margaret and Amos Best and their children: *Lowell Sun*, September 25, 1928

203. Nineteen people had gathered at the home of Pat Burke: "The Night 2,000 Died," produced by Glades-area students in the Gifted and Talented Program, 1988; from the collection of the Palm Beach County Public Library, Belle Glade, Florida

203. Jack Zuber noticed that the water in a nearby canal: *Miami Daily News*, September 24, 1928

204. "A little after seven the lull came": Frances Ball, letter to parents, September 17, 1928, from the collection of Palm Beach County Public Library, Belle Glade, Florida

204. The *Miami Daily News* later reported that the destruction: *Miami Daily News*, September 17, 1928

204. "So it was just a little bit before dark that the water began": "The Night 2,000 Died," produced by Glades-area students in the Gifted and Talented Program, 1988; from the collection of the Palm Beach County Public Library, Belle Glade, Florida

205. Zora Neale Hurston eloquently described: Hurston, Zora Neale, *Their Eyes Were Watching God* (New York, Harper Perennial Modern Classics, 2006) p. 158

205. San Felipe, in effect, was still over water as it roared inland: Interview with Michael Laca, producer of TropMet.Com, in Miami, October 8, 2014

205. In Belle Glade, Jabo Tryon was digging into his pie: "The Night 2,000 Died," produced by Glades-area students in the Gifted and Talented Program, 1988; from the collection of the Palm Beach County Public Library, Belle Glade, Florida

205. A few minutes before eight p.m., the barometric pressure reading in nearby Canal Point was 28.54: *Monthly Weather Review*, September 1928, p. 349

206. Jack Zuber walked into the kitchen of his house: *Miami Daily News*, September 24, 1928

206. At nine p.m., the barometer at Canal Point was reading 27.97: *Monthly Weather Review*, September 1928, p. 349

206. "Water was lapping up over the porch": *Miami Daily News*, September 24, 1928

206. In the Tedder Hotel in Belle Glade: "The Night 2,000 Died," produced by Glades-area students in the Gifted and Talented Program, 1988; from the collection of the Palm Beach County Public Library, Belle Glade, Florida

206. At Jack Zuber's farm, the water had risen: *Miami Daily News*, September 24, 1928

207. San Felipe's winds had driven more and more water against the dikes: Hurston, Zora Neale, *Their Eyes Were Watching God* (New York, Harper Perennial Modern Classics, 2006) p. 158

207. Water began filling the house where nineteen people, including Helen McCormick: "The Night 2,000 Died," produced by Glades-area students in the Gifted and Talented Program, 1988; from the collection of the Palm Beach County Public Library, Belle Glade, Florida; *Ocala Star-Banner*, October 30, 1981

208. The stalks closed around them, weaving a lattice-like trap: *South Florida Developer*, September 28, 1928

208. As the storm started rising, Vernon Boots and his family decided: "The Night 2,000 Died," produced by Glades-area students in the Gifted and Talented Program, 1988; from the collection of the Palm Beach County Public Library, Belle Glade, Florida

208. In Indiantown, a blast of wind lifted a small building: *South Florida Developer*, September 20, 1928

208. Frances Ball and her companions picked their way: Frances Ball, letter to parents, September 17, 1928, from the collection of Palm Beach County Public Library, Belle Glade, Florida

209. At about the same time Frances Ball went to bed, Margaret Best finished: *Lowell Sun*, September 25, 1928

209. Frances Ball, still picking bits of plaster: Frances Ball, letter to parents, September 17, 1928, from the collection of Palm Beach County Public Library, Belle Glade, Florida

209. Vernon Boots and his brothers began slogging: "The Night 2,000 Died," produced by Glades-area students in the Gifted and Talented Program, 1988; from the collection of the Palm Beach County Public Library, Belle Glade, Florida

210. "Water, knee-deep, covered all the land": Will, Lawrence E., *Okeechobee Hurricane: Killer Storms in the Everglades* (Belle Glade, Florida, The Glades Historical Society, 1990) pp. 131–132

210. Jack Zuber, still unconscious on the raft that had been a side of his house: *Miami Daily News*, September 24, 1928

210. But the Red Cross was getting alarming reports: Telegram, J. Denham Bird to American Red Cross Headquarters, Washington, D.C., September 17, 1928; Box 750, Folder 284, West Indies Hurricane 9-13-28, Donated Records Collection (Formerly Records Group 200), Records of the American National Red Cross 1917–1934, National Archives and Records Administration, College Park, Maryland

210. In Jacksonville, Red Cross officials received a message from an amateur radio operator: American Red Cross News Release, September 17, 1928; Box 750, Folder 284,

West Indies Hurricane 9-13-28, Donated Records Collection (Formerly Records Group 200), Records of the American National Red Cross 1917–1934, National Archives and Records Administration, College Park, Maryland

211. "If necessary, of course, I will act on the request.": Kleinberg, Eliot, *Black Cloud: The Great Florida Hurricane of 1928* (New York, Carroll & Graf, Publishers, 2003) p. 130

211. Without waiting for details of the Lake Okeechobee horror to emerge: *Tampa Morning Tribune*, September 19, 1928

211. As the storm spun northward, an announcer on WDBO radio: *Tampa Morning Tribune*, September 21, 1928

211–12. The *Palm Beach Post* said the Red Cross was estimating that fifty people had been killed: *Palm Beach Post*, September 18, 1928

212. The *St. Petersburg Times* reported that thirty bodies, most of them African Americans: *St. Petersburg Times*, September 18, 1928

212. "If you have made any winter plans about Florida, don't let any news reports": *Tampa Morning Tribune*, September 19, 1928

212. In Tallahassee, Governor John Martin also was following: *Stuart Daily News*, September 21, 1928

212. Around 1:45 a.m. on Tuesday, September 19, Red Cross vice chairman James Fieser: Transcript of radio messages to American National Red Cross, September 19, 1928; Box 750, Folder 284, West Indies Hurricane 9-13-28, Donated Records Collection (Formerly Records Group 200), Records of the American National Red Cross 1917–1934, National Archives and Records Administration, College Park, Maryland

213. But the editorial page in that day's edition of the *Tampa Morning Tribune*: *Tampa Morning Tribune*, September 19, 1928

213. "Cyclone or hurricane damage is essentially surface damage": *Wall Street Journal*, September 19, 1928

213. *Miami Daily News* readers got a jarring look at San Felipe's work: *Miami Daily News*, September 20, 1928

214. Cecelia Copeland, a reporter for the *St. Petersburg Times*: *St. Petersburg Times*, September 21, 1928

214. Howard Selby, the Red Cross chairman for Palm Beach County, sent a telegram to Peter Knight: *Palm Beach Post*, September 21, 1928

214. The two high-ranking state officials stopped there: *Stuart Daily News*, September 21, 1928

215. In Tampa, Peter Knight tried to deflect harsh criticism: *St. Petersburg Times*, September 21, 1928

215. "Conditions Lake Okeechobee region simply terrible": "Bulletin/The West Indies-Florida Hurricane," September 21, 1928; Box 750, Folder 284, West Indies Hurricane 9-13-28, Donated Records Collection (Formerly Records Group 200), Records of the

American National Red Cross 1917–1934, National Archives and Records Administration, College Park, Maryland

216. "It boils down to this": "Report of Paul Hoxie, Commander of the Legion Post St. Petersburg," September 24, 1928; Box 750, Folder 284, West Indies Hurricane 9-13-28, Donated Records Collection (Formerly Records Group 200), Records of the American National Red Cross 1917–1934, National Archives and Records Administration, College Park, Maryland

216. Around midnight, a weary and stunned Martin invited reporters: *Palm Beach Post*, September 22, 1928

216. The editorial followed the same formula as earlier ones: *Wall Street Journal*, September 22, 1928

217. "Just a few hours ago I saw the bodies of thirty-two colored men": *South Florida Developer*, September 28, 1928

217. "There is a political reason for the apparently senseless": *Wall Street Journal*, September 24, 1928

218. An editorial in the *Grand Rapids Herald*: *Grand Rapids Herald*, September 28, 1928

218. J.B. Ellis, chairman of the Lincoln County chapter of the American Red Cross: Letter, J.B. Ellis to W.M. Baxter, September 29, 1928; Box 750, Folder 284, West Indies Hurricane 9-13-28, Donated Records Collection (Formerly Records Group 200), Records of the American National Red Cross 1917–1934, National Archives and Records Administration, College Park, Maryland

218. Newspaper headlines such as one that appeared in the *Montreal Gazette*: *Tampa Sunday Tribune*, September 30, 1928

218. Red Cross officials and Palm Beach County leaders decided to confront: *Palm Beach Post*, September 29, 1928

218. On Monday, October 1, the *Journal*'s editorial page insisted the newspaper: *Wall Street Journal*, October 1, 1929

219. More than six hundred black victims of the storm: Kleinberg, Eliot, *Black Cloud: The Great Florida Hurricane of 1928* (New York, Carroll & Graf, Publishers, 2003) p. 130

219. The worst incident happened on September 23, when Knowlton Crosby: "A True Copy in the Matter of the Inquest on the Body of Cootie Simpson," November 19, 1928; Box 750, Folder 284, West Indies Hurricane 9-13-28, Donated Records Collection (Formerly Records Group 200), Records of the American National Red Cross 1917–1934, National Archives and Records Administration, College Park, Maryland

220. A few days after Simpson's death, an organization called the Negro Workers Relief Committee: *Indianapolis Recorder*, October 6, 1928

220. Bethune visited the hurricane area: Statement of Mary McLeod Bethune following her visit to storm-stricken are of Florida, October 8, 1928; Box 750, Folder 284, West Indies Hurricane 9-13-28, Donated Records Collection (Formerly Records Group

200), Records of the American National Red Cross 1917–1934, National Archives and Records Administration, College Park, Maryland

220. Du Bois wrote a letter to the Negro Workers Relief Committee: Du Bois, W.E. B., 1868–1963; letter from W.E.B. Du Bois to Negro Workers Relief Committee, October 4, 1928; W.E.B. Du Bois Papers (MS 312); Special Collections and University Archives, University of Massachusetts Amherst Libraries

220. In mid-October 1928, the Red Cross compiled statistics: "Relief Progress in Two Hurricane Areas," The Red Cross Courier, October 15, 1928, p. 23; Box 750, Folder 284, West Indies Hurricane 9-13-28, Donated Records Collection (Formerly Records Group 200), Records of the American National Red Cross 1917–1934, National Archives and Records Administration, College Park, Maryland

220. The death toll was still being calculated seventy-five years later: National Weather Service Memorial Web Page for the 1928 Okeechobee Hurricane

Chapter Twelve: Dreamland After All

221. A few weeks before his March 4, 1929 inauguration: *Miami Herald*, February 17, 1929

221. In the spring of 1927, he had coordinated the effort of local, state and federal agencies: "Herbert Hoover Timeline," Herbert Hoover Presidential Library and Museum website, available at http://www.hoover.archives.gov/info/HooverTimeLine.html

221. Preventing another flooding tragedy around Lake Okeechobee: *The* (New York) *World*, reprinted in *Miami Daily News*, February 17, 1929

221. . . . there were grim reminders: *Miami Daily News*, February 17, 1929

222. Crowds awaited him in other towns: *The New York Times*, February 17, 1929; *The* (New York) *World*, reprinted in *Miami Daily News*, February 17, 1929

222. A sixty-six-mile levee, 175 feet thick at its base and 34 feet high: *Miami Daily News*, August 11, 1935

222. "Facts and figures give indisputable evidence": *Miami Daily News*, February 17, 1929

222. And the city would have preferred that some winter visitors had stayed away: *New Yorker* magazine, March 2, 1929

222. The company insuring the Palm Island mansion had canceled the policy: *South Florida Developer*, September 21, 1928; *Miami Daily News*, September 13, 1928

222. On March 7, 1929, gangland violence from New York and Chicago: *Reading Eagle*, March 6, 1929; *Miami Daily News*, March 7, 1929; *Burlington* (NC) *Daily Times*, March 3, 1929; *Sarasota Herald-Tribune*, March 12, 1929

223. In his "Today" column of March 1, 1929, Arthur Brisbane: *The Ogden Standard-Examiner*, March 1, 1929

224. Had the Ashley Gang still been around: *Burlington* (N.C.) *Daily Times*, March 7, 1929

224. On March 19, the *Stuart Daily News*—now owned by Menninger*: Stuart Daily News*, March 19, 1929

224. Nor could the town pay its electric bill: *South Florida Developer*, October 4, 1929

224. Things were no better for the county government.: Martin County Chapter American Red Cross Report for April 1929, by Leora G. Field, Executive Secretary; Box 750, Folder 284, West Indies Hurricane 9-13-28, Donated Records Collection (Formerly Records Group 200), Records of the American National Red Cross 1917–1934, National Archives and Records Administration, College Park, Maryland

224. That sense of humor didn't desert him: Seebohm, Caroline, *Boca Rococo: How Addison Mizner Invented Florida's Gold Coast* (New York, Clarkson Potter Publishers, 2001) p. 175

225. In April 1929, the Mizner brothers, T. Coleman du Pont, Jesse Livermore, and other former directors: *New York Times*, April 5, 1929

225. Walter Fuller, who'd sold millions of dollars' worth of real estate in St. Petersburg: Fuller, Walter P. *This Was Florida's Boom* (St. Petersburg, Florida, Times Publishing Co., 1954) p. 64

225. Even Coral Gables was drowning in red ink: George, Paul, "Brokers, Binders and Builders," *Florida Historical Quarterly*, vol. 65, no. 1, July 1986, p. 49

225. "Though what we owe in bonds could only be properly estimated by a county-to-county": *South Florida Developer*, August 31, 1928

225. On April 6, citrus growers discovered Mediterranean fruit flies in groves near Orlando: *South Florida Developer*, August 2, 1929; author's interview with Robert Alicea, University of South Florida, Tampa, November 12, 2013

225. The state's citrus industry was nearly destroyed: Interview with Robert Alicea, University of South Florida, Tampa, November 12, 2013

226. But the market showed signs of shakiness in March: "The Crash of 1929," produced for "The American Experience" by Ellen Hovde and Muffie Meyer, written by Ronald H. Blumer, originally broadcast 1990 on Public Broadcasting System

226. On March 27, the *Stuart Daily News* published an editorial comparing the Wall Street edginess*: Stuart Daily News*, March 27, 1929

227. "The plumber, the iceman, the butcher, the baker": Marx, Groucho, *Groucho and Me* (Boston, Da Capo Press, 1995) pp. 188–199

227. On September 3, 1929, the Dow Jones Average climbed to its highest point in history: Ruggiero, Adriane, *American Voices from the Great Depression* (Tarrytown, New York, Benchmark Books, 2005) p. 1; "The Crash of 1929," produced for "The American Experience" by Ellen Hovde and Muffie Meyer, written by Ronald H. Blumer, originally broadcast 1990 on Public Broadcasting System.

227. That came on September 5, only days after the market's historic peak: *New York Times*, September 6, 1929

227. George Morse, executive manager of the Florida Motor Lines: *South Florida Developer*, September 13, 1929

228. "The trouble with this particular hurricane": *Schenectady Union Star*, reprinted in *South Florida Developer,* October 18, 1929

228. Stuart's streetlights were turned back on: *South Florida Developer*, October 4, 1929

228. "So many dirty things appear in the paper from time to time": *South Florida Developer*, September 20, 1929

228. The prediction was based on numbers tabulated at inspection stations: *South Florida Developer*, November 1, 1929

229. "There came a Wednesday, October 23, when the market was a little shaky.": "The Crash of 1929," produced for "The American Experience" by Ellen Hovde and Muffie Meyer, written by Ronald H. Blumer, originally broadcast 1990 on Public Broadcasting System

229. "Some of the people I know lost millions.": Marx, Groucho, *Groucho and Me* (Boston, Da Capo Press, 1995) pp. 188–199

229. "I believe that 1929 will go down in Florida history as our worst year.: *South Florida Developer*, January 3, 1930

230. In its issue of January 1930, *National Geographic*: La Gorce, John Oliver, "Florida: The Fountain of Youth," *National Geographic* magazine, January 1930, p. 4

230. "They once tasted excitement": *Stuart Daily News*, July 30, 1930

230. Menninger kept the *South Florida Developer* going: *Stuart Daily News*, January 9, 1964

230. When cash became almost impossible to come by: *The Stuart News*, February 21, 1995

231. "Visit Florida," the state's official Department of Tourism website: Morgan-Schleuning, "Florida's Tourism Industry Welcomed More Than 97 Million Visitors in 2014," posted March 3, 2015, "Visit Florida" website, available online at http://www.visitfloridamediablog.com/home/category/corporate-press-releases

232. ". . . run out the clock in Florida" "The Simpsons," Season four, Episode 67, "New Kid on the Block," air date November 12, 1992

232. In the wake of the subprime mortgage debacle: Author's telephone interview with Karen Procell in Orlando, Florida, December 6, 2010

Index